Adolescent Girls in Distress

Laura H. Choate, EdD, LPC, NCC, is an associate professor and counselor educator at Louisiana State University (LSU) in Baton Rouge. Her research interests include counseling issues and interventions for working with girls and women, eating disorders prevention and treatment, college student wellness, and counselor preparation. She is the author of the 2008 book, *Girls' and Women's Wellness: Contemporary Counseling Issues and Interventions,* and the 2013 edited book, *Eating Disorders and Obesity: A Counselor's Guide to Prevention and Treatment,* both published by the American Counseling Association Press. She has published over 40 articles and book chapters on issues related to girls' and women's wellness, and she was the guest editor of the recent *Journal of Counseling and Development* themed issue on eating disorders prevention and treatment. She was the 2004 to 2006 editor of the *Journal of College Counseling,* and is a three-term editorial board member of the *Journal of Counseling and Development.* She is a past recipient of the LSU Phi Kappa Phi Award for Outstanding Nontenured Faculty Member in the Humanities and Social Sciences, and the American College Counseling Association Research Award. She is a licensed professional counselor in Louisiana and serves as the Vice-Chair and the Discipline Committee Chair of the Louisiana Licensed Professional Counselors Board of Examiners. She has also volunteered as an outreach presenter to over 30 groups of girls and women in the Baton Rouge community on the topics of eating disorders prevention and sexual assault prevention.

Adolescent Girls in Distress
A Guide for Mental Health Treatment and Prevention

Laura H. Choate, EdD, LPC, NCC

SPRINGER PUBLISHING COMPANY
NEW YORK

Springer Publishing Company, LLC
11 West 42nd Street
New York, NY 10036
www.springerpub.com

Acquisitions Editor: Nancy S. Hale
Production Editor: Joseph Stubenrauch
Composition: diacriTech

ISBN: 978-0-8261-0954-5
e-book ISBN: 978-0-8261-0955-2

13 14 15 / 5 4 3 2 1

The author and the publisher of this Work have made every effort to use sources believed to be reliable to provide information that is accurate and compatible with the standards generally accepted at the time of publication. The author and publisher shall not be liable for any special, consequential, or exemplary damages resulting, in whole or in part, from the readers' use of, or reliance on, the information contained in this book. The publisher has no responsibility for the persistence or accuracy of URLs for external or third-party Internet websites referred to in this publication and does not guarantee that any content on such websites is, or will remain, accurate or appropriate.

Library of Congress Cataloging-in-Publication Data

Choate, Laura Hensley.
Adolescent girls in distress : a guide for mental health treatment and prevention / Laura H. Choate.
    p. ; cm.
Includes bibliographical references and index.
ISBN 978-0-8261-0954-5 — ISBN 978-0-8261-0955-2 (ebook)
I. Title.
[DNLM: 1. Adolescent Psychology. 2. Female. 3. Mental Disorders—prevention & control.
4. Mental Disorders—therapy. WS 462]
RJ503
616.89'140835—dc23

                    2013017162

Special discounts on bulk quantities of our books are available to corporations, professional associations, pharmaceutical companies, health care organizations, and other qualifying groups. If you are interested in a custom book, including chapters from more than one of our titles, we can provide that service as well.

For details, please contact:
Special Sales Department, Springer Publishing Company, LLC
11 West 42nd Street, 15th Floor, New York, NY 10036-8002
Phone: 877-687-7476 or 212-431-4370; Fax: 212-941-7842
E-mail: sales@springerpub.com

Printed in the United States of America by Gasch Printing.

I would like to dedicate this book to my daughter Abigail Choate, age 7. Abby, my hope for you is that you will stay strong as you are bombarded by cultural pressures that will cause you to want to doubt yourself, silence your true opinions, and to conform to societal ideals about how you "should" look and act. You are so full of life, fearless, witty, and confident—hold onto these qualities, as they will serve you well.
I am proud to be your mother and I hope these pages will help you and countless other girls to remain resilient as you swim upstream against the current toxic cultural tide.

Contents

Preface

I have a daughter who is 7 years old as this book goes to press. In imagining what her life could be like in the next few years, I try to view the world as it might appear through her eyes. Here is what I see:

At the mall, I see push-up bras and thongs for girls my age; in the toy aisle I view Bratz dolls and Monster dolls wearing high heels, lingerie, and heavy makeup; I look at pants designed with suggestive slogans on the backseat; I dial through the television channels and see girls fighting, gossiping, and competing with one another; I read about my favorite celebrity coming out of jail and rehab; I flip through girls' magazines that provide tips for kissing and pleasing boys. When I go online I can easily access websites teaching me how to starve or cut myself; I view a social media site filled with pictures of me taken at a friend's recent sleepover, followed by gossip about me; my friendship groups change from week to week, and I feel pressure that I can't keep up with all of the texts I receive. When I walk down the halls at school, I hear boys making rude comments about girls' bodies. Parents and teachers place high expectations for academics, athletics, and accomplishment upon me, yet the messages I receive everywhere else tell me that I need to spend my time on looking good and pleasing others. On top of all of this, I look in the mirror and see a girl going through the changes of puberty. The body I see is morphing into a new shape, and I barely know who she is anymore.

After this view of my daughter's potential future, I am over-whelmed and alarmed at the underlying messages and pressures today's girls are receiving at the same time they are undergoing major developmental transitions. It is no surprise that today's girls may feel lost as they attempt to navigate the pathways of adolescence. As stated in a slogan in a recent ad campaign by Dove, the "onslaught" is coming; girls are entering a battle.

This book is intended to address many of these current cultural trends and developmental transitions and how they impact adolescent mental health. While many other authors have focused specifically on physical or mental health, this book also focuses on the socialization processes that begin in early girlhood and how these challenges can influence the development of problems that are increasing in today's adolescent girls. While girls are achieving exceptional academic and professional levels, it is troubling that adolescent girls are increasingly vulnerable to potentially life-threatening issues such as depression, suicide attempts, self-injury, substance abuse, sexual trauma, and eating disorders, which are all on the rise in teenage girls (Hinshaw, 2009). For example, 20% of adolescent girls have experienced at least one episode of major depression before the age of 18, and this is twice the rate of boys (Evans et al., 2005; Forum on Child and Family Statistics, 2011). Further, the rate of depression triples for girls between the ages of 12 and 15 (National Survey on Drug Use and Health, 2012).

The suicide rate for girls is also increasing, with 1 in 10 girls attempting suicide during the adolescent period (Goldston, Sergeant, & Arnold, 2006). Further, sexual violence against girls continues to increase, as the World Health Organization's International Report on Violence and Health reports that nearly 33% of all adolescent girls describe their first sexual experience as being forced (Krug, Dahlberg, Mercy, Zwi, & Lozano, 2002).

In this book, I argue that an important component in the conceptualization and treatment of these mental health problems is the impact of current socialization trends for girls. Several of these trends were highlighted by the American Psychological Association's (APA) Task Force Report on the Sexualization of Girlhood (APA, 2007) and have received national attention in books written for the general public (e.g., Hinshaw, 2009; Levine & Kilbourne, 2008; Sax, 2010). Specifically, today's girls are increasingly socialized to conform to narrowly defined ideals regarding how they should look and act (APA, 2007). At a very young age, girls receive the societal message that they must be "hot and sexy," and that reaching this ideal is the most important avenue for achieving success and value as a woman. Further, they learn that in order to be acceptable they should behave in edgy, outrageous, and often sexually provocative ways in order to seek and keep attention from others. At the same time, girls receive the message that they can be and do anything to which they aspire, but a consequence of this expectation is that they are also experiencing pressure to be perfect in all areas: excel academically, be involved in multiple extracurricular activities, and achieve at high levels of athletic competence, while still maintaining their relationships and attempting to look effortlessly attractive (Hinshaw, 2009; Sax, 2010).

Throughout the book, I describe how the sexualization of girlhood and other related cultural trends are affecting girls at increasingly younger ages, leading girls to view themselves as sexualized objects and to define themselves through their physical appearance or accomplishments, thereby impeding their development of an authentic sense of self. The negative impact of current socialization experiences on girls' identity development and self-esteem is particularly critical during adolescence, as this is the developmental period in which a unique sense of self is formed. Without a core sense of self, girls are less equipped to manage the drastic transitions that occur in girlhood and throughout the adolescent years: family changes, school pressures, peer problems (e.g., sexual harassment, cyberbullying, sexual identity), and individual development (including physical, cognitive, identity, and social developmental transitions). Without the necessary skills for coping with harmful cultural influences and these rapidly occurring changes, girls are vulnerable to the development of mental health problems.

Because of these emerging cultural pressures, multisystemic changes, and increasing problems in today's girls, mental health professionals need a guide to assist girls in responding to these complex challenges. My primary goal for the book is to meet this need by addressing girls' socialization experiences, detailing treatments for mental health concerns that are increasing in adolescence, and providing prevention strategies for building girls' resilience to today's complex life demands. To this end, the book has three objectives: (a) to provide an analysis of contemporary girls' lived experiences through an ecological, multisystemic lens, examining macro (societal), micro (family, peer, school), and individual developmental influences and changes; (b) to describe detailed treatment strategies for problems that increasingly impact today's girls during adolescence, including treatment guidelines that are sensitive to timely factors such as cultural pressures and the diversity of girls' lived experiences; and (c) to highlight the necessity of early intervention for preventing these problems prior to their onset. The book includes general strategies to promote life skills for promoting girls' resilience to cultural pressures and for coping with complex life demands. It also infuses specific prevention interventions throughout each chapter as they are applied to particular mental health concerns.

The book consists of eight chapters, with Chapters 1 and 2 providing a multisystemic overview of girls' lived experiences. Chapter 1 addresses girls' socialization experiences at a macro-level. In Chapter 2, I provide an ecological, multisystemic analysis of the changes and transitions that girls will face as they enter the adolescent period, including family system transitions, peer group involvement, school changes, and individual developmental transitions. Chapters 3 through 7 address specific mental health problems that are increasingly impacting adolescent girls: Chapter 3 (depression), Chapter 4 (eating disorders), Chapter 5 (substance abuse), Chapter 6 (self-injury), and Chapter 7 (sexual trauma and dating violence). While specific prevention strategies are integrated throughout the previous chapters, in Chapter 8, I provide general strategies for the development of life skills that will enable girls to thrive in contemporary culture. Highlights from each chapter are detailed in the paragraphs to follow.

In Chapter 1, I first provide an introduction to the ecological systems theory (Bronfenbrenner, 1977) used as the book's frame for understanding today's girls' lived experiences. I review the influence of media in girls' lives, and provide an analysis of the messages conveyed through popular culture. I identify four trends from current culture that are affecting girls at increasingly younger ages. I provide specific examples from a variety of media forms and also describe how these influences are harmful to today's girls.

- *Trend One: Look Hot, Sexy, and Older Than You Are* is currently promoted as the basis of identity and worth for girls and women. I provide examples of clothing, products, music, advertisements, movies, and television to demonstrate the current socialization process for girls emphasizing sexiness above all else as the key to success. I also review the trend toward age aspiration, age compression, and the harmful consequences to girls when they are pressured to appear older than they really are.
- *Trend Two: Be a Diva* emphasizes the current trend that teaches girls to demand what they want with an "attitude" and to behave in edgy, outrageous, often sexually provocative ways in order to seek and keep attention from others. It also includes having a "passion for fashion," the trend toward shopping and acquiring more possessions, teaching girls to place high value on designer labels and consumerism.

- *Trend Three: Who Are You? Find Out by Plastering Yourself Online* describes girls' intense use of social media. Today's girls feel increasing pressure to cultivate and present the right online image, which ultimately impedes the development of an authentic sense of self.
- *Trend Four: You Can Have It All, and Do It All Perfectly* describes the pressures many girls feel to compete in all arenas—academics, athletics, extracurricular activities—while still maintaining their relationships and attempting to look effortlessly sexy. I describe how the pressure for perfection and for meeting unrealistic and often contradictory goals sets girls up for a sense of failure.

I also describe the process through which these themes are internalized by examining cultivation theory, social learning theory, and self-objectification theory.

In Chapter 2, I move from the macrosystems view to a microlevel perspective on three systems that often change drastically during the adolescent period. I first provide an overview of the importance of family connections in girls' lives. I discuss several recent trends in parenting styles, including the use of technology as a way to both enhance as well as place distance in family relationships. Next I examine changes that occur at the peer level. I first provide an overview of the importance of peer relationships, then discuss recent trends in relational and physical aggression and how this impacts girls' abilities to form authentic connections with peers. I also discuss the recent explosion of social networking and how girls' relationships with peers and romantic partners are impacted by technology. Finally, I provide an overview of girls' current academic achievements and successes at all educational levels, and then describe current educational problems girls face including academic pressures, sexual harassment, and the recent increases in school fighting, bullying, and cyberbullying. Finally, I highlight important developmental transitions by providing an overview of research on girls' physical, cognitive, identity, and social development, including recent research regarding earlier pubertal onset in today's girls.

After the ecological systems overview in the first two chapters, I then turn to mental health problems that are increasingly common in adolescent girls. In Chapter 3 I provide an overview of depression, including risk factors, prevalence rates, and gender differences. I then review multisystemic influences on girls' experience of these problems, and provide a discussion of effective prevention and treatment that incorporates an understanding of contemporary cultural context.

The effective treatments for adolescent girls' depression described in the chapter include cognitive behavioral therapy (CBT) and interpersonal therapy for depression in adolescents (IPT-A). In addition to specific treatment guidelines, I also provide examples of prevention programs designed specifically for adolescents.

In Chapter 4, I provide an overview of eating disorders in girls, including a description of the eating disorders continuum (including anorexia, bulimia, and binge eating). I then review risk factors, prevalence rates, and gender differences. As with the previous chapter, I outline multisystemic influences on girls' experiences of these problems, and provide a discussion of effective treatment for bulimia (CBT, IPT), anorexia (Maudsley family-based therapy), and for binge eating (dialectical behavior therapy and IPT). Specific prevention programs for adolescent girls at initial risk for eating-related problems are also provided.

In Chapter 5, I provide an overview of substance problems in girls, including a description of these disorders, risk factors, prevalence rates, and gender differences. After an overview of general factors needed for effective treatment, specific treatment approaches are reviewed including brief strategic family therapy, functional family therapy, multisystemic therapy, and multidimensional family therapy, and cognitive behavioral/motivational enhancement approaches. A review of protective factors and effective prevention programs is also provided.

Chapter 6 is dedicated to the problem of self-injury in adolescent girls. It is important for counselors to have an understanding of the risk and maintenance factors for this behavior, so as to understand the onset as well as the factors that contribute to the adolescent's continued engagement in the behavior. Because this issue has received high levels of media attention in recent years, I also discuss media influences on girls' experimentation with self-injurious behaviors (particularly from celebrity disclosures and demonstrations through YouTube video clips). Because dialectical behavior therapy (DBT) has the strongest research support for this issue, DBT treatment guidelines will be provided in detail. Components for prevention programs are also provided.

In Chapter 7, I provide an overview of sexual trauma in girls, including a description of types of sexual trauma, the relationship between childhood sexual abuse and later re-victimization, problems associated with early sexual experiences (including unwanted pregnancies and STDs), and risk factors for sexual assault and relationship violence. I then review multisystemic influences on girls' experiences of these problems, including the nature of the assault, the use of alcohol or other drugs during the assault, and a girl's available support systems. I also provide coverage of specific treatment for rape trauma, including trauma-focused CBT and cognitive processing therapy. Also included is a discussion of dating violence in adolescent girls, and prevention programs designed to enhance safe, healthy dating relationships.

The final chapter, Chapter 8, is titled: "Hope for the Future: Strengthening Resilience in Adolescent Girls." While specific prevention strategies are integrated throughout the previous chapters, in this chapter, I provide general strategies for the development of life skills for strengthening resilience that will enable all girls to thrive in contemporary culture. These skills and resources include: quality parenting; problem solving skills; coping skills; social skills and assertiveness; cognitive skills; sense of authenticity; sense of self-worth and efficacy; wellness and balance; positive support systems; positive physical self-concept; media literacy skills; and goal-setting skills for creating the future she wants for herself.

I opened this preface with a glimpse into the potential cultural atmosphere my 7-year-old daughter may face in the near future. As both a parent and professional counselor, this image highly concerns me. At the same time, it also inspires me to do whatever I can to create an empowered and healthy adolescence for my daughter and for all young girls. This task is not insurmountable, for at the same time that girls are being socialized to look and act in limiting ways, they are also poised at a time in history where the possibilities for their futures are endless. Girls are excelling academically, athletically, and professionally as never before. They possess strength for leadership and advocacy and have the potential to create a significant place for themselves in the world.

In addition to these strengths, the future is also encouraging because of the available research and resources for girls such as those provided in this book. In these chapters I have highlighted our field's increased understanding of girls' contexts, risk and protective factors, and skills they need to thrive. When girls develop problems, the book provides current evidence-based practices that can guide counselors' treatment approaches. The book also provides online and print resources, effective research-based curricula, and mentorship programs that are accessible to a diverse array of girls. Therefore, despite an often toxic cultural climate, counselors can help to provide girls with the foundation they need for navigating adolescence with courage and resilience. The remainder of this book is dedicated to assisting counselors with this critical task.

Acknowledgments

First I would like to acknowledge the support of my husband Michael and my children Benjamin (9) and Abigail (7) as they encourage me in my career path. They are truly my strongest supporters and gave me the inspiration I needed to complete this book. My parents, Judy and Lloyd Hensley, were also a great support as they provided meals, childcare, and carpool runs while I completed many long writing days during the past 2 years.

I would also like to thank my writing group members at LSU, Petra Hendry and Jackie Bach, who have read drafts of chapters in the book and who gave me invaluable feedback. Jennifer Curry, my colleague in the counselor education program, was also instrumental in helping me shape my initial ideas about girls' socialization trends. Mona Rocha, soon to complete her PhD in history at LSU, was a great asset to me as she supplied me with many of the examples I used in Chapter 1. Counselor Education graduate assistants are always essential to the completion of all of my published work, and I would especially like to thank Andrea Farris, Jennie Trocquet, Ainsley Pellerin, and Tenikka Sanders for the many hours of editing, typing reference lists, and conducting literature searches for me. I would also like to thank the students in my Girls' and Women's Wellness courses during the past 5 years. They have sparked my thinking, raised my awareness of contemporary cultural trends, and have helped me sort through many of the issues that adolescent girls face today. Their excitement and concern about girls' current challenges were highly motivating as I completed this book.

Finally, I would like to thank Nancy Hale and her team at Springer Publishing Company in believing in the idea for this book and providing support as I wrote, edited, and finalized the project.

1

Girl Power? Understanding Girls' Socialization Through the Lens of Popular Culture

A girl's mental health is a function of her experience of larger cultural systems operating in society, her family of origin and the values/behaviors they model for her, peer group influences, the neighborhood in which she lives, the school that she attends, her religious and/or community institutions and resources, and all of the ways in which these macro- and microsystems interact. In addition, individual biological factors related to her physical development and psychosocial factors stemming from her cognitive, identity, social, and moral development interact with and are affected by these other systems. Consequently, it is impossible for a counselor to understand a girl's increasingly complex inner life, her physical and psychosocial development, and her overall mental health and wellness when viewing her through only a unidimensional lens.

Bronfenbrenner (1979), an influential developmental psychologist, was one of the first social scientists to note the importance of understanding these types of intersections. According to his ecological systems theory, human development and behavior are functions of the interaction between the person and her environment, so that to understand a person, we should explore how all areas—society, family, political structure, local community, other environmental factors—impact psychological development and subsequent behavior. According to Bronfenbrenner, the ecological study of human development is the

> . . . Progressive, mutual accommodation throughout the lifespan, between the growing human organism and the changing, immediate environments in which it lives, as this process is affected by relations occurring within and between these immediate settings, as well as the larger social contexts, both formal and informal, in which the settings are embedded. (Bronfenbrenner, 1977, p. 514)

Bronfenbrenner identified four levels of nested systems, each located inside the next, that best describe the influence of person-environment interactions on human development. At the center of the systems is the individual, who is surrounded by multiple microsystems. A *microsystem* is an immediate social setting that surrounds and directly shapes an individual, such as family, peers, schools, religious institutions, and neighborhoods. At the next level, the *mesosystem* is comprised of a system of microsystems. It describes the interrelations among the major settings in which an individual is embedded at a particular point in life (e.g., the interaction among the parents, child, and members of the school system, or the interaction between the parents and a child's peer group). The *exosystem* involves the institutional structures, settings, and practices that do not contain the individual but do have an impact on the immediate systems in which the person may be found (e.g., a child's father loses his job because of an economic downturn, and this in turn affects the level of parenting quality and resources that the child receives). In this way, exosystems can include extended family, parent's work location, friends of family, legal services, community social services, or local educational, medical, and employment opportunities. Finally, surrounding and permeating all of the other systems, the *macrosystem* describes overarching cultural traditions, beliefs, and values of society. Most macrosystem beliefs are informal, implicitly accepted societal prototypes that are carried out through attitudes and behaviors (Bronfenbrenner, 1977).

Regardless of race or class, girls are bombarded from a very young age with macrosystem values about the ways in which they should look and act. In this chapter, I focus on this current macrosystem that transmits the messages of popular culture and how this system influences girls' socialization, development, and their subsequent mental health. As stated, this system includes unspoken, unwritten rules about how individuals in a society are supposed to act, and are powerfully conveyed through mass media (e.g., television, music, the Internet, video devices and games, magazines, books, movies, clothing, merchandise, toys). I will provide an analysis of four themes drawn from messages affecting girls' socialization in popular culture. The chapter covers messages girls receive from the preschool years through the adolescent period.

It is clear that girls are both exposed to and affected by media influences. For example, children in the United States are watching television at record levels, with children ages 2–5 watching 32 hours of television per week, and children ages 6–11 watching an average of 22 hours per week. When combining television, movies, and video games together, this number rises to 28 hours per week (McDonough, 2009). Another nationally representative survey indicates that among 11–17 year old girls, TV viewing takes up more time than any other activity during a typical week (Girl Scout Research Institute, 2011a). Not surprisingly, Internet use is also heavy among girls. Among preteens and adolescents, 93% use the Internet, 85% use social networking sites, 50% check their social networking profile more than once per day, and 22% check them 10 or more times per day (O'Keefe, Clarke-Pearson, & Council on Communications and Media, 2011).

Additionally, 75% of adolescents have a cell phone of their own, and when broken down by age group, 22% of 6–9 year olds, 60% of 10–14 year olds, and 84% of 15–18 year olds own a cell phone (Center on Media and Child Health, 2012). Fifty-four percent of 12–17 year olds send text messages daily (a higher percentage than those who report talking with friends face to face on a daily basis) (Pew Research Center, 2011). Further, recent statistics show that teen girls send an average of over 4,000 texts per month (compared with 2,500 texts for teen boys), which equates to roughly 135 text messages per day (Nielsen Company, 2010).

With such high levels of media communication and consumption, it is important for counselors to understand the specific messages conveyed through these sources. What are girls watching, hearing, purchasing, and consuming? One theme identified by many authors is the highly sexual content in TV programs and commercials, music videos, movies, magazines, and videogames (Starr & Ferguson, 2012). In addition, media are strong purveyors of sexualized, gender-stereotypical images and messages regarding gender and sexuality (Martino et al., 2006; Ward & Friedman, 2006). As an example, at least half of all girls watch music videos daily. Music videos are argued to be the medium through which a viewer is most likely to see representations of sexually objectified women (Grabe & Hyde, 2009). Further, the amount of popular music lyrics that degrade and sexually objectify women tripled between 1999 and 2009 (Hall, West, & Hill, 2012). Grabe and Hyde's (2009) study also indicates that the level of a girl's music video consumption is linked to holding traditional gender role attitudes, stronger acceptance of women as sexual objects, and being more accepting of attitudes about the treatment of women as objects through actual sexual harassment. In addition, girls (ages 12–14) who consumed more music videos were also more likely to place high value on physical appearance and to view themselves as sexual objects. This in turn increased their likelihood of experiencing negative body esteem, dieting behavior, depression, anxiety, and lowered math confidence (Grabe & Hyde, 2009).

There is also evidence that media consumption is related to actual sexual behaviors. When adolescents are not sure where to turn to get their questions answered about their sexuality, it seems many girls turn to the media as a "sexual super peer" (Brown, Halpern, & L'Engle, 2005). Brown et al. found that girls who reach puberty earlier than their peers were more likely to be drawn to popular, sexualized media in order to glean information about their emerging sexuality and to understand what is considered normal. Among 12–14 year old girls, early maturing girls were more likely report that they regularly view sexual content in movies, television, and magazines, view rated-R movies, and listen to sexual content in music. As both girls and boys view sexualized media, they are also more likely to imitate the behaviors they watch. O'Hara, Gibbons, Gerrard, and Sargeant (2012) analyzed the movie-watching patterns of 12–14 year olds and then surveyed them 6 years later. The adolescents who watched movies with more sexual content at a younger age were more likely to say that they had been influenced by what they watched, initiated sexual activity earlier than peers who had watched less sexualized content, and were more likely to report that they had imitated the sexual behaviors they had seen in the media.

In addition to influencing sexual attitudes and behaviors, girls' viewing of media images directly and negatively impacts their self-esteem and body satisfaction. For example, girls who watch more television are more likely than others to equate their physical appearance with their overall self-esteem (Girl Scout Research Institute, 2011b). This belief, in turn, can place her at risk for the development of body dissatisfaction and disordered eating practices. In support of this link, Grabe, Ward, and Hyde (2008) conducted a meta-analysis of studies in this area, and their results indicate that media use is directly related to girls' and women's body dissatisfaction, the internalization of the thin ideal, and disordered eating attitudes and beliefs.

While most studies in this area examine links between media consumption and girls' sexualized appearance and behavior, other primary socialization trends for girls have also emerged in recent years, such as those promoting the importance of consumerism, a diva attitude, a carefully crafted online presence, and the ability to appear and act as perfectly as possible. These and other messages will be described and analyzed in later sections of this chapter. In efforts to assist counselors in understanding the recurring messages that girls receive and *how* they have an impact on today's girls (Grabe & Hyde, 2009), the purpose of this chapter is to (a) present messages conveyed in popular culture through an examination of examples that comprise four themes; (b) understand the process through which these messages are internalized by using the framework of cultivation theory, social learning theory, and self-objectification theory; and (c) provide a rationale for the ways in which the current macroculture directly influences and also interacts with microsystem factors such as the family, peers, and school to influence girls' development and mental health.

The themes presented here are drawn from an analysis of clothing, television, movies, music, and toys from current girls' culture. I also cite other authors who have effectively described examples of trends in the current macrosystem (e.g., American Psychological Association [APA] Task Force on Sexualization of Girlhood, 2007; Hinshaw, 2009; Lamb & Brown, 2006; Levin & Kilbourne, 2008; Oppliger, 2008; Orenstein, 2011; Sax, 2010, and some of my previous work in this area: Choate & Curry, 2009; Curry & Choate, 2010). The four trends and examples follow.

PRESSURE ONE: LOOK HOT, SEXY, AND OLDER THAN YOU ARE

In today's popular culture, girls are bombarded with the message that their value and worth will be based on their physical appearance, and their sexual appeal will be the most important avenue to achieving success and popularity. The primacy of sexual appeal is emphasized to the extent that girls learn that a "hot and sexy" appearance should be pursued at all costs (APA, 2007). This pressure is now affecting even the youngest of girls, as they learn from an early age that "hot and sexy" is the norm for girls and women.

As noted by Hinshaw (2009):

Definitions of sexy and pretty have narrowed enormously in recent years—with the ever escalating demand that girls turn themselves into sexual objects. For a girl to fit the acceptable look now requires almost superhuman commitment to dieting, waxing, applying makeup, and shopping, and for some girls, plastic surgery has also come to seem like a minimum requirement. These trends begin at frighteningly young ages. (p. 9)

Both research and books for the public have critiqued this current trend. For example, books like *So Sexy So Soon* (Levin & Kilbourne, 2008), *Packaging Girlhood* (Lamb & Brown, 2006); *The Lolita Effect* (Durham, 2008), *The Triple Bind* (Hinshaw, 2009), *Girls on the Edge* (Sax, 2010), and *Cinderella Ate My Daughter* (Orenstein, 2011) describe the sexualization of girls and the harms associated with this media trend. The APA brought widespread attention to the issue of early sexualization with its 2007 Task Force Report on the Sexualization of Girlhood. According to the report, the sexualization of a person is defined in the following ways: (a) when a person's value comes only from his or her sexual appeal or behavior, to the exclusion of other characteristics; (b) when a person is held to a narrowly defined standard that equates physical attractiveness with being sexual; (c) when a person is sexually objectified, made into a thing for others' sexual use, rather than being seen as a person with the capacity for independent action and decision making; and/or (d) when sexuality is inappropriately imposed on a person (APA, 2007).

These conditions are increasingly frequent and prevalent in popular culture (Lamb & Brown, 2006). Girls are portrayed according to limiting gender stereotypes regarding their appearance and are measured against a narrowly defined standard of physical attractiveness as a determinant of their identity and worth (Choate & Curry, 2009). Various media, from toys, clothing, TV shows, and movies, emphasize the idea that girls from a very young age should appear as "hot and sexy" as possible (Lamb & Brown, 2006; Oppliger, 2008).

For example, both large-scale department stores and specialty girls' clothing stores sell tank tops with words such as "Hottie" and "Future Porn Star" in little girls' sizes. Popular retail stores sell t-shirts that promote the value of being "Hot" by selling "Cuties vs. Hotties" and "Hello my name is Hottie" printed on pajamas. Lingerie for young girls is now the norm, with thong underwear decorated with slogans such as "wink, wink," "eye candy," or "feeling lucky?"; even the question "Who needs credit cards?" is written on the crotch of a popular pair of girls' underwear. Mainstream stores sell padded bras in young girls' departments starting at size 30AA, and Abercrombie and Fitch recently marketed padded pushup triangle bikini tops for girls as young as age 7. Much media attention is also given to the recent trend of highly sexualized Halloween costumes for girls, and to the popularity of "Juicy" girls' fashions, with the word "Juicy" emblazoned on the backside of little girls' sweatpants. The sexualization process even starts at birth, with widely popular "Heelarious" high-heeled shoes marketed for infants in sizes 0–6 months. Offered in exotic animal prints with the tag line, "Her first high heels," these and other examples have led some commentators to coin the phrase "prostitot" or "pimpfant" for current girls' fashion, implying that dressing children in sexy clothing is part of having a "hip" baby, toddler, or young child (Oppliger, 2008).

In addition, television shows and movies for young children regularly feature characters with sexualized features (e.g., commonly female characters such as those on *Thumbellina* and *Winx Club* appear with bare midriffs, heavy makeup, and hour glass figures). As an example, the 42-year-old series *Scooby Doo*, now airing on Cartoon Network, has been recently updated to make its female characters more sexualized. Velma, the "smart" character known for her glasses and ability to solve mysteries, now wears red bows in her hair and spends most of her time on the show aggressively pursuing a romantic relationship with Shaggy, only to be rebuffed by him. Daphne, too, pursues a romantic relationship with Fred, who rejects her advances because he wants to remain friends. Instead of pouring their energies into solving mysteries, the female characters worry about looking and acting in a way to secure male attention (e.g., in one episode, Daphne sports a string bikini to get Fred's attention when he seems attracted to another girl).

As part of being hot and sexy, girls are also socialized to appear and act older than they actually are. Merchandise, clothing, and media programming often encourage girls to dress and act like older teens, to sell her an image of an older teen, not of a girl her age. The term "tween," referring to the age range between middle childhood and the teenage years (usually ages 9–12) was developed as a marketing concept in the 1980s when advertisers discovered that the top age of toy users had dropped from the age of 12 to the younger age of 8. To keep girls interested in toys and merchandise longer, toy companies began to offer products that would promote girls' identification with older girls' lifestyles (Lamb & Brown, 2006). This message is encouraged by marketers who promote age compression (marketing products intended for older teens toward younger girls), age aspiration (marketing to girls' desires to look/act like older teens), and the idea of Kids Are Growing Older Younger (KAGOY) (Schor, 2005) intending to capture girls' brand loyalty in their earliest years so that they might become cradle-to-grave consumers (Lamb & Brown, 2006). According to one brand management executive cited in Lamb and Brown, "If you don't target the consumer in her formative years, you're not going to be relevant through the rest of her life" (p. 17).

Along these same lines, Juicy Couture dolls are marketed to and are popular with very young girls, promoting the brand to young girls and capturing their loyalty early with their newly released babies' and children's wear lines, while older girls are drawn to the purses, fragrances and fashions of Juicy brand products. The Victoria's Secret "Pink" line markets lingerie and products (even stuffed animals) to younger girls with the intent of introducing them to their brand and holding onto them as they become adolescents and young adults.

Popular television series also attempt to hold onto girl viewers as they age. A highly popular TV series and product line including books, clothing, video games, DVDs and feature films, *Winx Club* features attractive adolescent girls who transform into beautiful fairies to save the world from villains. The fairies all have great friendships, use magic to help others, while also wearing bare midriff tops, short shirts, thigh-high boots or high heels, and have long, flowing hair and makeup. The complex message for girls is that they learn that they can be superheroes, but they must also look like sexy, magical fairies in the process. Because the show features both adolescent girls as well as cartoon fairies, younger viewers are attracted to the clothing and makeup of the older girls as well as the fairies, while presumably older girls will stay interested in the show and product line longer because of the age of the actors on the show.

Dolls have also been repackaged to appeal to both younger as well as older markets. For example, the popular *Dora the Explorer*, a young girl with t-shirt, shorts, and tennis shoes, has now been remodeled as a tall, thin adolescent girl, wearing a dress, leggings, ballet flats, and a pearl necklace. This new Dora is the basis for a toy that can grow longer or shorter hair with the touch of a button; another Dora toy is a head-only figure that is used for applying makeup and creating new hairstyles. In this way, marketers hope that girls will embrace the new, older Dora (whose defining characteristics are more about external beauty) and will stay interested in her as they enter the middle childhood years. Along the same lines, Barbie, developed by Mattel in the 1950s, was first marketed to 9–12 year old girls, but is now primarily marketed and advertised to 3–5 year olds. However, the same Barbies are marketed to the preschool set as to older girls, with the intent of keeping girls interested in Barbie as they age. For example, Mattel has developed a Lingerie Barbie line and a newly released Tattoo Barbie, advertised with "Ken" tattooed across her lower back. While these dolls might pique older girls' interests, they also teach preschoolers the importance of sexy lingerie and tattoos as part of being fashionable and successful.

Other highly sexualized dolls also influence girls in their message that they should appear hot, sexy, and older than they are. Monster High dolls, Mattel's biggest product launch since Hot Wheels was released in 1968, are dolls that feature heavy makeup and sexualized fashions, but who are also monsters (e.g., modeled after werewolves, vampires, Frankenstein), loosely based on the popularity of vampires with adolescent girls. They are the basis of upcoming movies, a TV series, and a clothing line. One of the dolls is named "Clawdeen," marketed as needing to spend a lot of time and effort plucking and shaving her unwanted hair so that she looks good in her fashions. Interestingly, the idea of waxing and shaving is becoming increasingly popular with preteens and adolescents; as an example, a national chain of waxing salons recently sponsored billboards that offered bikini and facial wax specials for all girls under the age of 15, while the show *Toddlers and Tiaras* regularly features girls as young as 5 receiving eyebrow waxes, spray-on tans, and wearing false teeth in order to win glitz pageant competitions (*Toddlers and Tiaras*, 2012).

Before the release of the Monster High dolls, the Bratz dolls were the most popular dolls for young girls, even outselling Barbie in recent years. Bratz, known for their long hair, heavy makeup, short skirts, fishnet stockings, stiletto heels, and feather boas, are highly sexualized representations of adolescent girls, but are also targeted to younger girls (with its "Baby Bratz" line), teaching girls to "hit the town and dance the night away" and to "know how important it is to be seen!" To attract additional girls, Bratz has recently released a "Bratzilla" line to compete with the Monster High dolls.

There is evidence that these toys and dolls do influence girls' views of themselves and others. When researchers showed 6-year old girls a pair of paper dolls (one that was highly sexualized with makeup, bare midriff, and high heels, and the other wearing fashionable but modest clothing; see Activity 1), the girls chose the sexualized doll as the one they would prefer as their ideal self, and as the one that they believe would be most popular. In contrast, they chose the regular doll as the one that they most actually look like and as the one they would prefer to play with (Starr & Ferguson, 2012). Even by age 6, girls have already learned that looking "hot and sexy" is something to aspire to and that will lead to popularity and attention from others, even though the sexy doll did not seem to look like them or appear more fun or interesting for play.

In sum, the current macrosystem message for girls primarily suggests that developing a sexy image is of utmost importance to girls' identity and success. As part of being valued as "hot and sexy," girls also learn that they must appear older and more mature than they are. In addition to messages about their *appearance*, girls also receive macrosystem messages about how they should *act*, as discussed in the following section.

Source: Dollz Mania's ChaZie Dollmaker, dollzmania.net/ChaZieMaker.htm

Activity One. In Starr and Ferguson's study, 6-year-old girls were shown these two images and were asked which one they would like to be like, which one would be most popular, which one they actually look like, and which doll they would prefer to play with. Try asking some younger girls these questions as they view the images and ask them why they think as they do. How do these answers compare with Starr et al.'s findings? What do you think are the most relevant influences on the way girls answer these questions?

PRESSURE TWO: BE A DIVA

The term "diva" is frequently used in popular culture not only to refer to celebrities known for their tendency to be demanding, entitled, and to engage in provocative behavior, but it is also used to reference all girls who are highly emotional and insistent about what they want. The new diva attitude still requires that girls act nice and polite to others, but at the same time encourages girls to demand what they want, to believe they deserve to be pampered, and to own the right merchandise. With labels like "diva" and "drama queen" regularly tossed out as labels for girls, "Diva" or "Princess" emblazoned on onesies, and t-shirts for girls printed with slogans such as "Professional Drama Queen" and "Spoiled Princess Soccer Club," it is not surprising that many girls grow up learning to act like a diva, with designer fashions, sense of entitlement, and a "bad is the new good" attitude (Sax, 2010).

One important aspect of being a diva is to have an attitude that is driven by a desire to have the "right" things, which currently include designer clothing and a "passion for fashion" (also the tag line for the Bratz dolls). Girls receive the message that they should "shop till you drop," engage in "retail therapy," and acquire the latest fashions in order to be happy. The importance of this passion is currently being marketed to girls through the phrase "girl power," which equates power with the ability to acquire and consume merchandise. In other words, to be powerful as a girl, one must also be powerful as a consumer; as stated by Harris (2004), today's emphasis on girls' consumerism "… commodifies girls' culture and connects the achievement of a successful identity as a girl with looking the right way and buying the right things" (Harris, 2004, p. 17).

As examples of the trend emphasizing that empowerment comes from shopping (Douglas, 2010), current fashion and beauty magazines that have been modified for adolescent audiences (e.g., *Teen Elle, Teen Vogue, CosmoGirl*), as well as many television shows popular with young adolescent viewers (e.g., *Gossip Girl, The OC*, or reality shows like *Teen Cribs, Keeping up with the Kardashians*), also send the message that owning designer brands and the right merchandise are necessary for success and happiness. In addition to girl power through consumerism, media images simultaneously promote idealized images of beauty and success that influence how girls think they should look. In a recent national survey, most girls ages 13–17 say that the fashion industry and or the media place a lot of pressure on teen girls to be thin, and 48% of girls in the survey say they wish they were as skinny as the models they see in magazines (Girl Scout Research Institute, 2009).

In addition to a "passion for fashion," the diva attitude also encompasses having a desire to be the center of attention and to be as famous as possible. More girls desire to be famous today than in the past (Girl Scout Research Institute, 2011a) and this is fueled in part by the popularity of reality television and Internet sites such as YouTube or Facebook, wherein a girl who posts a video clip or image that goes "viral" can become an instant celebrity. As girls observe the current celebrity culture of pop stars and the clips that are widely viewed, they see how acting out in edgy, rebellious, impulsive, and often sexually provocative ways can become the easiest avenue for gaining attention from others. Young women on reality shows are revered for sexually acting out and for fighting with one another. Further, as girls view the Diesel clothing ad campaign "Be Stupid," they see girls acting out in risk-taking, sexually provocative scenes (encouraging girls to be "risky" and "stupid" in order to be popular). The television program *Gossip Girl* often posts advertisements featuring adolescent girls in sexually suggestive poses, promoting the show as "parents' worst nightmare," "a nasty piece of work," and "mindblowingly inappropriate."

Girls also learn that they can gain attention for criminal behavior or for mental health problems. Young female celebrities such as Lindsey Lohan and Paris Hilton receive high levels of media attention for their arrests, jail time, and rehabilitation programs. Several others have garnered additional attention for their highly publicized criminal behavior, eating disorders, self-injury, and substance use disorders. While on the one hand it is positive that these celebrities are openly discussing certain mental health problems, the culmination of these stories is harmful, in that the overall message for girls is they can gain fame through acting rebelliously, dramatically, and through engaging in high-risk behaviors (Sax, 2010).

A third aspect of the diva attitude is that girls learn to view one another as competitors. From an early age, the message they receive is that they should watch out for other girls: "they are your competitors, not just your friends" (Lamb & Brown, 2006, p. 44). For example, the most popular show among older children and teens is *Pretty Little Liars* (TV.Com, 2012) in which girls compete with one another for their beauty, popularity, and ability to keep secrets from one another. In popular reality shows like *Jersey Shore, Real World*, and competition shows like *The Bachelor* and *Project Runway*, young women compete with one another for attention and a romantic partner. Surveys indicate that girls are paying attention to these messages: Girls who watch reality TV (compared with those do not watch these programs) are significantly more likely to agree that:

- "By nature girls are catty and competitive."
- "You have to lie to get what you want."
- "Gossip is a normal part of relationships between girls."
- "Being mean earns you more respect than being nice."
- "Girls often have to compete for guys' attention."
- "It's hard for me to trust other girls."

Often as part of their competition with one another, today's girls are also more likely to be physically aggressive toward others, and particularly toward other girls, than they were in the past (Garbarino, 2006). While girls' aggression is sometimes viewed as a sign of empowerment (e.g., girls are more likely to express themselves openly and fight back when they perceive they have been wronged), at the same time their behavior is an indication that they lack the skills for using positive coping strategies to deal with perceived rejections and insults in an adaptive manner.

This shift toward female competition and aggression is seen as a reflection of the glamorization of physically aggressive women. Women and violence is portrayed as an aspect of the diva role in the entertainment industry through films, music videos, television programs, teen magazines, and video games (e.g., Lara Croft in *Tomb Raiders*). These images result in a normalization of female physical aggression (Prothrow-Stithand & Spivak, 2005). According to Garbarino (2006), as girls grow up viewing television programs with verbally and physically aggressive female characters, girls learn to become desensitized to violence and to accept female aggression as normal and expected. Therefore, girls learn that not only is today's diva image one of fashion, beauty, celebrity, and competition, but it can also involve an aggressive attitude and the idealization of physical violence. According to Dellasega and Nixon (2003):

> Role models for today's teens are not powerful women who have succeeded because of their persistence and kindness to others, but rather superstar singers acting like sexy schoolgirls and movie stars firing machine guns or using martial arts on opponents while wearing skintight jumpsuits. No wonder young women find themselves in a state of extreme confusion, unsure of how to relate to either themselves or others. (p. 3)

In sum, the diva persona comprises fashion-consciousness, a sense of entitlement, provocative behavior, and even physical aggression. The macrosystem messages regarding acting like a diva are primarily geared toward how girls act in person. Next, I will turn to the pressures girls receive about online activities that occur not live but in cyberspace; nevertheless, their online image comprises an important part of girls' reality.

PRESSURE THREE: WHO ARE YOU?: FIND OUT BY PLASTERING YOURSELF ONLINE

Through almost constant use of the Internet, cell phones, and all social media, pre- and adolescent girls in essence live in a cyberbubble (Sax, 2010). The vast majority of preteens and adolescents have a cell phone and use the Internet, and this number will grow larger now that Facebook has announced plans to launch a preteen version of the site. However, many underage users are already using social networking sites. According to statistics in Consumer Reports cited by Orenstein (Too Young for Status Updates, 2012), 50% of parents with 12-year-olds said that their child already has a Facebook account and that most of those surveyed had lied about the child's age so that he or she could open the account. It is not surprising, then, that 38% of past-year users of Facebook are under the age of 13, and 25% are under the age of 10.

While the potential dangers of children's unsupervised use of the Internet in general and for social networking in particular have been well documented, less has been written about the effect of the ubiquitous cyberbubble on girls' development and mental health. The cyberbubble tends to emphasize the *appearance* of popularity rather than *actual* relationships, as counted by the number of social networking friends one has (currently an average of 351 friends for adolescent girls, Girl Scout Research Institute, 2010), tagged pictures, "like" statuses, and comments made by others. In essence, the expression of a girl's thoughts, feelings, and relationships is posted so that the world can see the activity (and inactivity) of her electronic life.

In addition to developing a face-to-face presentation based on her newly forming identity, today's girls are also required to assemble a social networking image that is the ideal combination of witty phrases, pictures, products, and "likes." As girls feel pressured to appear camera ready at all social events and to distill their lives into soundbites that can be posted online, girls become in essence a "micro-celebrity... having to carefully manage everything they say and do because they know it can end up online within a matter of minutes"(Sax, 2010, p. 65). This can create what Turkle (2011) terms a "presentation anxiety" regarding a girl's image on social networking sites. This anxiety causes her to spend hours of her life compiling her social networking pages, ensuring that she presents the right image. Presenting a "cool" online identity can be highly confusing for girls who are in the midst of trying to formulate an actual identity. Instead of expressing her authentic thoughts online, she "subtly adjusts what she is writing to suit what she thinks her friends want to read. After a while she might become the girl she is pretending to be"(Sax, 2010, p. 38). Not surprisingly, in a survey of 13–17 year old girls, 74% agreed that most girls their age use social networking sites to make themselves look "cooler than they are" (Girl Scout Research Institute, 2010). As a microcelebrity in her own social circle, her public and private lives are blurred, and she experiences the pressure of having to avoid social mistakes, always concerned about saying and doing the right thing.

This trend is also harmful in that being constantly connected is exhausting for today's adolescent girls, who feel pressured to follow hundreds of friends' status updates, pictures, and cell phone texts, often to the extent of neglecting their in-person relationships (Turkle, 2011). In addition, it can make them more body conscious and anxious about how their appearance is judged by others. For girls who are concerned about others' approval, checking Facebook provides a barometer about how much they are liked or how appealing they are. Research suggests that the more girls care about their looks, the more they check their Facebook profiles, and the more they check their Facebook profiles, the more they care about their looks (Orenstein, 2012). In one national survey of 600 Facebook users age 16 to 40, 51% of users reported that seeing photos of themselves and others on Facebook makes them more conscious of their body and weight, and 44% said they are always conscious when attending social events that photos of them might get posted on Facebook. This finding leads researchers to caution that Facebook might be fueling a social comparison and body conscious mentality among users (Center for Eating Disorders at Sheppard Pratt, 2012). While this study included both adolescents and adults, it is conceivable that the percentages would be higher if only adolescent girls were included.

In addition, if girls want to be popular on social networks, they learn that displays of sexiness in their pictures are a primary avenue toward attaining that popularity (Hinshaw, 2009). Through social modeling of this practice, teens and preteens are encouraged to post suggestive photos of themselves, so as to be highly tagged or rated on such sites as

Facebook but also on sites such as Facethejury.com or Formspring.me. There is also an increase in adolescents' use of sexting in recent years. According to a 2012 study of high school students, 28% of the sample reported having sent a naked picture of themselves through text or email, and 31% reported having asked someone else for sext. More than half of the students (57%) had been asked to send a sext. Girls (68.4%) more often than boys reported having been asked to send a sext. Girls who engaged in sexting behaviors were more likely to have had sexual intercourse and to have experienced a higher prevalence of risky sex behaviors (multiple partners, using drugs or alcohol) (Temple et al., 2012). It is important to note that while adolescents might be posting or sexting pictures to gain attention or popularity, these same girls may inadvertently send the wrong message about their willingness to participate in sexual activity (Oppliger, 2008). Clearly, sexualized images of girls posted through cell phones or online increases the risk of others viewing them as sexual objects and increases their vulnerability to sexual victimization (Curry & Choate, 2010).

Online use that can lead to inauthentic identity development, presentation anxiety, body monitoring, and vulnerability to sexualization are negative aspects of this cultural trend. However, most girls claim that social networking and texting helps them stay closer to their friends (Girl Scout Research Institute, 2010). While this is one positive aspect of online use for girls' friendships, heavy online communication is also related to relational aggression and cyberbullying. During the past decade, a large body of research has centered on this aspect of girls' friendships, termed relational aggression (RA): the act of hurting others through manipulating or harming their relationships (Crick & Grotpeter, 1995; Underwood, 2003). Since the inception of the term by Crick and her colleagues, researchers have demonstrated that RA is used significantly more by girls than boys and is a relatively normative conflict style in girls' peer groups (Crick & Grotpeter, 1995). According to Underwood (2003), girls' use of RA is powerful because it threatens the asset girls' value the most during this time: losing acceptance by friends and romantic partners.

Cyberbullying is a type of RA that takes place using electronic technology (e.g., devices and equipment such as cell phones, computers, and tablets, as well as communication tools including social media sites, text messages, chat, and websites). Examples of cyberbullying include mean text messages or emails, rumors sent by email or posted on social networking sites, and posting embarrassing pictures, videos, websites, or fake profiles (Stopbullying.gov, 2012). According to the 2011 Youth Risk Behavior Survey (Eaton et al., 2010), approximately

16% of 9th to 12th graders say that they have been bullied online, although this is likely to be an underestimate of the problem due to underreporting and ever-changing technologies. Several authors claim that cyberbullying is becoming increasingly common because it is faster to use than other methods, reaches more people, and the bully never has to face the victim (Dellasega & Nixon, 2003; Ophelia Project, 2007; Simmons, 2002). Cyberbullying decreases the responsibility and accountability aggressors feel for their actions, it can free aggressors to say things they might not otherwise say, and victims are even more negatively affected because they don't know who the aggressors are (Blair, 2003). Cyberbullying is also related to the previously discussed findings that girls report feeling as if other girls can't be trusted and that gossip and cattiness are normal parts of girls' relationships. If girls do not express their feelings toward one another openly, or are socialized to believe that being mean to others is a normal part of being a girl, then RA and cyberbullying behaviors will likely continue as part of girls' online experiences.

It is clear that girls experience pressures to look and act in a certain way, both online and in person. The next pressure explores how all of the previous themes interact in such a way that girls experience pressure to conform to all societal expectations simultaneously.

PRESSURE FOUR: YOU CAN HAVE IT ALL, AND DO IT ALL PERFECTLY

As reviewed previously, girls are socialized to look hot and sexy, to act like a diva, and to be dedicated to maintaining an active online image. These goals in and of themselves are impossible for most girls to achieve, but in addition, girls learn that they must also excel in academics and sports, and that they must make all of their efforts appear effortless. Indeed, if a girl looks as if she is trying too hard, then she is viewed negatively (Hinshaw, 2009). In his book *The Triple Bind*, Hinshaw identifies the bind for today's girls: to excel at what have traditionally been considered "girl" skills—care taking, relationship building, cooperation, empathy, and finding and keeping a boyfriend; along with displaying high levels of what have traditionally been considered "boy" skills—becoming a competitive athlete and scholar through assertiveness, competitiveness, and commitment to being a winner at all costs. To add to these two traditional pressures, girls must also become perfect, having and doing it all, whether she becomes a professional athlete, tenured professor, reality show star, or future CEO. According to Orenstein (2011), she must be both Cinderella and

Supergirl, aggressive and agreeable, smart and stunning, all the while undergoing paralyzing pressure to be perfect. The nonprofit organization Girls Inc. commented on the pressure for girls to be "supergirl" in 2000 with the publication of the report, *The Supergirl Dilemma: The Pressure on Girls to Be Perfect, Accomplished, Thin, and Accommodating,* noting that these expectations for girls are unrealistic and can result in negative outcomes for girls.

The pressure for perfection teaches some girls to work tirelessly in today's fast-paced culture to multitask her way toward the goal of meeting unrealistic and contradictory goals, setting her up for a sense of frustration and failure. For example, if a girl learns that she should be highly concerned about others' feelings and do whatever she can to maintain her relationships, how can she simultaneously be highly competitive on her volleyball team, competing against her teammates and friends for the top spot on the team? If a girl's strengths are rooted in her ability to connect with and care for others, how can she nurture this strength while also fighting to be the "winner" both academically and athletically? She is wondering, can she be expected to be a Diva, Bachelorette, or Real Housewife while also running a Fortune 500 company or becoming the next U.S. president?

In response, many girls are learning that they must overlook these contradictions in order to do it all, and to be it all. In her book, *Perfect Girls, Starving Daughters* (2007), Courtney Martin writes about the pressures that current girls and women have learned to place on themselves:

> We are the daughters of feminists who said, "You can be anything" and we heard "You have to be everything." We must get A's. We must make money. We must save the world. We must be thin. We must be unflappable. We must be beautiful. We are the anorectics, the bulimics, the overexercisers, the overeaters. We must be perfect. We must make it look effortless. (p. 18)

Susan Douglas (2010) also wrote about this conflict as becoming the price for success that girls (and future women) realize they must pay:

> We can excel in school, play sports, go to college, aspire to—and get—jobs previously reserved for men, be working mothers, and so forth. But in exchange we must obsess about our faces, weight, breast size, clothing brands, decorating, perfectly calibrated child-rearing, about pleasing men, and being envied by other women. (p. 16)

These pressures to measure up in all areas can be exhausting for girls, particularly if they perform out of fear of being rejected or viewed as unacceptable if they do not live up to supergirl expectations. The accumulation of these pressures and the belief that she must achieve these standards of perfection can lead to negative consequences for today's girls, as explored in the following section.

CONSEQUENCES OF CURRENT TRENDS FOR GIRLS' DEVELOPMENT AND MENTAL HEALTH

As illustrated through the preceding themes, girls are socialized to reach the unrealistic current ideal for females, and few will be able to measure up to this standard. In a culture in which girls have power in ways that they have never been able to enjoy before, there is also pressure on them to look and act in ways that are disempowering, contradictory, and inauthentic to their developing sense of self. Instead of thriving in this new world of "girl power," many girls are struggling and are developing mental health problems as they encounter the stressors of adolescence. It is important, therefore, for counselors to understand the processes through which these macrosystem pressures are experienced in earliest girlhood, internalized by the preteenage years, and then manifested as mental health symptoms in the adolescent period. Three theories offer a framework for conceptualizing the way that girls learn and internalize cultural pressures. First, Cultivation Theory (Gerbner, 1998) posits that the mass media projects a system of messages, images, and dialogues that construct a portrayal of reality for viewers. For those who are frequently exposed to this system, the message accumulates over a period of time, so that viewers adopt these same media perspectives as their own perspective on reality. As a result, viewers learn to internalize media views as their own beliefs and value systems (Gerbner, 1998).

While Cultivation Theory explains that media does strongly influence the beliefs of its viewers, Bandura's Social Learning Theory (1991) discusses more specifically how the belief system is learned. In the case of adolescent girls and gender role stereotypes discussed throughout this chapter, girls learn which behaviors are considered appropriate or inappropriate for girls, as well as those behaviors that will bring about desired rewards (e.g., if I look and act this way, I will be noticed, accepted, and have value). Social learning occurs through modeling (through viewing female sex models on television, which are also reinforced in her family and peer group), her lived experiences (e.g., opportunities or situations in which she is rewarded or discouraged from engaging in certain behaviors), and direct instruction from others (e.g., magazine articles tell her that if she dresses in a certain outfit, it will be certain to get a boy's attention). In other words, she learns of macrosystem pressures and expectations for girls, tries them out in real-world settings, and, based on the feedback she receives, she will adopt the attitude and behavior as part of what it means for her to be a girl.

Cultivation and Social Learning Theories are applicable to media influences on children's development in general, while Self-Objectification Theory is helpful to explore the specific process through which girls internalize cultural pressures regarding sexualized appearance and behavior. Self-Objectification Theory (Frederickson, Roberts, Noll, Quinn, & Twenge, 1998) asserts that if girls learn that sexual appeal will result in their social success, they learn to see themselves as sexual objects (APA, 2007; Choate & Curry, 2009). As they absorb these messages from the larger culture, girls may also have personal experiences that serve to reinforce these pressures. As girls are exposed to this same consistent message from macro- and microsystems, they begin to adopt these cultural attitudes as their own standards for self-evaluation and worth. Girls gradually begin to view themselves in an objectified manner, evaluating themselves in the third person (e.g., "How do I appear to others?"), critically judging their bodies and general appearance against idealized cultural standards. In turn, when a girl self-objectifies, she is likely to engage in excessive body monitoring, feelings of preoccupation with others' evaluations, and a feeling of being constantly "checked out" by others, particularly becoming aware of the "male gaze" (Frederickson et al., 1998).

McKinley explained self-objectification as consisting of three components: body surveillance, body shame, and control beliefs. Body surveillance refers to the pressure a girl feels to monitor her appearance, repeatedly checking to make sure she looks her best, and becoming overly concerned that she will be evaluated negatively by others (McKinley, 1999). Body shame occurs when a girl perceives that her body does not meet the media's standards of beauty, thinness, or sexiness. When she experiences body shame, she will not only feel negatively about her body, she feels like she is a bad person because she does not meet beauty ideals (Choate & Curry, 2009). Control beliefs refer to a girl's attitude that she should work her hardest in order to control her appearance and to do whatever it takes to achieve cultural standards of beauty.

Research indicates that the self-objectification is found in girls as early as age 11 (Lindberg, Grabe, & Hyde, 2007) and has been demonstrated experimentally with 6-year-old girls (Starr et al., 2012, as reported previously) and in 13-year-olds who engage in frequent music television viewing (Grabe & Hyde, 2009). Further, it is linked to negative psychological consequences that serve to impede girls' performance in a variety of domains including academic performance, career aspirations, and personal development (Davies, Spencer, Quinn, & Gerhardstein, 2002; Frederickson et al., 1998; Halpern, 2006; Hinshaw, 2009; Lamb & Brown, 2006; Tolman, Impett, Tracy, & Michael, 2006). It is concerning that when a girl is focused on body monitoring, self-control, self-evaluation, and concerns about how she is being evaluated by others, she has fewer resources available for other life activities. As she attempts to focus on her daily routine, her ability to concentrate becomes fragmented with feelings of being evaluated negatively by herself or others (Choate & Curry, 2009; Davies et al., 2002; Frederickson et al., 1998).

Harms to Academic Performance

Self-objectification can have a negative impact on girls' academic performance when girls are distracted, causing a decrease in their available mental resources needed for challenging academic tasks (Frederickson et al., 1998). When her consciousness is fragmented, a girl has decreased opportunities to experience peak motivational states (known as *flow*, Csikszentmihalyi, 1990). Also, spending many hours watching music or YouTube videos, texting, checking and posting on Facebook, and multitasking while using these forms of media is related to negative social outcomes in girls 8–12 years old. Researchers found that girls who frequently multitask with digital devices were actually more likely to report not feeling normal, feeling less social success, sleeping less, and having more friends with whom their parents perceive as bad influences (Pea et al., 2012).

A classic study by Frederickson and colleagues (1998) also demonstrates how self-objectification can distract from academic performance. In a sample of college students, participants were asked to try on either a swimsuit or a sweater and observe themselves in a full-length mirror (with no observers present). The women in the swimsuit condition performed worse on a subsequent complex math test compared to the women wearing a sweater, even though there were no differences in ability between the two groups at the outset of the study. The males in the study performed equally well under both conditions. While this study was conducted with college students, it is not hard to extrapolate that when an adolescent girl engages in body surveillance, self-evaluation, self-control behaviors, and concern about others, judgment of her, her mental resources are not fully directed to the required task. If she is overly concerned about what others are thinking about her appearance, she may be less likely to participate in the classroom setting and will be distracted from her academic performance. In turn, it is likely that she will not perform to her fullest potential in academic or future professional environments (Choate & Curry, 2009).

Another line of research that is related to women's internalization of gender stereotypes are *stereotype threat* studies. Stereotype threat occurs when a person's group membership is made salient at the time a cognitive test is being administered, so that stereotypes about one's group, such as "girls are not good at math" are activated for that individual. The tests taker is then threatened that she risks being judged by those stereotypes, or that the negative stereotype could provide a plausible explanation for her performance (e.g., "I worry they will think I am not good at math just because I am a girl"; Davies et al., 2002). Several studies found that young women asked to view gender-stereotypical commercials (e.g., clips of women who are only concerned about appearance and become overwhelmed with business-oriented tasks) actually performed worse on a math test when compared to women who did not watch those types of commercials. Although these studies measure the short-term effects of stereotype activation in women, it is plausible that these gender stereotypes are activated many times per day in girls when they frequently view popular media. As described previously in the chapter, because girls spend more time viewing television and using digital devices than any other activity, they are reminded of how current culture views girls' and women's worth and abilities on an all-too-frequent basis. If girls begin to believe pervasive gender stereotypes, they may be hesitant to enroll in upper-level math and science classes in both high school and in college (Halpern, 2006), which may in turn limit their future educational and/or career opportunities.

Harms to Mental Health

Self-objectification is also closely related to body dissatisfaction and negative body image, which is in turn associated with poor self-esteem, early smoking onset, unnecessary cosmetic surgery, and poor body esteem and eating disorders such as anorexia, bulimia, and binge eating disorder (Stice & Shaw, 2003; Tolman et al., 2006; see Chapter 4, this volume). Self-objectification and negative body image are also highly associated with anxiety and depression, which is increasing in adolescent girls in recent years (Rudolph, Hammen, & Daley, 2006; Substance Abuse and Mental Health Services Administration, 2012; see Chapter 3, this volume). As mentioned in a previous section, a recent study by Grabe and Hyde analyzed the relationship between adolescent girls, music television viewing and their psychological well-being, and found that music television is directly associated to self-objectification, which in turn is related to body esteem, dieting, depressive symptoms, anxiety, and confidence in math ability (Grabe & Hyde, 2009).

Another potential consequence of girls' self-objectification is sexual harassment and victimization (see Chapter 7, this volume). When both girls and boys are frequently exposed to sexualized media messages regarding women's value and worth, they begin to adopt these attitudes and learn to see girls and women as simplified types or objects, not as people. As this occurs in the early years of childhood, it becomes increasingly acceptable for children to treat girls and women with less respect, compassion, and empathy, and to act toward them in disrespectful and sexually degrading ways (Lamb & Brown, 2006). This can lead to the normalization of sexual harassment for both boys and girls. Unfortunately, girls regularly experience sexual harassment as part of their daily lives at school. For example, according to the most recent American Association of University Women [AAUW], Hill, and Kearl report (2011), fully half of students experienced some form of sexual harassment during the 2010 to 2011 school year and 87% of these students said it had a negative effect on them. Girls are more likely to be sexually harassed than boys (56% vs. 40%) both in person and via electronic means. Thirteen percent of girls said they had been touched in an unwelcome, sexual way, 9% were physically intimidated in a sexual way, and 4% report that they were forced to do something sexual at school.

Further, girls are more likely than boys to say they have been negatively affected by sexual harassment and were most affected by unwanted sexual comments, gestures, and having sexual rumors spread electronically about them. Girls were more likely than boys to report that these behaviors caused them to have trouble sleeping, to not want to go to school, to feel sick or nauseated, to find it hard to concentrate to study, and to change the way they went to or came home from school (AAUW et al., 2011). It is not difficult to imagine that frequent experiences of sexual harassment and its negative outcomes have a cumulative effect on both perpetrators and victims of harassment. Based on widespread harassment by peers and potential romantic partners, students may become desensitized toward viewing girls only according to their sexual appeal and what they have to offer sexually. In turn, both boys and girls may experience increasing difficulty in determining what constitutes consensual and nonconsensual sexual activity in their developing romantic relationships during the adolescent years.

In today's culture in which girls are socialized to be sexy in order to be acceptable or valued, girls may even confuse sexual harassment with the acceptance that they seek from others (Grube & Lens, 2003). When sexualized attitudes and behaviors are normalized through the media images they view and the relationships they observe, girls will be less confident in labeling or reporting offensive behaviors as sexual harassment. This may in turn influence their future decisions to report more severe forms of unwanted sexual behavior, including sexual assault and rape (Choate & Curry, 2009).

Finally, girls who self-objectify may also learn that the best way to achieve acceptance and to be noticed is to present themselves to others in an overly sexualized manner (either in person or online). Younger girls are learning to appear and act older than they are (see "Pressure One"), and generally this will involve a sexualized self-presentation. While girls may not be aware of the message that their appearance or behavior sends to others, this places them at risk for sexual victimization by predators. Particularly for girls who experience early pubertal onset, many girls may not have the developmental capacity for clearly understanding the dangers of potential exploitation and victimization. Concerned parents, counselors, and mentors are needed to assist girls in seeking affirmation from positive sources (and from providing it for themselves). They are also needed to provide guidance as they help to protect girls from high-risk online presentations and in-person activities.

CONCLUSION

In summary, the purpose of this chapter was to provide an overview of the macrosystem for girls as it exists in current Western societies and to discuss how the system impacts girls throughout their early years and into adolescence. Today's girls are learning that their appearance should be "hot and sexy," their actions should be diva-like, and their online presence should be even "cooler" than they are in person. Adding to these expectations, girls also learn that they should be "supergirls"— smart, athletic, kind, competitive, and beautiful. Clearly, these macrosystem messages can be complex and even contradictory for girls as they are in a developmental period in which they are trying to establish a sense of identity. These pressures can become an impediment to the development of a girl's authentic sense of self, affecting her ability to learn who she is and what she believes apart from what others expect of her. This is of great concern during adolescence as girls begin to prioritize their time and activities, focusing on what they perceive to be most important. While conforming to cultural norms, they might ignore the development of other important life areas such as spirituality, creativity, true friendship, or community service. As described in the previous section, this can lead to limited self-development, an over-focus on appearance, and negative academic or mental health consequences for girls who feel trapped underneath all of these pressures.

The four pressures discussed in this chapter will also be explored and integrated throughout the forthcoming chapters on the treatment of mental health concerns in adolescent girls. In the next chapter, I will turn from these macrosystem issues in order to highlight the microsystems that directly impinge on girls' lives—their families, peers, communities, and schools—and how these systems interact with an individual girl's physical and psychosocial development.

CASE EXAMPLE

Caitlyn is a 13-year-old girl who lives with her newly divorced mother and two younger brothers, ages 4 and 8. Before the divorce, she was a good student and was active in a local soccer league. She had always been excited to meet new people and try out new things, but now she is reluctant to do anything with her family. She is upset with her parents about the divorce and has a conflictual relationship with her mother, especially now that her mother frequently asks her to babysit her two younger brothers in the afternoons and evenings. She has stopped caring about school, her grades have dropped, and since her mother is unable to drive her to and from soccer practice, she has had to quit the team. Now when she is home, the only thing she likes to do is spend time in her room watching television and movies, visiting Facebook and texting her friends on her smartphone. Because her family leaves her alone when she is in her room with her door closed, she is free to watch whatever she wants on television and has unlimited access to the Internet. She loves to watch reality television shows and to follow her favorite celebrities on Facebook and Twitter. She loves to see how they dress and how they manage to get attention. Even when she is babysitting her brothers, she keeps her phone and laptop close by for texting and posting online. She feels anxiety when she cannot be near her computer or phone.

(continued)

CASE EXAMPLE (*continued*)

The more time she spends online, however, the more she becomes dissatisfied with herself.

Her mother is not aware of this, but she has started hanging out with a new group of girls at school and online after school. The girls tend to wear the latest fashions, including sexy lingerie and suggestive t-shirts, and they are also interested in boys who are in high school. These friendships have caused her to start becoming more self-conscious about her body. Caitlyn has recently started her period and has developed full breasts, which she likes, but she has also gained weight in her stomach, hips, and thighs, which she hates. She feels ashamed of her lower body, and she has tried several diets and exercise routines to help her lose weight. Her friends have told her about some diet pills that they can obtain for her, and she wants to take them so she will be as thin as the actresses she sees on TV. Her mother is always complaining about her own weight and is always on a diet, so Caitlyn and her mother sometimes compare their diet strategies.

Despite her negative view of her body, Caitlyn thinks she will feel better if she can wear lingerie and clothes like her friends. She knows that this is what older boys notice, and she really wants some older boys to pay attention to her the way that they do with her friends. Her mother has agreed to buy her these new clothes, but only if Caitlyn will babysit to earn the money for purchasing the items. Her mother doesn't like her dressing this way, but lately she is too tired to fight with her and just wants some peace in their relationship.

Caitlyn has also started spending lots of time at night posting flirtatious pictures to her Facebook page and in even posting some sexually suggestive statements in an effort to get noticed by a boy in high school that she is now interested in. One night he texts her, and they text until 4 a.m., all while her mother believes she is sleeping. She does not know how she will act the next time she sees him, because they have never actually met.

Discussion Questions

1. Which of the media messages described in this chapter seems to be having an impact on Caitlyn?
2. Which of the four macrosystem themes or pressures has Caitlyn internalized, and in what ways does this put her at risk?
3. Does Caitlyn need counseling, or is this just normal teen behavior? If you were her counselor, how would you want to intervene with her? What does she need in order to thrive?

RESOURCES

www.sparksummit.com
This website address the sexualization of girls and women. It also helps empower girls to take a stand against sexualization of girls in mainstream culture.

www.girlsinc.org
A non-profit organization that encourages girls to learn how to excel academically, physically, mentally, and financially. It also encourages girls to explore careers in the math, science, and technology fields.

www.poweredbygirls.org
A great tool to use to encourage media literacy by promoting media activism in girls.

www.missrepresentation.org
This site focuses on countering stereotypes and negative attitudes toward women in mainstream culture.

www.about-face.org
A site to teach girls and women media literacy skills to equip them with tools to resist harmful media messages.

www.braincake.org
A website that encourages girls to pursue interests in math, science, and technology careers and activities.

www.rachelsimmons.com
A website that has great resources and blogs for girls to explore to help deal with difficult issues in their lives. It also gives recommendations for books about different challenges and situations girls may experience.

www.hghw.org
Hardy Girls, Healthy Women promotes health, well-being, and independence in girls and women, and offers links to resources and programs for girls.

My World Is Spinning Upside Down: Family, Peer, School, and Developmental Upheavals

In Chapter 1, I discussed an ecological model for understanding girls' experiences and explored the recent shifts in our macrosystem messages conveyed to pre- and adolescent girls. These trends, primarily transmitted through the media, play a large role in the ways that girls are currently socialized. In addition, there are multiple micro-level influences operating in girls' lives at this time that can serve to mediate these cultural pressures. Parents, peers, and school environments can either exacerbate or provide a buffer against messages that limit girls' value and worth. It is important to understand these influences and how they moderate the impact of the macrosystem in girls' lives.

It is also striking that at the same time girls are receiving strong cultural pressures about how they should look and act, they are also undergoing major physical and psychosocial developmental changes during the transition through adolescence (Belsky et al., 2007; Steinberg & Silk, 2002; Weisz & Hawley, 2002). Simultaneously, they are also experiencing dramatic upheavals in their relationships with parents and peers, their family structure, their academic experiences, and their overall school environment (Laser & Nicotera, 2011; Straus, 2006). Counselors who work with adolescent girls, therefore, also need grounding in developmental literature to understand these seismic changes in girls' development.

The chapter begins with an overview of current trends in family structure and parenting styles as girls reach adolescence, followed by an exploration of changes in peer and school environments that are simultaneously operating in girls' lives. In the next part of the chapter, I provide an outline of the key developmental tasks of adolescence, highlighting the physical changes of puberty; changes in gender role, cognitive and identity development; and developmental shifts in relationships with parents and peers. Finally, the chapter covers strategies that counselors can use to work with girls and their parents in order to provide the connections, monitoring, and limit-setting that girls need during this period in their lives.

A TIME OF FLUX FOR ADOLESCENT GIRLS: FAMILY, PEERS, AND SCHOOLS

Current Trends in Family Structure

It is important for counselors to consider changes in family structure that have contributed to adolescent girls' socialization and their increased stressors in recent decades. One important trend is that more parents are working full time, working split shifts, or working more than one job in order to support their families in a time of economic downturn. There are higher numbers of dual earner households, and it is widely known that women's employment outside the home has increased dramatically over the past 50 years: 71.3% of women with children are currently in the labor force, and 62.4% of women with children under the age of 6 are employed (U.S. Department of Labor, Bureau of Labor Statistics, 2011). As a result of these economic changes, girls are more likely to spend time alone or to have more time without parental supervision. When parents are home, they may continue to work due in part to their 24-hour Internet connections that do not respect traditional 9-to-5 workday limits (Turkle, 2011). Therefore, even when parents are home with their children, it is difficult for them to spend unplugged, quality family time when they are multitasking and when they are exhausted from long, hectic days of work.

Parenting styles have also changed in recent years, affecting adolescent girls in significant ways. First, there is a style of underinvolved parenting that has evolved for several reasons. The first is due to the stressors already outlined—for example, single parents struggling to provide for their families may have few resources for providing the quality time, limit setting, and supervision that girls need during this time period. Another form of underinvolvement has emerged from what has been termed the *consumer culture of childhood* (Doherty, 2002), that a parent's job is to give children what they want and to please the child at all costs. Instead of instilling limits and boundaries, parents believe they should keep their children happy. Therefore, when adolescent girls demand unlimited freedom and insist on being left alone by their parents, some parents believe that they are obligated to fulfill these wishes so as to not disappoint their daughters (Taffel, 2009; Straus, 2006).

Yet another form of parenting that results in underinvolvement is due to the pervasive use of technology. This phenomenon is related to what Turkel (2011) calls spending time *"alone together"*—family members are home together, but each person may be quite alone in their pursuit of different virtual worlds (e.g., one is texting on a smart phone, another is playing video games, another is on Facebook, another is watching videos on a computer). Whereas in the past, families may have been able to spend quality time together when all individuals are home, now each member can be exposed to a vast external reality of which other people in the family are completely unaware. Therefore, even though there is time at home, families are not spending time together, nor sharing common activities and family rituals.

Second, parenting styles have also changed in recent years to reflect seemingly *overinvolved* parents— "tiger moms" or "helicopter parents" who micromanage their children's lives and leave nothing to chance in terms of involving them in every academic and extracurricular activity that will increase their likelihood of success (Levine, 2012). These parents are often competitive and pressure their children to become overly involved in activities. This can result in stress and developmental concerns in adolescent girls, especially when they are not prepared to take on so many responsibilities at one time (see the classic *The Hurried Child* [Elkind, 1981] and *Teach Your Children Well* [Levine, 2012]). Some authors claim that this parenting style, although seemingly encompassing a high level of involvement, may actually contribute to a lack of warmth and connection between parents and children. Life becomes hectic, with parents becoming very busy arranging children's lives, driving them to and from practices and events, and pressuring them to achieve, while in reality, they may have little time left over for downtime to truly connect with their children (Levine, 2012; Sax, 2010;

Straus, 2006). These parenting trends can be troubling when home is not a place where a child feels warmth and connection. When girls experience a void at home, they begin searching for the connections they crave at this point in their lives, which can lead to vulnerability to the adoption of a *second family* (e.g., a peer group, street gang, or even computer simulated life). According to Taffel (*Childhood Unbound*, 2009) many children without appropriate family connections will gravitate toward a socially disconnected or deviant peer group, and this can occur online, even if she never leaves the house.

An additional change in parenting style and family structure is the increase in divorced or single-parent families. In 2011, 26% of all children under the age of 21 lived with only one of their parents. This percentage differs widely by ethnic group—around 30% of White and Hispanic children lived with only one parent, while this living arrangement was the case for 62% of African American children (U.S. Department of Commerce, 2011). When girls are members of families undergoing divorce, girls face multiple family transitions (e.g., loss of resources, relocation, loss of contact with extended family, decrease in family time, decreased parental involvement and support, and decrease in parental monitoring and discipline). At the same time they are coping with changes related to divorce, they are undergoing major physical and psychosocial changes while also facing transitions with peers and school environments (Selekman, 2006). Even when the transition through divorce is relatively smooth, there still remains a general spillover from problems associated with the divorce into the parent/child relationship (Simpson, 2001). However, although many girls struggle through the initial stages of parental divorce, girls who have adequate parenting and coping resources do not necessarily experience major developmental problems. In fact, in some cases there can be positive outcomes for girls, particularly when a violent or dysfunctional parent exits from the home.

One of the challenges that girls experience after divorce is when the domiciliatory parent experiences depressive symptoms or other problems related to the divorce, and the adolescent daughter is called upon to perform the adult duties of parenting younger siblings, completing household tasks, serving as the parent's confidante, or even becoming triangulated between the parents for communication purposes. This process is called *parentification*. In cases when a daughter is parentified, the daughter's increasingly urgent needs for support, validation, and security during this time often remain unmet, and she will likely seek to meet these needs from sources outside the home (Selekman, 2006).

Another example of the impact of divorce on adolescent girls is the likelihood of decreased paternal involvement. After divorce, fathers are less likely to stay involved with their daughters. This lack of involvement is even more significant when considering that the relationship between all fathers and daughters typically weakens during this period. Fathers may feel a need to pull back from the relationship, uncertain of their role, giving mothers the responsibility for assisting their daughters through the challenges of adolescence. However, research indicates that girls benefit from positive connections with their fathers; strong father–daughter relationships are positively associated with school success, occupational competence, and a girl's sense of comfort in and mastery of the world around her (Straus, 2006). This protective factor will be further explored in Chapter 8.

Whether as a result of divorce or other circumstances, an increasing number of children are growing up in single-parent homes, and the majority of these homes are led by single mothers. Research across various cultural groups suggests that the impact of this type of living arrangement varies. For example, girls in single-mother families are overall at increased risk for problems than are girls living in two-parent households. These girls are at risk for early sexual intercourse and pregnancy, dropping out of school, or early employment (Merten & Henry, 2011). In addition, adolescents living with cohabiting stepparents or single unmarried mothers have lower psychological well-being than those living in two-parent married households (Worell, 2006).

However, these findings are tempered when examining cultural differences. For example, in contrast to Caucasian girls, African American girls do not face increased risks when raised in single-mother homes when compared to other family structures. These findings are explained by the fact that (a) there are unique strengths characteristic of African American families; that is, collective socialization of children by extended family systems and affiliated kin, and strong mothers who are independent role models for their daughters; and (b) the greater prevalence of single mother families in the African American culture (over 60% of children live in this type of arrangement) as it has become more of a normative context for African American girls (Merten & Henry, 2011).

Peer Group Transitions

The development and maintenance of friendships is an important developmental task in adolescence, and positive friendships serve as sources of support, intimacy, loyalty, and trust (Reynolds &

Repetti, 2006). In adolescence, a girl's peer group increases in importance, and she begins to spend more time interacting with her peers than with her parents (Basow, 2006). Peers play an essential role in the development of interpersonal competence during this time. Her skills in initiating and maintaining friendships have a long-term impact on her psychological health and well-being; girls who are accepted by peers and who have positive friendships are higher in self-esteem, are more socially skilled, and are more academically successful (Reynolds & Repetti, 2006). Affirming peer relationships also help buffer any negative relationships a girl is experiencing with parents or other peers (Rose & Rudolph, 2006) and peers can also serve as positive role models for healthy behaviors.

Unfortunately, the lack of a quality friendship group can also serve as a source of stress during this time period. Poor relationships are associated with academic failure, delinquent behavior, depression, anxiety, and low self-esteem in adolescent girls (Reynolds & Repetti, 2006). As reviewed in Chapter 1, girls often learn from media and other sources, including their own experiences, that other girls cannot be trusted and should be viewed as competitors (Girl Scout Research Institute, 2010). Problems also occur in developing friendships when a girl learns to suppress her true thoughts and feelings in order to be accepted by a particular peer group. In order to please her friends, she may not directly express her ideas or beliefs, hesitate to express anger, and learn to do what is needed to fit in with the desires of others rather than expressing her authentic voice. Termed "self-silencing" or "loss of voice," she may learn to wear a mask in relationships, failing to care for her own needs (Gilligan, 1991; Pipher, 1994).

Peers also serve as a source of stress in context of the multiple transitions that occur in peer group structure during this time. While friendship groups may have been stable in younger years, in adolescence a girl's peer group changes frequently and becomes highly fluid. In one study, researchers asked girls to name all of their friends, but when asked 2 years later to create another list of current friends, 75% of names on the new list had not been included on the original list (Schneider & Stevenson, 1999). A girl might change friendship groups every few weeks as she experiences rejection from one set of peers or acceptance by another. Increasingly, girls might be targeted as victims of bullying based on their appearance, gender identity, or even for their self-confidence and achievements. Whereas one week some girls are the target of bullying, in other weeks they may be part of a peer group that is bullying others. With such frequent changes in peer group affiliation and the inconsistent nature of friendships (friends one day, then enemies the next), girls often report that they do not trust their peers, feeling disconnected from classmates. This process makes it harder to develop the intimate friendships they desire, and leads them to view other girls as competitors rather than as sources of support (Straus, 2006).

A girl's peer group also has a strong influence on her own attitudes and behaviors. There is a strong relationship between peers' attitudes and behaviors and a girl's own attitudes and behaviors (Institute of Medicine and National Research Council, 2011). This is due to two effects: (a) a girl will be attracted to a peer group that shares her attitudes, values, and desired behaviors, and (b) once a girl joins a peer group, she will adopt the attitudes, values, and behaviors of those peers (Hall & Valente, 2007). Therefore, a girl's peer group is a reflection not only of who she currently is but also of who she sees herself becoming. For example, in a study of early adolescent girls, peers were a stronger contributor to the development of body dissatisfaction than were parents. Girls in the study report turning to their peers for appearance-related information and advice, and discussions about dieting, and that the pressure they receive from peers regarding thinness was more influential on body dissatisfaction than the pressure or support they receive from their parents (Blodgett, Salafia, & Gondoli, 2011). Girls may turn to peers for advice on dieting and improving appearance because they are dissatisfied with their bodies, but they also adopt the dieting behaviors and pressure to be thin that is shared by members of the peer group. A girl's peer group is also expanding in the sense that she can be part of an online peer community that also influences her attitudes and behaviors. As an example, a recent research team reviewed 400 to 500 websites promoting anorexia-related eating disorders (termed pro-ana sites) and competitive dieting and found that these sites were visited by thousands of young girls each day. In one year, 500,000 individuals visited the sites, many meeting on websites and then competing with each other to starve themselves to determine who can lose the most amount of weight (Bond, 2012).

In addition, a girl's peer group strongly influences her participation in risky and delinquent behaviors. Peer deviance is one of the strongest correlates of a girl's own delinquent behavior, and most antisocial behavior occurs in the presence of peers rather than in isolation. Further, girls who are aggressive, disruptive, emotionally disturbed, or marginalized tend to gravitate toward one another, thereby maintaining or even amplifying existing problems. It seems that when a girl begins to display mental health problems or delinquent behaviors, instead of seeking out peers who will be a positive developmental influence, girls tend to drift toward peers who are also struggling, thereby perpetuating attitudes and behaviors that put them at risk (Miller, Loeber, & Hipwell, 2009; Sontag, Graber, & Clemans, 2011). It is important to understand the important role of the peer group—either as a source of support or of stress (and often both at the same time)—in understanding the attitudes and behaviors of adolescent girls.

School Transitions

As girls progress from elementary to middle and high school, they are likely to move into larger (1,000 or more students) and thus more crowded schools. Because girls thrive in environments where they have authentic connections with others (Jordan, 2003), in large schools many girls feel lost and invisible (Straus, 2006). In large schools they are less likely to have meaningful relationships with both peers and adults, and it is easier for girls to slip by, unnoticed by others who could be sources of support, than in a smaller, more personal setting. Research indicates that the overall school climate—defined as a sense of safety, a sense that resources are shared, a perception of order and discipline, parental involvement, positive peer interpersonal relationships, the presence of teacher–student relationships, and a positive school building appearance—is significantly associated with students' overall life satisfaction and mental health (Suldo, McMahan, Chappel, & Loker, 2012). In school climates in which girls' abilities to learn are greatly disrupted by sexual harassment or bullying, or in which they have few positive peer or teacher relationships, it is not surprising that for many girls, school can become a source of distress that contributes to negative mental health outcomes. Research does indicate that in schools where sexual harassment is tolerated, peer harassment continues to increase, and the psychological and educational outcomes for students are diminished (Ormerod, Collinsworth, & Perry, 2008). As mentioned in Chapter 1, when the school climate is characterized as one of tolerance for sexual harassment, students are more likely to feel unsafe while at school, are more likely to withdraw from school, are highly distressed at school, and experience lower self-esteem (Ormerod et al., 2008).

On the other hand, statistics indicate that girls are thriving in school as never before. As a result of Title IX (1972) girls are not only doing well in the classroom, they are participating in athletics at higher rates than ever before (National Federation of State High School Sports Association, 2012). Further, the overall educational gender gap seems to have reversed in recent decades, with more women attending college at every level—2-year, 4-year, graduate programs, and professional degree programs (National Center for Educational Statistics, 2012). In one recent study of sister and brother pairs, researchers found the sisters made higher grades than brothers, their mothers had higher expectations for their daughters than for their sons, and that these sisters were more likely to attend college than were their brothers (Bissell-Havran, Loken, & McHale, 2012). While significant gender gaps still exist in the science, technology, engineering, and mathematics fields (National Science Foundation, Division of Science Resources Statistics, 2011), because of these gains, many researchers have now focused more of their attention on boys and their academic struggles (i.e., the "boy turn backlash"; Jones & Dindia, 2004).

While these positive strides in academics indicate good news for most girls, they can also translate into higher levels of expectations for girls to excel academically, athletically, and socially. As reviewed in Chapter 1, many girls feel that they must do it all, and do it all perfectly (Hinshaw, 2008). This might translate into girls placing inordinate amounts of pressure on themselves to make high grades while also competing on multiple sports teams, participating in clubs at school, maintaining a perfect appearance, and even keeping up with texting and her social networking sites. This pressure can be overwhelming for girls, particularly as they are working through the many developmental tasks of adolescence (Levine, 2012).

Unfortunately, at the other end of the continuum are the large numbers of girls who are increasingly uninvolved at school, who do not participate in any school activities, and may not have any authentic connections with adults during a time period in which they need strong mentorship, monitoring, validation, and support (Sax, 2010; Simpson, 2001; Straus, 2006). Without these supports in place, she is at risk for the development of mental health concerns, and it is these problems that will be the focus of Chapters 3 through 7.

DEVELOPMENTAL TASKS OF ADOLESCENCE

From the above review of family, peer, and academic changes that often occur simultaneously in girls' lives, it is of little surprise that adolescence can be a challenging period for many girls. However, even larger changes are occurring for her internally, both physically and psychologically, so that managing all of the developmental, environmental, and larger cultural pressures of adolescence becomes a highly demanding task. To understand adolescent girls' experiences, it is essential to understand the key developmental tasks that she is undertaking as she forges her way through the teenage years. The Harvard Education Project on Raising Teens (Simpson, 2001) identified 10 developmental tasks of adolescence in a comprehensive report on parenting. In the following sections, I review the identified tasks and provide a synthesis of relevant literature particularly applicable to adolescent girls.

Task 1: Adjust to Sexually Maturing Bodies and Feelings

Adolescence is a transition phase between childhood and adulthood, considered to begin at puberty (typically between the ages of 10–15), the age at which a young person becomes physically capable of sexual reproduction (Matlin, 2004). For girls, this involves the process of dramatic hormonal changes, breast development, the development of secondary sex characteristics, and the onset of menarche (LaGreca, Mackey, & Miller, 2006). Puberty also encompasses the most physical changes that have occurred to her since infancy; girls' circulatory and respiratory systems will change, she will grow over 3 inches per year, and she will experience increases in weight and body composition, mostly in the form of fat to her hips and thighs (Swarr & Richards, 1996).

The physical and hormonal changes that accompany puberty can pose challenges to girls' mental health. First, girls in adolescence become highly concerned about their appearance, weight, and shape, and this is occurring at the same time that they are undergoing weight gain and developing increased body fat. At the same time that her body is changing in significant ways, she also begins to place more importance on media messages regarding how women should look and act and begins to compare herself to the thin and beautiful ideals presented to her in the media. As her body is transitioning in a way that is increasingly discrepant from the thin ideal, this often causes her to experience body dissatisfaction, lowered self-esteem, and depression (LaGreca et al., 2006). Girls' experiences with body dissatisfaction and the development of eating disorders will be explored in Chapter 4.

A second avenue through which girls may experience problems during the transition to puberty is her increasing need for close interpersonal relationships and adjustment to her sexually maturing body and feelings. As she matures, she experiences increases in oxytocin, a hormone that stimulates her affiliative needs and behavior

(LaGreca et al., 2006), so she is drawn toward intimate relationships and toward attracting a romantic partner. At the same time, she is establishing a sexual identity, whether heterosexual, lesbian, bisexual, or transgender, and is learning the skills necessary to maintain a romantic relationship. While learning how to manage sexual feelings and deciding how she will participate in sexual activity is part of the normative developmental process for all girls, girls who engage in sex before the age of 16 are at higher risk for significant health problems, including unwanted pregnancy, sexually transmitted diseases, and HIV (Bingham & Crockett, 1996; Levine, 2012). In order to maintain a relationship with a male, some girls engage in sexual activity before they are psychologically ready to do so. In a national survey, 11% of high school girls report that their first sexual experience was unwanted (National Survey for Family Growth, 2011), and in another study, 38% of girls stated that they regretted their first sexual experience (Parkes et al., 2011). Younger girls may not have the social skills necessary to remove themselves from situations in which they do not feel comfortable. As will be reviewed later in this chapter, a girl's physical development is generally far more advanced than her cognitive and emotional maturity, so although she has the physique of a woman, she still has the cognitive developmental capacity of a young adolescent. This discrepancy can make it difficult for her when she finds herself having to make adult-level decisions (e.g., to engage in sexual activity, to use substances) but does not yet have the ability or experience to make these decisions in an informed manner that is also in her best interest.

Studies indicate that an adolescent girl's sexual behaviors are most influenced by her peer group, as a girl's sexual activity (including use of unsafe sexual practices) closely mirrors the behaviors of her peers (Reynolds & Repetti, 2006). Overall, when a girl experiences instability in close relationships either with romantic partners or with friends, and when her interpersonal needs are not met, she is at risk for the development of depression and other problems. A full discussion of girls' desires for interpersonal connections and risk factors for depression will be provided in Chapter 3.

A third and quite significant risk factor for problems in girls' mental health is related to the timing of pubertal onset. The timing of puberty is highly linked to girls' psychological health and risks for distress during this period (Graber, Nichols, & Brooks-Gunn, 2010). This is of concern as research suggests that the onset of puberty has fallen during the past 20 years. In a study published in the *Journal of Pediatrics*, 25% of African American girls, 15% of Hispanic girls, and 10% of Caucasian girls had started puberty at age 7 (readers should note that this refers to the onset of breast development and pubic hair development, not whether or not menstruation has started) (Biro et al., 2010).

During the past decades, a large body of research has linked girls' early pubertal timing (occurring before age 9) to elevated rates of a range of behaviors and disorders including depression, social anxiety, substance disorders, eating disorders, comorbid depression and substance disorders, as well as subclinical problems (e.g., increased peer victimization, negative body image, early and unwanted sexual activity, physical and verbal intimate partner violence, social exclusion, poor coping skills, disruptive or aggressive behaviors, low self-esteem, low support from friends and family) (Belsky et al., 2007; Blumenthal et al., 2011; Graber et al., 2010; Nishina, Ammon, Bellmore, & Graham, 2006; Sontag et al., 2011; Steinberg & Silk, 2002). This is likely to occur because early maturation is quite evident to a girl's peer group, causing her to feel as if all eyes are on her developing body. Her self-consciousness is compounded by normative developmental tendencies for social comparison, peer approval, and basing self-worth on social evaluation (Blumenthal et al., 2011). The self-consciousness and social anxiety can be compounded if she becomes the victim of peer teasing, bullying, and sexual harassment (Nishina et al., 2006).

Contributing to these other problems, early-maturing girls are also more likely to be heavier than their peers and to feel less comfortable about their body weight and shape, which can contribute to body dissatisfaction and disordered eating behaviors. Girls who mature earlier than their peers are also less likely to engage in exercise during adolescence. In one study, girls who mature early (by age 11) were less likely to engage in or to enjoy physical activity at age 13 (Davison, Werder, Trost, Baker, & Birch, 2007). In turn, body dissatisfaction and a poor physical self-concept can lead to long-term problems with eating and weight.

In addition, early-maturing girls will not have as much time as other girls to accomplish the developmental tasks of childhood. Instead, a girl must abruptly face new physical and psychological challenges in addition to coping with more complex interpersonal relationships with peers and potential romantic partners. This developmental gap can contribute toward less successful transitions into adolescence and adulthood (Weil, 2012). As she is forced prematurely into the adolescent subculture, she may appear physically mature but will still lack the emotional maturity and decision-making/coping skills needed for responding to the new challenges she faces (Steinberg & Silk, 2002), including attracting the attention of older romantic partners, being included in an older peer group, and being pressured to engage in high-risk behaviors. As will be explored later in the chapter, it is therefore important for counselors and other adults to respond to girls not according to the age they look but according to the age they actually are (Weil, 2012).

There are multiple reasons that a girl may experience early puberty, as it is largely influenced by complex interactions among biological and environmental factors. Some of the influences identified by researchers include the following:

CONTRIBUTORS TO EARLY MATURATION IN GIRLS

- *Genetics*: For example, there are strong links between her pubertal onset and her mother's pubertal timing (Biro et al., 2010).
- *Environmental toxins*: Some studies link chemicals added to food and products can act as estrogen mimics in the body, thus inducing early puberty (e.g., the chemical BPA commonly found in hard plastics) (Weil, 2012).
- *Diet and weight*: One of the highest contributors to earlier pubertal onset is prepubertal body fat and overall body weight, although the strongest link is to increased body fat content. In fact, higher level of body fat at age 5 predicts early pubertal development (Walvoord, 2010). This association is explained through the connection between body fat and increases in leptin, a hormone that contributes to early maturation (Walvord, 2010).
- *Stress*: Early pubertal timing is more likely to occur when a girl lives in conditions of uncertainty and moderately high psychosocial stress (termed the *psychosocial acceleration theory*; Arim, Tramonte, Shapka, Dahinten, & Willms, 2011). When there is a frequent stress response triggered in the body, there is a corresponding increase in androgens that are subsequently converted to estrogen in the breasts, thereby stimulating breast development. Through this process, uncertainty and general distress are contributors to early maturation in girls.
- *Interpersonal factors*: Research has determined certain family factors that contribute to early pubertal timing. Insecure attachment to parents is related to early maturation; girls who are insecurely attached to their mothers at age 15 months are 2.5 times more likely to begin puberty early compared to those were securely attached (Belsky, Houts, & Fearon, 2010).
- Overall negative family experiences and a parenting style that involves high conflict and harsh control, and that is low in warmth are significant contributors to early pubertal onset (Graber et al., 2010). In contrast, in one longitudinal study of 5-year-old daughters and their parents, researchers found that the more positive and affectionate interactions daughters received at age 5, the later their onset of menarche compared to other girls who did not receive as many positive interactions (Belsky et al., 2007).

The association between negative family experiences, parenting styles that lack warmth and affection, and pubertal timing has been examined through the evolutionary theory of Belsky, Steinberg, and Draper (BSD theory Belsky et al., 2007). BSD theory links early socialization and rearing to pubertal timing, predicting that stress-inducing and negative family environments would accelerate the onset of puberty. In essence, the theory posits that if girls learn that their home environment is not a safe place and that parents cannot be relied upon, it is in their best interest to mature early, seek out romantic and sexual relationships, leave home, and have as many relationships and children as possible. As presented here, there is evidence to support that negative, stressful home experiences, including harsh and controlling parenting, do predict the early onset of puberty, although there may be multiple explanations for this relationship (Belsky et al., 2007). Regardless of its cause, as early puberty onset is associated with so many risks for girls, it clearly adds an additional challenge to the development of girls' positive mental health during adolescence.

Task 2: Develop and Apply Abstract Thinking Skills

Recognizing the significant shift in adolescent girls' cognitive development is essential to understanding girls' thinking, emotional responses, and behavior during this stage. During early adolescence, most girls are still operating at Piaget's Concrete Operations stage (Piaget, 1972); they think concretely and remain unable to use abstract thinking or simultaneously hold multiple options or perspectives in their minds. A girl at this stage has a tendency to jump to conclusions, live in the present, think in only black-and-white terms, be unable to imagine the possible consequences of her actions, and may overgeneralize outcomes based only on the limited experience that she does have (Simpson, 2001). When unable to think abstractly or logically, many girls make decisions based primarily on their feelings, and are often unable to determine the most practical solution to a problem, reasoning instead with distorted thinking that might sound ridiculous or chaotic to adults (Straus, 2006). With the onset of Piaget's stage of formal operational reasoning in middle adolescence, a girl can begin to think through a problem with what is termed *multifinality* (i.e., the ability to envision various outcomes for the same situation); therefore, she can now consider multiple points of view and think through each of them using reason and logic (Piaget, 1972).

During this period of cognitive developmental shifts, girls are also living in a stage of egocentrism, remaining focused on themselves in the present. Elkind (1967) describes the egocentric adolescent who assumes that others are as obsessed with her appearance and actions as she is. She is unable to separate the reality of what others might be thinking about from her own preoccupation with thoughts about herself. In other words, her self-consciousness is in reaction to what Elkind terms the *imaginary audience*—the anticipation that others are scrutinizing her and reacting critically to her "performance." In actual social situations, this is generally not the case, as her peers are likely to be focused upon themselves rather than on her appearance or actions, but she nevertheless focuses heavily upon the potential reactions of the imaginary audience (Elkind, 1967). In current culture this is only exacerbated by social media outlets as she fears (but sometimes hopes) that her image is being viewed by hundreds if not thousands of spectators.

In addition to fears about scrutiny from the imaginary audience, she will also believe that her feelings and beliefs are unique and that no one has ever had these particular thoughts or feelings before. She believes a *personal fable*—a story she tells herself that is not true—and this fable contributes to her feelings of isolation and pain, as well as to her belief at times that she is more knowledgeable and capable than her parents and other adult figures in her life (Elkind, 1967). At times she might believe that she is the only person who ever thought about a particular issue in this way and will want to share her wisdom with all who will listen (Straus, 2006).

In sum, while she appears to be self-absorbed and overly focused on self, adolescence is also an important developmental period of self-discovery (Straus, 2006). Therefore at times she will appear overly confident, with grandiose beliefs about her capabilities, while at other times she will be in despair, believing that no one could possibly ever understand her (Straus, 2006). This uneven use of her newly developed skills makes it difficult for parents and other significant adults to know how to respond to her. It may also require a great deal of patience and understanding as she learns how to reason with both logic and emotions and to take in multiple perspectives as she makes decisions, as described in the following.

Task 3: Develop and Apply a More Complex Level of Perspective Taking

As she reaches the formal operations stage of cognitive development, a girl is now able to display empathy for others (i.e., to understand others' perspectives, hold both her perspective and another's perspective at the same time, and to use this skill to resolve problems and conflicts in relationships) (Eisenberg, Guthrie, Murphy, Shepard, Cumberland, & Carlo, 1999; Elkind, 1967). While in childhood she may have wanted to care for others to gain rewards or to avoid punishment, she now has the ability to think abstractly, understand other's perspectives, and to think about her actions toward others in terms of how they fit with her own beliefs and values; she can also consider in any given situation whether or not she wants to base her actions upon these particular beliefs and values (Eisenberg et al., 1999). Girls are best able to develop empathic understanding when they are raised in households that display a balance between warmth (responsiveness, support) and demandingness (conveyance of clear behavioral expectations) (Carlo, McGinley, Hayes, Batenhorst, & Wilkinson, 2007). In contrast, Miller and colleagues found that the development of emotional understanding is hampered when a girl is raised in a family environment that involves harsh parenting practices and that lacks parental warmth (Miller et al., 2009). It is evident that as girls develop abstract thought and perspective-taking, they also need positive role modeling from the family system in which they live in order to facilitate the development of empathy and prosocial actions toward others.

Task 4: Develop and Apply New Cognitive Skills Such as Decision Making, Problem Solving, and Conflict Resolution

This task involves the acquisition of new skills for decision making, problem solving, conflict resolution, planning for the future, and for moderating risk-taking behaviors so that they serve her goals rather than jeopardize them (Simpson, 2001). As with the previous two tasks, this involves formal operational thought to think abstractly and logically, and to consider multiple perspectives in decision making. However, brain development and functioning at this age significantly compromise the ability of an adolescent to engage in these processes consistently (Institute of Medicine, 2011).

Recent brain imaging studies show that the adolescent brain undergoes a major remodeling during the adolescent period. As it is pruned and rewired, it becomes more complex and more efficient. Studies also reveal the immaturity and pruning of the adolescent prefrontal cortex, which controls the executive functions (EF) of the brain (e.g., functions that control self-regulation, organize and direct cognitive activity, emotional responses, and behaviors, including functions such as self-initiation, flexibility in problem solving, planning tasks, and emotional regulation) (Levine, 2012). The prefrontal cortex is not fully reorganized and developed until an individual reaches his or her mid-to-late 20s, so adolescents do not yet have the capability to fully regulate and control their impulses or to engage in purposeful, logical, goal-oriented behavior. In addition, due to other rapid changes in the brain, the limbic system (that governs appetite and pleasure seeking) is developing more quickly than the prefrontal cortex, and this also makes her prone to taking risks and seeking novel experiences while she still lacks capacity for self-regulation (Institute of Medicine, 2011). Studies also indicate that adolescents tend to rate the benefits of certain behaviors as very high, so even when they do consider the risks involved, they rate the benefits as outweighing the risks, so they engage in the behavior regardless of the known risks (Institute of Medicine and National Research Council, 2011). It follows then, that an adolescent's tendency to engage in irrational, impulsive, or risk-taking behaviors can often be understood as normative based on her stage of brain development.

Counselors can help parents and other caregivers to understand the importance of continued parental oversight until the adolescent's executive functioning skills are more fully developed. Due to their unevenly and slowly maturing prefrontal cortex, they still need adequate amounts of adult support, monitoring, and guidance until they are consistently able to engage in goal-directed, planned, and purposeful behaviors (Levine, 2012; Straus, 2006).

Task 5: Identify Meaningful Moral Standards, Values, and Belief Systems

As adolescents enter the formal operations stage of cognitive development, they also transition to a more complex understanding of moral behavior and underlying principles of justice and care. They may begin questioning beliefs held by their family of origin, eventually adopting and using more personally meaningful values, religious views, and personally derived values to guide their choices and behavior (Simpson, 2001).

Moral development is generally conceptualized through the theory of moral decision making posited by Kohlberg (1972) and later expanded for girls and women by Gilligan (*In a Different Voice*, 1982). Kohlberg, who studied with Piaget, posited that younger children (under the age of 10–11) make moral decisions based upon rules that are fixed, absolute, and handed down from authority figures or God. These rules are to be obeyed without question. Children also make decisions based on the consequences of an action, not considering the intentions behind the behavior.

In contrast, after the development of formal operations, a young adolescent's views become more relativistic. She realizes that rules are not absolutes but are rather agreements formed to help people get along with one another, and that they can be questioned or changed if they do not fit with a particular situation. Adolescents can also begin to consider intentions driving a behavior in determining whether the action is right or wrong. Kohlberg (1972) defined this stage of moral development as *conventional morality*. In addition to the more relativistic thinking style described in the preceding, the adolescent begins to determine morality in terms of whether one lives up to the expectations of family and community, making decisions based on having good motives and positive feelings toward others in a given situation. While this moral judgment style works well in interpersonal relationships, adolescents also realize that they need a framework for understanding larger issues facing society. The subsequent phase in their moral development will therefore involve a concern with maintaining a social order, so that one considers not only the other person's feelings, but whether or not that good is maintained for society as a whole (Kohlberg, 1972). For example, in considering whether a friend should get away with stealing an item because he couldn't afford it, she might now say: "It may be best for this particular person, but if everyone did that, then society might fall apart."

Gilligan (1982) later proposed that Kohlberg's theory of moral reasoning favored the abstract, rights orientation of men and therefore did not adequately capture the nature of women's moral development. Gilligan believed that men and women have two distinct orientations or voices, with women having a voice of care, connection, and responsibility, and men possessing an abstract, impersonal, rights-oriented mode of reasoning. Gilligan's claim that men are favored by the research methods of Kohlberg, however, is not supported in reviews of the literature (Jaffee & Hyde, 2000). While Gilligan's assertions have been contradicted by empirical research, they have nevertheless broadened conceptualizations of moral development to include a greater emphasis on caring and responsiveness to the needs of others, which is critical to understanding the moral reasoning development of adolescent girls.

As her moral development becomes more relativistic, an adolescent girl starts to question previously unquestioned rules, family values, and religious beliefs. In many cases parents become distressed by these discussions and arguments, believing that their daughter is rejecting them as individuals and as parents. It is important for counselors to help families understand that it is normative for adolescents to think more relativistically and to question why she believes the things that she does (Steinberg & Silk, 2002). It is also normative for her to feel torn between making decisions based upon what she feels is best for her versus making a decision based upon pleasing significant others. Parents need to provide her with support and guidance, not rejection during this time. As written by Steinberg and Silk (2002), it is normative for a girl to flex her "newly developed cognitive muscles" in moral reasoning and value judgment as a part of her development (p. 107).

Task 6: Understand and Express More Complex Emotional Experiences

As she matures, an adolescent girl can better identify complex emotions, think about them in abstract ways, and understand the emotions of others. She can begin to learn to express her emotions appropriately and regulate her emotions so that her feelings do not dictate her decisions (Harter & Buddin, 1987). These new skills are discussed with regard to three primary aspects of emotional development: identification, expression, and regulation.

Emotion Identification

There will be many times during which girls may not understand what they are feeling, may not be able to put their feelings into words, and will not understand what their feelings mean. In early adolescence, girls are also often unable to understand why they are experiencing contradictory feelings about an event; for example, they can be furious at a boy for breaking off their relationship, sad that she no longer has a boyfriend, and relieved that she no longer has to rebuff his sexual advances. However, she may not have the developmental capability to understand that she is experiencing all three emotions at once, and so she will only label her experience with sadness. As girls mature, however, they are better able to identify their emotions and label them with specific feeling words, and to understand that individuals often respond to the same situation with several concurrent emotions (Straus, 2006).

Emotion Expression

While girls are socialized to be emotionally expressive, they are not taught how to appropriately express anger (Underwood, 2003). Girls often learn that in order to maintain relationships and secure others' approval, they should suppress their anger, even at a time in which they experience anger about different aspects of their world:

> The new angle on this old and familiar story is the anger. [Girls are] mad at themselves, their families, and their communities. Many are furious about living entrapped in a culture that seemingly offers them so many choices but insists that they kill so much time with concerns about how they look and behave. Just at the moment in life when they have the skills and experience to begin to really take a stand, they feel compelled to shrink and disappear. (Straus, 2006, p. 6)

As they learn to silence their anger, many girls turn any negative feelings toward themselves, leading to self-destructive behaviors such as eating disorders, self-injury, substance abuse, and depression, all reviewed in subsequent chapters in this book. Each chapter will emphasize that an important part of counseling for these problems is to provide a safe place for girls to express their anger and sadness and to teach the skills necessary for expressing negative feelings in an appropriate way.

Emotion Regulation

As discussed previously, emotion regulation is controlled by the prefrontal cortex, which is not yet fully mature in adolescence. Therefore, adolescents have strong emotional reactions to events but do not have adequate skills for managing these emotions. They still need adult guidance in emotionally charged situations for learning how to problem solve (when the situation can be changed) or to cope effectively (when the situation can't be changed and must be accepted/managed as it is). As part of her coping skills repertoire, she will need self-soothing responses for times of distress, as well as caring adults to provide her with support. The more parents and other adults consistently assist in providing her with comforting responses during difficult situations, the more she will begin to internalize these empathic and caring reactions, and eventually she will become able to provide these responses for herself (Selekman, 2006). Emotion regulation is discussed further in Chapters 4 and 6.

Task 7: Form Friendships That Are Mutually Close and Supportive

According to the Institute of Medicine and National Research Council, (2011), there are four key tasks for adolescents as they establish interpersonal competence: (a) to stand out (to develop identity and autonomy), (b) to fit in (to find comfortable affiliations and gain acceptance from peers), (c) to measure up (to develop competence and find ways to achieve, and (d) to take hold (to make commitments to particular goals, activities, and beliefs). In other words, girls want to stand out, to be unique, to establish an individual identity replete with goals, accomplishments, and dreams, while at the same time fitting in seamlessly with their peer group (Straus, 2006). This is quite a developmental challenge, as will be explored in the following section on identity development.

Task 8: Establish Key Aspects of Identity

The development of a positive self-concept is one of most important psychosocial tasks of adolescence. According to Erikson (1968), the adolescent period is a time to find and refine one's identity by resolving an identity crisis in discovering who you are. Essential aspects of identity are formed in adolescence, including the ability to function autonomously as well as in connection to valued people and groups. This also involves the development of an integrated identity around gender, physical attributes, sexuality, ethnicity, and sensitivity to cultural diversity (Simpson, 2001).

Gender identity is a particularly important aspect of identity development for girls. According to sex role developmental theories, girls are socialized to adopt the attitudes, feelings, behaviors, and motives that are culturally defined as appropriate for their sex (Gilbert & Sher, 1999). Social learning theories (e.g., Bussey & Bandura, 1999; see also Chapter 1) explain sex role development as occurring through an interaction among modeling, experience, and direct instruction.

- *Modeling.* Children watch others and imitate them, imitating their same-sex parent as well as role models from the media. Children observe differences between the sexes and then imitate the behavior to the extent that they believe that the model's behavior is ordinarily appropriate or inappropriate for that child's sex (Perry & Bussey, 1979). As they attend to same-sex models, girls increasingly learn about the importance of appearance in attracting a romantic partner, and about the importance of relationships (usually conveyed through the importance of having a boyfriend).
- *Experience.* Girls learn sex role behaviors by determining others' responses to a particular behavior as sex-appropriate or inappropriate. They learn through trial-and error, through a series of reinforcements (e.g., praise for behaving in a sex-appropriate way) or punishments (e.g., punishment for behaving in a sex-inappropriate way).
- *Direct Instruction.* Girls learn from being directly instructed regarding how girls or boys "should" look or act. Parents and families play a large role in encouraging or discouraging a child's sex role behavior (e.g., through encouraging chores that are divided as girls' jobs versus boys' jobs; what types of toys are purchased for girls versus boys; how girls are told to play with certain toys; and how certain activities and occupations are deemed appropriate for girls versus boys) (Bronstein, 2006).

In addition to social learning models, theorists have also examined children's cognitions about developing sex roles. Children develop *gender schemas,* cognitions formed about themselves and others based on cultural definitions of maleness and femaleness. With repeated use, these become automatic and are used to evaluate one's adequacy in living up to expected gender roles (Bem, 1993; Gilbert & Sher, 1999).

In current culture, as described in Chapter 1, the gender role for girls is changing, becoming more complex and often contradictory. Consider the following exercise:

SELF-AWARENESS ACTIVITY

In Gilbert and Sher's (1999) text on gender and sex in psychotherapy, the authors provide a list of traditional female gender role characteristics. After reviewing this list from 1999, which of these are still considered core to aspects of being a female? What has changed?

TRADITIONAL FEMALE ROLE

Please men
Not be competitive with men
Act inferior to men intellectually
Restrict personal ambitions
Be silent
Accommodate to the needs of others
Be dependent on men
Enhance one's status through associations with men
Be a desired sexual object
Give priority to marriage and children

1. After reviewing this list, which qualities should be added or deleted? Why do you think these changes have occurred?
2. If the list now contains contradictory qualities, how can a girl best resolve these contradictory expectations as part of her identify development? What can help her navigate these tensions?

Clearly, the formation of an identity for girls is an ambiguous process. Due to cognitive developmental limitations in the early adolescent period, girls do not yet have an organized self-system; she might be aware that she acts differently in different situations, but she will not know how these varying aspects of herself fit together as a whole (Piran & Ross, 2006). She does not understand when adults tell her to "be yourself" because she does not yet have a clear sense of what this means (Straus, 2006).

In addition to learning how to weave together a unified self, she is also observing and experiencing cultural pressures that tell her that "being yourself" means being what others want you to be. As she enters adolescence, she encounters an increasing tension between maintaining an authentic sense of self and doing what is necessary to please others (Travis, 2006). Termed the *crossroads* (Gilligan, 1991), between the ages of 10 and 13 girls enter a period in which their "journey toward self-development is challenged and potentially derailed" (Basow, 2006, p. 245). As girls are developing an increasingly interpersonal orientation, they are highly concerned with maintaining their relationships, keeping the peace, caretaking at the expense of their own needs, and keeping their own opinions and feelings silent. As stated by Gilligan (1991), "girls learn, be nice, and don't cause any problems" (p. 19). As reviewed in Chapter 1, today's girls also learn to "be a diva"—to demand what they want, to act out in entitled and edgy ways, and to behave aggressively in order to get attention. Many girls are confused as they receive both messages and feel lost in how to respond to others in order to get their needs met but also to maintain their relationships.

As a result, in contrast to the confidence they exert in late childhood, many girls lose their authentic voice, becoming less assertive and more subordinate in their interpersonal relationships (Travis, 2006). They may also respond by becoming less authentic by being more aggressive and competitive, shutting other girls out. Either of these orientations can also come into conflict with the development of instrumental achievement. As she reaches the middle and high school years, she is asked to begin the process of developing her career aspirations and to persevere toward personal goals (a process that requires autonomy and often competitiveness), while also maintaining her important relationships with peers, romantic partners, and family. This tension is often a source of stress for girls as they believe they must choose between pleasing others or fulfilling their own goals (Basow, 2006).

In addition, many girls are learning that physical beauty (including a sexualized appearance and a body weight and shape that resembles the thin ideal) is the most important determinant of a female's identity, worth, and value (Worell, 2006). Girls are learning to seek validation from others through their appearance and through attracting a romantic partner. Therefore, they place a strong emphasis on achieving an appearance that closely mirrors cultural ideals for beauty and thinness (i.e., "hot and sexy"), and feel as if they can never measure up. As a result, many girls become dissatisfied with their appearance and bodies during this period, which places them at risk for the development of eating- and weight-related concerns (Basow, 2006). This will be discussed further in Chapter 4. In sum, it is a challenge for girls to develop a strong sense of self that is unique and empowered yet is able to retain meaningful connections with significant others in their lives.

Task 9: Meet Demands of Increasingly Mature Roles and Responsibilities

An important aspect of adolescence is to learn the skills needed for launching into adulthood. As they take on increasing opportunities for employment, managing money, or making decisions about college and career readiness for life after high school, girls are able to develop increasing skills for self-regulation and responsibility (Simpson, 2001). As discussed in the section on identity development, girls will optimally develop a gender-balanced identity in which they are able to nurture their communal, emotionally expressive, and interpersonal strengths at the same time that they develop assertiveness, instrumental achievement, and an authentic voice and sense of self (Worell, 2006). A girl will thrive most optimally with a balance between these two aspects of herself, so that she can draw upon a full range of resources as she finds her way in the world. She will need encouragement from caregivers to develop and express her strengths, and to apply these as she makes plans for a career and for life as an adult.

Task 10: Renegotiate Relationships With Adults in Parenting Roles

While adolescence has been traditionally viewed as a time of separation from parents and other adults, developmental researchers and parenting experts now regard the adolescent years as a time when girls continue to need strong adult role models and meaningful connections with adults (Levine, 2012; Pipher, 1994; Simpson, 2001). The traditional mainstream media picture of an adolescent girl is one of increasing independence from her family, spending many hours alone in her room (even while she is online with the outside world), and spending increasingly large amounts of time away from home in order to spend time with peers and romantic partners. She is typically portrayed as argumentative with her parents, bored with school, and rebelling against rules. While there are many truths that undergird these stereotypes, the one finding that is not broadly conveyed is how often adolescents themselves say they want to be better connected to their parents, and how much they crave their parents' time and attention (Simpson, 2001; Taffel, 2009).

Because adolescents don't have as many physical and instrumental needs as they did in childhood, parents often pull back from the time and effort spent in connecting with their children. They are unsure about when to let go and when to hold on, and because of adolescents' unpredictable reactions to parental involvement, many parents decide to abandon their attempts to maintain close relationships or to provide appropriate supervision of their children (Straus, 2006). Regardless of their responses in a particular moment, however, adolescent girls need to be able to turn to their parents for needed emotional support and validation during this tumultuous time in their lives (Straus, 2006). Adolescents continue to desire that their parents provide a secure base; as they explore the world and try out new things, they still want to be able to come back to a home base they can count and depend on, even as they move away from parents and into the world of peers (Worell, 2006). As stated in the Harvard Project on Raising Teens (Simpson, 2001):

> Frustrating parents, teens want to be with them except when they don't, teens want their help except when they don't, and teens behave in excitingly more mature ways—except when they don't. Requiring moment by moment judgment calls, teens need an environment that provides opportunities for experimentation at certain times but not others; for privacy on some matters but not others; for peer influence in some areas but not others; and for negotiation and decision making on some issues but not others. Throughout, they need parents to remain available, taking the emotional high ground by providing opportunities for closeness that teens can sometimes accept and sometimes reject. (p. 41)

It is clear that adolescents and parents must develop a qualitatively different relationship, one that requires a great deal of wisdom necessary for discerning when to provide structure and limits, and when to accommodate to the adolescent's new capabilities and responsibilities. The evolving relationship requires a continued connection with the adolescent, even while enforcing key parental tasks of limit setting, monitoring, and enforcement of consequences. As demonstrated in the quote above, the new relationship requires consistency as well as flexibility and negotiation, and acceptance of conflict as a normal part of adolescent development. This process can be taxing on parents, and counselors can be helpful in assisting families as they forge this new type of relationship with their adolescent daughters.

DEVELOPMENTALLY BASED COUNSELING STRATEGIES

As explored in these first two chapters, adolescents are embedded within multiple ecological contexts—their families, peers, schools, communities, and society—and these in turn influence and are impacted by the developmental biological and psychosocial changes occurring during the adolescent period (Weisz & Hawley, 2002). In this section, I describe counseling implications for the developmental tasks presented in this chapter, first for counseling adolescent girls themselves, and next for working with their parents.

When working as a counselor for an adolescent girl, it is helpful to understand the tasks she must master in order to attain successful physical and psychosocial development. At the same time, it is also important to remain mindful that each girl is different based upon her unique genetic makeup and life circumstances. Therefore, even though the information presented in this chapter is crucial to counseling girls, it can only serve as a supplement to a strong counselor–client alliance and the therapeutic needs of each particular client (Weisz & Hawley, 2002). Some basic counseling strategies based on developmental themes are presented here.

DEVELOPMENTALLY BASED COUNSELING STRATEGIES

- Counselors should conduct an assessment of the developmental tasks of adolescence to determine the client's strengths and areas for continued growth. As examples, counseling strategies might need to involve psychoeducation to assist a girl in understanding the changes that are occurring in her brain and her body. She may benefit from skills training (e.g., social skills, empathy building, problem solving, coping, career development, values clarification). She may need a space for expressing her full range of emotions, including negative aspects such as anger, and she may need support and guidance for establishing an integrated identity.
- Counselors should be aware of developmental risk factors for girls. Knowledge of developmental trends is helpful when a girl displays risk factors such as early pubertal timing; negatively biased schemas regarding her identity and body image; affiliation with deviant peers or a lack of peers; lack of engagement at school or home; lack of goals or purpose; and initial internalizing and externalizing problem behavior.
- Counselors can use developmental risk factors to help prioritize the problems that a girl presents in counseling; for example, it is less worrisome if a girl reports fighting with her parents, but far more concerning if she has early pubertal onset and is socializing with older peers and is dating an older boyfriend (Weisz & Hawley, 2002). After consideration of development and risk, counselors are better equipped to make judgments about interventions; for example, there are some areas in which a counselor should provide support and validation while a girl resolves challenges on her own, while there are other areas in which counselors need to intervene immediately in order to protect her safety and well-being.

After a consideration of biological and psychosocial factors, counselors should also consider the influence of external systems on a girl's development. As reviewed previously, girls do not exist in a vacuum but rather within interconnected micro- and macrosystems (Bronfenbrenner, 1977). While many of these factors will be out of the counselor's or client's control to change, it is important to assess for strengths in these systems as well as the potential risks they may pose. First, I present factors shown to contribute to girls' ability to thrive in school, and then turn to factors relevant to neighborhood settings. The following are factors demonstrated to promote girls' resilience in school:

SCHOOL-LEVEL PROTECTIVE FACTORS

Students' experience a sense of belonging at school
Smaller size of school
Being involved in a school activity or club
Parental involvement with school
Positive relationships with peers who are also engaged with school
Teaching techniques that involve openness, group work, cohesion, cooperation
Providing experiences of accomplishment and praise
Providing high expectations for students
Providing an oasis, a buffer for students who are not doing well at home
Physical environment is attractive and well cared for
Presence of school mentors and/or teachers who take a special interest in students
Schools where students feel safe, with enforcement of discipline policies and an environment in which bullying and harassment are not tolerated

(Laser & Nicotera, 2011)

Outside of school and at the neighborhood level, the counselor can ask the following questions to determine whether the girl's neighborhood is a source contributing to her resilience or whether or not it contributes to problems (Laser & Nicotera, 2011):

- How does the client feel about living in the neighborhood?
- Do adults monitor what goes on in the neighborhood?
- Does she know other youth in her neighborhood?

- Does she have contact with neighborhood church or community leaders?
- What is her perception of the care of the neighborhood—for example, trash, graffiti, crime?
- Does the neighborhood climate prohibit her from accessing neighbors or neighborhood resources that might be a source of support for her?

Importantly, resources such as after-school programs in community youth organizations (e.g., Girl Scouts, 4-H Clubs, Boys and Girls Clubs, organized sports programs such as those offered through the YMCA or YWCA) and through faith-based organizations can provide multiple benefits to girls. These programs can provide a sense of belongingness, support, physical and psychological structure and safety, positive social norms through mentoring and skill building (Straus, 2006). Often, however, girls who would benefit most might have the least access to these programs (due to problems with the neighborhood climate), so accessibility issues must be addressed to ensure participation for girls in need (Laser & Nicotera, 2011).

DEVELOPMENTALLY BASED COUNSELING STRATEGIES FOR PARENTS

Adolescent girls still live at home with parents or caregivers, and these adults play a crucial role in the successful resolution of developmental tasks. There are five critical tasks of parenting adolescents as identified by the Harvard Project on Raising Teens (Simpson, 2001), which are summarized here.

Parenting Task 1: Love and Connect

An adolescent girl needs parents who are connected with her, who offer her warmth, nurturance, and support, and who communicate genuine interest, respect, and affection so that she feels acceptance and approval from her primary attachment figures (Simpson, 2001). She also needs connections that are maintained through the provision of continued family rituals and routines (e.g., enjoying regular family dinners, participating in holiday rituals). Ideally, adolescents need parents to be there for them at the times of day when they are most likely to talk and to share: when they get up in the morning, when they come home from school or activities, at family dinners, and when they go to bed (Straus, 2006).

Research supports the connection between caregiver warmth and support and positive adolescent outcomes: When an adolescent girl reports feeling close with her family, she will value her caregivers' opinions more highly, is more likely to seek guidance for difficult situations, wants to spend more time with her family, and is less likely to engage in deviant behavior (Fosco, Stormshak, Dishion, & Winter, 2012). Despite these benefits, ongoing connection is not easy in a world in which parents are working long hours at their careers, plugged into technology even when they are at home, or have their own emotional or behavioral problems. It is also difficult when the adolescent is behaving in ways that are highly critical toward parents, or when she refuses to participate in family activities, spends more time with peers, and is constantly fighting over family values and rules. Further, the more adolescent girls begin to display negative or delinquent behaviors, the more parents tend to become emotionally rejecting of their daughters. Studies indicate that while girls are more likely to engage in delinquent behaviors when they are raised in an environment that lacks warmth and attachment, if a girl begins to engage in delinquent behaviors, parents will pull back even further from the relationship, increasing the likelihood that the problems will continue (Gault-Sherman, 2012). A girl who displays the early onset of problems needs her parents to press in and remain connected, even though her behavior may tend to elicit the opposite response (Huh, Tristan, Wade, & Stice, 2006). In sum, for girls' optimal development, it is important that they remain connected with their families as they negotiate the difficult social, emotional, and cognitive challenges of adolescence (Fosco et al., 2012).

Parenting Task 2: Guide and Limit

While love and connection are key ingredients for successfully parenting an adolescent, the warmth must be balanced with structure and limits. In fact, the *authoritative* parenting style (Baumrind, 1991), characterized by high levels of parental warmth, support, limit setting, open communication, and parental supervision, is the parenting approach most associated with positive adolescent development (Carlo et al., 2007; Steinberg, Darling, Dornbusch, & Lamborn, 1992).

Within the context of a loving and supportive relationship, adolescents do best with clear limits that are consistently enforced, reflect important family values, and that are communicated explicitly. The expectations should be reasonable and the adolescent should have the skills and resources needed to attain these expectations consistently (Straus, 2006). It should be noted that appropriate parental limit setting is specifically associated with positive academic performance, social competence, and prevention of problem behavior such as substance abuse (Simpson, 2001).

However, parents should be encouraged to view family rules as an evolving set of boundaries that shift as the adolescent displays increasing autonomy and maturity. Parents should remain open to the adolescent's opinions and ideas when making rules, and allow room for flexibility and negotiation (Simpson, 2001). In sum, parents should work to maintain an ongoing balance between respecting her increased competence and responsibility, while also maintaining boundaries and limits that are intended to protect her health and well-being.

Parenting Task 3: Monitor and Observe

Parental monitoring refers to the practice of knowing the adolescent's whereabouts and communicating to her that they are aware of her activities. While the adolescent continues to spend more time away from home, it remains essential that parents know where she is and what she is doing. Parental monitoring is strongly considered a "cornerstone parenting practice" in that it is vitally important that caregivers track adolescent whereabouts and continue to provide a structured environment (Fosco et al., 2012). Monitoring is linked to lowered risk for a host of negative adolescent behaviors, including substance abuse, early sexual activity, pregnancy, depression, school problems, victimization, delinquency, and negative peer influences (Simpson, 2001). In one recent longitudinal study, sixth graders who were high in parental monitoring were significantly less likely to have developed problem behaviors in the eighth grade (Fosco et al., 2012).

Monitoring in childhood is often done through direct supervision and by providing a highly structured environment; that is, the parent is generally present and activities are planned. In adolescence, it is appropriate for parents to shift their monitoring away from direct supervision and more toward general structuring, frequent communication with the adolescent, occasional observation, and open communication and networking with other adults (parents of peers, teachers, coaches) (Straus, 2006). This shift should not occur too abruptly, as adolescents still need support and supervision, yet parents may not recognize the importance of continuing with consistent monitoring into the adolescent years. For example, in one study of parents of 700 sixth-grade girls, researchers found that only 4 of the parents thought their daughter had ever used alcohol, while 22% of the girls reported drinking during the past year. Thirty-eight percent of the girls reported "hanging out with older boys" or "kissing a boy for a long time," while only 5% of parents thought their daughter had ever engaged in this behavior. The parents in the study who underestimated their daughter's risk were also less likely to provide rules and parental oversight around these issues. It makes sense that if parents are not aware of the risk of early onset of these behaviors, then they will not see the need for monitoring or for communicating concern and setting rules related to these behaviors (O'Donnell et al., 2008). As with other aspects of parenting, appropriate monitoring requires a balance between respecting the adolescent's increasing need for privacy with the need to monitor her activities and whereabouts, and to conduct this monitoring in a way that respects her as an individual while also taking measures needed to protect her safety.

Parenting Task 4: Model and Consult

An adolescent girl needs positive models in her life for learning decision making, goal setting, handling social pressures, relating to peers and adults, and navigating both the adolescent and adult world. She also needs a predictable safe haven that she knows she can turn to for advice, guidance, and support. In addition, she also needs for parents and adult mentors to provide an environment that provides a balance between support and challenge. With too much responsibility or freedom, she will feel overwhelmed, while with too much support, she will feel restricted and will not have the room she needs to flourish and grow into adulthood (Straus, 2006).

Parenting Task 5: Provide and Advocate

Adolescent girls continue to need their parents to provide them with basic care such as food, clothing, shelter, and health care, while they also need a supportive, caring environment in which they can optimally develop and grow. Often, this means that parents will need to serve as advocates for their daughters as they seek out additional resources to provide their daughters with what they need in the way of guidance, training, and support (Simpson, 2001). This might involve seeking out better schools and educational programs, or connecting their daughters with community programs that promote positive development for adolescent girls.

CONCLUSION

As has been described in this chapter, a girl will encounter many challenges during her transition to adolescence and throughout the adolescent years. Not only are her brain and body changing in drastic ways, she simultaneously encounters pressures and upheavals in her academic life and in her peer and family relationships. She is becoming interested in attracting a romantic partner and in learning how to manage her emerging sexual identity. She is developing an overall sense of self that is often fragmented and confused about how she should look, how to act, and who to please. While girls are developing many strengths during these years, they are unclear as to the best way to express them. It is of no surprise, then, that these pressures and challenges from the multiple systems that influence a girl's life can potentially grow larger than what she can manage successfully, thereby leading to mental health problems. Counselors need the knowledge and skills to address these issues with girls and their families. In the remainder of this book, some of the most common mental health concerns are addressed: depression, eating and weight-related problems and disorders, substance use and abuse, self-injury, and sexual violence. Each issue will be viewed through a multisystemic lens, attend to developmental tasks, and provide specific evidence-based treatment and prevention guidelines.

CASE EXAMPLE

Amanda is a 14-year-old Caucasian girl who lives with her parents and one older sibling who is away at college. She is typically quiet and is interested in writing and art. She has two close friends who she knows through the yearbook club at her middle school. She wishes she had more friends, but she doesn't feel comfortable branching out beyond her small group in the yearbook club. As she entered puberty later than her peers, she is currently

---

(continued)

CASE EXAMPLE (*continued*)

very uncomfortable with the changes in her body and feels like a stranger in her own skin. She has grown to dislike school because it is so crowded and because she feels like everyone is staring at her when she walks down the hallways. Because she feels so awkward, she believes that they are all making fun of her behind her back.

However, she doesn't like being at home either. At home, Amanda's parents are both very busy with their careers. They both come home around 6 but continue working on their laptops and tablets throughout the evenings. Amanda feels like she has to interrupt them in order to get their attention to ask a question, and their communications are brief. When she does ask them if she can go on outings with friends, they typically refuse, stating that she is not old enough to leave the house unsupervised yet. As a 14-year-old, she believes she should have some additional freedoms beyond what she could do in elementary school, but her parents seem too busy to discuss her thoughts. In addition, they require that she keep her bedroom door open at all times and refuse to allow her to have a laptop or cell phone. She is growing increasingly frustrated with their restrictiveness and lack of flexibility; at the same time, she questions whether or not it is right for her to challenge her parent's decisions. However, she has no idea how to express her feelings to them without crying uncontrollably or screaming at them, so she keeps her feelings to herself.

At school, she has recently garnered some attention from the popular clique of girls because they realize she has some influence over how much they will be included in the yearbook. She likes their attention even though she is aware of their motives, and for a few days she ignores her two friends and hangs out with these popular girls instead. The girls gossip about her two friends, ask her questions about what will be in the yearbook, and ask her to come to their upcoming sleepover. She feels really torn; on the one hand, she knows that she does not really belong with this group of girls and that they are not really her friends, but on the other hand she wants to gain popularity and attention that she has never had before. She also feels she is outgrowing her two close friendships, but she does not know where else she *does* belong. She is also torn because she knows that her parents will not allow her to hang out with these girls, and she wants to avoid even bringing up the topic with them. She has no idea where to turn. She does respect her yearbook advisor, but she is wondering if her advisor would be willing to take the time to talk with her and help her sort this all out.

Discussion Questions

1. Which of the developmental tasks reviewed in this chapter seem particularly relevant for Amanda? How does she need to move forward in order to develop a sense of mastery around these tasks?
2. In reviewing the parenting tasks at the end of the chapter, how could a counselor work with Amanda's parents in order to help them develop a better relationship with their daughter?
3. What are Amanda's developmental risks at this point in her development?
4. What are her strengths? How could a counselor intervene in her situation?

RESOURCES

Sites for Information About Girls' Puberty

kidshealth.org
Information on girls and puberty from the American Academy of Pediatrics. Available at http://www.Healthychildren.org/English/ages-stages/gradeschool/puberty/pages/Whats-Happening-to-my-Body.aspx

www.pbskids.org
Understanding and raising girls. Video series available at www.pbskids.org/parents/raisinggirls

youngwomenshealth.org
Young Women's Health Center, Boston College. Available at http://youngwomenshealth.org/menstrual.html. The site explains the changes that occur in a girl's body during puberty through diagrams and medical explanations of biological processes.

Sites for Promoting Girls' Positive Development

Bullying.org
A site that aims to raise awareness about bullying for the purposes of prevention. Offers links to resources and programs that address bullying, and provides a forum for parents to connect and share their experiences.

Heyugly.org
A site that combats bullying and cyberbullying by teaching girls to be happy with their individuality. Great resources to encourage girls to change their negative self-talk.

Gemsandjewels.com
This program, created for preadolescent and adolescent girls, helps them transition through puberty, prepare for college/career, increase self-esteem and confidence, and become involved in community service.

Agirlsworld.com
This site provides a safe space where girls can visit to keep an online diary, connect with and encourage one another, play online games, and submit original articles.

Newmoon.com
This site is another place where girls can connect and support one another while creating poetry, artwork, stories, videos, and more.

Educatingjane.com
This site provides resources for girls regarding education, organizations, programs, and books that promote academic success in girls.

Daughters.com/Dadsanddaughters.com
The site offers activities that can help build a positive father-daughter relationship; also provides insight for single fathers to help raise adolescent girls.

A Cloud of Hopelessness:
Adolescent Girls and Depression

The number of adolescents who experience problems with depression is steadily increasing, with every generation since 1940 experiencing an increased risk for developing a depressive disorder (American Academy of Child and Adolescent Psychiatry [AACAP], 2007). This is particularly true for adolescent girls. It is commonly recognized that many girls experience occasional depressed moods, with 24% to 40% of girls reporting feelings of depression (Hankin, Wetter, & Cheely, 2008). However, this does not convey a complete picture of adolescent girls' distress. Between the ages of 12 and 15, the percentage of girls who have experienced a depressive episode triples (from 5% at age 12 to 15% by age 15). By the age of 18, at least 20% of all adolescent girls have experienced an episode of major depressive disorder (MDD), and 10% have made a suicide attempt (AACAP, 2007; Substance Abuse and Mental Health Services Administration [SAMHSA], 2012).

Adolescent depression is of serious concern for several reasons. First, depression onset at a young age is highly associated with recurrent episodes throughout adolescence and adulthood. Up to 72% of adolescents experience another depressive episode within 5 years of their first episode, and are at two- to four-times greater risk for depression as a young adult (AACAP, 2007). Second, adolescent depression is highly associated with suicidal ideation, suicide attempts, and other serious mental health problems. Adolescents who experience depression are four to five times more likely to have a history of suicide attempts than are adolescents who do not have a depressive disorder (Essau & Chang, 2009). Further, among depressed adolescents, 60% have experienced suicidal ideation and 30% have made at least one suicide attempt (AACAP, 2007). In addition to increased risk for suicide, 40% to 90% of those with depression also experience other comorbid disorders such as anxiety or disruptive behavior disorders, and those with comorbid disorders experience the greatest levels of overall impairment (AACAP, 2007).

Third, adolescent depression can have a significant negative impact on a girl's development of healthy emotional, cognitive, and social skills (Essau & Chang, 2009), essential components of the developmental tasks reviewed in Chapter 2. Adolescents who are depressed experience interpersonal problems such as social skills deficits, communication skills, and family/peer relational problems. For example, depressed adolescents experience problems with peer relationships (e.g., less likely to have a best friend and to have problems in making and keeping relationships), and are more likely to be teased than are nondepressed adolescents (Kochel, Ladd, & Rudolph, 2012). Because depression interferes with the development of social skills, interpersonal problems that develop during the adolescent period can persist into adulthood and have a negative lasting impact on a person's life. Compared with their nondepressed peers, depressed adolescents are more likely to experience low academic achievement, are more likely to drop out of school, and are more likely than others to have problems with work performance. They are also more likely to experience teen pregnancy and to have future marital distress. Depressed adolescents are also more likely to have a higher risk of future substance abuse, criminal offenses, legal problems, exposure to negative life events, physical illness, and overall poor work and social functioning as adults (AACAP, 2007).

CONCEPTUALIZATION OF ADOLESCENT GIRLS' DEPRESSION

Diagnostic Features

In assessing for adolescent depression, the *DSM-IV-TR*, the forthcoming *DSM-5* criteria, and the Practice Parameters for Child and Adolescent Depression (AACAP, 2077) are useful in determining symptoms. According to the *Diagnostic and Statistical Manual of Mental Disorders* (4th ed., Text Revision; *DSM-IV-TR*; American Psychiatric Association [APA], 2000), MDD consists of one or more major depressive episodes

(MDEs). An MDE is defined as a syndrome of at least five of nine depressive symptoms that persist for 2 weeks or more. These symptoms include depressed mood, loss of interest or pleasure in usual activities, appetite disturbance (decrease or increase), sleep disturbance (insomnia or hypersomnia), psychomotor agitation or retardation, fatigue or loss of energy, feelings of worthlessness or guilt, concentration problems or indecisiveness, and suicidal ideation or gestures. These symptoms must represent a change from previous functioning in the adolescent and must produce impairment in relationships or in performance of typical activities. Minor depression is characterized by at least two to four depressive symptoms that last for at least 2 weeks (APA, 2000).

While these adult criteria may be used in making a diagnosis, there are several differences in the way that depression is manifested in children and adolescents. Whereas adults are generally able to verbalize depressed feelings and experience long periods of depressed mood, children and younger adolescents are more likely to manifest depression as an irritable mood, mood lability, low frustration tolerance, temper tantrums, somatic complaints, and social withdrawal, interrupted by episodes of a more elevated mood. This is because children and young adolescents are more influenced by external events than are adults, so they can still find enjoyment in many life events and thus are still able to maintain periods of elevated mood. However, by later adolescence, the cognitive symptoms of depression (e.g., hopelessness, low self-esteem), are more pronounced, so that a client's negative thinking pervades her attitudes toward all aspects of her life and inhibits enjoyment of almost all activities that she might have previously found to be enjoyable (Stark, Hargrave, et al., 2006).

As described previously, another area that is particularly salient to assess is for the risk of suicide. Counselors should assess for suicidal or homicidal thinking when working with a depressed adolescent girl because depression is so highly associated with both suicidal ideation and behavior. Counselors should continue to assess for suicide risk not only during the initial assessment but also throughout the course of therapy, especially when the client is also taking antidepressant medications (AACAP, 2007). A recent national treatment trial for adolescent depression, Treatment for Adolescent Depression Study (TADS) compared the effectiveness of antidepressants (fluoxetine), cognitive behavioral therapy (CBT), and a combination of CBT/medication. The researchers found that the adolescents who were treated with medication alone were twice as likely as clients who received combination therapy or CBT alone to report suicidal ideation. Study findings led the national research team to conclude that a counselor should continuously assess for suicidal thoughts and behaviors in depressed adolescents, and should strongly recommend a psychosocial treatment such as CBT if a client is also taking an antidepressant (March, Silva, & Vitiello, 2006; TADS Team, 2009). More information about this study will be presented later in this chapter in the sections on treatment.

GIRLS' SOCIOCULTURAL CONTEXT

Gender Differences

Before adolescence, there are an equal number of boys and girls who experience depression. After puberty, however, girls are twice as likely as boys to develop depression, with these differences emerging sharply around age 13 (AACAP, 2007; Forum on Child and Family Statistics, 2011). Because of these differences, it is important for counselors to consider gender issues in the conceptualization and treatment of depression in adolescent girls (Essau & Chang, 2009). In other words, why are girls more likely to be depressed than boys? There is currently no comprehensive model to explain these gender differences, but the most plausible explanation is that there are multiple processes contributing to these differences (Hankin et al., 2008). The influences with the most research support are presented here.

Girls and Life Stressors

Viewed from a comprehensive perspective, girls have more cognitive, biological, and interpersonal vulnerability factors for depression prior to adolescence and then face more stressful events than do boys during the transition to adolescence. It is likely the combination of these vulnerability factors and life stressors that lead to higher rates of depression in girls (Hankin & Abramson, 2001). Common stressors, including the pubertal transition and changes in interpersonal relationships, are discussed in the paragraphs to follow.

Girls are more likely to experience multiple stressors during early adolescence than are boys, and girls are more likely to become depressed in response to these life stressors (Essau & Chang, 2009). It is noteworthy that counselors might think of depression as being associated primarily with major life stressors (parental death, illness, physical abuse), but for children and adolescents, depression is also highly linked with minor stressors such as daily life hassles and interpersonal problems like changes in peer or romantic relationships (Avenevoli, Knight, Kesslier, & Merikangas, 2008). A girl becomes particularly vulnerable to depression when she experiences the changes associated with adolescence simultaneously: the complex biopsychosocial changes of puberty, changes in peer and family relationships, increased parent–child conflict, increased media pressures regarding appearance, and the introduction of romantic relationships. Girls are also often transitioning to new, larger schools with more rigorous academic expectations and potential vulnerability to peer bullying and cyberbullying, both risk factors for depression and even suicidal ideation (Hinduja & Patchin, 2010). These changes can be highly challenging for a girl to navigate at the same time, leaving her vulnerable to the development of depression (Rudolph, Flynn, & Abaied, 2008). In contrast, boys are less likely to have to deal with these multiple stressors simultaneously.

One type of stressor strongly related to depression is the transition to puberty, and, as reviewed in Chapter 2, this is occurring at increasingly younger ages in recent years. Pubertal status is a better predictor of depression onset than is age, and girls who reach puberty at an earlier age are more likely to experience depression (Essau & Chang, 2009). In contrast, boys who reach puberty earlier are not more likely to develop depression. Girls who experience early puberty are more likely than other girls to suffer from a host of negative psychological outcomes: They are more likely to have lower self-esteem, a history of suicide attempts, and have a lifetime history of eating and disruptive behavior disorders (Essau & Chang, 2009). This is due in part because early maturing girls appear older than they actually are (which is already a message they received in early girlhood), which can cause them to be included in social situations in which they are pressured to participate in activities for which they are not cognitively or emotionally mature enough to handle. Because of their appearance, early maturing girls are also more likely to be sexually harassed and pressured into sexual activity before they are developmentally prepared to make these types of decisions, and these types of sexual experiences are also linked with depression (Kaltiala-Heino, Kosunen, & Rimpela, 2003).

Interpersonal Vulnerability

In addition to the experience of multiple and simultaneous life stressors, girls possess a greater interpersonal vulnerability to depression than do boys. Girls are socialized with a greater need for affiliation, so that girls are more likely than boys to base their self-esteem and worth on the success of relationships and on others' approval, making them more likely to be depressed if they are rejected in any way by their family or peers (Essau & Chang, 2009). For example, interpersonal stress is associated with higher levels of depression and lower self-esteem for girls but not for boys, and family conflict is more related to depression for girls than it is for boys (Hankin et al., 2008).

One way in which this interpersonal orientation and need for affiliation can become problematic is through a girl's overvaluation of her appearance in an effort to gain others' approval. Because peer approval is so valued, girls may become overly concerned with their appearance, weight, and shape in meeting cultural values for beauty and for gaining social success with peers and potential romantic partners. In fact, for girls, confidence in appearance is the most important contributor in determining self-worth, whereas for boys it is his confidence in his abilities (Gillham & Chaplin, 2011). As described in Chapter 1, girls who internalize the "hot and sexy" ideal as espoused in popular culture are more likely to have body dissatisfaction, which is strongly linked to depression in girls (Stice & Bearman, 2001). Conversely, depression is likely to contribute to negative body image; girls who are depressed are more likely to experience body image dissatisfaction, self-blame, and disappointment than are boys who are depressed (Gillham & Chaplin, 2011).

Another way in which an interpersonal orientation creates vulnerability to depression is when a girl places an over reliance on the success of her relationships. Girls' relationships are indeed a double-edged sword: Their relationships provide them with intimacy and emotional support, which are central to their growth and development. However, at the same time, the more girls invest in and identify with their relationships, the more they become vulnerable whenever they experience conflicts that threaten the stability of these same relationships. They also remain vulnerable when they lose their authentic self in order to maintain a relationship. Peer rejection or poor relationship quality are predictors of depressive symptoms in girls but not in boys. As girls become depressed, continued conflicts with peers only serve to exacerbate their depressive symptoms (Hankin et al., 2008; Rudolph et al., 2008).

Due to their socialization experiences emphasizing interpersonal relatedness, girls also have a tendency to display excessive empathy, causing them to experience feelings of guilt due to others' difficulties, taking on others' problems as if they were their own. Girls who experience excessive empathy, high levels of compliance (over concern about meeting the demands of others), and overregulation of emotions (working hard to keep her emotions in check) are also vulnerable to the development of depression (Hankin et al., 2008). Girls are also more likely than boys to minimize their feelings of anger and to inhibit their expression of assertiveness than are boys, and both of these qualities are linked to depression (Gillham & Chaplin, 2011).

This suppression of anger and use of excessive empathy is only compounded for girls when they also engage in a ruminative style of thinking about their problems or those of their friends, and ruminative thinking is highly associated with depression (Essau & Chang, 2009; Hankin et al., 2008). Girls are more likely than boys to use rumination as an emotion regulation strategy (Gillham & Chaplin, 2011). When depressed, girls are more likely to ruminate about their depressed mood and its cause instead of brainstorming possible solutions and actively trying to solve the problem. In addition, when something bad happens, girls will ruminate and blame themselves for their perceived incompetence (Durbin & Shafir, 2008).

In addition, girls frequently engage in *co-rumination*—the excessive talk about problems within friendship groups—which is also linked to depression in adolescent girls. This is especially likely to occur when an adolescent girl is involved in a romantic relationship and her friends communicate frequently about problems in that relationship (Starr & Davilla, 2009). Interestingly, even though the use of social media has not been directly measured as a source of girls' problems, this co-ruminative tendency among friends has been recently termed "Facebook depression" (O'Keeffe & Clarke-Pearson, 2011). In the American Academy of Pediatrics report on adolescent use of social media, girls who engage in excessive co-rumination (communicating about their interpersonal problems with one another, either verbally or electronically through social networking, texting, etc.) are more likely to become depressed over time. The authors of the report cite that heavy social media use can cause problems if a teen is: (a) spending too much time online when she is already at risk for depression, preventing healthy development of coping and social skills; (b) co-ruminating online about problems with friends who don't have the problem solving skills to take action on solving the problem, thus contributing to further co-rumination rather than problem solving; or (c) comparing herself frequently to peers' Facebook or other social networking pages and feeling like she doesn't measure up (e.g., has fewer friends, is not being invited to participate in as many activities, etc.). This tendency toward co-rumination instead of active problem solving will be addressed in the section on treatment for depression, as problem-solving skills play a central role in both of the psychosocial treatments for adolescent depression described later in this chapter.

Ethnicity and Culture

There are no consistent findings to indicate racial or ethnic differences in prevalence rates of depressive disorders in children and adolescents. In addition, while depression is related to lower socioeconomic status in adults, studies are less consistent regarding this finding with children and adolescents (Avenevoli et al., 2008). Clearly more research is needed in this area to determine specific cultural differences. It is important to consider that members of different cultural groups may hold varying beliefs about the nature of depression, the meaning of their symptoms, and the ways in which they personally experience these symptoms (Durbin & Shafir, 2008). For example, one study found that African American adolescent girls reported higher rates of depression than did Caucasian girls but that they were less likely to receive mental health services, and were more likely to drop out of treatment early when they did participate in treatment. It is hypothesized that African American girls might tolerate more distress before seeking help, have reservations about seeking help from a mental health professional, or might more often seek help from alternative resources such as church, family, and leaders in the community (Durbin & Shafir, 2008).

Family Influences

As stated previously, one of the most consistent risk factors for adolescent depression is being female. A second risk factor that is highly linked to adolescent depression is having a family history of MDD (AACAP, 2007; Commission on Adolescent Depression and Bipolar Disorder, 2005; Gilliam & Chaplin, 2011). Having a depressed parent places a child at two to four times greater risk of developing MDD, having an earlier age of onset of MDD, and having a greater likelihood of recurrent episodes. The link between family history and depression is not only related to genetic factors but also to the negative impact of parental depression on parents' interpersonal interactions with their children and on their parenting behaviors.

In addition to parental depression, family dynamics also play an important role both in an adolescent's initial vulnerability to depression as well as in the way she experiences life stressors. Compared to nondepressed adolescents, families of depressed adolescents are more likely to contain chaos; hostility; abuse and neglect; a lack of support and approval; poor early attachments; or a critical, punitive, belittling, or rejecting parenting style (Gilliam & Chaplin,

2011). Families, however, can serve as a protective factor when they help provide a buffer against the many stressors of adolescence, or when they use positive parenting practices, display high levels of warmth, use low levels of psychological control, and are appropriately involved in their daughters' lives (Laser & Nicotera, 2011; see also Chapter 2).

There do appear to be gender differences in family influence on the development of depression. Research indicates that the family has a greater influence on girls' social and emotional adjustment, while peers play a greater role in boys' adjustment (Essau & Chang, 2009). Interestingly, a father's interactions with his child have more of an impact on a girl's experience of stressors than they do for a boy, and a positive paternal relationship seems to protect an adolescent girl from experiencing stress and the subsequent development of depression. Conversely, negative interactions between fathers and daughters create a more harmful home environment that impacts girls more negatively than it does for boys (Commission on Adolescent Depression and Bipolar Disorder, 2005).

Recent research indicates that these types of risk factors described above do not in and of themselves lead to depression, but rather it is the accumulation of risk factors across multiple domains that place an individual at highest risk (Abela & Hankin, 2008a). This becomes particularly problematic for girls, who face multiple transitions and life stressors simultaneously as they transition to adolescence, as was reviewed in this section. Because girls need early intervention when depressive symptoms begin to develop, the rest of the chapter is dedicated to effective treatment and prevention approaches for reducing depression in adolescent girls.

CASE EXAMPLE, PART ONE

Kelsey is a 12-year-old girl and only child living with both of her parents. Her family just moved to a new state after the death of her maternal grandmother, who had lived with them prior to her death. Upon arrival in her new city, Kelsey's parents enrolled her in a large public middle school (whereas before she had attended a private elementary and middle school in her previous state). The middle school is 25 minutes from her home, and she has to take

(continued)

CASE EXAMPLE, PART ONE (*continued*)

a 40-minute bus ride to get to school each morning. During the past year she has gone through significant pubertal changes, and her physical appearance suggests that she is much older than 12. When she arrives at her new school, most of the girls make fun of her because of her breast development and curvaceous figure; she seems so different from them that they immediately begin to treat her as an outcast. The older boys at her school, however, stare at her as she walks down the hall, and several of them try to get her cell phone number. Because she is so lonely, she gives her number to an 8th grader and begins to respond to his texts. Gradually he passes her texts around to his older friends, and soon she is texting a 16-year old boy who is in high school. She finds him much more exciting than the boys at her school, so soon they start to meet after school. He tells her that he can drive her home so that she doesn't have to take the bus. She quickly becomes romantically involved with him and also starts to hang out with his friends. She does not understand when he begins to pressure her sexually, as she has never even kissed a boy before. She rejects his advances but still wants to be his girlfriend. He tells her that she is just a "tease" and that he wishes he had never wasted his time on her. In less than a week, he stops texting her and does not respond to any more of her calls.

Kelsey is devastated. She had never told her parents or anyone else about her romantic involvement with the 16-year-old, but now she starts to text her friends back in her hometown regarding what happened and begs them to help her know what to do. She posts lengthy comments on Facebook about how badly she feels, and her friends from home try to be supportive, but soon grow tired of her repeating the story. They just tell her to move on. Soon they no longer respond to her either.

At home, she stays quiet. Her father has a history of depression and she doesn't want him to become upset. Her mother is busy with working and adjusting to their new home, so she doesn't want to bother her either; in addition, she knows her mother is still grieving the loss of her mother. Kelsey also misses her grandmother but pushes these feelings away because she worries that she will never stop crying from all of the pain she is going through right now. All she can do is think about how stupid she is, how ugly she must be, and how hopeless her situation is. She believes she will never have friends at her school and that she will be an outcast for life. Slowly she stops caring about her schoolwork, she loses interest in eating or in going out with her family, cries for no apparent reason, and wants to sleep all of the time. In fact, she goes to sleep as soon as she comes home from school and only comes out of her room if her parents make her have dinner (which is only 3 to 4 nights per week). Her parents do not seem to notice; she guesses that they are relieved that they do not have to spend time with her. Over a period

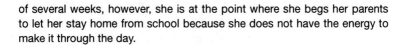

of several weeks, however, she is at the point where she begs her parents to let her stay home from school because she does not have the energy to make it through the day.

Discussion Questions

1. What are the risk factors for depression that Kelsey possesses? Which are intrapersonal and which are interpersonal factors?
2. Could Kelsey's depressive episode have been prevented? What in her environment could have been changed to make her situation better?
3. If you were Kelsey's counselor, where would you start in your treatment with her? What do you see as her strengths, and what are her obstacles to change?

MENTAL HEALTH TREATMENT APPROACHES FOR ADOLESCENT DEPRESSION

Both CBT (primarily in group format) and interpersonal therapy (in individual format) are well-established therapeutic modalities for adolescent depression (David-Ferdon & Kaslow, 2008). These two treatment approaches will be described in detail in the sections that follow.

CBT Approaches for Depression in Adolescent Girls

According to cognitive behavioral theory, depression results from an interaction between stressful life events and a preexisting cognitive vulnerability to depression. Under normal conditions, girls with a vulnerability to depression might be indistinguishable from the general population. Only when faced with certain stressors do the differences between vulnerable and nonvulnerable girls begin to emerge. For example, in Kelsey's case, she is undergoing the stressors of the death of her grandmother, a move to a new state and school, and the stresses of early puberty all at the same time. According to Beck's schema construct (1983), a girl is cognitively vulnerable to depression when she possesses a negative attributional style (tending to make global, stable, and internal attributions for negative life events) and when she develops negatively biased beliefs, leading to a highly negative view of self, others, and the future (Commission on Adolescent Depression and Bipolar Disorder, 2005). This *negative triad*, often referred to as a cognitive gateway to depression, includes beliefs such as negative self-beliefs (e.g., I am deficient, inadequate, a failure), negative views of others (e.g., others are critical and rejecting; life experiences and relationships are likely to turn out badly), and negative beliefs about the future (hopelessness and helplessness to change one's difficulties). According to cognitive theory, once a girl develops this negative triad, she is likely to develop depressive symptoms in response to life stressors (Abela & Hankin, 2008a; Reinecke & Ginsburg, 2008). It is interesting that research indicates that fathers have a greater influence on the development of girls' cognitive triads than do mothers, as messages from fathers have a greater influence on whether or not a girl develops negative beliefs about herself, others, and the future (Essau & Chang, 2009). In Kelsey's case, she has learned from her father to retreat from her feelings and to view the world as a negative and lonely place.

In addition to negative core beliefs, girls vulnerable to depression also possess dysfunctional or perfectionistic standards, biased information processing, pessimistic cognitive styles, and poor coping and problem-solving strategies (e.g., passivity, rumination, or aggression). Once a girl possesses these negative cognitive and behavioral styles, these can lead to downward spiral or self-fulfilling prophecies in which these same thoughts, beliefs, and actions only serve to exacerbate her depressive symptoms (Gillham & Chaplin, 2011; Reinecke & Ginsburg, 2008). For example, if she already possesses a negative belief about herself, she will more likely attend to negative feedback from others and rule out positive feedback in order to confirm and reinforce her already negative self-concept (Remmel & Flavel, 2004). Further, she will become less likely to implement active coping and problem-solving skills when she attributes negative meaning to her experiences and believes that her attempts to make her problems better will only be futile. In addition, when she believes that others are likely to be rejecting or unsupportive, she may push others away and behave in such a way that only serves to increase her social isolation (Abela & Hankin, 2008a; Davila, Stroud, Starr, Miller, Yoneda, & Hershenberg, 2009). For Kelsey, she only notices when girls are making fun of her, and not when she receives praise or positive attention from teachers or peers. As she believes others do not like her, she becomes increasingly unfriendly and aloof, thereby perpetuating her social isolation.

General Components of CBT Treatment

Based on this theoretical framework, CBT interventions address deficits in cognitive, problem solving, and coping skills contributing to depression by assisting the client in changing beliefs, attitudes, and thoughts to effect a change in mood and behavior. While there are a variety of CBT intervention programs available, most research-based treatment programs include the following components (Brent, Poling, & Goldstein, 2011; Kennard et al., 2009; Reinecke & Ginsberg, 2008):

Psychoeducation

Counselors should educate parents and daughters about the nature of depression, and how it is determined by multiple causes including cognitive, behavioral, emotional, biological, and environmental factors. It is also helpful to provide girls and their families with a rationale for the CBT techniques what will be used and why these will be helpful. Resources and web/bibliotherapy (see resources at the end of this chapter) are also helpful.

Therapeutic Collaboration

Effective programs emphasize the collaborative nature (termed *collaborative empiricism*) of treatment. They include motivational interviewing principles to increase the client's internal motivation and readiness for change and to instill hope that change is possible. Counselors work to join with the client, checking in frequently to determine that he or she is correctly understanding the client.

Goal Setting, Monitoring, and Homework

In CBT, all techniques are designed to gain information about the problem, understand or restructure cognitions, or develop a new behavioral skill. Clearly defined, measurable goals are deemed essential to client progress, and monitoring is important for tracking thoughts and mood, and helping clients to recognize that certain beliefs or activities cause them to feel better or worse. Homework is assigned each week to give clients opportunities to self-monitor, test out the validity of a belief, or practice a new behavioral skill.

Activity Scheduling/Behavioral Activation

Clients are encouraged to increase pleasant activities throughout the week and institute self-rewards to help motivate them to overcome initial reluctance to engage in pleasurable events.

Cognitive Restructuring

These techniques are used to assist a client in identifying automatic thoughts and cognitive distortions about self, others, and the future. The client is then encouraged to develop more realistic counter thoughts. To do this, the counselor asks the client a series of questions to help the client to recognize errors in thinking and how a particular belief may be unhelpful and contributing to depression. To develop adaptive counter thoughts, adolescents are taught to talk back to their thoughts. For example, "What is the evidence for this belief?" "Is there another way to think about it?" "Is there another course of action I could take?" It should be noted that the client should be at a cognitive developmental stage in which she can utilize abstract thinking skills in order to be able to use cognitive restructuring effectively.

Social Skills and Communication Training

This component is one of the most effective in decreasing depressive symptoms (Kennard et al., 2009). It consists of training the clients in areas such as assertiveness (e.g., avoiding passivity and aggression); compromise (e.g., active listening, reflection, negotiation, conflict resolution); social interaction skills (e.g., starting conversations, joining groups, listening, using I-statements); and family communication (e.g., reducing blame, clearly identifying problems without name calling, increasing trust) (Kennard et al., 2009).

Problem Solving

This component has also been identified as one of the most effective for effecting client change. It involves teaching clients a five-step model for solving problems: (a) defining/operationalizing problems, (b) defining goals, (c) generating potential solutions, (d) evaluating consequences, and (e) implementing action and evaluating results (see also Chapter 8).

Affect Regulation and Distress Tolerance

These strategies teach clients skills for either interrupting the chain of events that lead to distressing emotions or for providing self-soothing or relaxation strategies for coping when emotionally arousing situations occur. This might include progressive muscle relaxation, deep breathing, guided imagery, imagery, seeking social support, or connecting to religious and spiritual resources. For example, one study found that girls who used positive coping resources such as religion and spirituality were less likely to have depressive symptoms (Durbin & Shafir, 2008).

Relapse Prevention

Clients are encouraged to review the communication, cognitive, coping and problem-solving skills learned in treatment, to monitor mood, to determine potential triggers for relapse, and to develop a specific plan for relapse prevention.

These components cut across CBT treatment programs, although they are packaged in different ways depending upon the treatment setting and particular client population. Two of the most highly studied CBT interventions designed specifically for adolescent depression are the *Coping with Depression-Adolescent* program (CWD-A) and the *ACTION* program. These are described in detail in the paragraphs that follow.

PROGRAM HIGHLIGHT: COPING WITH DEPRESSION-ADOLESCENTS

CWD-A is among the most studied and effective CBT programs for adolescents (Clarke & DeBar, 2010; David Ferdon & Kaslow, 2008; Garber et al., 2009). It is helpful that the training manual and student workbook in individual and group format are available free of charge online at www.kpchr.org/acwd/acwd.html. It is designed for adolescents ages 13 to 17, and sessions are conducted in eight weekly 90-minute, mixed-sex group meetings. These sessions are followed by continuation sessions that meet monthly for an additional 6 months. At least two family sessions are also incorporated. CWD-A is based on a social learning model that focuses on

(continued)

PROGRAM HIGHLIGHT: COPING WITH DEPRESSION-ADOLESCENTS (continued)

teaching the following skill modules: (a) cognitive restructuring to address negative beliefs, guilt, hopelessness, and worthlessness by identifying and implementing challenges to negative thoughts; (b) behavioral techniques to address social withdrawal and interpersonal interactions by increasing pleasant activities; (c) problem solving, communication, and negotiation skills to address poor problem solving and ineffective interpersonal interactions with family and peers; (d) relaxation training to ease social anxiety and tension; and (e) goal setting to identify short- and longer-term life goals.

PROGRAM HIGHLIGHT: ACTION TREATMENT PROGRAM

The *ACTION* CBT-based treatment program, specifically designed for young adolescent girls ages 9 to 13, also has strong empirical support for its effectiveness (Stark et al., 2008; Stark, Sander, et al., 2006; Stark, Streusand, Krumholz, & Patel, 2010). This is a treatment based on the conceptualization of depression as resulting from negative thinking and skill deficits. The self-regulation program helps girls learn to recognize negative thoughts or moods and then to use these as cues to begin using coping, problem solving, and/or cognitive restructuring skills. Leaders teach these skills in groups of 4 to 6 girls, meeting twice weekly for 11 weeks. The group format is deemed important for its instillation of universality, hope, and for reliance on other members as sources of emotional support and for assisting in the countering negative beliefs. In the first half of the group sessions, girls learn coping and problem solving strategies. Girls are taught to recognize situations in which they cannot change the outcome as opportunities to use a coping strategy. The coping skills are presented in terms of five categories: (a) do something fun and relaxing; (b) do something that uses energy; (c) do something soothing and relaxing; (d) talk to someone; and (3) change the way you think about it. Problem solving skills are taught for situations in which action is needed in order to improve the situation. The steps are as follows: (1) problem definition, (2) goal definition, (3) solution generation, (4) evaluating consequences, and (5) self-evaluation.

In the second half of the group sessions, girls learn cognitive restructuring skills and continue to practice coping and problem-solving strategies. Girls are taught to recognize their negative thoughts and to counter them by learning how to be "thought judges" who use two primary questions to evaluate whether or not a thought is valid: "What is another way of looking at it?" and "What is the evidence?" The leaders also present this skill symbolically as being able to talk back to the "muck monster" in which negative thoughts are visualized as keeping her "stuck in the muck." Girls are encouraged to talk to the muck monster, dispute the negative thoughts, and replace them with more positive thoughts. In final sessions girls are given action kits that consist of color-coded cards to serve as reminders of the skills taught in the program. These include (a) when to use either coping skills, problem-solving skills, or cognitive restructuring, (b) how to identify emotions, (c) five categories of coping skills, (d) the five problem-solving steps, and (e) the two primary questions used to evaluate negative thoughts.

CASE EXAMPLE, PART TWO

To help Kelsey overcome her depressive symptoms, Kelsey's parents enrolled her in a small counseling group that followed the ACTION model. While she was reluctant to join a group at first, her parents believed that she would benefit from the interactions with other people in her group. In the first few sessions, Kelsey began to trust the leaders and members as she realized that they cared about her feelings and what she had to say. They helped her to recognize her negative thoughts and triggers for her sad moods. She learned to recognize these as cues to alert her to the need to implement problem-solving or coping skills, or cognitive restructuring. To develop her problem-solving skills, she chose the most pressing problem—no friends. She then learned the steps for problem solving, eventually coming up with three strategies (e.g., talk to someone in class, join an after-school group away from school, make eye contact as she walks down the hall). Within the group, she also identified coping skills for when she is in situations that cannot be changed (e.g., she is not able to move back to her hometown, but must remain in her current school). She agreed to try some new pleasant events (go to a free yoga class, prepare dinner for her family), some energy-producing events (go for a walk on the track near her house), self-soothing strategies (light a candle and listen to relaxing music), talk to someone (she does like her English teacher, and maybe her mom would be more open if she knew what was going on with her). She also learned to change the way she thinks about herself, others, and the world. For example, she learned to

(continued)

CASE EXAMPLE, PART TWO (*continued*)

visualize her negative thinking as a muck monster and her thoughts as keeping her stuck in the muck. She learned how to talk back to the muck monster by evaluating her thoughts in the following manner:

Thought: I am an outcast here and no one will ever like me.

Talking back to the muck monster:

Q: What's another way of thinking about it?

A: I just moved here and these girls have been friends with each other since elementary school. They haven't had time to get to know me. Besides, if they are this mean, maybe I don't want to be friends with them either. Maybe I can find friends through a group or club outside of school.

Q: What is the evidence for this belief?

A: It's true that some of the girls are making fun of me and my boyfriend stopped calling me. It's true that this really hurts my feelings. But there is no evidence that no one will ever like me; I had lots of friends at my old school and there are lots of guys here that seem to want to talk to me.

INTERPERSONAL THERAPY FOR ADOLESCENTS

While there is strong evidence for CBT effectiveness, it also important for counselors to be aware that interpersonal therapy for adolescents (IPT-A) has clear research support and there is some initial indication that it might be more effective for girls in particular due to its interpersonal focus. As reviewed previously, girls cope with depression differently than boys, tending to be more internally focused and ruminating about problems in relationships, while boys are more externally focused (Ferdon & Kaslow, 2008). It follows then that a treatment approach focused specifically on important interpersonal relationships, building interpersonal skills, and increasing social support might be highly appealing and well-suited to the needs of adolescent girls.

Theoretical Conceptualization of IPT-A

IPT-A is a time-limited brief therapy initially developed to treat unipolar depressed adults (Klerman, Weissman, Rounsaville, & Chevron, 1984; Weissman, Markowitz, & Klerman, 2000). It is based on the theoretical assumption that interpersonal problems and skill deficits contribute to the onset of depression, and that regardless of the underlying cause, the depression is intertwined with the client's interpersonal relationships. It is assumed that dysfunctional communication patterns and negative interactions with early significant others tend to be replayed throughout the many relational transitions that occur in adolescence. Until these maladaptive interpersonal patterns are changed, relational problems and the vulnerability to depression will continue.

IPT-A also assumes that depressed adolescents interact with others in ways that elicit negative feedback and loss of social support, thus perpetuating the depression. It is hypothesized that as the client improves interpersonal relationships, builds support, and enhances interpersonal competence, depressive symptoms will be reduced (Mufson & Dorta, 2000). While IPT-A does not focus on symptoms directly, it addresses relational issues and interpersonal stressors that are most pressing for adolescents such as family and peer problems (Mufson & Dorta, 2000). Specifically, IPT-A examines areas such as family conflict, affective expression, and effective problem-solving and communication skills, and takes into account relevant developmental tasks such as individuation, romantic relationships, managing peer pressure, and coping with death and loss (Mufson & Dorta, 2000). Because of its focus on interpersonal stressors, it is most appropriate for adolescents for whom an identifiable interpersonal problem preceded or contributed to the current depressive episode (Mufson & Dorta, 2000).

Most counselors are not as familiar with interpersonal therapy as they are with CBT, but there is a strong line of research supporting its effectiveness with both adults and adolescents. Three randomized clinical trials have been conducted to conclude that IPT-A, delivered in an individual format, is more efficacious than treatment as usual, clinical monitoring, and wait list. It is also as effective as CBT (Jacobson & Mufson, 2010; Mufson, Dorta, Wickramaratne et al., 2004). IPT-A has also been successfully modified for group (Mufson, Gallaher, Dorta, & Young, 2004), for pregnant adolescent girls (Miller, Gur, Shanok, & Weissman, 2008), and for school-based mental health clinics (Mufson, Dorta, Olfson, Weissman, & Hoagwood, 2004).

IPT-A Treatment Approach

IPT-A is described fully in a treatment manual published in book form (Mufson, Dorta, Moreau, & Weissman, 2004). A summary of the treatment format is provided here. According to IPT-A, there are four therapeutic tasks: (a) to create a therapeutic relationship; (b) to conceptualize the adolescent depression through an interpersonal context by identifying interpersonal problems in one of four areas: grief, interpersonal role disputes, role, transitions, and interpersonal deficits; (c) to assist the client in recognizing maladaptive communication patterns and change them so she can better get her relational needs met; and (d) to help the client to develop a stronger social support network.

Treatment begins with a pretreatment evaluation in which the counselor meets with family members to explain the counseling process and to obtain an interpersonal history. Part of the purpose of this evaluation is also to determine if the client will likely benefit from IPT-A. Research indicates that she is most likely to have treatment success if the family is supportive, if she can establish a therapeutic relationship, and if she is motivated to decrease her depressive symptoms. She should be in agreement that her interpersonal problems are contributing to her depressive symptoms. Finally, according to the treatment manual, IPT-A is only recommended as a short-term treatment for adolescents aged 12 to 18 who meet the criteria for acute-onset MDD or dysthymia. It would not be appropriate if the client is suicidal, has psychotic symptoms, or if her primary diagnosis is bipolar disorder, substance abuse, anxiety, or conduct disorder (Mufson, Dorta, Moreau, & Weissman, 2004).

The counselor then meets with the adolescent alone to begin to build the therapeutic relationship by discussing confidentiality and assessing reasons for seeking help. The counselor conducts an assessment to diagnose the depression, to obtain information about current and past depressive symptoms, to ascertain a history of current depression, including a possible precipitant, course of previous illnesses, psychosocial history and current psychosocial functioning, and family/personal medical history. With adolescents it is also important to discuss associated problems such as suicidality, nonsuicidal self-injury, drug abuse, antisocial behavior, or other comorbid problems. It is recommended that the counselor meet with the parents separately to confirm the results of this assessment and to attempt to reconcile any discrepancies between client and parent reports.

Initial Sessions

Initial sessions include psychoeducation in which the counselor helps the adolescent to understand that her symptoms are part of being depressed, and she and her family members should be encouraged to provide her with some relief from the pressure of performing at the same level as prior to being depressed. She might need some extra support at this time, but she should still be encouraged to go to school, complete tasks, and to do as many of her usual activities as possible. Parents' concerns should be validated, but they should be encouraged to refrain from expressing frustration at their daughter's lower performance quality while she is depressed.

Next, the counselor should conduct an interpersonal inventory. The inventory helps to examine the client's relationship problems and history. For example, general questions such as: "Do you think you have problems in your relationships with people? What are the problems? Who in your family do you feel closest to, that you could count on and go to for help? What makes the relationship special to you? Who can't you count on? What makes it hard for you to be close to that person?"

Client can then examine current relationships through a "closeness circle" exercise. The client is asked to draw a series of concentric circles, with an X in the center to indicate the client. The client is asked to name others in her life and to place them on the circles according to the level of closeness she feels with each of them. The counselor can then discuss the most important relationships in greater depth. For example, for the person who is closest on the circle, what do they do together? How frequently do they interact? What are the terms and expectations for the relationship? What are the positive and negative aspects of this relationship? What changes does she want to make? Is there anything that they can't agree on? What happens when they try to talk about it? What has she tried already that was or was not helpful? How has the client's depression affected the relationship with this person?

The next part of the inventory is to assess for life events that occurred around the time of depression onset, including changes such as changes in family structure, transitioning to a new schools, moving to a new location, death or illness in the family, onset of sexuality and/ or sexual relationships. As the client begins to link the onset of depression with interpersonal and life stressors, the counselor can explain the connection between the interpersonal problem and the depression and can encourage the client that as changes are made in her relationships, she will subsequently have more energy and begin to feel better, and will develop relationships that are more mutually satisfying. At this point the counselor will help the client select one or two problem areas for treatment focus: grief, interpersonal role disputes, role transitions, interpersonal deficits (Mufson, Dorta, Moreau, & Weissman, 2004).

Middle Sessions

In sessions 5 to 8, the counselor and client will clarify the problem area, develop strategies for improving the problem, and implement strategies for improving the relational difficulties. The counselor will use such techniques as education; clarification of feelings and expectations; encouragement of affect; clarification of her roles in the family, peer, group, community; facilitation of social competence through communication analysis (impact of words on others, the feelings they convey, the feelings that are generated, and how they can modify these exchanges); and decision analysis (basic problem-solving skills, compromise, negotiation skills, modeling, and role playing).

Four Areas of Treatment Focus

Grief. In this problem area, the adolescent is coping with the loss of a relationship, such as the death of a parent or other loved one. The IPT-A approach to grief resolution is helpful for adolescent girls who are currently experiencing depression, but can also be beneficial for those who are at risk of depression following a loss. This may be particularly important for adolescents who have been depressed in the past and who might be vulnerable to its recurrence given the stress of the loss. It might be also helpful for girls who lack an understanding of death, have lost significant others due to multiple or sudden deaths including suicide or homicide, have a conflicted relationship with the deceased person, or have an overly dependent surviving parent, as these are all risk factors for developing depression during the bereavement period (Mufson & Dorta, 2000).

To assess the impact of the loss on her life, the counselor can examine the nature of the relationship with the deceased person, her current support system, her coping skills and psychological maturity, and any signs of distorted grief including behavioral problems such as acting out, drug or alcohol use, or sexual promiscuity. It is also helpful for counselors to know that with adolescents, the grief response may be more episodic than pervasive across time.

The first step in IPT-A grief work is to assist the client in connecting the loss with the onset or increase of depressive symptoms. Once this link is made, it is helpful to provide her with education about normal bereavement patterns. She might be experiencing a range of feelings, from sadness, excessive guilt, anger, a belief of responsibility that she could have done something differently to prevent the loss, concern that the same thing will happen to her, or over identification in order to maintain the deceased person's presence in her life. It is important for her to understand that her feelings are normal, that grieving takes time, that grief is experienced differently by each individual, and that grief might put a strain and cause the potential for conflict in existing relationships in her life. These conflicts can increase her vulnerability to depression at a time when she needs supportive relationships in her life. Next, the client is encouraged to actively mourn the loss by thinking about and describing it in detail. What happened right before, during, and after the loss? How was her relationship with the person around the time of the loss? What types of things did they do together? If the loss was a death, how did she find out about it? How did she react to it? What was the funeral like for her? How did she grieve during the funeral?

Next, she can explore her feelings about the relationship and the loss in the present. For example, what is she struggling with *most* now that the person is not present in her life anymore? It is especially helpful for her to create a realistic picture of the relationship, recalling both the good and bad qualities, because exploring a balanced view of a lost relationship helps to facilitate the mourning process (Weissman, Markowitz, & Klerman, 2000). During the recounting of past events and current feelings, the counselor can assist her by normalizing and validating the client's painful feelings. She can be reassured that it is normal to have both positive and negative feelings about the person, and that it is also normal to fear being overwhelmed and unable to control her emotions. The counselor can help her to move slowly at her own pace and discuss aspects of the loss as she feels ready to do so. Finally, the counselor can examine her need for strengthening existing relationships or establishing a new social network that will provide support. This is important because she might have friends who are currently avoiding her because they do not know how to discuss the loss. She might also need additional support if she is in a relationship with a parent or loved one who is overly relying on her for support. Because of these problems, she might need to practice new styles of communication, learn to set boundaries, practice ways to develop supportive relationships, and be encouraged to become involved in activities that might strengthen her support system (Mufson, Dorta, Moreau, & Weissman, 2004).

In the case of Kelsey, the recent loss of her grandmother should be explored, as Kelsey is actively trying to suppress her feelings about the death. When her counselor asked her to share her feelings, she admitted that she is carrying a lot of guilt, with beliefs such as "I should have been there when she died; instead, I stayed at my friend's house" and "I must be a terrible person because I am not sad all of the time about it; actually I am mad at her because if she hadn't died, we wouldn't have had to move here." Her counselor normalizes her grieving process, letting her know that it is normal to have both positive and negative feelings about the loss. During sessions, Kelsey described her tension-filled relationship with her grandmother; she had loved her and often looked forward to spending time with her when she was younger, but once she became sick and moved in with her family, Kelsey started to avoid her and was angry with her mother for paying more attention to her grandmother than to her. At the funeral, Kelsey did not even cry, and her mother let her know that she was disappointed in her because she didn't seem to care about her grandmother. All of this had led Kelsey to develop guilt and true regret that she had not been a good granddaughter. She and her counselor decided that the person she could turn to for support through this time is her mother, but they have not ever even discussed the loss. After a few sessions of practicing sharing her feelings, Kelsey decided to invite her mother to join her in session and to allow the counselor to facilitate their discussion about her grief so that it would be easier for her to bring it up at home.

Role Disputes.   Role disputes is a relevant area when the client and significant others have conflicting expectations in their relationship. Such interpersonal conflict can cause an adolescent girl to feel helpless, powerless, out of control, and misunderstood. In turn, she might increase social withdrawal and poor communication with others, furthering her inability to communicate her feelings and expectations with the other person, resulting in depression. The goal in this problem area is to assist the client in successfully resolving a conflict with the identified significant others in her life. For example, many girls have experienced conflicts as a result of unmet expectations, mistreatment, and betrayals in their relationships with parents, best friends, teachers, or significant others. To assess the history of the dispute, the counselor might ask such questions as: When did you first become aware of the dispute? What are your expectations of this person and how have they changed? What do you fight about? How do you communicate your needs? How do your fights end? How do you feel when this happens? How do you wish the other person would respond to you? How do you think your relationship can be helped or improved? What have you already tried to do to resolve the dispute? What prevented these attempts from working? (Weissman et al., 2000).

   To address disputes, the counselor can first determine the stage of the dispute: *negotiation* (ongoing attempts to improve the relationship), *impasse* (neither individual is attempting to change), or *dissolution* (the relationship is beyond repair). The client's action plan will be dependent upon the stage of the dispute. For example, if she is at the negotiation stage, she may spend time closely examining her patterns of communication with the person with whom she has a conflict. She can receive feedback about the ways she communicates her needs, how she expresses anger, and how she responds to the conflict (Weissman et al., 2000). The counselor can assist her in problem solving and in practicing new ways of communicating, or work to change her expectations of relationships if these have been unrealistic. She may also benefit from role playing with the counselor and to observe modeling of appropriate communication. She might also benefit from having the person attend a session with her to practice the skills and to try to decrease the conflict.

If the member is at the impasse stage in her relationship, she can brainstorm alternatives for making a decision to either move the relationship back toward negotiation or to facilitate its movement toward dissolution. To move toward negotiation, she might have to invest more energy in the relationship, take risks in sharing her feelings, and open up the conflict in order to resolve it. If she decides that dissolution is the best solution, the counselor can assist her in taking action to end the relationship. In this case, she may need to spend time mourning the loss of the relationship, incorporating aspects of grief work, and accepting the loss as a role transition (as described in the next section; Weissman et al., 2000). If the dispute is with a parent, she can examine the most effective ways to cope with the situation, develop realistic expectations, and increase pleasurable activities that do not involve the parent. She might also try to identify an alternative family member who might be able to provide the support and caregiving that this parent is unable to give (Mufson, Dorta, Moreau, & Weissman, 2004). In Kelsey's case, it is likely that her father (who is currently experiencing an episode of depression) will not be able to provide the support she needs. Her mother seems willing to come to sessions, but she is likely dealing with her own grief and transition issues. After discussing her situation with the counselor, the mother agrees to seek her own counseling with another counselor so that she can be better able to serve as a support for her daughter. She also agrees to work on having more open communication with Kelsey.

Role Transitions. Like role disputes, role transitions are common difficulties in girls with depression. Role transitions include difficulties in releasing a previous life role and in embracing a new one, such as managing changes related to puberty, family structure, onset of sexual desires and decision making, the initiation of romantic relationships, or taking responsibility for her future (Mufson, Dorta, Moreau, & Weissman, 2004). Transitions might also occur unexpectedly due to a change in the adolescent's role in the family due to a move, separation/divorce/change in family structure, or family illness. An adolescent girl might experience problems with transitions when she and her parents have difficulty accepting the inevitable changes that occur with adolescent transitions, or when she lacks the skills for meeting others' expectations associated with these life changes (Mufson & Dorta, 2000). For an adolescent girl who is facing problems related to a role transition, the first step is to assist her in clearly identifying the nature of the actual transition. Once the roles are defined, she can focus first on her old role, fully validating and exploring her feelings about it, and mourning the loss of a role that is comfortable and familiar. She can also explore how the loss affects her sense of identity and relationships with others. The counselor might also provide parents with education regarding normal adolescent developmental transitions.

She can then begin to examine her feelings about the new role. For example, what is causing her to experience anxiety or ambivalence about her new role? What are the potential benefits and opportunities that the new role may yield? How does the new role fit with her overall life goals? It may be helpful to assist her in creating a chart, comparing and exploring the pros and cons of both the old and new roles in an effort to create a balanced picture of the transition (Weissman et al., 2000). The next step will be for her to examine the specific demands of her new role. What does it require? Are there things she needs to learn? How can she go about developing these skills? What are the strengths she already possesses that she can bring to the new role? Finally, she can examine her support system and the ways in which she may need to ask for help in transitioning to the new role. It might also be helpful for her to become involved in activities that she might enjoy and in which she might meet new friends with similar interests (Mufson, Dorta, Moreau, & Weissman, 2004).

In Kelsey's case, her counselor recognizes that this is likely the area most relevant to her life. She has undergone changes in transitioning from girlhood to adolescence in a short period of time, moving to a new state, new type of school, loss of friends, and loss of a potential boyfriend. To move past her former roles, her counselor helps her to first acknowledge what she is giving up and to mourn the loss of her old roles and relationships. Only then can she begin to identify her new roles (an adolescent girl with new opportunities, a new larger school with more activities, a time to develop a new friendship group based on mutual interests, and an increased ability to evaluate potential relationships with romantic partners). As she learns to appreciate the positive things about her new life, she realizes that she needs to take some steps in order to embrace the transition. For example, she can evaluate her talents and interests and then investigate the opportunities that are available in her new city/school. She can make efforts to join these new activities and make some new friendships (rather than expecting others to reject her).

Interpersonal Deficits.   This problem area is identified when a client has a history of difficulty in initiating or maintaining intimate relationships. When an adolescent girl has trouble developing and maintaining relationships with peers and becomes socially withdrawn, she is less able to overcome her social deficits, which contributes to depression and subsequently leads to further withdrawal. Social isolation and a lack of a network of peers are particularly problematic in adolescence because the successful establishment of social relationships is an important aspect of many of the developmental tasks of adolescence (Mufson, Dorta, Moreau, & Weissman, 2004).

To make improvements in this area, the counselor can assist an adolescent client in assessing her interpersonal problems by discussing her current relationships, past relationships, and relationship with the counselor. As part of this review, the counselor can provide the client with specific feedback about her communication style and how it might be improved. To help reduce her social isolation, establish new relationships, and strengthen existing ones, the client may benefit from basic social skills training exercises that can be practiced both within and outside of the counseling sessions. Family members may also be involved so they can encourage the development of these new skills. For example, the client can identify people who can be a support to her, practice ways to express her feelings more clearly, role play a conversation with peers, and identify activities in which she can participate that will enable her to meet peers with similar interests. Mufson and colleagues recommend that it is most helpful to be specific, and to stay focused on improving one relationship or building one particular skill set in order to make progress during the limited time frame of counseling.

In Kelsey's case, she seems to have developed a group of friends in her former city, and she does not display any apparent social skills deficits. Now that she has experienced setbacks in her sense of self (with negative thoughts about herself and that others will likely reject her), she will have to overcome these negative thoughts in order to assert herself in social situations in which she might be able to establish some healthy relationships. It will also be helpful for her to learn to communicate more openly with her mother so that she can serve as a source of support during this time of transition.

Conclusion and Maintenance

The last phase of therapy helps the client plan for how she will manage interpersonal stressors after therapy has ended and to review the progress she has made during treatment. Some termination tasks include: (a) elicit feelings about ending treatment; (b) review signs of depression and warning signs that might indicate the need to return to counseling; (c) acknowledge the client's interpersonal strengths and progress made in developing these competencies; (d) identify areas where continued work is needed and develop a plan for action steps she will take once counseling has ended; (e) schedule maintenance or booster sessions for the near future (once per month maintenance sessions are suggested in the treatment manual).

Adaptations of IPT-A

IPT-A has recently been adapted to a group format (IPT-AG) with promising results (Mufson, 2010; Mufson, Gallagher, Dorta, & Young, 2004). Belonging to a group provides adolescents with a place where they can practice the communication and relational skills they are learning and provides them with an experience of universality that they are not alone with their problems. The current format of IPT-AG includes two individual pre-group sessions with adolescent and parent in order to conduct the interpersonal inventory and to determine areas of focus, followed by 12 consecutive group sessions. It also includes one mid-treatment family session with each adolescent. The standard IPT-AG model has also been modified to include family members in every session. In this format, weekly sessions are divided into two parts: individual meetings with adolescents followed by joint or dyadic meetings with parents. Additional studies are needed to establish the effectiveness of incorporating parents into all weekly sessions (Dietz, Mufson, Irvine, & Brent, 2008).

IPT-AG has been studied in a group of primarily Latina female adolescents ages 12 to 18 in a school setting, and results demonstrated that IPT-AG group is effective (as compared to a control group who received primarily supportive psychotherapy); however, the results were strongest for those who were in highly conflictual relationships with their mothers or with friends (Gunlicks-Stoessel, Mufson, Jekal, & Turner, 2010). There is also some initial evidence that IPT-AG was effective in reducing depressive symptoms in a group of adolescents who were displaced survivors of war in northern Uganda, and the effects were stronger for girls than for boys (Bolton et al., 2007).

IPT-AG has been further modified for more specific client populations. One such innovative approach is IPT-PA (pregnant adolescents). IPT-PA follows a similar format to the IPT-A described in this section, with the exception that it adds a fifth problem area, single parent family concerns. Initial studies confirmed the effectiveness of this treatment for pregnant adolescent girls from a public school designed for pregnant adolescents who received IPT-PA in group format (Miller et al., 2008). In addition to the treatment goals already described, treatment goals for the additional fifth area include: issues around the new role of motherhood within the context of adolescence, identifying needed social and material resources for sustaining health and security, adding increased levels of responsibility, encouraging the value of motherhood, skills for self-advocating for needed resources, obtaining social support from experienced mothers, obtaining practice in negotiation during conflict, and avoiding dangerous situations that threaten the health and well-being of mother and infant (Miller et al., 2008).

Antidepressant Medications and Psychotherapy

No discussion of treatments for depressed adolescent girls would be complete without further mention of the TADS and the need for the assessment for antidepressant medication. As stated previously, TADS is a randomized controlled clinical trial to evaluate the effectiveness of CBT alone, antidepressant medication (fluoxetine) alone, and combination therapy (both CBT and medication). In a 36-week study, adolescents treated with both fluoxetine and CBT/medication combination had the greatest recovery rates. Combination treatment reached maximum benefit at Week 18 with a response rate of 85%, reaching peak effectiveness 3 months earlier than either therapy alone. When fluoxetine and CBT alone were compared, the medication produced symptom reduction more quickly than CBT, but adolescents who only received medication were twice as likely as clients with combination therapy or CBT alone to report suicidal ideation. This concerning finding led researchers to conclude that clinicians may want to begin treatment with CBT alone to avoid risk of antidepressant-induced suicidality, and only adding medication to the treatment regimen if the response to CBT is inadequate. By starting treatment with CBT, there is no increased risk for suicidality, and adding CBT to medication helps protect from suicidality because it helps the client learn skills for managing stressful events, family conflicts, and negative affect (TADS Team, 2009).

Using this information to assist in decision making regarding treatment, the counselor should consult with appropriate medical professionals and should consider the recommendations of the American Academy of Child and Adolescent Psychiatry Best Practice Guidelines for Child and Adolescent Depression (2007), which incorporates the TADS findings:

- For uncomplicated or brief depression with mild psychosocial impairment, counselors should provide psychoeducation about depression (causes, courses, treatments, and risks associated with each treatment), supportive management through the use of active listening skills and instillation of hope, teach general coping and problem-solving skills, collaborate with the family and school, and conduct ongoing monitoring of symptoms.
- After 4 to 6 weeks, if there is no improvement, then a trial with CBT or IPT is recommended for clients who are nonsuicidal and whose symptoms remain in the mild range.
- For clients who have more moderate to severe depression, it is recommended that treatment should begin with combination therapy to minimize the risk of medication-induced suicidality (TADS Team, 2009). As reported previously, antidepressant medication alone may increase a client's risk of suicidal ideation (TADS, March et al., 2006), while adding CBT can provide a protective effect. It should be noted that IPT was not included in the TADS.

It should also be noted that studies revealed that depressed adolescents who had greater than nine CBT sessions were 2.5 times more likely to have a positive treatment response than were those who had less than nine sessions (Kennard et al., 2009), and that clients who received 6 to 9 months of counseling had the greatest benefits from therapy (March & Vitello, 2009; TADS Team, 2009). This indicates the importance of longer term treatment, even if a client is also receiving antidepressant medication. Best practice guidelines indicate that the best indicator for relapse prevention is to continue treatment for 6 to

12 months, even offering monthly, quarterly or "booster" sessions after primary treatment has ended (AACAP, 2007).

PREVENTION OF ADOLESCENT DEPRESSION

Prevention interventions designed to prevent the onset of depression are particularly important in the early adolescent period. As reviewed previously, rates of depression triple for girls during early adolescence, so teaching preadolescents those coping skills that target risk factors for depression are particularly important during ages 10 to 14 (Gillham, Brunswasser, & Freres, 2008) because preventing the onset of depression during this period may prevent the development of depressive episodes throughout the life span. Young adolescents at risk (those who have already developed symptoms, those who have had a previous episode, or family history) benefit the most from these targeted prevention programs.

Several prevention programs have been developed for the prevention of depressive symptoms in adolescents, but there are common components that cut across programs. These general modules include:

COMPONENTS OF PREVENTION FOR ADOLESCENT DEPRESSION

(a) Emotional literacy and regulation (learning to recognize the link between thoughts and feelings, how to increase positive mood),
(b) Stress reduction skills (awareness of body signals, how to stay calm, learning ways to cope with challenges),
(c) Social skills (developing and *maintaining* relationships, conflict resolution skills),
(d) Problem solving skills (following the 5-step model reviewed previously),
(e) Cognitive skills (learning ways to think rationally and constructively),
(f) Building positive support systems,
(g) Participation in pleasant events,
(h) Awareness of mental health issues and how to access services (Essau & Chang, 2009).

PROGRAM HIGHLIGHT: PENN RESILIENCY PROGRAM

The Penn Resiliency Program (Gillham et al., 2008, Gillham & Chaplin, 2011) is one of the best researched prevention programs and has demonstrated effects in preventing the onset of depression, anxiety, and behavioral symptoms in children and adolescents ages 10 to 14. It is taught in a group format in weekly 1- to 2-hour sessions. It targets cognitive and behavioral risk factors for depression to promote overall resilience, and to prevent symptoms of depression from developing. It contains two major components. The first addresses cognitive skills. The students learn the ABC (adversity-beliefs-consequences) model to understand the links between activating events, and our automatic beliefs in reaction to them that lead to our subsequent emotional or behavioral distress. Students learn to recognize pessimistic or optimistic thinking styles, recognizing the need for flexible, accurate approaches to thinking. Next, they learn about cognitive restructuring. This is taught to children using the example of two detectives. The good detective makes a list of suspects and looks for clues before drawing any conclusions, while the bad detective just blames the first suspect that comes to mind. To illustrate this, the leaders give students an essay written by a character containing his problems and pessimistic beliefs. Students then examine his "file," which contains report cards, diary entries, notes from teachers, family, friends, to look for evidence that supports or refutes the character's beliefs. They are then encouraged to examine their own beliefs and to analyze the evidence that supports or refutes these beliefs.

Next, students learn problem-solving and coping skills for handling difficult life events and uncomfortable emotions. Some skills that are taught include: deep breathing, relaxation, distraction, seeking social support, assertiveness and negotiation, strategies for overcoming procrastination, and interpersonal problem solving (Gillham & Chaplin, 2011).

PROGRAM HIGHLIGHT: GIRLS IN TRANSITION (GT)

Based on the same principles as Penn Resiliency Program, GT is targeted specifically to risk factors for early adolescent girls who are navigating the transition to adolescence. It adds a specialized focus on emotion regulation, interpersonal relationships and conflicts, and contextual risk factors. It can be facilitated in small groups in 12 or more sessions, and can be led by school or mental health counselors. It is divided into four primary units:

(a) *Thinking skills*: Teaching girls skills to address common problem areas, such as unrealistic negative thoughts about appearance and changing relationships with peers.

(b) *Problem solving and coping*: This component includes problem-solving and assertiveness skills for interactions with peers and friends and for dealing with relational aggression, popularity, and cliques. The girls are encouraged to talk about gender roles around assertiveness and to explore ways to manage emotions such as sadness, anxiety, and anger, and how to break the cycle of rumination.

(c) *Challenging media messages*: First girls focus on identifying their personal strengths and goals, then they are taught to think more critically about media messages and their unrealistic standards for girls and women. Girls put these in perspective by thinking about the qualities that are important in their lives. They identify their own strengths and identify positive role models.

(d) *Reviewing the major concepts and skill review*: This component involves a review of the concepts and skills learned in the group and prepares girls for termination.

Interpersonal Therapy: Adolescent Skills Training

IPT has also been adapted to a prevention format, termed IPT-AST (IPT-adolescent skills training) that is targeted to adolescents who display initial depressive symptoms and who are at risk for developing depression. IPT-AST is titled, "Teen Talk" for adolescents and includes two individual pre-group sessions, followed by eight weekly group sessions. The purpose of the group is to focus on psychoeducation and skill building in the areas of role transitions, role disputes, and interpersonal deficits. Some of the psychoeducational topics include education about depression and understanding the relationship between feelings and interpersonal interactions. The skills taught and practiced include communication and interpersonal skills that can be practiced within the group. Initial evaluations of the prevention program's effectiveness indicate that IPT-AST group members had fewer symptoms and better functioning at 3- and 6-month follow up than did students who were assigned to a school counseling as usual group, indicating some initial evidence that the format is effective (Young, Mufson, &

Davies, 2006). However, a more recent study comparing IPT-AST with school counseling as usual in students with elevated depressive symptoms indicated that while the IPT-AST group had significantly fewer depression diagnoses in the first 6-month follow up, by 12 months there were no differences in the two groups. The authors suggest that post-group booster sessions might be necessary to sustain the prevention effects (Young, Mufson, & Gallop, 2010).

CONCLUSION

The purpose of this chapter was to provide an overview of the development and maintenance of depression in adolescent girls and also to present effective treatment and prevention approaches for this population. While research on the conceptualization and treatment for adult depression is well established, less is known about the complexities of depression during the adolescent period, particularly for girls. With today's girls experiencing the earlier onset of puberty, multiple life transitions and stressors in their schools and families, and strong cultural pressures about their appearance and actions, it is not surprising that more girls are becoming depressed during childhood and early adolescence. Because these trends are not likely to change in the near future, it is important for counselors to develop an understanding of the multiple influences that operate to trigger the onset of depression in many girls, including the specific processes related to girls' socialization (e.g., excessive empathy, rumination, indirect expression of anger) that increase girls' vulnerability. It is important that counselors are prepared to provide effective, evidence-based treatments for girls who are experiencing depression, including the CBT and IPT approaches reviewed in this chapter. Finally, it is essential that counselors engage in prevention programs that target the prevention of depression in adolescent girls.

As reviewed throughout this chapter, when depression develops in adolescence, it causes impairment in the development of healthy emotional, cognitive, and social skills, thus leading to significant interpersonal problems that will follow girls into adulthood. In contrast, prevention programs can help to prevent the onset of depression while also strengthening the development of prosocial skills. In addition, the prevention of depression in early adolescence provides protection against chronic depression. This is highly important to girls' and women's mental health, as not only can effective interventions prevent the onset of depression during the adolescent period, they also serve to prevent the recurrence of depressive episodes throughout a girl's lifetime.

RESOURCES

www.kpchr.org/acwd/acwd.html
Coping with depression/adolescents treatment manual for individuals and groups can be downloaded at this site.

helpguide.org/mental/depression_teen_teenagers.htm#. Tlum9Sh4xPM.email
HELPGUIDE.org gives tips and tools for teenagers that can help themselves and their friends cope with depression.

kidshealth.org/teen/your_mind/mental_health/depression.html#
Kidshealth.org gives an overview of what depression looks like in teenagers and information on how to get help.

www.about-teen-depression.com/teen-depression.html
This site addresses teenage depression symptoms, signs, screening tools, and risk factors.

www.teendepression.org/stats/teenage-depression-statistics/
Statistics about teenage depression are included on this site.

www.nimh.nih.gov/health/publications/women-and-depression-discovering-hope/how-does-depression-affect-adolescent-girls.shtml
The National Institute of Mental Health describes how depression affects adolescent girls as compared to adolescent boys.

4

Weighted Down: Disordered Eating in Adolescent Girls

There is a high prevalence of maladaptive eating practices in adolescent girls including binge eating, dieting, weight concerns, and diagnosable eating disorders. According to the 2009 Youth Risk Behavior Surveillance (YRBS) study of 9th to 12th graders (Eaton et al., 2010), weight loss behaviors are extremely common. In the survey, 59% of girls reported that they were trying to lose weight, 52% reported dieting, and 68% reported exercising to lose weight or to keep from gaining weight. More disturbing, 15% stated that they did not eat for 24 or more hours to lose weight or to keep from gaining weight, 6.3% took diet pills, powders, or liquids, and 5.4% reported vomiting or taking laxatives to lose weight. In addition, binge eating has emerged as an increasing problem in adolescent girls during recent years, with 20% to 60% in community samples reporting episodes of binge eating (Ackard, Neumark-Sztainer, Story, & Perry, 2003; Hudson, Hiripi, Pope, & Kesler, 2007; Shisslak et al., 2006; Sierra-Baigrie, Lemos-Gioraldez, & Fonesca-Pedero, 2009).

While eating-related problems were once considered a concern only in Caucasian, middle-class girls and women, recent studies indicate that body dissatisfaction and disordered eating are increasingly appearing among all Westernized racial and ethnic populations (Becker, Franko,

Speck, & Herzog, 2003; Cachelin & Striegel-Moore, 2006; Commission on Adolescent Eating Disorders, 2005; Grabe & Hyde, 2006; Rich & Thomas, 2008; Talleyrand, in press), although symptoms may manifest differently in different cultural groups (Alegria et al., 2007). For example, in the YRBS survey cited, Hispanic females (6.9%) were significantly more likely to have used laxatives or vomited than were White (5.2%) or Black (3.6%) females, and in other studies, African American and Latina women experience binge eating rates comparable to their Caucasian peers (Alegria et al., 2007; George & Franko, 2010; Striegel-Moore, Wilfley, Pike, Dohm, & Fairburn, 2000).

In addition to the high number of girls who engage in the weight loss behaviors described above, approximately 10% of adolescent girls have a diagnosable eating disorder, including anorexia nervosa (AN), bulimia nervosa (BN), or eating disorder not otherwise specified (EDNOS), which currently includes binge eating disorder (BED) (Hudson et al., 2007; Stice, Marti, Shaw, & Jaconis, 2009; Wade, Bergin, Tiggemann, Bulik, & Fairburn, 2006). These disorders are considered complex and challenging to treat, as they are associated with high levels of comorbidity, anxiety and mood disorders, functional impairment, substance abuse, suicidality, and morbidity (Swanson, Crow, le Grange, Swendsen, & Merikangas, 2011). Researchers also note that even girls who have subthreshold eating disorders (those who do not meet criteria for one of the *DSM-IV-TR* diagnoses) can experience the same levels of distress and impairment as those with AN or BN (Swanson et al., 2011).

Because disordered eating symptoms and eating disorders remain such a significant problem among adolescent girls, and because adolescence is a high risk period for the onset of these problems (around age 12; Swanson et al., 2011), the purpose of this chapter is to outline risk factors for disordered eating in the multiple systems operating in girls' lives, and to provide models for understanding the development and treatment of BN, EDNOS, BED, and AN. Prevention models are also provided.

RISK FACTORS FOR DISORDERED EATING ONSET

Genetic factors play a role in the development of eating disorders, in that there is a greater lifetime prevalence of disordered eating among relatives of clients with eating disorders when compared to controls, and twin studies also confirm these familial links (Commission on

Adolescent Eating Disorders, 2005). Hormonal changes during the onset of puberty may also play a role in the development of eating disorders, with early adolescence being a high-risk period for the onset of eating disorders (American Psychiatric Association [APA], 2006). Girls also struggle with the physical changes of puberty, including weight gain in the hip and thigh areas. However, these genetic and biological mechanisms that contribute to a girl's vulnerability to disordered eating do not fully account for the numbers of girls who develop eating disorders. In addition to genetics and biological changes during adolescence, researchers agree that environmental influences, primarily sociocultural influences from media, family, and peers, play an instrumental role in increasing a girl's risk for the disorder, as described in the following.

Sociocultural Theory

Sociocultural theories attempt to explain the impact of social and cultural influences on the development of eating-related problems in Western societies. Pervasive cultural pressures to achieve thinness result in girls' and women's normative discontent with their bodies (Rodin, Silberstein, & Streigel-Moore, 1984), as the majority of females cannot achieve this standard. It is evident that in recent years, the thin ideal has become progressively thinner while the average woman has become larger. The current beauty ideal encompasses often unattainable and frequently contradictory characteristics including extreme sexiness, thinness, white and flawless skin (or light colored skin for women of color), thin waist, long legs, tall, young, physically fit, muscular, and angular while also espousing a curvaceous and full-breasted body type (Levine & Smolak, 2002). The pervasiveness of these messages leads researchers to conclude that becoming dissatisfied with one's appearance is a natural outcome of extreme social pressures to achieve the thin and beautiful cultural ideal. This dissatisfaction is often a precursor to the over evaluation of weight and shape in determining one's worth, low self-esteem, and negative affect, and is the driving force behind dietary restriction, all of which place an individual at risk for the development of an eating disorder (Wilfley, Kass, & Kolko, 2011).

One of the leading sociocultural models, the *tripartite model* (Thompson, Heinberg, Altabe, & Tantleff-Dunn, 1999) identifies three sources of thin-ideal messages: media, family, and peers. These sources can directly contribute to the development of negative body image and disordered eating attitudes/behaviors. These sources also facilitate the development of thin ideal internalization and appearance comparison, which mediate the relationship between sociocultural variables and eating disturbance (Smolak & Chun-Kennedy, 2013). These mechanisms are discussed in the following sections.

Media Influences

One of strongest and most effective conveyors of the importance of thinness and appearance is the mass media (e.g., movies, the Internet, television, magazines, media-related merchandise such as toys and games). Adolescent girls are highly exposed to these messages, as they report watching 3.5 hours of television per day, and using the computer 1.5 hours per day (Media Literacy Clearinghouse, 2012). Meta-analyses indicates a consistent relationship among adolescent girls' body image dissatisfaction, eating behaviors, and their exposure to media images that promote the thin and beautiful ideal (Grabe et al., 2008; Groesz, Levine, & Murnen, 2002; Want, 2009). As discussed in Chapter 1, girls also receive messages that they should look "hot and sexy," appearaing curvaceous as well as thin (APA, 2007). Smolak and Chun-Kennedy (2013) note that girls who are repeatedly exposed to beauty ideal images will grow up believing the message that women should be thin and sexy and virtually all women could look this way if they try hard enough and buy the right merchandise. In turn, girls will believe they must strive to do whatever it takes to achieve this ideal. As also addressed in Chapter 1, girls also receive the message that they should achieve perfection in other life areas (e.g., relationships, career) while also attaining the beauty ideal. This pressure to achieve superwoman status also contributes to the development of negative body image and subsequent eating-related problems (Snapp, Choate, & Ryu, 2012).

Family Influences

The family has also been researched as a form of influence on body image development and subsequent disordered eating, with parental influences being the most studied. Parental influence can be classified in two ways: parental modeling of maladaptive attitudes and behaviors, and parental negative comments about their daughter's body and/or appearance. Specifically, a girl's sense of body dissatisfaction is strongly related to her mother's personal attitudes toward her own body (McKinley, 1999). Daughters observe the ways in which their mothers cope with cultural pressures and are highly influenced by maternal modeling. When girls observe their mothers engaging in chronic dieting and excessive exercise regimens and when mothers frequently center family discourse around the importance of thinness for success, girls are more likely to feel negatively about their own bodies (Haworth-Hoeppner, 2000).

Girls are also highly influenced by the comments they receive from their parents regarding their body shape, size, and appearance. A girl's *perception* of her family's approval of her overall appearance (versus their *actual* approval) is positively related to her body esteem. Girls who are pressured to diet and who receive negative parental comments about their weight exhibit higher levels of weight and shape concerns, higher levels of dieting, lower levels of social support, and lower levels of self-esteem than girls who do not receive such comments (Barr Taylor et al., 2006). In addition to specific comments, the emphasis that her parents place on beauty and thinness will affect the importance a girl gives to appearance in determining her overall self-concept (Smolak & Chun-Kennedy, 2013).

Peer Influences

A third source of influence comes from peers, including being part of a thinness subculture in which body dissatisfaction and maladaptive eating are modeled. When girls have friends who diet, have a strong drive for thinness, and are concerned about their appearance, they are also likely to have these same concerns (Paxton, Schutz, Wertheim, & Muir, 1999). This can also occur through participation in peer group activities that emphasize body shape, weight, and appearance, such as ballet, cheerleading, and gymnastics (Smolak & Chun-Kennedy, 2013). A girl's peer group also negatively influences her body satisfaction when her friends engage in frequent appearance-related conversations (e.g., discuss dieting and other weight-loss behavior, make fun of others regarding appearance). These types of discussions are termed "fat talk," a common form of communication among females that includes criticism of self and others based on weight and appearance (Salk & Engln-Maddox, 2011).

Finally, being the victim of peer teasing is also associated with negative body image and disordered eating (Wertheim, Paxton, & Blaney, 2009). Boys are more likely to make critical comments about a girl's weight and shape than are other girls. If girls place great importance on the opinions of others, particularly on the approval of males, it is not surprising that male peer teasing can result in body dissatisfaction and a focus on thinness as the key to social approval.

Social Comparison

In addition to these influences, which can create a direct pathway to disordered eating, these influences are often mediated or moderated by other factors, including the internalization of the thin ideal and body dissatisfaction. While most girls are exposed to cultural influences to some extent, girls also begin to compare themselves against the thin ideal and notice a discrepancy between their own body and the expected standard. They also begin to compare themselves with other girls to determine how they measure up in terms of culturally defined standards. This social comparison process generally results in body dissatisfaction. While some girls are able to accept this discrepancy and not allow it to overly influence their self-esteem, other girls believe they must achieve the ideal in order to be successful. In turn, they internalize cultural messages conveying that thinness and beauty are the primary determinants of girls' and women's self-worth. Girls who overvalue weight and shape as the basis for their sense of self tend to be heavily invested in their appearance and spend a great deal of time and effort in the pursuit of thinness (i.e., excessive dieting and exercising). They may believe that regardless of biological predisposition, with enough work and effort they can control their appearance (McKinley, 2002) and achieve the culturally defined weight and shape ideal. They might also begin to engage in self-objectification, constantly monitoring themselves as though they are being observed, making comparisons with other girls, and paying a great deal of attention to others' perceptions of and reactions to their appearance.

In sum, researchers have espoused theories to account for body image development in girls and women, taking into account the contributions of genetics, biological changes in puberty, and the strong sociocultural influences of media, family, peers, and how social comparison can mediate these three influences. In the following sections of the chapter, I focus on the importance of considering these factors in the assessment, conceptualization, treatment, and prevention of disordered eating in adolescent girls.

CASE EXAMPLE, PART ONE

Emilie is a 15-year-old Caucasian girl who lives with both of her parents. She is an exemplary student in her first year of high school, and she is a cheerleader and dancer at her school. Because of her strong grades and her involvement in cheer and dance, her parents are already discussing with her the possibility of a college scholarship. If she works hard enough, they claim, she can win either an academic or athletic scholarship, or possibly both. Emilie wants to go to college, but she isn't sure that she wants to keep up with the demands of cheerleading and dance. In addition, she is starting to feel pressure about her grades now that her classes are more challenging. She feels increasingly frustrated with her parents for placing so much pressure on her, and she is also resentful that she does not have any down time to just hang out with friends or choose something she would like to do.

This year she began to take dance lessons from a new instructor, who insists that she follow her prescribed exercise and diet routine. The diet involves restricting all dairy, carbohydrates, and fat, and eating only protein, fruit, and vegetables. The instructor tells her that this the only way she can have a dancer's body and that without this body type she should quit dance. Emilie is offended that her instructor thinks she doesn't "look the part" and she is also embarrassed that she may be perceived as overweight. She follows her advice and informs her parents that she must follow a new diet plan. They applaud her efforts, telling her that it will help her have the self-discipline and the body shape she needs to be successful.

After several weeks on the diet, Emilie continues to work out 2 hours per day, plus work on homework until midnight on most nights. She feels very hungry on her diet, and very stressed over her workload between school, cheerleading, and dance. Late one night after her parents had gone to bed she decides to eat one piece of cake left over from dinner. After eating the cake, she feels out of control, and starts to eat all of the foods she "can't" have—cereal and milk, ice cream, buttered bread, a box of cookies. After the binge is over, she is in disbelief about what she has done, and she wants to undo all of the damage she perceives that she has done to her weight and shape. She forces herself to vomit, and goes to bed feeling disgusted, leaving half of her homework undone. The next day she restarts her diet in earnest, only to binge again the following night. Soon she feels trapped in a cycle of dieting, bingeing, and purging.

TREATMENTS FOR EATING DISORDERS IN ADOLESCENT GIRLS

The first step in any treatment approach is a multisystemic assessment of the presenting problem. In this section, assessment guidelines are reviewed, including diagnostic criteria for AN, BN, EDNOS, and BED.

ASSESSMENT OF EATING DISORDERS

When a client initially presents for counseling, it is often difficult to determine the full extent of her problems related to disordered eating. She may initially present with adjustment problems or other concerns (Schwitzer, Rodriguez, Thomas, & Salimi, 2001), only admitting her problems with eating after she has established a trusting relationship with a counselor (APA, 2006; Huebner et al., 2006). To assess for the presence of an eating disorder, counselors can use the Eating Disorders Examination, a comprehensive structured clinical interview (Fairburn, Cooper, & Shafran, 2003). For a more time efficient self-report instrument, the Eating Disorders Inventory-3 (EDI-3; Garner, 2004) is also commonly used to make an accurate assessment of actual symptoms, to ascertain the appropriate level of treatment (i.e., either outpatient or a more intensive level of care), and to be able to tailor treatment to the specific core issues experienced by the client. Counselors should also assess for the presence of comorbidity, including mood or anxiety disorders, substance misuse, self-injury, clinical perfectionism, core low self-esteem, and personality traits or disorders, as all are problems that frequently co-occur in clients with eating disorders and can interfere with treatment outcome (APA, 2006; Fairburn, 2008). This assessment process should be conducted by a multidisciplinary treatment team, ideally consisting of a psychiatrist to monitor the need for medication if appropriate, a physician or nurse practitioner to evaluate ongoing medical issues, and a dietitian to collaborate with nutritional education and counseling (APA, 2006).

According to *DSM-IV-TR* criteria (APA, 2000), a client with a diagnosis of AN is dedicated to the achievement of thinness through extreme dietary restraint and other compensatory behaviors. To meet criteria for AN, the client's weight loss must have resulted in a body weight of less than 85% of what is expected for normal weight and height or a body mass index of less than 17.5. A client with AN is intensely fearful of gaining weight or becoming fat and has strong fears of losing control and becoming overweight. During this period of extreme weight loss, significant changes to her mood, behavior, and physical health can occur, including depression, social withdrawal, food pre-occupation, amenorrhea, decreased metabolism, and increased risk of medical emergencies. In addition, she will over-value the importance of weight and shape to her sense of self, experience disturbance in the way her body is perceived, and possess a general denial of the seriousness of problems associated with her low body weight (APA, 2000, 2006; Wilson, Grilo, & Vitousek, 2007). The *DSM-IV-TR* also includes two subtypes of AN. The restricting subtype is used to identify individuals who do not engage in regular binge eating or purging (i.e., self-induced vomiting, laxative misuse, or diuretic misuse), and the binge-eating/purging subtype is used to identify individuals who engage in regular binge eating, regular purging, or both.

As identified by Berg and Peterson (2013), the *DSM-5* includes three major changes to the diagnostic criteria for AN (APA, 2012).

- In contrast with the *DSM-IV-TR* (which gave 85% ideal body weight [IBW] as an example of what might be considered a minimally normal body weight), *DSM-5* will eliminate this from the weight criterion and will require counselors to use clinical judgment when determining whether an individual is underweight.
- The B criterion for AN have been modified to read, "intense fear of gaining weight or becoming fat, or persistent behavior that interferes with weight gain, even though at a significantly low weight." This criterion change means that if an individual denies fear of weight gain, but regularly engages in behavior to prevent or avoid weight gain, the individual would still meet this criterion.
- The D criteria is eliminated, which means that amenorrhea or the loss of menstrual cycles will no longer be required for a diagnosis of AN.

Clients experiencing BN possess many of the same symptoms as AN, as they tend to over-evaluate weight and shape and engage in dietary restraint in order to lose weight. A distinguishing feature of BN, however, is the recurrent episodes of binge eating, in which the client consumes large amounts of food and experiences a lack of control over eating during the binge episode. To compensate for the binge eating, clients engage in recurrent, inappropriate compensatory behaviors to prevent weight gain. These include self-induced vomiting, laxative abuse, diuretics, fasting, or excessive exercise. To meet criteria, episodes must occur at least 2 times per week for a period of at least 3 months (APA, 2000, 2006). Similar to AN, the *DSM-IV-TR* recognizes two subtypes of BN: the purging subtype identifies individuals who engage in regular purging compensatory behaviors (i.e., self-induced vomiting, abuse of laxatives, or diuretics), and the nonpurging subtype, which identifies individuals who regularly engage in nonpurging compensatory behaviors (i.e., excessive exercise or fasting), but not purging behaviors.

As summarized by Berg and Peterson (2013), *DSM-5* criteria for BN largely remain the same (APA, 2012), with the exception of two changes:

- The frequency criterion for binge eating and compensatory behaviors will decrease from twice per week for 3 months to once per week for 3 months
- BN will no longer include subtypes

Clients with significant impairment due to eating and weight concerns but who do not meet criteria for either AN or BN are likely experiencing EDNOS. The *DSM-IV-TR* describes client presentations that would meet criteria for EDNOS: (a) all criteria for AN are met, except amenorrhea, (b) all criteria for AN are met except that the individual is at a normal weight, (c) all criteria for BN are met except that the binge eating and compensatory behaviors occur less frequently than twice per week or for a shorter duration than 3 months, (d) regular purging without binge eating, (e) chewing and spitting food out without swallowing and no regular compensatory behaviors, (f) binge eating without the use of compensatory behaviors (i.e., BED; APA, 2000).

One of the problems with EDNOS is that it captures a wide range of problems, with rates as high as 60% among children and adolescents (Lock, LeGrange, Agras, Moye, Bryson, & Booil, 2010). These rates are significantly higher than both AN and BN combined (Loeb et al., 2011). However, assuming that these are subthreshold disorders with less need of clinical attention is problematic in that researchers have demonstrated that women with EDNOS often experience similar problems and levels of distress as those with AN or BN, so that differences between disorders may be a difference of degree rather than a difference in kind (Stice, Killen, Hayward, & Taylor, 1998; Walsh & Garner, 1997). Further, a recent large-scale study indicates that EDNOS mortality rates are similar to rates for AN, indicating the potential severity of this disorder (Crow et al., 2009). Further, it should be noted that the majority of clients with eating problems fluctuate frequently between eating disorder diagnoses, so that a client often migrates among AN, BN, and EDNOS (Fairburn, 2008).

The criteria for *DSM-5* attempts to reduce the prevalence of EDNOS (APA, 2012). One of the biggest changes to the eating disorders criteria is that BED is formally recognized by *DSM-5* as a full-syndrome eating disorder. BED is now characterized by both objective eating episodes (eating within a discrete period of time an amount of food that is definitely larger than most people would eat in a similar time period and under similar circumstances), and loss of control (feeling that one cannot stop eating or control what or how much one is eating). Binge eating episodes may also be associated with eating more rapidly than normal, eating until feeling uncomfortably full, eating in the absence of hunger, eating alone due to embarrassment over how much one is eating, or feeling disgust, depression, or guilt after overeating. While *binge* eating in BN is often followed by compensatory behaviors (such as purging through vomiting or laxatives), the binge eating that occurs with BED is not associated with purges to compensate for binge episodes. Because a large amount of calories are consumed during binge eating episodes, weight gain often ensues. As such, binge eating is linked with obesity and its associated medical complications. Binge eating is also related to body image dissatisfaction, low self-esteem, depression, suicide attempts, medical complications, and increased risk for current and future psychiatric problems (Ackard et al., 2003; Stice et al., 2009; Tanofsky-Kraff et al., 2007).

The preceding assessment section is based upon adult criteria for eating disorders as defined in the *DSM-5*. In addition, the counselor should develop a treatment plan that is based on an assessment of the adolescent client's clinical presentation and her developmental needs. As emphasized throughout this book, the counselor must consider her situation within the context of normal adolescent growth and development, which might look very different than that of an adult client living on her own. Her level of cognitive development should be strongly considered in the assessment, as her ability for abstraction, consequential thinking, and hypothetical reasoning is required for many of the recommended approaches to be effective (Weisz & Hawley, 2002). Treatment goals and time frames might need to be shortened and visual/written aids might be used in order to structure the session to match her developmental level. Her social development must also be considered (e.g., ability to maintain relationships, to accept responsibility, to engage in perspective taking), particularly within the context of her identity development. Effective treatment should incorporate the importance of relationships in her life at this time, her need for interpersonal skills (including assertiveness), and her fears of being judged by others (the *imagined audience*, Elkind, 1967; Weisz & Hawley, 2002).

In addition to her level of psychosocial development, because of her age, she is likely still living at home and is therefore embedded within her family system. Best practices indicate that the family should be involved with treatment (APA, 2006) and that counselors should provide families with psychoeducation about eating disorders and the model of treatment provided, and should address overall family dynamics and communication patterns (Campbell & Schmidt, 2011). In addition, skills training for parents may be needed to assist them in balancing necessary parental control, boundaries, and consistency with emerging adolescent autonomy (Campbell & Schmidt, 2011; Weisz & Hawley, 2002).

TREATMENTS FOR EATING DISORDERS IN ADOLESCENT GIRLS

There has been a great deal of research in the treatment of eating disorders in recent decades, but many practitioners report that best practice treatments are not well disseminated. The purpose of the following sections is to provide an overview of the leading treatments for BN, EDNOS, BED, and AN, and to describe ways they may be adapted to the specific needs of adolescent girls. First, I discuss cognitive behavioral therapy (CBT)-enhanced for the treatment of BN and EDNOS. Next, I provide an overview of CBT, dialectical behavior therapy (DBT), and interpersonal therapy (IPT) as adapted for the treatment of BED. Finally, I highlight the major tenets of family-based therapy (FBT), the treatment with the largest evidence support in the treatment of adolescent AN.

CBT ENHANCED FOR BN AND EDNOS

CBT is the leading evidence-based therapy for BN and EDNOS among adults and is also recommended for the treatment of adolescents (Commission on Adolescent Eating Disorders, 2005). Even though there are limited data to support its effectiveness specifically with adolescents, CBT is recommended because it has a strong evidence base for treating other adolescent disorders such as anxiety and mood disorders (Campbell & Schmidt, 2011). Best practice guidelines currently recommend that clients will respond well to a form of CBT that was originally developed for BN (APA, 2006; Fairburn, 2008; Fairburn, Marcus, & Wilson, 1993; Wilson et al., 2007). Over the past two decades, many research studies and meta-analyses have demonstrated the superiority of manualized CBT for BN when compared with medication and other psychotherapeutic approaches, including

IPT, behavioral therapy, supportive counseling, and nutritional counseling (APA, 2006; Shapiro, Woolson, Hamer, Kalarchian, Marcus, & Bulik, 2007; Wilson et al., 2007).

The standard CBT treatment was recently reformulated and enhanced by Fairburn (CBT-E; 2008) so that it now takes a transdiagnostic approach to the conceptualization and treatment of eating disorders. The enhanced treatment is designed to treat clients across the eating disorder spectrum, and assumes that all clients with eating disorders share underlying core beliefs regarding overvaluation and control of weight and shape. The treatment is targeted to disrupt the cognitive and behavioral patterns that have emerged from these core beliefs. Because of its transdiagnostic nature, CBT-E is appropriate for clients with all eating disorders (Wilfley et al., 2011), although the specific treatment adaptation for clients with AN will not be presented here (see Fairburn, 2008). While less research has been conducted to date regarding the CBT-E version presented here, recent trials indicate its effectiveness (Byrne, Fursland, Allen, & Watson, 2011; Fairburn et al., 2009).

CBT-E Model

The CBT-E model of disordered eating is central to conceptualizing the mechanisms maintaining the problem (Fairburn, 2008). According to CBT dietary restraint model, as a girl faces increasing cultural pressures that equate her worth with beauty and thinness, she may learn to determine her identity solely by her evaluation of her weight, shape, and control over her appearance. As stated previously, over time, she internalizes the thin, sexualized ideal as the most important aspect of her worth and value as a person and develops body dissatisfaction as a result.

In response to these maladaptive cognitions and attitudes she begins to engage in chronic dieting and weight loss regimens in attempts to control her weight and shape. Many begin to diet in an effort to achieve the thin and sexualized ideal (Stice, Presnell, & Spangler, 2002). Between 60% and 80% of middle school and high school girls report dieting (Lock & Le Grange, 2006), which is of concern in that dietary restriction is a strong predictor of binge eating onset in adolescent girls (Stice et al., 2002). Because of physiological drives when the body experiences deprivation, diets ultimately cause girls to fail in their attempts to reach an ideal weight or shape, which sets them up to lose control and engage in binge eating (Fairburn, 2008). In fact, girls who engage in the most extreme dieting behaviors such as fasting are at the highest risk for binge eating (Stice, Davis, Miller, & Marti, 2008). Dieting also puts a girl at risk for binge eating due to the abstinence-violation effect (i.e., the belief that once she has violated the rules of her diet plan, she might as well eat everything she desires). Further, dieting leads a girl away from relying on her physical hunger as a cue for eating. Instead, she begins to rely on cognitive control strategies to regulate when and what she eats ("I will only eat one meal per day, and it will only consist of salad"). As cognitive control is highly susceptible to changes in a girl's thoughts, emotions, and circumstances, binge eating can result when cognitive control strategies are disrupted (Fairburn, 2008).

It is clear that dieting will not be sustainable over a long period of time, and eventually a girl will experience a sense of deprivation and loss of control that will result in a binge eating episode. In individuals with BN, binge episodes are followed by attempts to purge the body of unwanted calories, usually through vomiting, laxative or diuretic abuse, or excessive exercise. The client subsequently experiences a sense of failure for losing control and will resolve to work even harder to maintain her diet/exercise routine in the future. These episodes are often triggered by life stressors or negative affect. Binges, excessive exercise, or the restriction of food intake can serve as a way to regulate emotions or modify these negative mood states (Fairburn, 2008; Stice, Bohon, Marti, & Fischer, 2008; Waller et al., 2007). The client perceives herself as trapped in a vicious cycle in which she continually fails in her efforts to reach her ideal weight and shape, so that her attempts for control that were originally intended to improve her self-esteem actually contribute to increased feelings of failure (Fairburn, 2008; Fairburn et al., 1993).

The treatment phases described below are drawn from Fairburn's (2008) CBT-E treatment manual, following the CBT-Ef (focused) version of the approach. It should be noted that the enhanced version now includes treatment modules to address four additional mechanisms that are known to maintain an eating disorder and that can impede the progress of cognitive and behavioral change. The additional mechanisms are included in the CBT-Eb (broad) version of the approach:

- *Mood intolerance*: Addresses the client's difficulties with intense mood changes and regulation, impulsivity, and distress tolerance
- *Interpersonal problems*: Addresses the client's problems in relationships
- *Clinical perfectionism*: Addresses the client's perfectionistic standards not only toward eating, weight, and shape but also as they extend to other life areas
- *Core low self-esteem*: Addresses the client's pervasive negative view of self and hopelessness that can interfere with self-efficacy for change

The reader is referred to Fairburn (2008) for more information about these modules.

Further, the core treatment principles presented in this chapter do not take into account unique client characteristics and preferences, so it is important for counselors to apply these principles with flexibility (Waller et al., 2007).

CBT-E Treatment Approach

The overall goal of CBT-E treatment is to normalize eating, to reduce the over-valuation of weight and shape concerns, and to enhance motivation for cognitive and behavioral change. CBT-E is focused on the present and emphasizes the reduction of maladaptive eating behaviors before targeting a change in cognitions (Fairburn et al., 1993; Pike, Loeb, & Vitousek, 1996). The four phases of treatment, generally comprising 20 sessions, are outlined next. A version of this approach adapted for college women with EDNOS was also described in Choate (2010).

Phase 1

Phase 1 is designed to address four primary therapeutic tasks by meeting twice weekly over a period of 4 weeks (Fairburn, 2008; Wilson, Fairburn, & Agras, 1997):

- Build a therapeutic relationship with the client to enhance motivation and commitment
- Provide psychoeducation
- Establish weighing procedures
- Introduce regular eating patterns

Relationship Building, Motivation, and Commitment

Clients experiencing eating disorders are rarely motivated for treatment and are often secretive about the extent of their symptoms. Clients with AN experience their symptoms as ego-syntonic, meaning that they value their symptoms and do not perceive any need for change. Adolescent girls with BN, however, often experience guilt and disgust at their secretive behaviors, and desire for the binges (and purges) to stop. In contrast, they do not generally want to give up control over dieting or engage in any changes that might lead to weight gain. When these clients do seek counseling, therefore, they fear that counselors will pressure them to gain weight (APA, 2006; Vitousek, Watson, & Wilson, 1998). The initial goal for counselors then will be to create a strong therapeutic alliance in which the client feels validated and safe in disclosing her problems related to eating and weight, and in which the client is fully aware of what information will and will not be reported to her parents. The counselor will also need to enhance motivation and increase client commitment to changing her maladaptive eating patterns and attitudes (Constantino, Arnow, Blasey, & Agras, 2005).

Knowing that the client is likely fearful of being forced to give up her behaviors and beliefs, the counselor can first validate the client's feelings of anxiety. Using reflective statements, the counselor can demonstrate an understanding of the function that her disordered eating symptoms likely serve in her life and the reasons that she would want to hold on to them as a coping mechanism for control and for dealing with negative emotions. At the same time that a counselor demonstrates acceptance of the client as she is and conveys a belief that the client is coping the best that she can, he or she also helps the client focus upon her need to change and provides information that will help the client make informed choices about moving toward recovery (APA, 2006; Waller et al., 2007). One way to begin this process is to emphasize both the pros and cons of change so that the client can begin to hear in her own words how change really is in her best interest (Miller & Rollnick, 2002). Wilson and Pike (2001) recommended using a cost–benefit analysis by comparing the costs and benefits of maintaining her symptoms with the costs and benefits of changing her attitudes and behaviors. First, she is asked to list positive consequences of *changing* her symptoms (e.g., "If I don't binge, I won't have to lie all of the time about the missing food from the pantry"; "I will probably get better grades in school if I don't think about food so much"), then the negative consequences of change (e.g., "I might gain weight if I don't diet"; "I will lose control and never stop eating"). Next, she can list the positive consequences of *continuing* with her symptoms (e.g., "I feel in control when I am thin"; "I like the feeling of escape I feel when I binge") and the negative consequences of continuing (e.g., "I am tired of always being on a strict diet;" "I think it's vain and boring to worry about my appearance all of the time"). She can also look at the answers to the following questions adapted from Garner, Vitousek, and Pike

(1997): "Besides thinness and appearance, what other values are important to me? How does thinness relate to achieving them? Will I really be able to fulfill my long-range goals if I continue with these attitudes and behaviors?" As she feels both accepted and challenged, the client begins to realize that there are multiple benefits to change and she will gradually become more invested in the counseling process.

Establish Weekly Weighing Procedures

Clients are encouraged to weigh themselves weekly so they can recognize that they are not gaining weight while they are stabilizing their eating patterns. It is also important for the client to weigh herself no more than once per week, as body weight fluctuates on a daily basis. Fairburn (2008) and Waller et al. (2007) emphasize the importance of weekly weighing conducted in-session by the counselor rather than by the client. Weekly weighing can also be conducted by a nutritionist, but results should be communicated to the counselor so that weight monitoring can be used as part of treatment. The client's goal should be to accept a medically acceptable weight range rather than to aim for a specific number on the scale (Wilson et al., 1997). For clients who may be underweight or excessively restricting food intake, a set lowest weight limit should be negotiated between the treatment team and client. The client will need to stay above this weight in order to remain in outpatient treatment (Pike et al., 1996). This needs to be agreed to in advance with both the adolescent and the family in order to keep underweight clients motivated to stay out of the hospital.

Provide Psychoeducation

To alleviate her fears and to instill confidence in the CBT approach, an overview of the treatment approach, structure, and goals should be provided to the client and her family in early sessions. As part of this education, the counselor should emphasize the importance of self-monitoring and other homework assignments that are crucial to the success of the CBT approach (Fairburn, 2008). At the outset of counseling, the client is asked to complete a daily self-monitoring record that is recorded in real-time. This log will include the time, place, food consumed, type (i.e., meal, snack, or binge), whether or not a binge or purge occurred, and the circumstances around the food consumption. As the client collects baseline data throughout the week and brings her record to sessions, the counselor and client can review this information to identify themes, patterns, and high risk situations for eating problems (e.g., attending social situations where food will be served). Self-monitoring records are continued on a weekly basis throughout treatment.

In addition, the counselor should provide education about the CBT model for eating disorders. As the client learns about the processes that drive and maintain her disordered eating, it is helpful for the counselor to create a personalized diagram as an aid to help her visualize these components. Fairburn (2008) encourages this exercise as it empowers a client to view her problem more objectively and to determine the functions that the disorder serves in her life (see also Fursland & Watson, 2013).

Further, as the client is ready, it is helpful for counselors to provide information about such topics as the physiological and psychological consequences of extreme dieting (e.g., food preoccupation, binge eating, unusual eating habits, social withdrawal, poor judgment, decreased concentration, or sleep disturbance). Clients also benefit from learning about the ineffectiveness of vomiting, laxative, and diuretic abuse in promoting weight loss. Information about the adverse effects of dieting (i.e., that sudden weight loss only leads to changes in metabolism designed to help the body return to its previous weight level) can be reviewed. To reinforce this information, the book *Overcoming Binge Eating* (Fairburn, 1995) is also recommended as reading for clients. Further, clients might also benefit from information on nutrition and nondieting approaches to eating (APA, 2006). Finally, is also helpful to examine the thin and sexualized ideal that is currently perpetuated for women in Western cultures. This information might also be conveyed by the nutritionist on the treatment team, if this resource is available.

Introduce Regular Eating Patterns

Introducing a pattern of regular eating is the most important CBT component, as it serves the following functions:

1. By eating on a regular schedule, she will have more available energy for other life tasks
2. Her urges to binge are highly reduced as she no longer experiences feelings of hunger or deprivation
3. She learns that she will not gain weight if she eats on a regular basis, but rather her weight will settle around a range that is physically best suited for her

To normalize eating, the clients is taught to plan and eat three meals per day plus two snacks, with no more than a 4-hour interval allowed between eating. If necessary, counselors can assist clients and their families in planning their eating routine, as many clients have dieted for so long they may have difficulty in contemplating how to eat meals and snacks that do not involve dieting or subsequent binging. Counselors can also help clients understand that the initial feelings of fullness, discomfort, or anxiety they may experience when eating on a regular basis are normal, will subside with time, and will not result in weight gain (Wilson et al., 1997). Clients and their families are encouraged to take an experimental approach to eating at this point and to focus on the eating routine per se instead of being concerned about the actual type of food consumed (Pike et al., 1996). The client's food intake should be recorded in her monitoring form (Fairburn, 2008; available at www.psych .ox.ac.uk/research/researchunits/credo/cbt-and-eating-disorders-fairburn-2008-pdf-files/A%20blank%20monitoring%20record.pdf).

During the next several sessions, the client can begin to develop a list of situations that put her at high risk for binging and then create a plan of action for coping with each situation. For example, a client can create a menu of pleasurable activities that are incompatible with binges or excessive exercise (e.g., going for a leisurely walk with her family). She can also devise delay strategies (e.g., leaving the house for an activity after eating so that she won't be around foods that might lead to a binge), limit availability of high risk foods (e.g., instructing family not to purchase typical binge foods for home), or discard leftover food after meals (Pike et al., 1996; Wilson et al., 1997).

CASE EXAMPLE, PART TWO: EMILIE'S TREATMENT

In the case of Emilie, when she begins work with her counselor, she feels like a failure as a person if she can't reach her goal weight and shape, and that if this doesn't happen, then she did not work hard enough. Her counselor spends time validating Emilie's desire not to give up her diet or to gain weight, but she also helps Emilie to evaluate whether or not she wants to be free of the binge—purge behaviors. Through psychoeducation, Emilie begins to learn that she cannot continue with her extreme dieting behaviors while trying to eliminate her binges; the more deprived she feels, the more likely she is to binge. Still, Emilie is resistant to trying anything different.

(continued)

CASE EXAMPLE, PART TWO: EMILIE'S TREATMENT
(continued)

Her counselor helps her evaluate the pros of change (no more stealing food from mom's pantry, no more excuses about where the food went, no more unfinished homework and sleep deprivation) versus the cons of change (I might gain weight, I won't have anything good to eat, I won't have binges as a stress relief). She then evaluates the pros of continuing the behavior (I can eat as much as I want at night and not gain weight; I can please my dance instructor), against the cons of continuing the behavior (I will remain tired, guilty, disgusted at myself, and I probably won't be able to dance or cheer my best). When she evaluates her binges and purges against her life goals, she realizes that she can't be a happy person attending college if this still haunts her life. Slowly she agrees to try the CBT model. She agrees to weighing herself once per week, and only at her counselor's office. She agrees to eat every 4 hours, even though it might just be a small snack like fruit or carrots. She does not agree yet to add dairy, carbohydrates, or fat back into her diet, but she will eat other foods on a regular basis. She also agrees to go to bed earlier at night, when her parents do, because the primary time that she binges is late at night.

Phase 2

Phase 2 begins after the first 4 weeks of counseling (or eight sessions). This is a transitional stage comprised of two sessions during which the counselor reviews client progress to date, identifies any obstacles, and identifies the treatment components that need to be addressed in phase 3. At this stage it is important for the counselor to assess for client improvement in functioning, as early response to CBT is a clinically significant predictor of positive treatment outcome (Wilson et al., 2007). If the client does not experience symptom reduction during phase 1 she will not likely benefit from the strategies used in phase 3 (Fairburn, 2008). If she is not making progress, the counselor may need to spend additional time on the components of phase 1, revisit the client's readiness for and commitment to change, or abandon the CBT approach in the hopes that a different theoretical model will be more effective.

Emilie has made slow progress during phase 1. She is eating more often and recognizing the connection between eating more and her desire to binge. Because of her progress, she feels motivated to continue. She still finds it hard to go to bed earlier when she has so much homework, so she and her counselor brainstorm options to find other ways to keep her from binging late at night. Once these ideas are put into place, she feels ready to move to phase 3.

Phase 3

Phase 3 is generally comprised of eight sessions and begins with a focus on the client's beliefs and behaviors that stem from her over evaluation of weight and shape. One helpful exercise is to help the client to construct a self-evaluation pie chart. The client is asked to think about all areas of her life upon which she judges herself (e.g., "Name some areas of your life that make you feel good if they are going well, and badly if they are not going well"). She can fill in the pie with appropriately proportioned slices (Fairburn, 2008; Waller et al., 2007). As she examines her pie chart, she can better see the need for reducing the proportion of the pie that is related to weight and shape and for increasing the proportions in other areas.

To reduce the importance of weight and shape in her self-evaluation, behavioral experiments (e.g., reducing frequent shape checking or comparing oneself to others) are also helpful for testing out the validity of her dysfunctional beliefs (Fairburn, 2008). Cognitive restructuring is also helpful in identifying and changing belief patterns in this area. To address broader societal messages, the client can examine negative cultural pressures for today's girls and analyze how these messages and images might be influencing her current thought patterns. The counselor can assist her in exploring examples of harmful messages such as: Girls should be perfect in all areas, achieve at high levels, do everything boys can do, but above all else, also look "hot" and sexy (Hinshaw, 2009). They should claim "girl power" but also allow others to treat them as sexual objects (APA, 2007). Girls also learn that they should be caretaking and conforming in order to preserve their relationships, but at the same time they should be competitive and demand what they want with an aggressive attitude (Garbarino, 2006). Further, they learn that to be acceptable they should appear effortlessly sexy, but not to be overtly sexual or to be seen as promiscuous (Hinshaw, 2009).

After examining these cultural messages, the counselor can help a client to separate these external expectations from her personal beliefs (Choate, 2011). The client can explore what it would be like to trust her own values regarding how she should look and act. She can begin to recognize that she does have a choice in how she allows sociocultural pressures to influence her sense of self-worth and her lifestyle. As she begins to develop an internally derived value system and an internal locus of control, she can begin to rely less on others' opinions regarding the importance of appearance (Choate, 2008).

To begin developing other life areas, the counselor can encourage the client to identify strengths in multiple dimensions, including spiritual, intellectual, social, and physical competence (Choate, 2010; Myers & Sweeney, 2005). As the client learns to view her identity as extending beyond her appearance, she can be encouraged to dedicate her time and energy to more meaningful activities, pursuits, and goals. When she begins to accept and value herself in ways not contingent upon externally derived standards for appearance, she will be less likely to revert to the chaotic eating and binging patterns that caused her distress at the outset of counseling.

Another important aspect to address in phase 3 is reducing dietary restraint. Whereas in phase 1 the goal was to normalize eating *times* and *patterns*, the goal in phase 3 is to eliminate dieting by addressing both the *type* and *amount* of food eaten. The client can begin to introduce typically avoided foods and to expand the range of foods that she eats (Fairburn et al., 1993). As part of this process, she can first identify any dietary rules she has created and explore the consequences of breaking one of these rules (e.g., "I will not eat lunch at school, but if I do eat, I usually end up binging after school"). The counselor and client can plan ways to intentionally break each rule and then determine alternative responses. Another step is to create a hierarchy of "forbidden" foods (i.e., foods avoided due to their perceived high calorie, carbohydrate, or fat content), and progressively incorporate them into meals, beginning with the least threatening and working up the hierarchy toward the consumption of anxiety-producing foods (Wilson et al., 1997). For example, if her list includes avocados as the *least* threatening food she avoids and ice cream as the *most* threatening, she can start experimenting with adding an avocado to one of her salads on a designated day. She can record her thoughts and feelings after consuming the food, and these patterns can be reviewed in session. She can conduct these types of experiments as she works her way up the hierarchy.

The client is also encouraged to examine the *amount* of food she eats throughout the day. Clients with BN often limit their food intake during the day, then overeat or binge in the evenings due to feelings of hunger and deprivation. While the client will have already been practicing the skill of eating on a regular routine, at this point the counselor or nutritionist can assist the family with planning and eating well-balanced meals and snacks that will provide adequate energy for her to function effectively. If she has problems with eating regularly, it may be helpful to provide information that will dispute some of the client's erroneous beliefs about eating. For example, the client may believe: "If I start eating pizza I will definitely get fat" or "If I don't diet, I will become out of control and will eat everything in sight." She might need reassurance that most individuals (unless they are severely underweight at the outset of treatment) do not gain weight as they normalize their eating, and that eating in moderation will actually lead to feelings of satisfaction and decreased urges to binge (Garner et al., 1997).

The final aspect of phase 3 is addressing the ways in which a client manages stressful events and negative moods, as these often serve as triggers for continued binges or difficulties in maintaining regular eating patterns. Many clients with disordered eating have poor coping skills for dealing with emotions related to their relationships or life circumstances. Instead of coping directly with the situation or feelings that emerge, they have learned to use eating-related behaviors (e.g., binges, food restriction) as a way to avoid or reduce negative emotional states (Waller et al., 2007). To deal with stressful situations, Fairburn (2008) recommends basic problem solving. Problem-solving steps are outlined as follows: (a) identify a situation in which the client exhibited maladaptive eating or dieting practices in response to a stressful situation, (b) identify other possibilities for coping with the stressor, (c) assist the client in evaluating the effectiveness of each proposed solution, (d) assist the client in choosing the most effective solution, (e) assist the client in clarifying the steps she needs to take in future situations, and (f) ask the client to monitor her implementation of the identified solution and to evaluate its effectiveness. These steps are helpful for planning ahead for potentially stressful events (e.g., social gatherings, parental conflict, academic exams) in the hopes of preventing future problems.

CASE EXAMPLE, PART THREE: EMILIE'S TREATMENT

In the case of Emilie, the counselor asked her to complete a self-evaluation pie chart in order to evaluate how much importance she places on weight and shape in her life. When she revealed 80% of her self-worth comes from her weight and shape, 10% comes from her accomplishments in dance and cheerleading, and 10% from her grades, her counselor helped her reevaluate where she would like to be in terms of these proportions. Emilie reported

(continued)

CASE EXAMPLE, PART THREE: EMILIE'S TREATMENT
(continued)

that she would like to reduce the weight/shape to 10% so that it is balanced with her other interests. In addition, she said she would like to increase her value on relationships with friends, family, and in spending time listening to music. These were then used to help set goals for Emilie in how she prioritizes her time. The counselor also used cognitive restructuring to help reduce the importance of weight and shape in her life, helping her examine where these messages came from; after much questioning and reflecting, she realized that she only feels valued for her accomplishments, not for who she is as a person. Through cognitive techniques, the counselor helped Emilie to challenge her irrational thinking ("I am only loveable if I perform and look perfect"), to surround herself with a support system that valued her apart from her appearance or accomplishments, and to learn to value all of the strengths she possesses in multiple life areas, including her character.

The last and most difficult stage of CBT-E for Emilie was to eliminate her food rules and especially her list of forbidden foods. For her to give up her lengthy list of forbidden foods was tantamount to admitting failure, that she was not strong enough to meet her weight and shape goals. Only after realizing that these were not meaningful goals and that this narrow focus was keeping her from having the life she wanted, she agreed to try to intentionally break her food rules by eating three planned meals plus two snacks, and by first allowing herself to add dairy foods back into her diet. At first this only meant having milk in her morning coffee, and later she was able to have a bowl of cereal with milk. Gradually she added all food groups back into her diet, and was very surprised that as she did so, her urges to binge were greatly reduced and after an initial gain of two pounds, she did not gain any more weight.

Discussion Questions

1. How does Emilie's dietary restriction actually lead to a cycle of binge eating?
2. How does the abstinence violation effect help explain the onset of her first episode of binge eating?
3. How do the pressures that Emilie experiences in multiple life systems contribute to her eating-related problems?
4. If you were Emilie's counselor, where would you want to start first in addressing her symptoms?

Phase 4

The fourth and final phase of CBT helps a client experiencing EDNOS to explore the idea of termination and of employing CBT behavioral and cognitive strategies on her own without the ongoing support of a counselor. This phase is generally comprised of three sessions, scheduled once every other week. To prepare for termination, a client needs to renew her commitment to refrain from dieting, her willingness to eat meals on a regular basis, and her acceptance that occasional setbacks are inevitable. She can be reassured that relapses are just slips that can be viewed as an opportunity for learning or growth. If she can spot slip ups early, she can identify triggers and work to put procedures in place to prevent further lapses. She will also benefit from identifying areas of continuing vulnerability (e.g., "What are high risk situations for me? How will I know if I am slipping back into my old habits? What will I do if I slip up?"). Further, the counselor and client can discuss some indicators that might necessitate a return to counseling if the maintenance plan is not effective (Fairburn, 2008; Garner et al., 1997).

CASE EXAMPLE, PART FOUR: EMILIE'S TREATMENT

Emilie was able to identify her high-risk situations (staying up late, depriving herself of a wide range of foods, allowing herself to experience too much stress over her competitions and tests) and develop a plan for each of these potential areas of vulnerability. She recognized that she might need to return to counseling if she found herself resorting back to dieting and thinking negatively about herself, or if she began to view herself only in terms of her appearance or accomplishments.

TREATMENTS FOR BINGE EATING

In the previous section, I presented a synopsis of CBT-E as the treatment with the strongest evidence base for treating clients who engage in dietary restraint, binge eating, and purging. I now turn to a description of models for the treatment of binge eating only; that is, binge eating in the absence of compensatory behaviors to rid the body of unwanted calories consumed during the binge. Before addressing specific treatments for binge eating, it should be noted that many adolescents who binge eat may gain weight over time, becoming overweight and at risk for obesity (APA, 2006). Instead of addressing the binge eating, parents and even physicians may recommend dietary restriction without assessment for binge eating episodes and without any consideration of the mechanisms that are driving the binge eating behavior. In many cases, the adolescent does not simply need a weight loss program but needs specific treatment targeted to binge eating (Commission on Adolescent Eating Disorders, 2005).

BED, as newly defined in the *DSM-5*, includes objectively large eating episodes, as well as the experience of loss of control during certain episodes of eating. It can also involve eating in the absence of hunger and the tendency to continue eating while ignoring feelings of fullness (APA, 2012). Due to child and adolescent variation in what is considered "normal" food intake, studies with this population have found that loss of control is a better determinant of aberrant eating than is an examination of what is eaten during a particular eating episode. Adolescents who have abnormal eating patterns also display behaviors such as eating in secret, eating in absence of hunger (instead they may rely on social cues, or use food as entertainment), and emotional eating (Commission on Adolescent Eating Disorders, 2005). Loss of control, eating in secret, eating in the absence of hunger, and emotional eating are all associated with adolescent binge eating, being overweight, and being at high risk for obesity. It is clear that an assessment of these characteristics should be considered and that these behaviors should be targeted in the treatments described below.

There are two primary models to explain the onset of binge eating in adolescent girls: the *dietary restraint model* and the *emotion dysregulation model*. The dietary restraint model was presented in the previous section on CBT-E. The *emotion dysregulation* model explains binge eating as related to an adolescent girl's inability to regulate her emotions. Research indicates strong links between negative mood states and binge eating (Polivy & Herman, 2002), as binge eating may serve as a learned coping response for reducing uncomfortable emotions. In a cultural climate in which girls experience multiple pressures for achievement and appearance, it makes sense that they might resort to binge eating as a way to cope with or escape from overwhelming feelings of powerlessness or being overwhelmed (Smolak & Murnen, 2004). While it has negative long-term consequences, the binge eating behavior is maintained over time due to its short-term effectiveness in temporarily numbing or decreasing the intensity of unwanted emotions (Safer, Telch, & Chen, 2009).

Whether or not a girl engages in binge eating to cope with her emotions or develops binge eating in response to dieting and over-valuation of weight and shape is influenced in part by ethnicity. One study that examined cultural differences in maladaptive eating found that Hispanic adolescent girls were the most likely to report any disordered eating behaviors (e.g., binging, vomiting, fasting, using diet pills) (Ackard et al., 2003). Further, compared to other adolescent girls, African American girls are the least likely to engage in weight control behaviors and appear more comfortable and satisfied with their body weight and shape (Chao et al., 2008). However, binge eating is the most common disordered eating pattern among African American women, although it manifests differently than for women from other cultural groups. For example, when African American and White women with binge eating are compared, Black women weigh more, report more binge eating episodes, and have more realistic perceptions about the importance of weight and shape in determining self-worth. For African American women, binge eating appears to be a strategy for coping with stressors rather than a response to perceived pressures for thinness (Striegel-Moore, Dohm, Pike, Wilfley, & Fairburn, 2002).

CASE EXAMPLE: CHERIE

Cherie is a 14-year-old African American girl who lives with her single mother and her brother. She is also close to her grandmother, who lives a few houses away from her. Now that she is in middle school, members of her extended family frequently ask her to babysit and her mother requires that she prepare dinner for the family each evening. She also has to take care of the majority of household duties because her mother works long hours.

She is overweight according to her doctor's medical chart, but this does not bother her because her mother tells her that she is a "big girl" and that it "runs in her family." Many of her cousins and extended family are also overweight and she sees it as normative. Her family likes to have large meals in which overeating is viewed positively.

Cherie prides herself in being a good student and in not causing trouble in school like her brother. Her mother often praises her for being such a good daughter. Lately, however, some girls at school have been bullying Cherie, calling her cruel names, and threatening her to fight them. Cherie

---

(continued)

CASE EXAMPLE: CHERIE (*continued*)

does not want to tell anyone about this because she thinks it will only make the matter worse. She thinks her mother and grandmother will blame her for causing problems. She is frightened to go to school, and every day she worries that these girls will catch her alone and harm her. She can feel the rage building up inside of her, but she does not know how to handle these feelings. Some days she yells at the girls, but then runs away so that she can't hear them respond. Lately at home she has started bringing food into her room so that she can watch television and eat in private. She notices that she goes into trance-like behavior while she eats, and often does not realize how much she has eaten until the episode is over. It is getting increasingly hard to cover up the amount of food she is eating in secret. She still eats large meals and multiple snacks with her family, but she looks forward to the times when she can escape and numb herself with food. As a result, she is spending increasing amounts of time alone, is lying frequently about the missing food, and is gaining weight rapidly. Her mother and grandmother have not noticed these changes in her behaviors.

Discussion Questions

1. What are the stressors in multiple systems that Cherie seems to be experiencing?
2. If Cherie is satisfied with her weight and is not dieting, how can she have an eating disorder? Explain.
3. Why might Cherie have turned to food to cope with the stressors in her life?
4. What skills or resources does Cherie need in order to begin recovery from her binge eating?

TREATMENT MODEL FOR BINGE EATING IN ADOLESCENT GIRLS

Based on research findings regarding binge eating in adolescent girls, it is important for counselors to introduce counseling strategies designed to address both subtypes of binge eating identified in the literature (Grilo et al., 2009; Stice et al., 2002); that is, binge eating maintained by dietary restraint, and binge eating maintained by its effectiveness as a coping strategy for managing negative affect. The model first presented in Choate (2011) includes:

- Feminist therapy approaches that emphasize client empowerment and recognize the importance of sociocultural context
- CBT to address the elimination of dieting, introduce regular eating patterns, eliminate behaviors related to eating patterns such as eating in secret, eating in the absence of hunger, decrease the overvaluation of weight and shape, and strengthen cognitive coping skills for challenging negative societal messages for girls and women
- DBT to teach mindfulness, emotion regulation, and distress tolerance skills that enhance a client's ability to identify, regulate, or express her emotional experiences
- IPT to address relational concerns, including family, friendships, and romantic relationships, and to assist girls in more effectively expressing emotions in their relationships

Empowerment Component: Feminist Therapy

Feminist therapy approaches to working with girls and women assert that counselors should recognize the impact of gender as well as the influences of other social variables (e.g., social class, race/ethnicity, health status, and sexual orientation) on girls' and women's development. Feminist therapies also assert the importance of understanding clients' unique experiences within the context of larger social forces that shape their private lives, recognizing that women's individual problems cannot be separated from their sociocultural context (Piran, Jasper, & Pinhas, 2004; Worell & Remer, 2002). These social forces include the effects of media's limited definitions of the ideal girl and woman in popular culture; the contradictory social messages that girls and women receive, and the emphasis on weight, shape, and appearance as the primary determinants of women's self-worth (APA, 2007). Because of these influences, the counselor conceptualizes a client's binge eating as an understandable method for coping with the contradictory cultural messages and life stressors that emerge during the early adolescent period.

Feminist therapy approaches also emphasize client empowerment, so that the client is viewed as her own expert who may be in need of support and information in order to find her own answers to life problems. To promote client empowerment, feminist therapists promote egalitarian relationships both within and outside of counseling. They emphasize ways to share power *with* the client rather than asserting power *over* the client (Cummings, 2000) by demystifying the counseling process, working collaboratively with the adolescent and her family in setting treatment goals, and working to decrease the power differential in the relationship whenever possible (Worell & Remer, 2002). It is helpful to remember that adolescent girls are struggling with issues of autonomy and control and in maintaining an authentic voice without resorting to self-silencing in order to protect their relationships (Gilligan, 1991). Therefore, providing a space for the client to have a voice, to make treatment choices, and to share power in treatment is an important first step toward creating a trusting alliance and in empowering her to reach her goals (Piran et al., 2004).

Counselors can also work to value girls' and women's strengths and perspectives that are often devalued by the larger culture. This is exemplified through relational cultural therapy, an outgrowth of early feminist therapies (Jordan, 2010). Compared with traditional theories of development that prioritize increasing individuation, the goal of relational cultural therapy is to promote connections with self and others and to build relational competence (Trepal, Boie, Kress, & Hammer, in press). Therefore, instead of dampening girls' need for connections with others, counselors can emphasize the importance of relationships as central to girls' development and reinforce qualities such as empathy, nurturance, cooperation, intuition, and interdependence (Piran et al., 2004; Worell & Remer, 2002). As girls learn to value these strengths, they can develop coping skills for challenging limiting gender role expectations and for freeing themselves from roles that do not fit with their own personal values (Choate, 2008). Because feminist principles are foundational to therapy with girls, these base tenets can be woven throughout the three approaches described in the paragraphs to follow.

Cognitive and Behavior Change Component: CBT

As with BN, CBT is the best researched and supported psychotherapy for the treatment of binge eating (APA, 2006). As reviewed in the previous sections of the chapter, CBT is recommended as the first step in treatment for adolescent girls who are engaged in a cycle of dieting and binge eating, and who over evaluate the importance of weight and shape in determining their identity and worth (Fairburn, 2008). The overall goal of CBT for binge eating is to support the client to eliminate dieting, normalize her eating patterns, and change her maladaptive thinking around the importance of weight and shape (Fairburn, 1995, 2008); the treatment strategies are primarily the same as those reviewed for BN. Fairburn's (1995) self-help manual for binge eating is often recommended as a first step in treatment. As stated previously, some girls do not struggle with these issues and would be able to begin treatment by focusing on the DBT and IPT strategies that follow this section.

Emotional Component: DBT

Emotion regulation is a key component that drives binge eating in many adolescent girls and should be considered as an important element of therapy (Safer et al., 2009). DBT, a form of behavioral therapy originally developed for work with clients with borderline personality disorder (Linehan, 1993a, b), specifically focuses on building skills for emotion regulation and has recent support for its application to the treatment of binge eating (Safer et al., 2009). It differs from CBT in that while CBT is most effective for changing maladaptive eating behaviors and thought patterns related to over evaluation of weight and its control, DBT is targeted to assisting clients with identifying, tolerating, and regulating their emotional reactions to daily life stressors.

DBT assumes that girls who binge eat may not have developed skills for coping effectively with daily stressors of adolescence, for regulating their often fluctuating emotions, or for tolerating uncomfortable, painful feelings (Crowther, Sanftner, Bonifazi, & Shepherd, 2001; Safer et al., 2009). Disordered eating symptoms such as binge eating become a girl's attempt to regulate intense emotions and to cope with stressors (Telch, Agras, & Linehan, 2000). Clients are taught skills to enhance their ability to monitor, evaluate, and modify their emotional reactions and to accept and tolerate feelings in stressful situations. It is assumed that with the use of more effective regulatory strategies, the need for binge eating will be eliminated. As also suggested by feminist therapy, the approach also assumes a collaborative therapist–client stance and a commitment to accepting the client where she is, while also strongly encouraging her to make changes to improve the quality of her life (Safer et al., 2009). Only a summary of core DBT skills is presented here; for the entire treatment manual, see Safer et al. (2009) and the original treatment manual and skills workbook by Linehan (1993a, b).

Core Mindfulness Skills

Mindfulness involves paying attention to one's emotions, thoughts, and physical experiences without necessarily trying to end them, numb them, or avoid them. It involves observing, describing, and experiencing emotions in the moment and learning to be in control of one's attention. As a client become more mindful of the present, she learns to understand how her emotions naturally ebb and flow; they are only temporary (McCabe, LaVia, & Marcus, 2004). Specific skills requiring mindfulness are listed here: *mindful eating* (i.e., giving full attention and awareness to the act of eating by savoring and fully tasting the food being eaten), *urge surfing* (i.e., observing urges to binge in a detached, objective way, without following through on the urges), and *alternate rebellion* (i.e., instead of using binges as a way to rebel against others, the client learns to rebel in a more creative manner that honors her rights and quality of life).

Emotion Regulation Skills

Emotion regulation strategies are used to reduce emotional vulnerability and change intense and painful emotions. As the client practices emotion regulation, she recognizes that she does have control over how she reacts to emotional experiences. She begins to learn the function her emotions serve and how she can better manage her reactions. Some specific skills for emotion regulation include *identifying the trigger of the emotion* (i.e., identifying the prompting event that contributed to the emotion, analyzing her interpretation of the event, her associated physical and body changes, her actual emotional expression, and any aftereffects of the emotion), *reducing vulnerability* (i.e., decreasing the likelihood of intense reactions by caring for herself physically, eating a nutritious and balanced diet, getting enough sleep and exercise), *increasing positive emotions* (i.e., increasing daily pleasant events that do not involve food), *building mastery* (i.e., completing daily activities that contribute to a sense of competence and mastery), and *acting opposite to current emotions* (i.e., learning to change her emotional reactions by acting in a manner opposite to the emotion she is currently experiencing, such as approaching a friend who gossiped about her rather than avoiding that friend).

Distress Tolerance Skills

Distress tolerance is the ability to effectively tolerate emotional pain in situations that cannot be changed, at least in the present moment (Linehan, 1993a). By accepting a situation that cannot be changed and not struggling against it, a client is able to cope with it more effectively (Safer et al., 2009; Wisniewski & Kelly, 2003). Distress tolerance skills are categorized as either skills for accepting reality or skills for crisis survival. Accepting reality skills assists clients in accepting life in the moment, just as it is, even when it is painful or uncomfortable. These skills include *observing one's breath* through deep breathing and *half-smiling* (triggering positive emotions associated with a smile). Skills for crisis survival involve engaging in activities that help her remain functional without resorting to behaviors that make things worse. These might include ways to comfort and provide self-nurturance, including relaxation, mental imagery, and other self-soothing techniques (e.g., listening to music, taking a bubble bath). It could also involve doing activities to improve the moment in a small way, whether it is through prayer, taking a break, or using positive thoughts.

While Safer and colleagues developed the DBT treatment protocol for groups, therapists can also adapt this model to work with clients on an individual basis when groups are not available (Safer, Lock, & Couturier, 2007; Safer et al., 2009). DBT skills are particularly helpful for empowering adolescent girls as they cope with the stressors of an eating disorder, developmental pressures in adolescence, and also with obstacles they increasingly face in family life (e.g., parental divorce; parental substance abuse or mental illness; physical, sexual, or emotional abuse).

CHERIE'S DBT TREATMENT

In the case of Cherie, her counselor believed that the DBT approach for assisting her in better regulating and tolerating her emotional reactions would help reduce her binge eating symptoms. Cherie first learned about mindful eating, recognizing that she needs to be present when selecting, eating, and digesting her food, and also learned about urge surfing, realizing that she does not have to follow every urge she experiences to binge. She learned to identify those triggers that lead to negative emotions (which then lead to binge eating); for her, they were shame from being targeted by a bully, rage at the girls, and frustration at feeling there are no options to make the situation better. She also learned to take better care of herself by exercising, sleeping enough, and increasing positive events in her life that do not involve food. Finally, she learned some self-soothing skills to help her tolerate her distress such as taking a break, journaling about what she would actually like to say to the girls, and listening to music on her iPod. By putting these skills into place, she was eventually able to replace binge eating with more helpful problem-solving and coping strategies.

Relational Component: IPT

IPT, a treatment originally developed for the treatment of depression (Klerman et al., 1984), focuses on assisting clients in making improvements in their interpersonal relationships, directly targeting social difficulties. Research indicates that IPT is effective in the treatment of binge eating and is the only treatment to show comparable outcomes to CBT (Wilfley, Kass, & Kolko, 2011). Because of the potential for peer teasing, stigmatization, and social rejection among adolescents who are overweight or obese, IPT also has demonstrated effectiveness for adolescents at high risk for adult obesity (Tanofsky-Kraff et al., 2007). Further, IPT is appealing for adolescents due to the fact that their social network is becoming increasingly important to them, and having a chance to improve their relationships may motivate them to participate (Wilfley et al., 2011).

IPT assumes that as an adolescent girl expresses her emotions more openly, takes steps to improve communication in her relationships, and strengthens her support system, her binge eating will decrease (Wilfley, MacKenzie, Welch, Ayers, & Weissman, 2000). It is recommended that IPT can be incorporated into therapy when a client has significant impairment in her relationships, when she lacks support, and when she possesses ineffective communication skills for expressing her feelings openly with others (Wilfley et al., 2000). As also reviewed in Chapter 3, IPT focuses treatment on one of four problem areas: grief, interpersonal role disputes, interpersonal transitions, and interpersonal deficits. Because of their specific relevance to adolescents and binge eating, only interpersonal role disputes and transitions are discussed here.

Interpersonal Role Disputes

Previous research indicates that interpersonal role disputes is the most common IPT problem area for clients with binge eating (Fairburn, 1997). Relationships become more conflicted in adolescence, as many girls highly value their relationships and are socialized to be passive in order to keep their relationships intact and conflict free. Many girls do not develop the skills necessary for resolving their conflicts in a direct, assertive manner, choosing to internalize their feelings. On the other hand, girls are increasingly socialized to resort to manipulative, relationally aggressive methods of communicating negative feelings such as anger (Crick & Grotpeter, 1995; Underwood, 2003) or to be physically aggressive or even violent with others in order to receive attention and to get their needs met (Garbarino, 2006). Whether they self-silence or act out in violent ways, both communication styles contribute to inauthentic relationships and are ineffective in resolving conflicts. Because of their frustration and lack of effectiveness in relationships, girls may turn to binge eating as a result.

In the IPT approach, the counselor first assists the client in assessing the history of her specific relationship conflict. The counselor can ask the client to describe her expectations for each of the important relationships in her life, how she communicates her needs, and the ways in which she has already tried to resolve the conflict she is currently experiencing (Fairburn, 1997; Weissman et al., 2000). Next the counselor can help her to determine the particular stage of her conflict: *negotiation* (ongoing attempts to improve the relationship), *impasse* (neither individual is attempting to change), or *dissolution* (the relationship is beyond repair). The client can then develop different coping strategies depending upon the stage of her dispute. As described, she can examine the unhealthy ways in which she responds to conflict: passive responses, relational aggression, or physical aggression. The client might also benefit from changing her expectations regarding her relationships if these have been unrealistic.

If the client is at the negotiation stage of a conflict, she can brainstorm ideas for actively promoting resolution of the problem. If the conflict is with her family, they can be invited for a session so that the client can have support in expressing her needs and in receiving feedback on her communication style. If a client is at the impasse stage in her relationship, she can generate alternatives for making a decision to either move her relationship back toward negotiation or to facilitate its movement toward dissolution. To move toward negotiation, she might have to invest more into the relationship, take more risks in sharing her feelings, and open up the conflict in order to resolve it. As stated previously, this may be difficult for many girls when they believe that asserting their opinions or feelings will result in the loss of her relationship. In contrast, some girls may resort to relational aggression or physical violence, but this also does not move her toward healing her relationship or toward ending it in a healthy manner.

Regardless of the stage of the dispute, an adolescent girl could benefit from discussing cultural pressures that provide girls with limited options for voicing their authentic selves in relationships (Pipher, 1994). In addition, the counselor may need to assist her in developing assertiveness skills, taking the time to practice the differences between being passive, assertive, and aggressive. Ultimately, the client can learn to express herself in an authentic way, understanding that she does have the right to directly assert herself, to ask for what she wants in relationships, and to say no to requests, as long as this does not harm the rights of others. Through this process, she can become empowered to take control in her life and manage conflicts directly rather than turning to food to numb her feelings or to avoid problems.

CASE EXAMPLE: CHERIE'S IPT TREATMENT

In the case of Cherie, the counselor helped her to recognize that she is in the dissolution stage with the girls in this scenario. This means that she will need assertiveness to confront them and let them know that she does not want them to be involved with her anymore. She will have to tell them what she wants ("I need for you to leave me alone and I am not going to fight you") and for what she does not want ("I don't want you to wait for me again after school"). She will also need to develop skills for sharing her feelings with others, whether it is with the school counselor, an outside counseling agency, or with her mother. This is particularly crucial as her initial attempts to communicate with the girls at school will not likely be successful, and Cherie needs encouragement to continue with her resolve to end the relationships.

Role Transitions

Role transitions are also common difficulties in individuals with binge eating (Fairburn, 1997; Wilfley et al., 2000). Role transitions include difficulties in letting go of a previous life role and in embracing a new one, such as those that girls experience in adolescence. Girls undergo many simultaneous transitions: starting new schools with increased academic and extracurricular pressures, dealing with pubertal changes, handling the onset of dating, managing changes in their parental relationships, and losing old friends/gaining new ones. In the IPT approach for resolving role transitions, a counselor will first assist the client in defining the old and new roles. Once the roles are identified, she can focus first on her old role, fully exploring her feelings about it, and mourning the loss of a role that might be comfortable and familiar. She can also explore how the loss of her old role affects her sense of identity and her relationships with others (Wilfley et al., 2000).

The counselor can then help her to examine her feelings about the new role. For example, if she is transitioning from middle school to high school with increased academic and athletic pressures, what in particular is causing her to experience anxiety or ambivalence about being in high school? What are her strengths that she already brings to being a student? What are the potential benefits that the new role may yield? How do the opportunities at the high school fit with her overall life goals? The next step will be for her to examine the actual demands of her new role. In this example, what will it require for her to be successful as a student and an athlete at the high school? How can she develop the necessary skills? Does she need to change her study habits or practice requirements? Finally, she can examine her support system, including her parents and friends, and develop new sources of social support. She might also discover ways in which she may need to ask for help as she transitions to her new role.

As the client identifies her role disputes or transitions, develops new skills for expressing her feelings to others, sorts through her ambivalence and fears around adolescent transitions, develops a stronger support system, and makes active steps toward improving her relationships, the IPT approach assumes that the need for binge eating will be reduced. As adolescent girls thrive in the context of supportive relationships with parents, peers, and adult role models (Jordan, 2010), the IPT approach can be important in empowering girls to strengthen their existing relationships and in developing relational competence (Choate, 2011). As with the case example in Chapter 3 (Kelsey), Cherie is undergoing multiple transitions at once: academic challenges in maintaining good grades, increased responsibilities at home now that she is older, physical changes of puberty, and moving from stable friendships to a climate of bullying and mistrusting other girls. She needs to identify her old roles, mourn their loss, and begin to identify the opportunities that her new roles will bring. Cherie has many strengths to bring to her new roles (e.g., responsibility at home, good student, desire to stay out of trouble), so with some additional support and communication skills it is likely that she can learn to cope with her negative feelings more directly rather than turning to food for comfort.

FAMILY-BASED TREATMENT FOR AN

As reviewed previously, AN is a life-threatening disorder with the highest mortality rate of any psychiatric illness; according to Katzman, (2005) approximately 10% to 20% of those who experience AN will die within 20 years of onset. Due to the severity and complexity of the disorder, AN has a profound impact on both clients and their families, with the entire family experiencing extreme distress as the disorder progresses (Read & Hurst, 2012). Best-practice guidelines for children and adolescents with AN recommend FBT as the most effective intervention for clients with AN, having garnered the most research support to date (APA, 2006; Bulik, Berkman, Brownley, Sedway, & Lohr, 2007; Treasure, Claudino, & Zucker, 2010). The Maudsley approach, first developed in the 1980s at the Maudsley Hospital in London, is now known as family-based treatment (FBT). FBT has been manualized by Lock, Le Grange, Agras, and Dare (2001) and has demonstrated success in several randomized controlled trials (Lock et al., 2010). The treatment has also shown success for adolescents with BN (Le Grange, Crosby, Rathouz, & Leventhal, 2007) and has been manualized for the treatment of BN (Le Grange & Lock, 2007). Because the theoretical underpinnings and treatment approach for BN are very similar to AN, only FBT for AN is presented here.

FBT is an intensive outpatient treatment that involves all family members. FBT is not concerned with the etiology of AN but rather focuses on empowering the family as the necessary and essential resource for restoring the weight and health of their daughter. FBT assumes that the AN has impeded the daughter's normal developmental progression, so even though she is chronologically an adolescent, she is now functioning like a younger child in terms of her food and eating (e.g., her impaired thinking abilities, her inability to make rational decisions, her fear of weight gain). At the heart of the treatment is the counselor's support of the parents in temporarily taking control of their adolescent daughter's eating in order to restore her weight and health. In many cases, the parents have become paralyzed from taking direct action to control their daughter's eating, fearing it will make the situation or their relationship worse. By prescribing an executive role for the parents, the food restriction and eating-related problems are directly addressed without criticism or blame (Loeb et al., 2012). Once the adolescent is back in better control of her thinking and overall functioning, the parents can return the control of eating back to their daughter and can go back to their original role of supporting her in achieving the normal developmental tasks of adolescence. To this end, FBT is based upon the following assumptions:

- For treatment to be effective, the family must learn to refrain from blaming the adolescent or themselves for the AN by externalizing the anorexia from the client.
- The parents should assume the executive position of taking charge of restoring their daughter's weight. Siblings are encouraged to serve as a support and encouragement for the adolescent client.

- Because the family functions as a system, the entire family needs to attend therapy sessions together.
- Family therapy should directly address the goal of weight gain and teaching parents how to assist their daughter in eating enough to gain weight.
- The parents will gradually return control over eating to the adolescent when she has gained sufficient weight and will begin to work through adolescent developmental issues and family relationships only after her weight restoration has been accomplished (Robin & Le Grange, 2010).

There are three phases of treatment that occur over 20 to 24 sessions over a 12-month period: phase 1: parents are temporary placed in control of their adolescent child's eating and weight restoration; phase 2: negotiation for family relationships in which eating and food decisions are returned to the adolescent; and phase 3: adolescent developmental issues are addressed and termination is conducted (Lock et al., 2001). These phases are discussed in greater detail below. For further reading on this approach, the reader is referred to the treatment manual of Lock et al. (2001) and to an article by Hurst, Read, and Wallis, 2012.

Phase 1: Re-Feeding the Client

The initial sessions are designed to accomplish the following tasks: engaging the family to increase motivation for treatment, providing referral for medical monitoring and assessment in cases when hospitalization might be necessary, emphasizing the seriousness of the disorder, providing a thorough rationale for the necessity of parents' taking control over their daughter's eating and weight loss behaviors, and insisting that weight restoration will remain the primary goal of counseling in phase 1. The counselor should spend time in sessions helping family members to reduce blame and criticism both of their daughter as well as of themselves. This is best accomplished by separating the client from the disorder by using the narrative therapy technique of externalizing the AN (White & Epston, 1990): "So AN wants Carrie to continue to lose weight and causes her to believe she is fat, but all of you, including Carrie, want her to be strong and healthy again." Session 2 involves an in-session family meal where the parents are encouraged to get their daughter to eat one more mouthful than the *AN wants her to* (Lock & Le Grange, 2006). As the counselor observes the family as they encourage their daughter to eat, the counselor can provide in vivo coaching so that the family can learn new strategies for maintaining their executive position over their daughter's eating. The counselor can also provide positive support for the family during this difficult and stressful phase of treatment, as the parents must stay committed to reorganizing their lives (taking time away from work or other activities) in order to exert total control over their daughter's food intake and in providing a high level of supervision to prevent behaviors such as secret purges or exercise (Hurst et al., 2012).

Phase 2: Negotiation for a New Pattern of Relationships

Phase 2 can begin when the client's weight is at a minimum of 87% of her ideal body weight and when parents report that there are no longer significant struggles with their daughter in getting her to eat regular and balanced meals. Now that the parents feel more confident in their ability to re-feed their daughter, it is time for them to gradually release their control over her eating and to allow her to make some decisions over how and when she eats. Lock and Le Grange (2006) recommend that the parents start this process by carefully negotiating a small trial period to see if the adolescent can cope with one change (e.g., our daughter can eat one lunch at school unsupervised). This process may be difficult for parents as they fear that she might relapse into behaviors that put her life at risk again. Gradually and through the support of the counselor, the parents can hand autonomy over eating-related decisions back to their daughter.

Phase 3: Adolescent Issues and Termination

In this phase, the counselor can begin to discuss adolescent developmental issues (e.g., client socializing, dating, academics, independence) and how the family will address each of these issues through using problem solving. The counselor can also encourage the family to plan for the return to a normal life (i.e., how things were before the anorexia) so their sole focus can shift away from their daughter's recovery back to other aspects of family life.

TREATMENT CONCLUSION AND RECOMMENDATIONS

In concluding this review of treatments for eating disorders, it should be noted that the included treatments are outpatient approaches that are targeted as a first level of care for the majority of clients entering treatment. However, depending on the severity of the disorder, a more intensive level of care may be warranted. Services can range from outpatient, weekly counseling (as described here) to partial hospitalization programs, residential settings, and intensive inpatient programs in which the client receives specialized medical treatment, nutritional counseling, and/or individual, group and family counseling (APA, 2006). An adolescent girl should begin treatment in the least restrictive setting and remain at this level unless she refuses to comply with treatment, continues to lose weight, or her health becomes medically compromised. If she does not comply with treatment, the team can first add an additional treatment modality (e.g., adding more frequent sessions, family counseling, nutritionist appointments, weight monitoring, and activity restrictions) before proceeding to the next level of care (Werth, Wright, Archambault, & Bardash, 2003). If she refuses this step and/ or her health continues to decline, a more intensive level of care will be needed.

According to best-practice guidelines, the highest level of care (inpatient hospitalization) is deemed to be required when there is rapid or persistent decline in oral intake, a decline in weight, the presence of additional stressors that interfere with the client's ability to eat, co-occurring psychiatric problems that require hospitalization, and a high degree of client denial and resistance to participate in her own care in less intensively supervised settings (APA, 2006). In making treatment decisions about level of care, the counselor should be consulting closely with a treatment team and should include the family as part of decision making and as part of treatment (APA, 2006).

PREVENTION STRATEGIES

Due to the young age of onset and due to the strong sociocultural nature of these largely preventable disorders, prevention programs are particularly important to consider for the population of adolescent girls (Stice et al., 2009).

As reviewed elsewhere in this book, there are three different types of prevention programs: universal, selective, and indicated. *Universal* prevention includes interventions offered to all individuals in a particular population (e.g., adolescent girls). Many universal programs promote healthy weight regulation, discourage dieting/calorie restriction, and address ways in which body image is influenced by developmental and sociocultural factors such as: (a) resisting unrealistic and unhealthy attitudes about the importance of weight and shape; (b) understanding biological processes related to weight gains in puberty; and (c) developing strategies that enable girls to analyze and then resist persistent media messages about the importance of attaining the Western thin ideal. Other universal programs focus on more general qualities that girls need to cope well with life demands and that reduce vulnerability to eating disorders. According to Levine and Piran (2004), these include life skills such as stress management, decision making, and communication skills, which can lead to greater self-esteem and empowerment.

Prevention components can also be drawn from studies of protective factors. In an empirical study by Snapp et al. (2012) that tested the body image resilience theoretical model of Choate (2008), several protective factors emerged that were associated with positive body image: family support, rejection of the superwoman ideal, active coping skills, and positive physical self-concept, which all contributed to overall wellness when they were associated with positive body image. The resilience model is helpful for counselors who can work to strengthen these body image protective factors in all adolescent girls. The protective factors are summarized in the following text box:

BODY IMAGE PROTECTIVE FACTORS

Family support: As reviewed previously, family criticism and messages about weight can serve as a risk factor for eating disorders, but family support and positive messages can help girls develop and maintain a positive body image. Specifically, when girls perceive lower levels of family pressure to achieve the cultural ideal, they are more likely to have a positive body image. As also mentioned in a previous section, parents need to be aware of the influence their own attitudes about the importance of thinness and dieting will play in their daughter's developing body image. In addition, if girls experience open communication, support, secure attachment, quality time with family members, and the ability to turn to family members as a source of advice or for problem solving, they are not as likely to experience the need to seek approval through meeting cultural standards in order to feel acceptance and worth.

Rejection of superwoman myth: Girls need assistance in evaluating and becoming comfortable with the multiple and often contradictory cultural expectations placed upon them as emerging women in today's society. They will benefit from increasing their awareness of pressures they receive from multiple sources (including media, family, and peers), and from receiving psychoeducation regarding the historical nature of the thin ideal and how it has changed over time, and how it is an unrealistic standard for the vast majority of girls and women. They can also learn media literacy skills for increasing their ability to recognize and challenge negative media messages for women.

Active coping skills: Girls can learn coping skills that help them to manage life demands more effectively. Instead of avoiding their problems by binging or food restriction, girls can learn to use active coping skills for dealing directly with their problems and concerns.

Positive physical self-concept: Girls can learn to develop a more positive physical self-concept (e.g., appreciation of fitness, health, agility, strength) through exercise and nutrition, and for appreciating the body for what it can do, not just for how it appears to others.

Holistic wellness and balance: Girls can learn the importance of developing a sense of mastery and competence in multiple life dimensions. It is particularly important for girls to develop a sense of self-worth that is not solely based upon appearance and to build resilience to pressures they may receive from family, friends, and the media.

In contrast with universal programs, *selective* prevention programs are offered only to individuals who are at risk for eating-related problems (e.g., body image or weight concerns), while *indicated* prevention programs are provided for girls already displaying initial symptoms of binge eating or other disordered eating problems. Currently, the Body Project, a selective prevention program, has the strongest evidence base to date (Stice, Rohde, Shaw, & Gau, 2011). The Body Project has been found to be successful in effectiveness trials where professionals outside of a clinical setting such as school counselors, nurses, or teachers are responsible for recruitment and delivery of the program. After receiving training, counselors or other professionals can also train others to recruit for and deliver the intervention (Shaw & Stice, 2013). The program has been manualized in book format, and a revision of the facilitator's guide for the Body Project is forthcoming (currently Stice & Presnell, 2007; see also www.ori.org/thebodyproject/).

Body Project Rationale and Program Outline

In the Body Project program (Shaw & Stice, 2013; Stice & Presnell, 2007), young women with body image concerns critique the cultural thin ideal in verbal, written, and behavioral exercises (Stice, Mazotti, Weibel, & Agras, 2000). According to the theory of cognitive dissonance, arguing against the cultural standard for women will cause dissonance that motivates participants to reduce pursuit of the thin ideal, which in turn will decrease body dissatisfaction, unhealthy weight control behaviors, negative affect, and eating disorder symptoms. The Body Project was developed as a four-session, 4-hour program and has been studied with girls and women aged 13 to 22. Girls and women are recruited by advertising a group in their schools or communities that is a four-session project designed for young women who have some concerns about their bodies. More recruitment information is available at the Body Project website.

Session 1

The leaders inform group members that the program is based on the idea that discussing the costs of the thin ideal in current society can improve body satisfaction. After eliciting their verbal consent for participation, members are asked to discuss the definition and origins of the thin ideal; how it is perpetuated; the impact of messages about the thin ideal from family, peers, dating partners, and the media; and how corporations profit from this unrealistic standard. For homework, leaders assign two tasks: (a) to write a letter to a hypothetical younger girl that discusses the costs of pursuing the thin ideal, and (b) to examine her reflection in a full- length mirror and to record positive aspects of herself.

Session 2

Leaders begin the session by asking members to share their reactions to writing the letter regarding the costs of pursuing the thin ideal. Second, members explore the self-affirmation mirror exercise and the feelings and thoughts she experienced during this activity. Third, the leaders conduct a counterattitudinal role play, in which each member attempts to dissuade the group leaders from pursuing the thin ideal. For homework, leaders again assign two tasks: members are to provide three examples from their lives concerning pressures to be thin and then to generate verbal challenges to these pressures. The second homework task is to create a top-10 list of things girls/women can do to resist the thin ideal.

Session 3

Members first discuss one of the pressures to be thin that they identified and explain how they might verbally challenge this pressure. After sharing individually, members next generate "quick comebacks" that challenge thin-ideal statements made by peers. Members then discuss the reasons they originally signed up for the class and openly share their body image concerns. Leaders subsequently ask them to undertake a body image behavioral experiment in the next week that will help to challenge their negative beliefs about their bodies (e.g., wearing shorts if they have avoided doing so because of body dissatisfaction; attending a pool party they might have otherwise avoided). Next, leaders ask the members to share items from their top-10 list of things girls/women can do to resist the thin ideal. For a second homework assignment, leaders ask the members to actually implement one of their body activism ideas from their top-10 list.

Session 4

In the final session, each member shares her experiences with and reaction to her body image experiment. The leaders encourage members to continue to challenge their body-related concerns in the future. Next, members report on their progress with the body activism exercise. The leaders also introduce more subtle ways in which they might be unknowingly perpetuating the thin ideal (e.g., joining in when friends complain about their bodies). Leaders provide participants with a list of these types of subtle statements and ask them to identify how each perpetuates the thin ideal. Leaders next review difficulties participants might encounter in resisting the thin ideal, as well as how each could be addressed. Finally, group members discuss how to talk about one's body in a positive, rather than a negative, way. For final homework assignments, leaders ask members to write a letter to a hypothetical younger girl about how to avoid developing body image concerns, and select a self-affirmation exercise to complete at home (e.g., when given a compliment, rather than objecting, "No, I'm so fat," they can practice saying "Thank you"). Leaders ask them to email the facilitator about their experiences with these exercises (Shaw & Stice, 2013).

CONCLUSION

This chapter addressed a problem that is increasingly common among adolescent girls: the development of negative body image and subsequent disordered eating practices such as dieting, over-exercising, binging, or purging. In today's cultural climate where girls receive messages that in order to be acceptable they should look hot, sexy, curvy, while also being very thin, it is not surprising that girls develop negative attitudes about their bodies and undertake extreme eating-related behaviors with the hope this will help them achieve the beauty ideal. Resulting body dissatisfaction and disordered eating puts these girls at high risk for a variety of mental health problems, including the development of life-threatening and chronic eating disorders.

Because of the increasing stressors that girls encounter as they undergo puberty and reach adolescence, girls are also turning to binge eating as a way to cope with negative and often overwhelming emotions that often occur during this developmental period. With so many adolescent girls engaging in binge eating behavior, it is troubling that binge eating can lead to a disorder that is contributes to both harmful psychological and medical consequences.

Fortunately, counselors can draw upon effective treatment models in order to best serve their adolescent clients. In this chapter, CBT-E was reviewed as the treatment with the most research support for BN and EDNOS. I also provided an overview of models for working with girls who binge eat, including CBT, DBT, and IPT. Finally, I described FBT as the model of service delivery that currently has the most success for the treatment of adolescent AN. Universal prevention components based on a body image resilience model and the research-based Body Project (Shaw & Stice, 2013) were also provided. While no treatment will be effective for every client, it is important for counselors to be familiar with these recommended first-line approaches for the treatment and prevention of disordered eating in adolescent girls.

RESOURCES

NationalEatingDisordersAssociation.org
The National Eating Disorders Association (NEDA) is a nonprofit organization dedicated to supporting individuals and families affected by eating disorders. The site provides a wealth of information regarding prevention and treatment, including downloadable handouts for students, parents, loved ones, and educators.

www.newmovesonline.com
Dedicated to the New Moves program, a school-based physical education program aimed at improving body image and self-image in adolescent girls. New Moves strives to provide an environment in which girls feel comfortable being physically active, regardless of their size, shape, or skill level.

Maudsleyparents.org
Maudsley Parents is an independent, volunteer organization of parents who have helped their children recover from anorexia and bulimia through the use of a family-based treatment known as the Maudsley approach (as reviewed in this chapter).

Media-awareness.ca
Media Awareness Network features information and images about digital alterations of photographs used in print media.

www.mediaed.org
Media Education Foundation site features information and educational materials for educating adolescents to become more critical viewers of the media

www.CampaignForRealBeauty.com
Dove campaign for real beauty features educational videos and information to help promote body acceptance and self-esteem.

Adiosbarbie.com
This website contains articles to spark discussion and awareness about issues that girls face including sexism and body image issues.

Girlshealth.gov
This is an interactive site for girls with information on body image, fitness, nutrition, safety, and relationships.

Girlscouts.org
A Girl Scouts/Dove Self-Esteem Fund joint program entitled Uniquely Me.

5

Fitting in and Numbing out: Substance Use Disorders in Adolescent Girls

Substance use disorders (SUDs) among adolescents is a prevalent, significant public health concern and is particularly harmful for adolescent girls. While it was once the case that boys significantly outpaced girls in terms of their substance usage, this gap has considerably narrowed and in some cases has disappeared (Greenfield, Back, Lawson, & Brady, 2010). In fact, girls' use of alcohol and other drugs remains surprisingly high and compares directly to boys rates of usage, with 23% of 9th to 12th grade girls reporting binge drinking and 19% taking prescription drugs without having a doctor's prescription (Youth Risk Behavior Survey [YRBS], 2009). Seventeen percent of girls report smoking marijuana in the past 30 days, with marijuana remaining the most highly abused drug by adolescents in the United States (Johnston, O'Malley, Bachman, & Schulenberg, Monitoring the Future Survey, 2012). In addition girls are *more* likely than boys to have sniffed glue, breathed contents of an aerosol spray can, or inhaled paints to get high (13%). They are also more likely to say they are currently misusing controlled prescription drugs than are boys (National Institute on Drug Abuse, 2010). When examining age groups more specifically, 8th grade girls show higher prevalence rates of alcohol use than do boys, and 10th grade girls and boys show equivalent rates of use (YRBS, 2009).

While this is a problem that cuts across all ethnicities and social classes, it is important to note that there are gendered, ethnic/racial group differences among adolescent substance users. For example, Caucasian high school girls are more likely to drink and experiment with drugs than are African American girls. For example, current alcohol use is reported by a significantly higher percentage of White females (46%) and Hispanic females (44%) than by Black female (36%) students; binge drinking is also highest among White female students (26%), followed by Hispanic females (23%) and Black females (12%). White female high school students also demonstrate significantly higher rates of cigarette use and misuse of prescription drugs (23.3%) than do Hispanic (16.6%) or Black girls (10.3%) (YRBS, 2009). Therefore, it is important to consider the potential of both gender and ethnic/racial group membership as a contributor to risk and protective factors in understanding adolescent girls' substance use and problems.

Although around 75% of all adolescents experiment with addictive substances during their teenage years, a substantial number of these students progress to addiction (substance abuse or dependence) (CASAA, 2011), and girls now develop problems related to their substance usage at similar rates as boys (8.1% of girls vs. 8.0% of boys ages 12–17). Given that boys have historically outpaced girls in terms of SUDs, researchers have termed this new trend the *convergence effect*, which indicates how the gender gap in rates of substance use and abuse has significantly narrowed for individuals born after the 1960s (Stewart, Gavric, & Collins, 2009).

Because substance use and abuse can be so problematic for girls, the purpose of this chapter is to first provide an overview of developmental risk factors for adolescent girls' substance use problems, including environmental factors, family history, and individual factors such as brain development, early age of onset, and social/emotional development. Following a review of risks, the rest of the chapter details current treatments for adolescent substance abuse, including general factors for effective treatment, family approaches (Brief Strategic Family Therapy, Functional Family Therapy [FFT], Multisystemic Therapy, and Multidimensional Family Therapy [MDFT]), and Cognitive Behavioral/Motivational Enhancement Therapy). The chapter concludes with a review of protective factors and effective prevention programs that have demonstrated success in preventing the onset of substance use or of substance-related problems.

DEVELOPMENTAL RISK FACTORS

As reviewed throughout this book, the adolescent period is a time of major physical, cognitive, emotional, social, and behavioral change that offers girls both great opportunity as well as increased risk for dysfunction (Weisz & Hawley, 2002). These developmental shifts are particularly important to consider in our understanding of adolescent substance use, as the major transitions that occur in adolescence strongly influence the onset and progression of substance use (Weisz & Hawley, 2002). Because the goal of adolescence is to develop a sense of identity and personal goals, develop relationship with peers and romantic partners, and achieve a greater sense of independence from parents, many adolescents experiment with and use substances in an effort to try new activities and roles, engage in risk-taking behavior in order to fit in with peers, and challenge parental and legal authority figures (Botvin & Griffith, 2002; Upadhyaya & Gray, 2009).

In some sense the use of substances might be considered normal and expected behavior as it fits with the adolescent's need for experimentation, risk taking, and identity development. In fact, girls with higher social self-esteem are more likely to initiate substance use during adolescence than are girls with lower scores in this area (Fisher, Miles, Austin, Camargo, & Colditz, 2007); yet these might not necessarily be the same girls who develop significant problems related to their use. In contrast, girls with lower global self-esteem are more likely to be heavy drinkers later in adolescence (National Center on Addiction and Substance Abuse, 2011), demonstrating the importance of understanding a girl's motivations for experimentation versus her engagement in a pattern of heavier use that might lead to future abuse or dependence. In the following section, environmental, family, and individual differences (brain development, comorbidity, early onset of use, and socioemotional development) are described.

Environmental Factors

Certain environmental factors contribute to the risk for developing adolescent substance use problems. Examining factors from a macrosystems level, cultural attitudes about adolescent substance usage (e.g., attitudes about underage drinking), media promotion of substance use (e.g., popular movies in which female stars are featured drinking heavily with few negative consequences; Internet videos of female teen stars smoking marijuana or being intoxicated), and law enforcement practices regarding adolescent substance usage all contribute to societal level influences on adolescent use. At the neighborhood level, extreme economic deprivation, neighborhood norms regarding use, low neighborhood attachment and disorganization, and ease of obtaining substances all contribute to whether or not an adolescent is likely to use alcohol and other drugs. At the school level, risk factors include a lack of school attachment and commitment to school, and being offered substances at school. For example, a recent survey of 9th to 12th graders indicated 19% of girls and 26% of boys say that they have been offered, sold, or given drugs on school property (YRBS, 2009). Other risk factors include school mobility, school dropout, and lack of family involvement in the school (Arteaga, Chen, & Reynolds, 2010).

Peers also have a strong influence on whether or not an adolescent uses substances and whether or not he or she will become involved in a pattern of heavy use. While peer factors are risks for both boys and girls, some research has examined peer influences specifically for girls. When an adolescent girl has a best friend or a peer group who uses, she is more likely to try substances, and if she affiliates with peers who engage in deviant behaviors (including delinquency and high risk substance use) by the time she is 16, she is more likely to have a substance use problem by age 26 than girls who do not have this type of peer affiliation. A girl is also more likely to develop problems if her siblings also use and when her parents are not closely involved in her life (AACAP, 2005; Commission on Adolescent Substance and Alcohol Abuse, 2005; Schinke, Fang, & Cole, 2008).

Family History

Adolescents are particularly at risk for substance use problems when they have a family history of substance abuse or dependence. This is due in part to the genetic component of substance problems. For example, children of alcoholics are at increased risk for developing alcoholism themselves, even when they are adopted at birth and raised in a home by nonalcoholic parents. Some studies indicate that up to 66% of adolescents who seek treatment have at least one parent with a SUD (CASAA, 2005). Being raised in a home in which parents engage in heavy substance use also contributes to increased risk by fostering an environment in which there is poor parent–child communication, minimization of the dangers of drug use, and poor parental supervision and limit setting (AACAP, 2005).

Beyond family history of SUDs, risk factors associated with the adolescent's family also include child abuse or neglect, parent–adolescent conflicts, inadequate parental monitoring of children's whereabouts, insufficient rules about nonuse of substances, and inconsistent discipline practices (Schinke et al., 2008). While these are risk factors for all adolescents, poor attachment to parents is more related to girls' substance use than it is with boys, (Schinke, Di Noia, Schwinn, & Cole, 2006). This underscores the importance of family involvement in adolescent girls' lives, and parental monitoring and limit setting will be highlighted as important treatment components in the section on treatment found later in this chapter.

Individual Influences

Brain Development

The brain is changing and developing throughout adolescence, propelling the adolescent to engage in both reward-seeking and risk-taking behaviors. Further, as highlighted in Chapter 2, the executive function of the brain is still developing throughout adolescence and into early adulthood. As this function involves inhibitory control, goal-directedness, metacognition, decision making, abstract and logical reasoning, and reward appraisal, it is clear that many adolescents will not have the cognitive capacity to make responsible decisions about their substance use (Brown, McGue, Maggs, Schulenberg, Hingson, Swartzwelder, & Murphy, 2008). Those adolescents at most risk for problems are those with high levels of thrill seeking and risk taking, low levels of harm avoidance, impulse control problems, and decreased perception of reward from familiar stimuli over time (Upadhyaya & Gray, 2009).

Further, when an adolescent begins to regularly engage in heavy substance use, her problem-solving ability becomes impaired. In studies examining cannabis use in adolescents, due to its long half-life, individuals who use the drug over an extended period of time will have impaired cognitive functioning (e.g., attention, memory, processing of complex information) not only while intoxicated, but also for months and even years after the cessation of use (CASAA, 2005).

In addition to brain development, substance use and abuse also negatively impact girls more so than boys in terms of psychological and overall physical impact, and once girls begin using substances they are more likely to become dependent more quickly than are boys (Liddle, Rowe, Dakof, Henderson, & Greenbaum, 2009).

This phenomenon is termed the *telescoping effect*—once females begin using substances, they develop problems and progress to dependence more rapidly than males (Stewart et al., 2009; Tuchman, 2010; Zilberman, 2009). In addition, as mentioned previously, compared to boys, girls are more vulnerable to the negative effects of substance use and abuse and are particularly susceptible to health-related problems associated with abuse (Zilberman, 2009). Further, girls who abuse multiple substances have increased adverse psychological and social consequences than do girls who only use one substance, and these effects are more negative for girls than they are for boys (Spoth, Randall, Trudeau, Shin, & Redmond, 2008). Girls who use substances in adolescence can experience both short- and longer term effects on their health, development, and well-being as they age; for example, girls who drink even moderate amounts of alcohol can experience disrupted growth and puberty (Liddle et al., 2009; Center on Alcohol Marketing and Youth, 2013).

Comorbidity

One of the reasons that girls experience more negative health and psychological-related consequences is the fact that they are also more likely to experience additional mental health problems. Up to 75% of females in treatment for substance-related problems also have additional psychological problems (Sussman, Skara, & Ames, 2008) and comorbidity is more prevalent in females than in males (Zilberman, 2009).

Comorbid disorders commonly include disruptive behavior disorders such as conduct disorder and ADHD, both of which have been found to precede the onset of the SUD (CASAA, 2005). Further, conduct disorder and behavior problems are a leading risk factor for substance use (Schwinn, Schinke, & Trent, 2010). Mood disorders are also common in adolescents with SUDs, with prevalence rates of 24% to 50% (Greenfield et al., 2010). While not as well studied in adolescents, an adult with alcohol dependence is four times more likely to develop major depressive disorder (MDD) than someone who does not (CASAA, 2005). In another national report, 29.7% of those women with SUDs were also diagnosed with mood disorders (Greenfield et al., 2010). Anxiety disorders such as posttraumatic stress disorder (PTSD), sexual and physical violence, and social phobia are also commonly associated with SUDs; among those women seeking treatment for substance abuse, rates of physical or sexual abuse range from 55% to 99%, with many of these also manifesting the symptoms of PTSD (Greenfield et al., 2010). While many of these percentages refer to both girls and women, social anxiety disorder in particular is related to a 4.5 to 6.5 times increased risk for a girl's development of alcohol and cannabis dependence.

Many girls with SUDs also experience eating disorders, with comorbidity rates between 17% and 46%, and girls with either eating disorders (ED) or SUD are over four times more likely to develop the other disorder than are females in the general population (Harrop & Marlatt, 2010). Another study specifically with Spanish adolescent girls seeking treatment for bulimia nervosa (BN) (average age 15), 25% of the sample also engaged in a high level of regular or risky use of substances (Castro et al., 2010). These two disorders are a particularly dangerous combination, as alone they are challenging, but when a girl experiences both she is likely to have worse outcomes for both disorders (Harrop & Marlatt, 2010).

Another gender difference in comorbidity is that while it is some-times difficult to determine the direction of the influence of multiple disorders on one another, females are more likely than males to expe-rience psychiatric problems prior to the onset of substance use prob-lems, leading researchers to speculate that women are more likely to use substances as a means of self-medication or to cope with stressful events (Briggs & Peperrell, 2009). For example, girls with untreated depression, anxiety, or a history of abuse are more likely to become addicted to substances than are girls who do not have these problems (Zilberman, 2009).

Early Age of Onset

Longitudinal studies indicate that when an adolescent begins sub-stance use at an early age, he or she is at very high risk of developing later serious and chronic SUDs. For example, 90% of adults who have addictive disorders report that they started drinking or using drugs before the age of 18, and 44% of those who started drinking before age 15 developed a later alcohol dependence problem (versus only 10% of those who started drinking after age 21) (CASAA, 2011). Further, early use is a strong predictor of other negative developmental outcomes. Those adolescents who start using substances and who have conduct problems before the age of 15 are far more likely to be chronic offend-ers; experience depression, school failure, and unemployment; develop relational problems with peers and family members; engage in risky sexual behaviors that can lead to unplanned pregnancies, STDs, and HIV; and experience low self-esteem throughout adolescence and adulthood (Liddle et al., 2009).

While early age of onset is a risk factor for both boys and girls, once a girl starts using substances she is at risk of progressing to addiction in a shorter period of time than it takes for boys (Zilberman, 2009). It is also important to note a trend in gendered ethnicity differences in early age of substance onset for girls. While White girls in high school have the highest rates of current substance use (followed by Hispanic girls), Black and Hispanic female students are significantly more likely to initiate the use of substances at an early age. For example, the highest percentages of alcohol use before age 13 occurred among Black females (21.9%) and Hispanic females (23.2%) versus White female students (15.55%) (YRBS, 2009). This indicates that when understanding the statistics regarding problems associated with early onset, it is important to examine differences by both gender and ethnic/racial group membership.

The physical changes that occur in adolescence also play a role in whether or not an adolescent girl will experiment with substances at an earlier age. Body changes that occur during puberty influence girls' social roles and expectations regarding their newly mature bodies, and when the timing of this change occurs early, girls may be forced into negotiating a new, sexualized identity before they are psychologically prepared (Tanner-Smith, 2010). As discussed in Chapter 2, girls who experience early puberty are at risk for early onset substance use, particularly because they are more likely to become involved with older peers and romantic partners who will expose them to alcohol and other drugs at an earlier age, often before they are prepared to handle these opportunities. The differences between early maturing and other girls' rates of use are most striking in the early adolescent years, when there is the most contrast between physically mature girls and their same-aged peers (Tanner-Smith, 2010). Girls who mature early are also more likely than other girls to be victims of sexual assault and to suffer from depression and anxiety, all of which are associated with higher risk of adolescent substance use (Brown et al., 2008).

Social and Emotional Development

The adolescent period requires major role transitions such as increasing responsibility for daily life and the future, developing more mature relationships with family, establishing greater overall independence, undergoing school transitions and greater academic expectations, exploring romantic and sexual relationships, and preparing for adult occupational roles (Brown et al., 2008). All of these developmental changes require tremendous social adjustments and social skills development (e.g., communication skills, assertiveness, autonomy, coping skills) that will in turn affect whether or adolescents will develop problems with substance use and abuse (Chung & Martin, 2011).

Girls' identity is a key component of this aspect of development, as girls draw a large proportion of their worth and value from their ability to obtain and maintain relationships with peers. Because their sense of identity is so tied to their relationships, girls might be more likely to use substances as a way to belong to a peer group, maintain their status in a romantic couple, and to fit in with male peers. In fact, research indicates that girls report using substances to gain peer approval and to please dating partners more so than do boys (Schinke et al., 2006). Girls who are marginalized, feel alienated from peers, or who have poor social skills might turn to substance use as a way to feel accepted among peers. If she has low self-esteem or is overly concerned about her weight and appearance, she might become more vulnerable to substance use. For example, girls with poor self-esteem at age 12 are 2.5 times more likely to use heavily at age 15 than are those girls with higher self-esteem (SAMHSA, 2012). Girls who long for social connection, acceptance, and attention from peers might succumb to pressures to conform to the behaviors of her peers (often including substance use and sexual activity), even if this is not congruent with her authentic values and sense of self.

Younger girls are likely to use substances at an early age in an effort to achieve developmental goals, particularly when they do not believe they can achieve them in any other way (Botvin & Griffin, 2002). Learning to bond with others through experimentation and intoxication may preempt the normal development of social skills necessary for negotiating future healthy relationships with peers and romantic partners (Brown et al., 2008). If a girl continues to use throughout adolescence, her association with other peers who use substances will also disrupt her connections with protective relationships such as family and school, leaving her with even greater and continued exposure to those with deviant attitudes and behaviors (Liddle et al., 2009).

In addition to derailing healthy social skills development, girls who engage in early and sustained use of substances often experience a conflict between what they truly want for themselves and their desire to conform to the behaviors of peers, resulting in tension and distress. This internal conflict places a girl at higher risk for addiction as she begins to use more heavily in an attempt to assuage these negative feelings (Briggs & Pepperrell, 2009). It is noteworthy that girls are more likely to report using substances to increase confidence, reduce tension or stress, or to cope with problems than are boys. For example, girls who believe that drinking alcohol will help them deal with sadness or repression drink more alcohol than those who do not (CASAA, 2007). In other words, while boys or men tend to engage in substance use for pleasure-seeking reasons (e.g., to enhance their emotions or to get high), girls and women tend to use as a means to suppress or numb negative emotions or to cope with stressors (Briggs & Pepperrell, 2009; Greenfield et al., 2010).

Sustained and heavy substance use can ultimately lead to significant and lasting disruption to adolescents' social and emotional development. Even moderate use during the adolescent years may impair motivation, school achievement, and identity development (AACAP, 2005; Brown et al., 2008). For adolescent girls who do progress to substance abuse and dependency, there is often impairment in psychosocial and academic functioning, including family conflict, interpersonal problems, and academic failures as a result of substance usage (Brown et al., 2008; Upadhyaya & Gray, 2009). Further, adolescents who abuse substances are also more likely to experience lower educational and occupational attainment, violence and gang involvement, crimes such as stealing, vandalism and violence, reduced satisfaction with one's relationships and life, and even premature death (Sussman et al., 2008; Wisdom, Cavaleri, Gogel, & Nacht, 2011). One particular problem associated with adolescent girls' substance use is that it is associated with high-risk sexual behaviors that often result in unprotected sex, date rape, sexual assault, STDs, or unplanned pregnancies. In a study of girls ages 14 to 21 who had experienced unplanned pregnancies, one third reported that they had been drinking alcohol when they had sex, and 91% reported that the sexual activity had been unplanned (Center on Alcohol Marketing and Youth, 2013).

In sum, when an adolescent girl has a family history of substance abuse problems, reaches puberty earlier than her peers, or begins using substances at an early age, she is at risk for developing a SUD and for experiencing a host of negative physical, psychological, interpersonal, academic, and occupational substance-related problems that can last well into the adult years. Given an understanding of the developmental risk factors that increase girls' vulnerability to substance use problems, treatment and prevention approaches can be tailored to address these areas. In the following sections, I review family approaches and cognitive behavioral/motivational enhancement strategies, the approaches with the most research support for adolescents. This review is followed by a discussion of prevention strategies that incorporate identified risk and protective factors.

CASE EXAMPLE

Audrey is a 13-year-old girl living with her parents who were divorced when she was 5. As part of the custody arrangement, she lives for 1 week with her mother, alternating with 1 week with her father. She has a room at both parents' homes, but she has never liked the arrangement and is resentful toward her parents because she feels like doesn't really have a "home." Soon after her parent's divorce, her mother's new boyfriend moved in with the two of them. Audrey never felt comfortable around him, and tried to hide in her room when her mother was not home. One day when she was 6, he came in her room unannounced and molested her, then told her that he would hurt her badly if she ever told anyone about what had happened. She was highly frightened by this experience, so she did not tell her mother or father, even when the man was later accused of molesting his 7-year-old niece. Audrey experienced anxiety and guilt about what happened to the other girl, but decided that it would upset her mother too much if she ever told her what had happened. She began to spend increasing amounts of time in her room at her mother's house as well as at her father's house. When she did have to interact with others, she frequently argued with her parents, having conflicts with others at school, and engaged in several physical fights on the playground during elementary and middle school. Her parents, who fought frequently prior to their divorce, excused her behavior as "diva-like" and "having a mind of her own." By the time she was 10, Audrey presented herself as angry, aggressive, and demanding, although she frequently felt lonely, afraid, and numb.

When Audrey reached puberty at age 11 and began to look much older than she was, she began to hang out with older girls at school who were known for their high-risk behaviors. She admired the way they dressed in sexy clothes, could hang out with older boys late at night, and how cool they seemed when they smoked and talked about drinking and drugs. Soon she began to make plans to meet them after school, and when at her father's house, she began to sneak out at night to meet them because he never checked up on her after he thought she had gone to bed. Soon she began to try this behavior while at her mother's home, and found that her mother did not notice either.

While with these friends, she drank heavily to prove that she could fit in with the older crowd. When they offered her marijuana or prescription pills, she always took them. Because of her young age and size, at first she became intoxicated quickly and blacked out on most occasions. There were many nights when she didn't remember how she got home or anything she did during the drinking episode. She realized that she was engaging in sexual activity during these blackouts, but had no memory of it.

(continued)

CASE EXAMPLE (*continued*)

When she woke up with hangovers and no memory of what she had done, she felt guilty and scared, but soon learned to put it out of her mind and said to herself, "so what, it's only sex..." By the time she was 13, she also learned to trade sexual favors in exchange for alcohol and drugs, so she never had to be concerned about losing her supply of substances. Over time, she could tolerate increasing amounts of alcohol, but she continued to black out on most occasions when she drank alcohol, especially when combined with other drugs.

Because she had hangovers in the mornings before school, she learned to sneak into her parent's liquor cabinets to take a few shots of vodka to help her get through the mornings. She also took prescription pills to get through her days until she could meet up with her friends and drink or get high again. While she was relieved that she didn't have to deal with her parents trying to stop her from her substance use, she was also shocked that they didn't seem to care that she was gone for hours or that she sometimes didn't slip into the house until 5 a.m., just before they awakened for work. She often felt hurt that they didn't ever comment on her hangovers, her late nights, or her total lack of communication with them.

After one occasion in which she blacked out and stayed gone for 2 days, she finally returned to her mother's home. When her mother saw her 13-year-old daughter coming home after 2 days of drinking, drugging, and not sleeping, she finally recognized that Audrey had a problem and needed treatment. Audrey told her mother to leave her alone and that all she needed was a good night's sleep.

Discussion Questions

1. What are the macro- and microsystems factors that might have placed Audrey at risk for substance abuse? What contributed to her early age of substance use onset?
2. As a counselor, what concerns you the most about Aubrey and how would you prioritize your treatment with her? Would you work at the family or individual level, and why?

TREATMENT OF SUDs FOR ADOLESCENT GIRLS

The Academy of Child and Adolescent Psychiatry Best Practice Guidelines indicates that all adolescents with substance use problems should receive treatment specifically targeted for substances prior to receiving treatment for other issues. Research strongly supports treatment effectiveness for adolescent SUDs (Williams, Chang, & Centre for Adolescent Research Group, 2000). In this section, I review general treatment issues, screening, and assessment. I then provide a description of two of the most researched and effective strands of treatment for adolescent substance abuse: family approaches and cognitive behavioral therapy (CBT) paired with motivational enhancement therapy.

The first decision in treatment provision is assessment to determine level of care. The counselor will have to determine the motivation and willingness of not only the adolescent but of the family to participate, the existence of other medical or comorbid conditions, the need for client safety, the parental ability to provide structure and limit setting, the feasibility of other types of treatment in the area, and whether or not the adolescent has already experienced treatment failure in a less restrictive setting (AACAP, 2005).

Screening and Assessment

Several brief screening instruments have been developed to help medical professionals and counselors detect the potential for problems in adolescents related to SUDs. Several of these are not copyrighted and are readily available online.

SCREENING INSTRUMENTS FOR PROBLEMATIC ALCOHOL AND DRUG USE HERE

Alcohol Use Disorders Identification Test (AUDIT): This was developed by the World Health Organization to assist helping professionals in detecting alcohol use disorders in both adolescents and adults (Babor, Higgins-Biddle, Saunders, & Monteiro, 2001). The manual and test is available online at no cost at http:// whqlibdoc.who.int/hq/2001/who_msd_msb_01.6a.pdf.

Problem Oriented Screening Instrument for Teenagers (POSIT): This screening instrument, available at no cost from the National Institute for Drug Abuse and Alcoholism (www.positpc.com), assesses for problems in 10 areas of adolescent functioning.

Rutgers Alcohol Problem Index (RAPI): This instrument is available at no cost from the Center for Alcohol Studies at Rutgers University (http:// alcoholstudies.rutgers.edu/research/prevention_etiology/health_human_ development/RAPI23.pdf). It is an 18-item screen to assess adolescent problem drinking and associated negative consequences.

(continued)

SCREENING INSTRUMENTS FOR PROBLEMATIC ALCOHOL AND DRUG USE HERE (*continued*)

CRAFFT: The CRAFFT is brief screening tool designed specifically to detect both alcohol and drug use-related problems. It is verbally administered, simple to score, and designed to be an easy acronym to remember:

C: Have you ever ridden in a car driven by someone (including yourself) who was high or had being using drugs or alcohol?

R: Do you ever use alcohol or drugs to relax, feel better about yourself, or fit in?

A: Do you ever use alcohol or drugs while you are by yourself, alone?

F: Do you ever forget things you did while using alcohol or drugs?

F: Do your family or friends ever tell you that you should cut down on your drinking or drug use?

T: Have you ever gotten into trouble while you were using alcohol or drugs? (Knight, Sherritt, Shrier, Harris, & Chang, 2002).

Two commonly used instruments must be ordered from the test publisher for a fee:

Adolescent Drinking Index (ADI) is a 24-item rating scale measuring the severity of drinking problems in adolescents (Psychological Assessment Resources, 2012).

Substance Abuse Subtle Screening Inventory Adolescent Version (SASSI-A2) is a 100-item instrument that is designed to detect adolescents who have a high probability of having a substance-related disorder. It includes subtle items to identify those adolescents who may be unwilling or unable to admit substance abuse or related problems (Miller & Lazowski, 2001). It is available for purchase from the SASSI institute (www.SASSI.com)

The availability of screening instruments designed specifically for adolescents is helpful, as it is difficult for researchers and practitioners to accurately diagnose substance abuse disorders especially among adolescent girls. Many of the accepted *DSM-IV-TR* criteria do not necessarily identify problem users accurately. According to the *DSM*, to meet criteria for substance *abuse*, the individual must display one of the following four behaviors in a 12-month period:

- Recurrent use resulting in failure to fulfill major role obligations at work, home, or school
- Engaging in physically dangerous behavior or resulting in physically dangerous situations

- Use of the substance has caused legal programs
- Continued use despite social or interpersonal problems caused by use of the substance. (APA, 2000)

To meet criteria for *dependence*, three of the following seven must apply within a 12-month period:

- Withdrawal (substance taken to relieve withdrawal)
- Tolerance (escalation of substance doses to achieve the desired drug-induced effect)
- Larger amounts of the substance are consumed than intended
- Unsuccessful attempts to stop have been made
- An excessive amount of time is spent on obtaining, using, and recovering from the substance
- Important social or occupational activities are given up or reduced
- There is continued use despite the person's awareness of the negative effects of drinking. (APA, 2000)

Applying *DSM-IV-TR* criteria for substance abuse and dependence to adolescents becomes problematic, however, because these criteria were developed for adults and have not yet been established for adolescents (AACAP, 2005). For example, some of the criteria such as tolerance do not accurately distinguish problem adolescent drinkers from experimental drinkers. Further, adolescents tend to show less physical problems related to their use, yet when they do begin to use more heavily, adolescents develop dependence much more quickly than do adults. As another example, withdrawal is infrequently reported by adolescents, as this takes years of involvement with a substance before it develops (CASAA, 2005).

While adults' regular use of alcohol and other drugs may not necessarily be considered abuse, adolescents are at high risk when they use because of the potential of certain substances to interfere with their brain development and growth, and heavy use can cause chronic damage to brain development (Sussman et al., 2008). Conversely, while certain behaviors would be considered highly symptomatic in adulthood, some high-risk behaviors and sensation seeking might be expected as part of a normal transition to adolescence (Briggs & Pepperell, 2009).

Given the inconsistency in fit identified in previous research, the CASAA (2005) proposed the following definition for adolescent substance abuse:

- Disturbances in mental life in the form of obsession-like ruminations or cravings for drug-related experiences

- Disturbances in behavior in the form of compulsive-like repetitive drug-taking or drug-related behaviors to the detriment of normal activities
- Manifestations of neuroadaptation to drug exposure, in the form of tolerance and sometimes observable and characteristic withdrawal when there is abrupt cessation of drug use
- Usage may also include loss of control during cycles of euphoria and craving
- Usage exists on a continuum of severity that ranges from minimal use/limited consequences to compulsive use/serious impairment. Some adolescents show progression along this continuum while others remain relatively stable

Components of Effective Treatment

Given the difficulty in diagnosing adolescent SUDs, treatments have been developed that address the spectrum of substance use problems. The vast majority of adolescents are appropriately treated in an outpatient setting, with up to 80% of adolescents receiving treatment at this level of care (AACAP, 2005). It is important to note, however, that girls who enter treatment tend to have higher levels of substance use, experience more problems with use, report harder drug use as their primary substance, and have higher rates of psychiatric comorbidity as compared to boys (Stevens, Andrade, & Ruiz, 2009). Therefore, when girls do seek treatment, they are more likely to have more medical, behavioral, psychological, and social problems than do males, despite the fact that they may have been using fewer substances or have used for a lesser amount of time (Greenfield et al., 2010). For the purposes of this chapter, the focus will be on psychosocial treatments that can be provided for girls in an outpatient setting, while remaining mindful of the fact that girls need to be assessed carefully to ensure that they do not need a more intensive level of care.

Best practices indicate that treatment should target not only interventions that target motivation and initial reduction of use, but also multimodal interventions that teach skills and that create those environmental changes that are required to maintain behavior change over time. This includes the following components:

(a) Motivation and engagement, ideally through individual counseling
(b) Family involvement to address needs of adolescents as well as parents in order to improve supervision, monitoring, and communication

(c) Improved problem-solving skills, often taught in a group counseling format

(d) Treatment for comorbid psychiatric disorders

(e) Improvements in social ecology, increasing prosocial behavior, peer relationships, involvement with school, and academic functioning

(f) Adequate duration of treatment and posttreatment aftercare, which is related to improved treatment outcomes (AACAP, 2005).

Research strongly indicates that duration of treatment is associated with better outcomes (Deas & Clark, 2009). Other factors related to positive treatment outcomes include programs that provide a wide range of services such as mental health treatment, legal advocacy, academic tutoring, and parent training (AACAP, 2005). Unfortunately, most treatment programs are not designed specifically to meet the needs of adolescents, do not have the capacity to offer multimodal treatments, and do not take individual differences into consideration (e.g., gender, ethnicity, and readiness to change (McWhirter, 2008).

In contrast, factors that tend to complicate treatment include adolescents who abuse multiple substances, have comorbid psychiatric disorders (particularly conduct disorder), and lack of parental concern about the seriousness of the problem (e.g., parent thinks the teen will grow out of the problem or their lack of concern that treatment is necessary) (Wisdom et al., 2011). Treatment is also complicated by the presence of substance abuse in the client's immediate family (AACAP, 2005). Treatment outcomes are also negatively affected when there is need for intervention in multiple systems, including medical, legal, and educational realms. Further, because adolescents who identify as lesbians show higher levels of alcohol abuse than do heterosexual girls, and because of the challenges of the coming out process during adolescence, treatment is also more complex for lesbian girls (see http://kap.samhsa.gov/products/manuals/pdfs/lgbt.pdf for a downloadable treatment manual for substance abuse treatment for lesbian, gay, bisexual, and transgender individuals developed by the Center for Substance Abuse Treatment). The involvement of multiple systems paired with the unique context of the adolescent and her family can make treatment extremely difficult (CASAA, 2005).

Before moving to a discussion of specific treatment approaches, it is important to highlight three treatment issues that are debated in the literature: the issue of harm reduction versus abstinence, the issue of group versus individual counseling, and the inclusion of gender-sensitive or single-gender treatment services. While any use of a non-prescribed substance by adolescents is illegal and therefore should not be endorsed by counselors, harm reduction is often a recommended temporary goal in order to engage the client in treatment (Marlatt, Baer, & Larimer, 1995). Harm reduction focuses on assisting the client in reducing the negative effects or consequences of use so as to improve her overall quality of life. Rather than setting abstinence as a goal that might seem initially unattainable, a client might be more open to learning skills for reducing use and related harms, which will then provide her with greater self-efficacy for setting a goal of abstinence in the future (Miller & Rollnick, 2002). However, this issue should be balanced with ethical and legal concerns for client safety and with parental rights to knowledge of their child's high-risk and illegal behaviors (Remley & Herlihy, 2010). This is a difficult balance for counselors to attain as they recognize the need for abstinence but also the need to motivate the client for continued treatment (which is more likely to occur when harm reduction is introduced as a goal).

Another somewhat controversial issue often discussed in the literature is the use of group modalities for adolescent substance abuse treatment. There are some data that indicate that group treatment can have a negative effect on outcomes, as deviant adolescents can serve as negative peer role models. More recent studies show that negative group effects might be limited to groups that include high proportions of adolescents with conduct disorders (CASAA, 2005). On the other hand, other studies show positive effects for substance abuse treatment groups with adolescents (Liddle et al., 2009). Large-scale studies of adolescent marijuana abusers did not find any iatrogenic (negative) effects of group treatment when compared to individual and family therapy (Dennis et al., 2004). Nevertheless, it is recommended that practitioners prescreen and take caution when forming groups for adolescents with substance abuse problems, and should consider referring more conduct-disordered clients to other forms of treatment such as family-based or individual treatment (CASAA, 2005).

Another related issue to group work with adolescents is the referral of adolescents to Alcoholics Anonymous (AA) or Narcotics Anonymous (NA) groups. Twelve-step–based intervention models were developed from the AA model, which is widely used and effective with adults, and was initially targeted to middle-aged male alcoholics. Some researchers suggest that these groups may not be developmentally appropriate for adolescents because of the difficulties in accurately diagnosing an adolescent with substance abuse or dependence, as many adolescents mature out of problem drinking and might not benefit from being forced to accept the term "alcoholic" or "addict" as part of their identity. In fact, while most adults have a sense of identity that was formed prior to the addiction, many adolescents might have formed their only sense of identity around their alcohol or drug use. Because of this, they might cling to the only identity they know ("addict") and will require a significant adjustment to form a new way of being and coping in the world. Other authors have noted that 12-step–based groups are not necessarily sensitive to girls' and women's needs (Briggs & Pepperrell, 2009). Therefore, it is helpful to consider 12-step groups as a form of support and aftercare for adolescents in treatment, while remaining mindful that they will not necessarily be appropriate for all adolescent girls (Kassel & Jackson, 2001).

A third issue particularly relevant to this chapter is whether or not treatment should be tailored to gender differences, particularly to the extent of providing separate programs for males and females. Because there are gender differences in risk factors, history, motivation for treatment, reasons for relapse, and because girls and women have a greater likelihood of abuse history, increased likelihood of comorbidity, and are likely to have a more severe presentation at the onset of treatment, it is suggested by several scholars that males and females are best served in single-gender programs and services in order to motivate and engage them in treatment (Green, 2006; Greenfield et al., 2010; Stewart et al., 2009; Zilberman, 2009). At minimum, it is suggested that women be offered some separate treatment modules to meet their specific needs. As part of these services, girls and women will also likely need treatment accommodations that include such programs as mental health services for comorbid disorders; access to medical, legal, and financial services; the provision of child care (for those who are mothers); stress management, assertiveness training, or parenting skills training; treatment for sexual trauma and victimization; domestic violence services; and educational or vocational guidance (Briggs & Pepperell, 2009; Stevens et al., 2009). Despite these recommendations for adults, there is little research available on gender-specific treatment interventions for adolescent substance abuse (Upadhyaya & Gray, 2009). As a way to begin to narrow this gap in the literature, I will integrate suggestions for gender-sensitive treatment considerations throughout the treatment descriptions to follow.

In the following sections, I describe the most researched treatment approaches for adolescent substance abuse. Because family therapy approaches are so strongly supported by empirical research, I will give considerable coverage in the chapter on family therapies (brief strategic family therapy, family focused therapy [FFT], multi systemic therapy, and multi dimensional family therapy [MDFT]). Other studies confirm the effectiveness of both cognitive behavioral therapy (CBT) alone and when paired with motivational enhancement therapy (MET; AACAP, 2005). Because MDFT and group CBT in particular have received the most empirical support to date (Perepletchikova, Krystal, & Kaufman, 2008), I will devote the most attention to these two forms of therapy. As lengthy descriptions are beyond the scope of this chapter, I refer readers to seminal articles and manuals for each approach.

FAMILY-BASED TREATMENT APPROACHES

Family approaches are the most studied modality in the treatment of adolescents with SUDs, have the most supporting evidence for positive treatment outcomes, and provide significant decreases in substance use from pre- to posttreatment (CASAA, 2005). Outpatient family therapy that includes work with multiple systems is superior to other forms of outpatient treatment, with more adolescents entering, engaging in, and completing family therapy than any other treatment type (CASAA, 2005; Stanton & Shadish, 1997; Williams et al., 2000). As such, family therapy or significant family involvement is now an expected component of treatment for adolescents with substance use problems (AACAP, 2005; CASAA, 2005; Liddle, Dakof, Turner, Henderson, & Greenbaum, 2008).

Family therapy approaches treat the adolescent within the context of the family and social systems within which substance problems develop and are maintained, and understand adolescent substance usage as a symptom of maladaptive family interaction patterns. Treatment approaches therefore target family interactions to improve overall family functioning. While there are differences between the approaches, all family therapies have the following overarching goals: (a) provide psychoeducation about SUDs, (b) assist parents to initiate and sustain efforts to engage the adolescent in treatment, (c) assist parents to establish family structure with consistent discipline practices such as limit setting and monitoring of adolescent activities and actions, (d) improve communication skills among family members, and (e) motivate other family members into appropriate treatment or support groups (AACAP, 2005). A brief description of several family approaches is provided in the sections to follow.

Brief Strategic Family Therapy

BSFT (Horigan, Suarez, Morales, Robbins, Zarata, Mayorga, Mitrani, et al., 2005) is an empirically supported family therapy that targets patterns of interactions in the family that are specifically known to influence adolescent substance abuse. The family is seen as a natural social system that can be disrupted by the system's way of reorganizing or self-regulating itself when forced to cope with internal or external changes and stress. Because drug use is seen as resulting from problematic family interactions, the goal is to improve family relationships and the relationship the family has with other important systems that influence the adolescent's life. In sum, instead of just focusing on the substance use, therapy focuses on the interaction patterns that permit, maintain, or encourage the substance use.

According to Horigan et al. (2005), the strategies of BSFT include joining, diagnosing, and restructuring the family. First, joining occurs at both the individual and family level so that each family member feels engaged with treatment. In order to understand/diagnose the interactions that have allowed for the adolescent to turn to substance use, the therapist attempts to create an enactment so that family members interact in their typical style of communication and behavior. The therapist assesses for problems in family functioning in such dimensions as organization (e.g., leadership, subsystems, coalitions, triangulation), resonance (e.g., sensitivity and caring displayed for one another; the presence of boundaries, enmeshment, or disengagement), and developmental stage of the family (e.g., how does the family adapt to developmental milestones and changes in the family). After this assessment, the therapist begins the restructuring process, helping the family move toward a new and more functional way of interacting. The therapist will attempt to restructure certain boundaries and alliances, starting with a stronger parenting subsystem that provides leadership for the family and has the ability to carry out consistent parenting practices (limit setting, monitoring). During this stage, the therapist will assign tasks for the family to practice different interactions both at home and in session. Therapy generally lasts 12 to 16 weeks, ending when the family has the skills to manage crises without the therapist's assistance (Perepletchikova et al., 2008).

Family Focused Therapy

FFT also shows empirical support for its effectiveness and is very similar to BSFT in its conceptualization of the problem at a systems level. It emphasizes relational goals along with a structured approach (Sexton & Alexander, 2005). The first phase involves engagement and motivation, wherein the therapist attempts to reduce any family negativity toward treatment or toward the adolescent. The second phase involves behavior change, including promoting family communication skills, problem solving, identification and building of within-family protective factors, and working with extra-familial systems such as juvenile justice and schools to help facilitate the generalization of what is changing at home to be extended to the adolescent's interactions at school and in the community (Sexton & Alexander, 2005).

Multisystemic Therapy

MST (Henggeler, Schoenwald, Borduin, Rowland, & Cunningham, 2009) is a manualized approach to family therapy that addresses the multiple factors that lead to drug use and antisocial behavior. It is effective in reducing both substance abuse problems as well as juvenile delinquency. Research indicates that it has high completion rates and can reduce re-arrest rates up to 64% (Henggeler et al., 2009). In a 4-year longitudinal study of substance abusing and substance dependent juvenile offenders, findings support the long-term effectiveness of MST, including significant reductions of both substance use and aggressive criminal behavior. A particularly noteworthy finding was that 55% of marijuana users who completed MST were still abstinent at the end of a 4-year period (Henggeler, Clingenpeel, Brondino, & Pickrel, 2002).

As with BSFT and FFT, MST conceptualizes adolescent substance use and other problem behaviors as best understood in terms of the multiple systems in which the adolescent is involved (family, peers, school, neighborhood). Based on an assessment of these systems, treatment focuses on addressing the risk factors in each system that are unique to the adolescent, and also promotes general protective factors (e.g., positive social support, problem solving, parenting competence). Another major focus of MST is on the parental/caregiver subsystem of the family. The MST therapist works to empower caregivers to increase their self-efficacy and competence as they gain the resources and skills needed for effective parenting. Caregivers are seen as the agents of change in all systems in which the adolescent is involved; therefore, the therapist spends time with caregivers by assisting them in developing a plan to better monitor, supervise, and support their children. For example, a primary focus is the development of discipline strategies (e.g., clearly defined and consistently enforced family rules with appropriate consequences; consequences are enforced 100% of the time by all caregivers). Parents/caregivers are also assisted in identifying a support system that can be counted on for help with the monitoring and supervision of children (Henggeler et al., 2009).

At the peer level, therapists encourage parents to take leadership in providing opportunities for the adolescent to begin engaging with more prosocial peers, to help the adolescent become involved in extra-curricular activities in which she might be exposed to more prosocial peers, and to establish rules that discourage affiliation and time spent with deviant peers. Strategies often include increasing parental contact with the adolescent's friends and their caregivers, monitoring her activities with peers more closely, and associating with competent parents who can serve as role models. Finally, the therapist also focuses on the educational/school level. Knowing that an increased commitment to school is a protective factor against the development of substance use problems, the therapist works to promote an active collaboration among teachers, school administrators, and caregivers so that interventions established at home are also reinforced at school (Perepletchikova, et al., 2008). For additional reading about MST, see the manual by Hennggeler, Schoenwald, Borduin, Rowland, and Cunningham (2009).

Multidimensional Family Therapy

MDFT (Liddle, 2002) is also a manualized, integrated, outpatient family therapy approach that has some of the highest levels of research support of any treatment for adolescent substance abuse (Liddle, Dakof, Parker, Diamond, Barrett, & Tejeda, 2001; Liddle, Rodriguez, Dakof, Kanzki, & Marvel, 2005). Its effectiveness has been established in five large-scale clinical randomized controlled trials where it has been compared against other family therapies, peer group treatment, group CBT treatment, and comprehensive residential treatment. It reduces drug and alcohol usage between 41% and 82% from intake to completion, and treatment gains are consistently maintained when adolescents are reassessed at 1-year follow up (Dennis et al., 2004; Liddle et al., 2009). It is also effective in reducing problems related to substance use, including comorbid symptoms, school functioning, family functioning, and delinquent behavior/arrests, and convictions when compared to other types of treatment (Liddle et al., 2009).

Mirroring the ecological systems approach used throughout this book, MDFT conceptualizes adolescent substance abuse through the lens of ecological theory, examining the web of social influences that impact an adolescent's development (Liddle et al., 2009). It blends family therapy, individual therapy, substance abuse counseling, and multisystems interventions. MDFT addresses risk and protective factors at multiple system levels and also includes the most relevant domains of adolescent functioning: intrapersonal level (identity, competence); interpersonal (e.g., family and peer relationships); and contextual/environmental (school, community support). Intervening in multiple systems and at multiple domains is deemed central to providing a complete clinical picture that will lead to accurate assessment, case conceptualization, treatment planning, and successful implementation of the treatment plan (Liddle, 2010).

MDFT is conducted one to three times per week both in the home and in a clinical setting and generally lasts 3 to 6 months. The therapist works simultaneously at four levels: the adolescent, the parents, the family/adolescent conjointly, and with other systems to promote family collaboration with all other pertinent social systems (e.g., school, medical, juvenile justice, etc.). This helps to actively coordinate the different services that are available to the adolescent. An initial multidimensional assessment is conducted by meeting with all of the key members of these systems.

Stage One

The therapist first meets with the entire family to assess family interaction patterns, then meets with every family member alone to obtain his or her perspective of the problem. Next, the therapist meets with the adolescent alone. The goal of the initial sessions with the adolescent is to increase her motivation and to give encouragement, helping her to see that there can be a benefit of this treatment for her. The therapist begins by discussing the adolescent's story (e.g., what life is like in her family, school, and neighborhood) in an effort to build the therapeutic alliance and to promote hope that things can be better for her. The therapist works to help her identify goals such as better communication with family and peers, better management of anger, and enhanced problem-solving skills. The therapist also begins to explore the role of alcohol and other drugs in her life, and encourages her to explore what she enjoys outside of using substances. A final issue in initial sessions is to help the adolescent prepare for forthcoming parent/adolescent meetings in which she will be encouraged to share her perspective about her involvement in a substance-using lifestyle (Liddle, 2010).

In early parent-only sessions, the therapist's goal is to strengthen the parenting relationship (if both parents are involved), validate their previous efforts to make the problem better, encourage hope that treatment will be effective, and enhance and strengthen feelings of love for/ commitment to the adolescent so that these feelings might be better expressed to their daughter. Even though the parents might be frustrated and discouraged, they can be encouraged to increase their warmth and involvement with their daughter through initiating more conversations, spending more quality time with her, and showing an overall increased interest in her and her activities. At the same time, the therapist spends time in parent sessions teaching basic parenting competencies (e.g., basic skills for increased parental monitoring, limit setting, and follow through), while balancing this discipline with the necessary emotional support that their daughter needs (Liddle et al., 2005).

After these meetings, the counselor meets with the entire family again, working to improve how the family communicates with one another, and collaboratively deciding on the most urgent family topics to address. As described in BSFT, the therapist relies on the structural family therapy technique of *enactment* (asking the family to discuss issues as they typically do at home) to better see how the family interacts and to determine how to discuss and solve problems in more innovative, productive ways that do not elicit blame or defensiveness (Liddlet et al., 2005).

At the social systems level, the counselor helps the family to first identify needed social services, then assists them in navigating the complex social bureaucracies that might present barriers to accessing these services (legal, employment, mental health, or health systems). This will alleviate some of the burden on parents as they are able to successfully obtain the services that they need to function more optimally as a family.

Stages Two and Three

During stage two, the adolescent's individual sessions will continue to emphasize preparation for a session with her parents and family in which she will talk openly about her experiences. In addition, the counselor helps the client weigh the pros/cons of change as well as the pros/cons of substance use. The counselor assists the client as she envisions short- and longer-term goals for her life and whether or not her current substance-using lifestyle will help or hinder the achievement of these goals. The counselor also uses this time to teach life skills such as communication, decision making, problem solving, anger management, and coping skills. Drug screens are also instituted to increase accountability and to open dialogue about use with both the counselor as well as with parents.

At this stage, the counselor assists parents by devising a specific plan for providing age-appropriate discipline (e.g., monitoring, limit setting, enforcing consequences) and for decreasing the adolescent's time spent with delinquent peers. Because these are demanding tasks and the parents are likely to already feel depleted, one or both parents might need to engage in higher levels of self-care during this time (e.g., seeking personal counseling, health care, or increased support). The parents should be further prepared for family sessions wherein they can listen to their adolescent relate her story without reacting defensively or in anger.

At the family systems level, the counselor will direct the adolescent when she is ready to talk openly about her experiences without being interrupted by other family members. The counselor can then invite family members' reactions and can intervene if these are not conveyed in a helpful manner. Throughout, the counselor can keep a focus on validating the family members' feelings of love, support, and warmth toward one another. In addition to these disclosures, the counselor will address the important family issues identified in earlier sessions, attempting to bring relational conflicts into the sessions so that they can be enacted and resolved. To help the family move toward change, the counselor can teach skills for effective conflict resolution and negotiation so that the family can practice these both in session and at home.

At the social systems level, the counselor maintains an ongoing collaboration with all systems to ensure that there is consistency between family changes in supervision and discipline and those that are enforced at school or in the neighborhood. Part of the reason that MDFT is effective is the emphasis on reconnecting the family and adolescent with school to institute commitment to school success. Academic achievement and school connection promotes a positive trajectory for adolescents and is seen as a protective factor against substance use and delinquency (Liddle et al., 2005). Along these same lines, conduct problems and juvenile delinquency are a strong risk factor for substance use, so MDFT counselors make every effort to promote prosocial peer relationships and to collaborate with the juvenile justice system when appropriate to reduce any risks for delinquency (Liddle et al., 2005).

In stage three, for all modules, the therapist works to prepare for termination, consolidate learning among family members, and to create a family dialogue around what has been most helpful in treatment. For an overview of the MDFT approach reviewed here, see www.med.miami.edu/CTRADA/x7.xml for information, related publications, and resources. The reader is also referred to Liddle et al. (2009) for a clinician manual and DVD. A more recent clinical manual is also in press with Guilford Press.

Strengths Oriented Family Therapy (SOFT) Approach

With less empirical support than MST or MDFT, SOFT is a nationally recognized multimodal approach that incorporates the use of multiple-family groups (MFGs) where multiple families attend sessions together and also provide one another with family peer support. It is mentioned here so that counselors can consider the potential use of MFGs for the families with whom they work. The SOFT approach integrates solution-focused family therapy, family communication skills training, and targeted case management for adolescents (Hall, Smith, & Williams, 2008). In the MFGs, families learn to give and receive positive feedback, listen assertively, give and receive criticism, cope with peer pressure, solve problems, build healthy relationships, manage stress, manage anger, and prevent future substance use and abuse (Smith & Hall, 2010).

CASE EXAMPLE: AUDREY'S FAMILY-BASED TREATMENT

By the time Audrey arrived at her counselor's office, her parents were both aware of her substance use problem and both agreed to support her in counseling. The counselor recommended MDFT due to Audrey's age, ability to work on an outpatient basis, and her family context. During the first session with Audrey alone, the counselor tried to connect with Audrey, who insisted that she was just a party girl like her friends and that there was nothing wrong with her. Instead of arguing, the counselor asked Audrey to tell her about her daily life and the role of substance in it. She also asked Audrey some screening questions to help evaluate the extent of the problem. Audrey relaxed a little when she realized that the counselor would not try to unduly pressure her and wanted to believe her when she said that she would always look out for her best interests.

In the parent session, the counselor asked both the mother and father to attend the session. The counselor wanted to get each parent's view of the problem and how it played out in their relationships with Audrey at their respective homes. Audrey's father said he was fed up with her and had just stopped trying to connect or even show interest in her whereabouts.

(continued)

CASE EXAMPLE: AUDREY'S FAMILY-BASED TREATMENT
(continued)

He felt like it wouldn't do any good to try to stop her from what she wanted to do. Her mother, on the other hand, wanted to be close to her daughter again, but didn't want to place limits on her so as to make their relationship even more strained. She said she had been letting Audrey have her own space just so they could get along. Neither recognized that Audrey had been using substances to such a heavy extent, but both agreed they would think about additional ways to monitor Audrey's activities while she was at either home and they would stick by the same rules at both houses. The counselor also emphasized the importance of not only instituting some consistent rules, but also trying to show warmth and love to Audrey, even during this time when she was trying to push them away. The counselor then invited Audrey into the session and asked the parents to discuss their feelings and new rules with Audrey. She initially argued with them, frequently cursing at them, but then shut down and remained silent when she realized that they were not going to back down from their new rules and limits. After this session, the counselor also went to Audrey's school to meet with the school counselor and all of her teachers. They agreed to call the counselor with any concerns about Audrey's absences, tardiness, or poor performances at school, and the counselor informed them of a schedule for checking in at the school. The school counselor also agreed to meet with Audrey weekly. In this way, Audrey would have to function within the same frame of responsibility both at home and at school.

In phase two of treatment, Audrey continued to meet individually with her counselor with the goal of being able to share her feelings openly with her parents and also disclosing how involved she was in a life of alcohol and drugs. Audrey began to recognize her anger at her parents for asking her to live in two different homes, as Audrey did not feel at "home" in either place. She also revealed her anger at her mother for having a live-in boyfriend who sexually abused her. She believed that this man caused her to become "damaged goods" at a young age, so that she had learned that she did not deserve to take care of herself or to form sexual boundaries with which she felt comfortable. She stated that when she was intoxicated, she didn't have to experience these painful feelings, and she felt others' approval of her as she used substances with them and when she was chosen as a sexual partner.

Being part of a "cool" crowd had become an important part of her identity and Audrey was highly reluctant to let go of that part of herself. The counselor helped Audrey to look beyond her daily life and to create goals for her future, something Audrey had never envisioned. Audrey did not want to still drink and use drugs at age 25; she wanted to go to college and have a professional job some day. Audrey admitted that if she kept going in her current direction then she would not have this future life. She also admitted that she would enjoy having some friends her age and even a boyfriend who valued her for herself and not just for her sexual availability. Audrey recognized that she needed new skills for making friends and maintaining relationships without the use of alcohol or drugs. She also wished she could move past the hurt and fear related to the sexual abuse, and she admitted that part of the reason that she became intoxicated so frequently was to distance herself from that pain. Finally, she realized that she needed to communicate all of this to her parents so that they could serve as a support system for her.

On the parents' end, each parent began enforcing ground rules and instituting close parental monitoring. For a time, Audrey was not allowed to leave the house at night and could only go out with parental supervision. Because she was home more, Audrey began to spend time with her father at home, even sharing in activities that they both enjoyed. She also began to talk more with her mother and they even went on a weekend trip together. Although Audrey was angry and resentful that she had lost her social life, she was also a little relieved that her parents both cared enough about her to keep her at home. The counselor spoke weekly with the school counselor, who informed her that Audrey's attendance had improved and that she was slightly more alert and motivated in class. She also seemed to be distancing herself from her former clique of friends.

Finally, Audrey felt ready to have a joint session with her parents where she shared her feelings about their divorce and custody arrangement. She also shared the experience of her sexual abuse and how she had made the decision not to tell anyone until now. All three of them sobbed as the parents assured her that she could have told them about the abuse and that they would have supported her. Audrey's mother apologized that she had ever let someone into her home who would hurt her daughter. Audrey described how much time she had been spending with older peers who she felt understood her and actually liked hanging out with her. She told them that she was drawn to this because she felt like such an outcast at home. The parents listened intently and cried, but did not act defensively or aggressively. Audrey was surprised that they really wanted to listen and to help her, and she eventually asked for their support so that she could make a better life for herself.

It was finally agreed that the family would: (1) revisit the custody arrangement in way that made more sense for Audrey's well-being; (2) continue individual counseling with the counselor and weekly checkins with the school counselor; (3) monitor Audrey's whereabouts after school and in the evenings; (4) provide consistent limits and enforce consequences when family rules are violated; (5) check in with the school as needed to ensure that Audrey is attending classes and completing her assignments; and (6) hold several additional family sessions so that Audrey can continue to express her continually evolving feelings toward her parents.

CBT/MET APPROACHES

Because CBT is so efficacious with adults who experience SUDs, CBT has been applied to adolescent SUDs with successful outcomes (AACAP, 2005; CASAA, 2005). It conceptualizes substance use as a learned behavior that develops in the context of social interactions with others (e.g., observations of family members, peers, media models) and is then maintained through contingencies in the environment (e.g., settings, cravings for use, using with certain friends). Treatment therefore focuses on a functional behavioral analysis to examine these triggers and the context in which substance use generally occurs, and identifying alternative reinforcers that can take the place of drug use (or avoiding high-risk situations that might lead to drug use). CBT also takes a cognitive approach by identifying disordered thinking patterns and developing more healthy coping strategies. It also teaches important life skills such as communication, problem solving, substance refusal skills, and often includes assertiveness, relaxation, anger management, and relapse prevention (Waldron & Turner, 2008).

While CBT adolescent programs differ in specific content, most contain the same basic components, as outlined in Kaminer and Slesnick (2006). In phase one of CBT programs, the therapist will determine the most pressing client problems and develop a treatment plan in conjunction with parents' input. As part of this, a problem list is created and each problem is prioritized according to the following hierarchy: (1) life threatening; (2) threat to physical well-being; (3) mental health and physical health problem; (4) therapy interfering behavior; and (5) quality of life interfering behavior (which would include substance abuse). Once problems are prioritized, the therapist and client have a more realistic idea as to where to start treatment.

In the middle phase of treatment, CBT strategies are used to help the adolescent develop more effective coping skills and to assist her in reducing those behaviors that threaten her safety, health, and quality of life. This includes such components as: information and education about substance use; contingency contracting; self-monitoring; problem solving training; substance refusal skills; communication skills training; identifying cognitive distortions; increasing healthy leisure activities; and anger management. The session structure includes modeling, behavioral rehearsal, feedback, and homework assignments. The ending stage consists of skill review, relapse prevention, and termination of the counseling relationship (Kaminer & Slesnick, 2006; Perepletchikova et al., 2008).

CBT is often most effective when supplemented with MET, also known as the motivational interviewing (MI) approach (AACAP, 2005; Bukstein & Horner, 2010; Dennis et al., 2004). In a large-scale study comparing effective treatment approaches for adolescents using cannabis (the Youth Cannabis Treatment Study), MET/CBT was considered one of the most cost-effective interventions for adolescents (Dennis et al., 2004). Motivational approaches are designed to be brief sessions that will minimize treatment dropout, produce rapid, internally motivated change, and enhance goal setting for individuals who are heavy substance users (Miller & Rollnick, 2002).

A book by Naar-King and Suarez (*Motivational Interviewing with Adolescents*, 2010) provides a practical overview of the MI approach as adapted specifically for adolescents. The following description provides a brief overview of principles and techniques. For further reading, the reader is referred to the Naar-King and Suarez book, as well as *Motivational Interviewing* by Miller and Rollnick (2002). MI is not a grouping of techniques but rather is a therapeutic style for interacting with clients. First, the counselor is *supportive of the adolescent client's autonomy*, providing her with options, valuing her personal choices, and encouraging her to take responsibility for her life (within the constraints that current authority figures in her life have placed upon her). As the client views the counselor as someone who is not forcing her to change but is on her side in helping her find ways to make her life better (e.g., fewer conflicts with parents, better grades, fewer difficulties with law enforcement), the client becomes willing to *collaborate with the counselor* around these issues. In their partnership, the counselor and client can devise goals that will satisfy the tension she is experiencing between the need for increasing autonomy and the desire to have less conflict with the authority figures in her life.

Another key counselor stance in MI is *evocation*. When the client comes to treatment, she likely expects that she will be corrected and lectured to about her substance use problem. Instead, the MI counselor listens attentively to her thoughts and feelings, demonstrating an understanding of her perspective on the problem. Rather than giving advice, the MI counselor will provide reflections that help her feel understood and that also help her better understand her own reasons for and concerns about change. When the client is able to verbalize her own reasons for change and when she is able to recognize that change is in her best interest, she is far more likely to act on this change (Naar-King & Suarez, 2010).

The four basic principles of MI as described by Naar-King and Suarez, 2010 provide the basis of the techniques used in sessions. They are described as follows.

Principles of Motivational Interviewing

Express Empathy

To join with the client, it is important for the counselor to provide reflections that clearly demonstrate that he or she values what the client has to say. It is recommended that the ratio for reflections should be two reflections for every one question. The counselor can give the client choices about what she would like to discuss in the session, asking her permission before beginning a task in the session. If the client is hesitant to talk about her substance use, the counselor can ask her about a typical day and explore all areas of her life, including family, peers, and school. She can reflect upon what others are thinking and saying about her current substance use.

Types of reflections used can be *simple reflections.* For example, when Audrey says: "I did the same thing all of my friends were doing last weekend. I don't see what the big deal is," a counselor might respond: "You're really frustrated. All these other people are doing it, yet you are the one who has to be here." A *double-sided reflection* might include the response "You said that keeping your grades up and being accepted to a good college is an important life goal for you. But from what you just said, when you go drink with your friends during the day, it is not unusual for you to skip class and even miss tests at school. Help me understand that." An *amplified reflection* would include a reflection that slightly amplifies the truth so that the client has to verbalize some of the negative consequences of use: "So your parents and teachers are not bothered AT ALL when you drink before school." Finally, an *omission reflection* would reflect on the things the client does not seem to want to discuss: "You seem uncomfortable talking about this area of your life." Summaries are also used to connect the major themes of the session.

Develop Discrepancies

The client can be encouraged to share her values and goals for the future, so that the counselor can attempt to clarify and magnify the discrepancy between what she says she wants for her future and where her current behaviors will likely lead. The counselor can ask questions to develop discrepancies such as "What is the best thing that might happen if you stop drinking? What is the worst thing that might happen if you don't stop? If you look at your life 5 years from now, what might it be like if you decide not to stop drinking at your current level?" These answers can then be reflected to the client in a double sided reflection (e.g., "So you are having a lot of fun now, but you believe that you might not be able to earn good enough grades to go to college if you keep drinking this way"). To help her make a decision about change, it is also helpful to assist her in developing a pros/cons list. The counselor can help her decide about the pros and cons of her decision to change to a more positive behavior to help her determine whether or not change is in her best interest. This can be far more effective than the counselor attempting to convince her that she should change.

A final method recommended for developing discrepancies is for the counselor to provide her with personalized feedback about how her substance use level compares with normative data. For example, the counselor can give her personalized feedback regarding data from the national or local level that helps her see how she compares to others and to become more aware of the potential risks that are involved with continuing at her current level of use (Hernandez, Barnett, Sindelar, Manning, Chun, & Spirito, 2011). This helps her develop more concern about her use and again creates a discrepancy between her current behaviors and her future goals for her life. It is important for the counselor not to give too much information at once or the client will not be responsive. The counselor should first ask permission to give the information, provide the information in two or three sentences, then elicit her thoughts or reactions to the information. In this way the collaborative effort between client and counselor will be maintained.

Roll With Resistance

When the counselor perceives resistance, he or she should overcome the initial tendency to correct the client or interpret her behavior. Instead the counselor should use the *Stop, drop, and roll technique*: Stop, consider what is currently happening in the relationship; drop whatever approach you are using because it is not working; and roll with the resistance, reflecting your understanding of the client's perspective.

Support Self-Efficacy

The MI counselor will work toward building the client's self-efficacy for changing her behaviors. This is best accomplished through exposing her to similar models that have been successful and in helping her start with small steps that will ensure initial success. For example, if Audrey currently drinks 10 drinks per week and decides she will drink less during the week, the counselor will work with her to establish a reasonable goal that she can accomplish: "So you think you might be able to drink 1 drink less per night on the nights you go are allowed to go out... so that would be a total of 7 drinks this week?" As mentioned previously, this approach is controversial with adolescents due to the fact that all substance use is illegal; however, research supports that change will not be lasting unless the client has internal motivation for change, and this can only occur if the client develops the self-efficacy for abstinence (which might take several successful attempts at reduction until this goal is approached). When the client's safety or well-being is threatened, it is certainly prudent for the counselor to follow ethical and legal obligations for notifying parents and legal guardians when their child is at risk (Remley & Herlihy, 2010).

The MI approach has been successfully combined with CBT (e.g., CBT/MET5; Dennis et al., 2004). In this manualized, research-supported approach developed by Sampl and Kaddin (2001), two individual MET sessions are followed by three group CBT sessions conducted over a period of 6 to 7 weeks. In the individual sessions, the therapist uses MI techniques to help the adolescent recognize the negative consequences of marijuana use in an effort to recognize that the cons of use actually outweigh the benefits. The sessions are also used to prepare the adolescent for the group sessions. The CBT group sessions teach important coping skills such as how to refuse offers of drugs, how to establish a social support network that is supportive of recovery and nonuse; how to develop alternative activities that the adolescent can do instead of using; problem solving; and coping with high-risk situations (Mason & Posner, 2009). The entire CBT/MET5 manual is available online at www.chestnut.org/li/cyt/products/mcb5_cyt_v1.pdf.

PREVENTION PROGRAMS FOR ADOLESCENT SUBSTANCE USE

While family and cognitive behavioral-based treatment programs are effective for adolescents who have already developed problems, it is preferable for counselors to intervene with girls before problem usage patterns are ever developed. There has been much research in the area of substance abuse prevention in recent years, and there are three national registries that list evidence-based programs: National Registry of Effective Programs and Practices (www.nrepp.samhsa .gov/), the Blueprints for Violence Prevention Center (www.colorado .edu/cspv/blueprints/), and the U.S. Department of Education Office of Safe and Drug Free Schools (www2.ed.gov/about/offices/list/ osdfs/index.html). There are many effective programs available to practitioners, but due to space limitations, only three major programs are mentioned here.

Given that delayed age of initiation is a strong protective factor against SUDs, many prevention programs have been designed for the prevention of early substance use. There is a developmental window to work with young adolescents who have not yet initiated substance use, and therefore prevention programs are most effective when targeted to students in middle childhood (Spoth et al., 2008). Because it is most effective to work with adolescents before they develop problems, universal prevention approaches are used to reach large numbers of individuals who might be at risk for later substance use problems but who do not currently need treatment. Prevention programs are designed to intervene at either the student level or the family level (providing families with guidance about the importance of parental connection, limit setting, and monitoring).

At the adolescent level, current evidence-based approaches in primary prevention indicate that programs should focus on both managing negative peer and social influences as well as competence enhancement/life skills approaches. Social influence approaches teach students to recognize the role of various social influences (peers, media, advertising), how to resist these pressures, how to avoid high-risk situations where they will experience pressures, and how to handle social pressure in these situations (Botvin & Griffith, 2002). On the other hand, competence-enhancement approaches target the enhancement of both social as well as personal skills. These approaches emphasize general personal and social skills such as decision making, interpersonal communication, and coping skills.

The Life Skills Training approach of Botvin (Griffin, Botvin, Nichols, & Doyle, 2003) incorporates both of these aspects and is currently the most commonly used prevention curriculum in elementary schools (Hanley et al., 2010). The Life Skills Training program consists of three major components: personal self-management (i.e., decision making, goal setting, problem solving, resisting media influences, self-control for coping with anxiety and anger); social skills (i.e., interpersonal skills to overcome shyness, strategies for giving and receive compliments, skills for initiating social interactions, skills related to dating and assertiveness), and drug-related information and skills (i.e., providing information about the short-term consequences of drug use, correcting normative expectations, teaching techniques for resisting media and peer pressure to use substances). Research indicates that this is an effective approach in delaying adolescent onset of use and reduced usage levels over time (Botvin & Griffith, 2002).

While the Life Skills approach focuses on the adolescent, it is clear that the family also plays a critical role in preventing the onset and development of substance use problems. Family protective factors include families who provide high levels of emotional connection, warmth, support, and communication; quality time spent together as a family; positive expectations about school performance; and high levels of parental supervision and consistent discipline practices (Liddle et al., 2001, 2009). In fact, research has demonstrated that when parents institute adequate monitoring of their children and provide positive, consistent parenting practices, adolescent drug involvement can be delayed or decreased, even after the adolescent is already engaging in substance use (Mason, Kosterman, Hawlins, Haggerty, & Spoth, 2003). The more a family is involved with their daughter and the more they provide her with appropriate structure and limits, the less likely she will experience substance use problems. As an example, young girls who say they have dinner at home every day are less likely to initiate alcohol use than are girls who eat at home on only some days or never (Fisher et al., 2007).

Cultural values taught at home are also an important protective factor that can be emphasized in family prevention approaches. One study of adolescents found that the cultural values of filial piety and familism were associated with a lower risk of substance use. Filial piety emphasizes obedience to parents, providing support for parents, and avoiding any behaviors that would disgrace the family. Familism is the sense of obligation to and connection with one's family, so that an adolescent might refrain from alcohol or drug use out of respect for her family. In this study, these values were associated with reduced substance use regardless of ethnicity, indicating that it is the value set taught and not the cultural group in particular that is important (Unger et al., 2002). Another protective factor generally taught in the family is the importance of religion and spirituality. Religious and spiritual values are considered critical protective factors, and these values are highly related to abstinence from substances among adolescents (Wallace, Brown, Bachman, & LaVeist, 2003).

Examples of Prevention Programs for Families

The Life Skills Parent Program is designed as a parenting curriculum to be learned at home with a manual and accompanying DVD. In the 15-session curriculum, the authors provide parents with an overview of substance abuse issues, protective family factors (e.g., appropriate parental monitoring and communication), and ways to promote positive self-management and social skills development in their children. With initial research to support its effectiveness, it can serve as a supplement to parents who are not able to attend sessions at an office or school (Griffin, Samuolis, & Williams, 2011).

One study combined the Life Skills Training program for young adolescents in schools (ages 10–14) with the Strengthening Families Program for Youth (SFT; Spoth et al., 2008). The SFT program met for 7 weeks, and each session included separate, concurrent 1-hour parent and youth skills training, followed by a 1-hour family session where family members could practice their newly learned skills. Parents learn risk factors for substance use, how to enhance parent–child bonding, how to monitor their children, enforce rules, and impose consequences, and how to manage anger and family conflict. The children practiced resisting peer influences. These families were compared with those who only received the LST program and a control group who received minimal attention, and were followed over 5 years. The LST only and LST+SFP programs were both effective in delaying onset of use and severity of use over the 5 years compared to the control group, but there were unexpectedly no significant differences between the two treatment groups (Spoth et al., 2008; National Registry of Evidence Based Programs and Practices, 2008).

Guiding Good Choices is another effective substance abuse primary prevention program focused on improving parenting practices (www.channing-bete.com). Designed for parents of children ages 9 to 14, it is intended to enhance bonding within the family, teach skills for resisting drug use, and strengthen consistent expectations and discipline within the family. It is a five-session program that provides information about the risks and dangers of early substance use, ideas for promoting family closeness through regular interactions with one another, establishing consistent discipline practices, teaching kids skills about how to resist peer influences, and providing skills for reducing and managing family conflict (Mason et al., 2003). Research from a line of studies indicates that compared to those who did not receive the program, the program is effective in improving abstinence rates among adolescents who participated in the program, and at 4-year follow up, substance use increased at a slower rate for the program participants than for the nonparticipants. Parenting outcomes indicated that parents demonstrated better child management skills, possessed more positive and consistent discipline practices regarding substance use, and had better family communication than did those parents in a control group (Kosterman, Hawkins, Haggerty, Spoth, & Redman, 2001; Mason et al., 2003).

One other prevention program was designed specifically for African American mothers and their adolescent girls ages 11 to 13. This computer-based intervention intended to strengthen mother/ daughter communication, warmth, and closeness, all of which are protective factors against early substance use. In the module for mothers, parents were provided with parenting information such as the importance of monitoring their daughters' behavior and activities, of establishing rules about substance use, of creating family rituals, of refraining from communicating unrealistic expectations, and to provide support. In the modules designed for girls only, girls learned skills for managing stress, conflict, and mood; for reducing peer, pressure; and for enhancing body esteem and self-efficacy. There were also modules designed to promote better interactions between mothers and daughters to encourage closeness and communication (Schinke et al., 2006). At 1-year follow up, the intervention group had initiated substance use at significantly lower rates than did the control group, thus indicating the importance of maternal closeness, communication, and supervision.

CONCLUSION

It is clear that the majority of girls experiment with alcohol and many progress to trying other drugs during the adolescent period. While most girls' usage patterns are part of a normal developmental trajectory, the earlier a girl begins using substances and the more risk factors she displays (e.g., family history, poor social skills, association with peers engaging in deviant behavior, poor school or family attachment), the more likely she will be to progress to a pattern of heavy substance use, abuse, or dependency. As girls begin to engage in more frequent and heavy use, it is important that counselors not dismiss this as typical adolescent behavior but to take these risks seriously by assessing for a potential SUD. Because girls are more likely than boys to progress to addiction more quickly once they begin using (the *telescoping effect*), early identification is crucial.

Research has also identified the necessity of building client motivation and engagement early in the treatment process. MI/MET is currently the most successful approach in working with initial adolescent resistance. Instead of correcting, lecturing, or blaming, the counselor uses a MI style to join with the client, understand her perspective on the problem, and to gently help her recognize for herself that change is in her best interest. If the counselor pushes for change instead of facilitating conditions in which the client is internally motivated to change her behaviors, client resistance is likely to ensue. While this approach might be difficult to balance with counselors' mandate to protect clients from harm, this is the best initial approach for helping clients become open to creating lasting change.

The research reviewed in this chapter also reveals the need to intervene at multiple levels, including family, school, peers, and community. An adolescent girl is embedded in multiple systems, so it will be difficult for her to change on an individual level without also making adjustments in each system that supports her efforts at change. As emphasized throughout this chapter, family involvement is considered an essential element of treatment, not only to enhance family communication and problem solving, but also to strengthen the parental system. Parents/guardians need guidance in developing better skills for supervising their children, monitoring their whereabouts, remaining aware of their daughter's peer group, encouraging relationships with pro-social peers, and establishing contact with her peers' parents. Further, parents need the skills to set limits and family rules, and then to persist in consistently enforcing these rules. These parenting skills are difficult for parents who are engaged in substance abuse or have other mental health or physical problems themselves. They are also difficult for single parents or guardians who have little social support to assist with monitoring and rule enforcement. Counselors can be instrumental in helping parents to access resources in order to obtain their own treatment and can provide assistance in helping parents to build stronger social support networks. Counselors can also ensure that key school personnel are on board with the treatment plan, encouraging frequent communication between the school and the parental system.

For girls in particular, treatment also needs to address issues of comorbidity. Instead of overlooking other problems, girls often need treatment that simultaneously addresses substance abuse as well as other disorders that frequently co-occur with girls' substance abuse (eating disorders, depression, anxiety disorders). Finally, as emphasized in all treatment approaches, girls need general life skills in order to effectively manage the many stressors of the adolescent period. Not only do they need alcohol and drug refusal skills, they also need problem solving, self-management strategies, and active coping strategies, as well as social skills training to assist in developing and maintaining relationships without relying on drugs or alcohol to facilitate social interactions.

Girls also need treatment approaches that are flexible enough to include components designed specifically to address the specific needs of adolescent girls, including managing the stressors of early puberty, social pressures for girls to obtain a culturally defined, often unattainable ideal regarding how they should look and act, and how to establish healthy relationships with romantic partners that are based on mutuality and respect. Clearly this problem is a serious concern that can significantly impact girls' physical and mental well-being, and it is no surprise that the challenges for treating substance use problems can seem insurmountable to some professionals. However, by detecting problems early, engaging and motivating the client, intervening at multiple levels, and teaching girls the skills that are most relevant for navigating their daily challenges, counselors who invest their time and energy into this multi systemic approach are more likely to have positive treatment outcomes.

RESOURCES

National Registry of Evidence-Based Programs and Practices (NREPP). www.nrepp.samhsa.gov/

Treatment manuals for MET/CBT sessions and a MDFT treatment manual. http://kap.samhsa.gov/products/manuals/cyt

Treatment Manual for Providers introduction to substance abuse treatment for Lesbian, Gay, Bisexual, and Transgender Individuals. Developed by the Center for Substance Abuse Treatment, Substance Abuse and Mental Health Services Administration (2009). http://kap .samhsa.gov/products/manuals/pdfs/lgbt.pdf

Center for Substance Abuse Treatment. www.samhsa.gov/about/ csat.apsx

Center for Substance Abuse Prevention. www.samhsa.gov/about/ csap.aspx

National Institute on Drug Abuse (NIDA) home page. www.nida
.nih.gov/NIDAHome.html

Motivational Interviewing home page. www.motivationalinterview.
org

Monitoring the Future Survey. www.monitoringthefuture.org

Youth Risk Behavior Survey (YRBS), U.S. Department of Health
and Human Services, Centers for Disease Control and Prevention.
Available: http://www.cdc.gov/HealthyYouth/yrbs/index.htm

Center on Addiction and Substance Abuse at Columbia University:
Girls and Alcohol. www.casacolumbia.org

Girls Incorporated: Girls and Substance Abuse. www.girlsinc.org

Adolescent Substance Abuse Knowledge Base contains statistics,
signs and symptoms of drug use, information for teenage parents, resources, and more. www.adolescent-substance-abuse.com/
girls12-17.html

Expressions of Pain: Counseling Adolescent Girls Who Engage in Nonsuicidal Self-Injury

Self-injury, once a highly misunderstood and under reported behavior, is now frequently represented in popular culture. According to the International Society for the Study of Self-Injury (2007), nonsuicidal self-injury (NSSI) is defined as the deliberate, direct, intentional, and self-inflicted destruction of one's own body tissue that results in immediate tissue damage and is conducted for purposes not socially sanctioned and without intention to die. Unfortunately, NSSI has become a familiar piece of the adolescent landscape, as it is an alarmingly common behavior in adolescents of both sexes and across all racial and ethnic groups, with estimated rates of 13% to 45% in community samples and 40% to 60% in clinical samples (Hilt, Nock, Lloyd-Richardson, & Prinstein, 2008b; Latzman et al., 2010; Muehlenkamp, Williams, Gutierrez, & Claes, 2009; Nock & Favazza, 2009; Rodham & Hawton, 2009). With an average

Note: This chapter is adapted from Choate, L. (2011). Counseling adolescents who engage in nonsuicidal self-injury: A Dialectical Behavior Therapy approach. *Journal of Mental Health Counseling, 34*, 56–71. Adapted with the approval of the American Mental Health Counseling Association.

age of onset between 12 and 14 years (Nock, Teper, & Hollander, 2007), middle-school populations have the highest prevalence rates of self-injury (Whitlock, 2009).

The early onset and prevalence of NSSI during early adolescence is of particular concern for girls, especially because it appears that girls' transition to adolescence may be a period of vulnerability for the development of self-injury and other negative psychological symptoms (Guerry & Prinstein, 2010; Nock, 2010; Prinstein et al., 2010). For example, in one ethnically diverse community sample of young girls ages 10 to 14, 56% of participants reported engaging in at least one NSSI behavior, and 36% reported a behavior within the past year (Hilt, Cha, & Nolen-Hoeksema, 2008). As reviewed elsewhere in this book, girls are at risk for psychological distress and experience more stressors during adolescence, and thus may be prone to using NSSI as a way to cope with these stressors and problems (Adrian, Zeman, Erdley, Lisa, & Sim, 2011).

It should be noted that while self-injury is often associated with White, middle- to upper-class girls, there are few studies that actually support this profile (Whitlock, 2009). For example, research is largely inconsistent in demonstrating any racial differences in rates of self-injury; most current studies indicate no significant differences between racial groups (Whitlock, Muehlenkamp, et al., 2009). In addition, few differences emerge when examining self-injury rates by socioeconomic status. There are consistent findings, however, that do link self-injury with sexual orientation. Lesbian/gay/bisexual/transgender/questioning (LGBTQ) adolescents are at higher risk for self-injury than are heterosexual adolescents, and more specifically, adolescents who identify as bisexual or questioning have the highest levels of risk compared to other sexual minority groups or to heterosexual peers (Whitlock, Eckenrode, & Silverman, 2006).

In examining other demographic variables, according to some studies, NSSI is more common in girls than in boys, but current large-scale research indicates inconsistent results regarding gender differences, often demonstrating no difference in prevalence rates between girls and boys (Muehlenkamp, Williams, et al., 2009; Whitlock, Muehlenkamp, et al., 2009). As an example, in a large sample of middle and high school students in the rural south, researchers found no gender differences in rates of NSSI (Latzman et al., 2010). In contrast, a recent study by Moran et al. (2011) followed a group of adolescents over a 15-year period and found that during the early phase of the study (when adolescents were between the ages of 14 and 19), significant gender differences emerged (10% of girls vs. 6% of boys reported NSSI), and while more girls than boys reported self-harm during every phase of the study, the gender difference was greatest during the younger adolescent years. Therefore, NSSI seems to cut across gender, race, class, and sexual orientation, causing it to be a concern for counselors who work with adolescents from a variety of backgrounds. Another reason these behaviors are of concern is that rather than being viewed as harmless adolescent experimentation, NSSI is associated with a high potential for health risks and severe physical harm, as it generally involves skin cutting with a sharp instrument (occurring in 70%–90% of individuals who self-injure), and can also entail scratching, hitting, inserting objects under the skin, or burning the skin (Nock & Favazza, 2009). Further, NSSI is associated with other serious disorders that emerge for girls during puberty (also discussed elsewhere in this book), including eating disorders, substance abuse, and depression (Kerr & Muehlenkamp, 2010; Klonsky & Muehlenkamp, 2007; Muehlenkamp, Engel, et al., 2009). In addition, although NSSI by definition does not constitute a suicide attempt, 50% to 75% of those with a history of NSSI have also made at least one suicide attempt (Nock & Favazza, 2009). Further, NSSI is one of the strongest predictors of completed suicide in adolescents (Moran et al., 2011).

Because of its prevalence, severity, and onset during a high-risk period of adolescent girls' development, it is important for counselors who work with girls to have a model for understanding the complex functions of this behavior and to be familiar with effective approaches to treatment. Counselors, however, report a general uncertainty about the conceptualization and treatment of NSSI (Healey, Trepal, & Emelianchik-Key, 2010). To address this need, in this chapter I will first discuss NSSI risk factors from a multisystemic perspective and provide models for understanding the maintenance of these behaviors. Next I describe general cognitive behavioral therapy (CBT) treatment approaches for NSSI, including assessment, replacement skills training, and cognitive restructuring. I then present the dialectical behavior therapy (DBT) approach, a promising treatment for adolescents who engage in NSSI. I conclude the chapter with suggestions for prevention and provide resources for counselors, parents, and adolescent girls.

RISK AND MAINTENANCE MODELS FOR NSSI

According to Nock (2010), individuals who self-injure often possess genetic and environmental risk factors that contribute to the likelihood that they will engage in NSSI. For example, there is evidence to indicate that adolescents who engage in NSSI have a genetic predisposition toward high emotional/cognitive reactivity. Compared to adolescents who do not self-injure, adolescents who engage in NSSI display higher physiological reactivity during distressing tasks, demonstrate poorer ability to tolerate this distress, and show deficits in social problem solving (Nock & Mendes, 2008). Further, adolescents who engage in NSSI report that they experience little or no pain during episodes of NSSI, possibly indicating that they might have a high tolerance or decreased sensitivity to pain (Nock & Mendes, 2008). For example, in a diverse sample of young adolescent girls, the majority of participants report little or no pain when engaging in NSSI episodes (Hilt et al., 2008b).

In addition to genetic predisposition, adolescents who engage in NSSI are also more likely to report traumatic experiences in childhood (including experiences such as chronic illness, major surgeries, parental loss) and are more likely to report receiving harsh or critical parenting during their childhood years (Yates, Tracy, & Luthar, 2008). Further, they are likely to have endured aversive childhood experiences, with up to 79% of self-injuring individuals reporting a history of child abuse, maltreatment, and neglect (Yates, 2009).

The presence of these types of risks in a child's life creates intrapersonal and interpersonal vulnerability to NSSI and other types of maladaptive coping behaviors such as eating disorders or substance abuse. Such intrapersonal vulnerabilities include deficits in emotional regulation (e.g., problems with the experience, awareness, and expression of emotions; high levels of aversive emotions; suppression of aversive thoughts and feelings; poor distress tolerance; and poor ability to tolerate negative emotional states; Guerry & Prinstein, 2010; Nock & Mendes, 2008). They are also likely to engage in self-derogation and self-directed anger (Klonsky & Muehlenkamp, 2007). At the same time, these adolescents may develop an interpersonal style that involves poor verbal skills, communication skills deficits, and poor social problem solving. These intra- and interpersonal characteristics all place an adolescent girl at high risk for psychological distress, which can then lead to behaviors such as NSSI.

In sum, certain risk factors (e.g., genetics, childhood maltreatment) create intrapersonal (e.g., emotional dysregulation) and interpersonal vulnerabilities and stressors (e.g., unsupportive social contexts) that increase the likelihood of NSSI. These vulnerabilities also increase the likelihood that a person will develop other maladaptive behaviors that serve the same affective/cognitive regulatory and relational function. For example, eating disorders are very common in individuals with NSSI, and some authors suggest that NSSI serves the same emotion regulation function as that served by certain disordered eating symptoms (e.g., binges, purges). Further, for some individuals, eating disorders and NSSI behaviors often replace one another, so that if NSSI behaviors are controlled, disordered eating symptoms reemerge, or when the disordered eating symptoms become controlled, the NSSI recurs (Muehlenkamp, Engel, et al., 2009). It is therefore important for counselors to examine not only general maladaptive coping strategies but also NSSI-specific risk factors in order to understand why certain individuals choose NSSI as a preferred strategy for coping.

NSSI Specific Vulnerability

Cultural Influences

According to Nock (2010), several processes may serve to operate in the selection of NSSI as a coping strategy versus other types of maladaptive behaviors. First, adolescents are highly affected by cultural messages and ideals. Girls in particular are socialized to believe they should measure up to a physically perfect feminine ideal that can lead to limited forms of self-expression and a negative view of her worth and value (Zila & Kiselica, 2001). They also learn to turn to media images and representations for understanding who they are supposed to be and how they are supposed to act. NSSI is regularly featured in popular media and is very familiar to today's adolescents. High profile icons in popular culture have publicly discussed their personal use of NSSI (e.g., Johnny Depp, Angelina Jolie, Princess Diana, Courtney Love, Fiona Apple, Demi Lovato, Megan Fox, Christina Ricci), and NSSI is prominently featured in many current movies, television programs, books, music, and Internet sites. A recent study examined popular YouTube video clips for examples of self-injury and found that graphic videos of individuals engaging in NSSI are viewed frequently and are rated positively by viewers. Of the 100 most frequently viewed of these videos, many of the videos depicted explicit imagery of individuals who were cutting or burning their wrists, arms, and legs. Of these videos, 80% were accessible to a general audience and 58% contained no warnings about their content. The videos were selected as a "favorite" over 12,000 times, and were viewed over 2 million times by YouTube viewers (Lewis, Heath, St Denis, & Noble, 2011).

This type of prevalence of NSSI images in popular culture serves to normalize and sensationalize the behavior for adolescents and to prime them to consider experimenting with NSSI behaviors that they might not have otherwise considered (Whitlock, Purington, & Gershkovich, 2009). Some research does seem to suggest that NSSI is more common in adolescents who frequently interact with these Internet videos or images (Whitlock et al., 2009). Counselors therefore need to assess for an adolescent girl's Internet and media use history to determine how much it might have introduced her to NSSI or how it reinforces her NSSI behaviors (Whitlock et al., 2009). Counselors need to consider that while certain online communities can serve as an important support system for adolescent who engage in NSSI, other websites might serve to reinforce NSSI attitudes and behaviors (Whitlock, Lader, & Conterio, 2007).

Peer Influences

Peers serve as another primary source of influence, as most adolescents who engage in NSSI report that they learned about it from their friends, siblings, and the media (Nock, 2010). When adolescent use of NSSI behaviors is widespread or highly publicized in a community, there are often reports of contagion effects (i.e., NSSI increasing because individuals have seen, known, or heard about others self-injuring) that have been observed in school, college, community, and treatment settings (Prinstein et al., 2010; Walsh, 2006).

Research indicates that there is a complex association between NSSI and peer NSSI use, and this association is particularly strong for young adolescent girls, as peer relationships are highly important to them during this period (Prinstein et al., 2010). As adolescents observe their peer group, they may learn about NSSI as a viable option for self-regulation, for fitting in with peers, or as a method for gaining attention (Heilbron & Prinstein, 2008; Nock, Prinstein, & Sterba, 2009). In addition to connecting with others, NSSI might be negatively reinforced when an adolescent's behaviors are used as ways to avoid certain peers and activities (Hilt et al., 2008a) and to distance herself when she is already feeling marginalized from peers, school, family, and her community (Moran et al., 2011). Further, NSSI is used to cope with interpersonal stressors that often intensify in adolescence (e.g., arguments with significant others, breakups with romantic relationships, peer victimization). Compared to girls who do not engage in NSSI, girls who use NSSI report more unpleasant stressful events in the year preceding the onset of NSSI, and most of these stressors are related to interpersonal events (Hilt et al., 2008a). The fact that the decision to engage in NSSI is associated with a desire to connect with peers, avoid peers, cope with peer problems, or to shock peers makes it important for counselors to assess the client for the peer-related function that NSSI serves in her life.

Individual Beliefs

An additional influence on whether an adolescent girl uses NSSI is whether or not she believes it is an effective method for communicating the pain or distress she is experiencing. In many cases, when she tried to give voice to her pain through words, crying, or screaming to parents or significant others, she may have been invalidated or ignored. In turn, she may have learned to suppress her feelings and communicate only those things that she believes others will want to hear; however, her true feelings remained unexpressed (Pipher, 1994). In contrast, she also learned that engaging in NSSI sends a strong signal to others that cannot be overlooked and that her scars describe her pain in a way that words could never express. The book, *A Bright Red Scream* (Strong, 1998), describes the signaling and communication function of NSSI in vivid detail. The young adult fiction novel *Cut* by Patricia McCormick (2011) also describes this function.

Finally, young adolescent girls in particular may choose NSSI for pragmatic reasons; it is readily available and easy to use. While 12-year-old girls might have difficulty obtaining alcohol, drugs, or even binge foods, they can easily have access to methods for NSSI. Even in a highly structured environment, adolescents can escape to a bathroom stall at school to cut their thigh with a paper clip or lock themselves in the bathroom at home to burn an arm with a hair curling iron. As stated previously, most girls express that they experience little to no pain during NSSI episodes, and it is powerfully reinforced: NSSI works quickly and is highly effective as a strategy for self-regulation. Many individuals who use NSSI report that it is much more rapid and effective in relieving distress than any other form of maladaptive behavior, including alcohol and other drugs or food binges and purges (Strong, 1998).

In sum, adolescent girls are at risk for NSSI when they:

- Have difficulty verbalizing their feelings
- Feel invalidated and marginalized by their support systems
- Have high levels of psychological distress and emotional reactivity
- Are vulnerable to cultural and media messages about NSSI
- Experience intrapersonal stressors
- Possess few effective strategies for connecting with or creating boundaries between peers or family

198 ADOLESCENT GIRLS IN DISTRESS

Once she begins using NSSI behaviors for coping, the behaviors are maintained over time by several functions, which are described in the sections that follow.

Maintenance of NSSI Behaviors

Once an adolescent girl begins to engage in NSSI, the behavior can serve a variety of complex functions that serve to reinforce the NSSI over time. According to Nock (2010), Nock and Cha (2009), and Klonsky and Muehlenkamp (2007), these functions most commonly include:

Affect Regulation. The use of NSSI to regulate affect is its most prevalent function. Prior to an NSSI episode, adolescents report that they typically experience intense feelings of anger, anxiety, and/or frustration, and believe that the NSSI will release urgent emotional pressure, block negative feelings, or manage stress (Nock, 2010). Many adolescent girls feel out of control in many areas of their bodies (e.g., weight gain, menstrual cycles, body changes) and may believe that the NSSI enables them to reestablish a sense of control that they can't achieve through any other means. Adolescents also report that they use NSSI to resist suicidal urges when they are able to release the pain and tension they are experiencing.

Antidissociation. Adolescents who engage in NSSI often report feeling "nothing," "empty," "numb," or "unreal" and NSSI helps to interrupt these episodes of dissociation or depersonalization. Adolescents report that the behavior helps them to "feel something" even if it is pain, and to "feel real again" when their sense of self is disrupted.

Self-Punishment. Many adolescent girls report that they experience extreme self-hatred and self-directed anger, and believe that there are aspects of themselves that deserve punishment. Girls who have experienced sexual abuse and the trauma of early sexual experiences often want to punish or get rid of sexualized parts of the body that are seen as "bad" (e.g., cutting the breasts or genitals). Through the use of NSSI, they believe they can punish themselves and subsequently report feeling "cleansed" or "satisfied" after NSSI episodes.

Establishing Interpersonal Boundaries. Adolescents may use NSSI as a way to affirm boundaries between self and others. By using the skin as a way to visibly mark the boundary between the self and the external world, they may feel more independent and in control.

Interpersonal Influence. As noted previously, self-injury serves a social function in that it can be an attempt to influence others by communicating the extent of one's suffering (showing a romantic partner how much she is hurt by a breakup), to gain attention (cutting to get parents' attention), fit in with peers (showing peers her scars), or to disrupt family conflict so that the attention is refocused on the adolescent's self-injury (having an NSSI episode so parents will stop arguing to focus on assisting the adolescent).

Sensation Seeking. NSSI can generate feelings of excitement, resulting in a rush or high that comes from the release of endorphins. This function may be particularly salient when NSSI is performed around friends.

NSSI behaviors are effective in achieving these functions in an adolescent girl's life, and they are maintained through intrapersonal and interpersonal reinforcement processes that perpetuate NSSI over time. As suggested by Nock (2010), research supports four specific reinforcement processes that maintain NSSI behavior: (a) intrapersonal negative reinforcement when the NSSI behavior is followed by tension release or the cessation of negative thoughts and feelings; (b) intrapersonal positive reinforcement, occurring when the NSSI behavior is followed by an increase in desired thoughts or feelings (e.g., feeling satisfied that one has adequately punished oneself); (c) interpersonal positive reinforcement, when the NSSI behavior is followed by an increase in a desired social outcome (e.g., attention, support, such as when adolescents feel more connected with their peer group or receive attention from their parents); and (d) interpersonal negative reinforcement, when the NSSI behavior is followed by a decrease in an undesired social outcome (e.g., peers stop bullying, parents stop fighting) (Nock, 2010). Because the NSSI behaviors are effective and are reinforced, many girls do not view them as problematic and are not interested in eliminating NSSI, which can be a significant impediment to treatment (Hoffman & Kress, 2010).

These research findings indicate the importance of understanding the function that NSSI serves in adolescent girls' lives and how it is reinforced over time. The findings also indicate the necessity for a counselor to take the time to engage the client in treatment, as she will not likely be motivated to stop these behaviors because they are so effective in helping her cope with stressors. They also suggest the need for treatment that addresses the actual NSSI behaviors, but also the intrapersonal and interpersonal vulnerabilities associated with NSSI (including affect dysregulation, inability to tolerate uncomfortable feelings, self-invalidation, and interpersonal deficits). These areas will be emphasized in the section that follows.

CASE EXAMPLE

Julia is a 15-year-old girl from a rural town. She lives with three brothers and an older sister in a small home in much need of repair. Her father is currently unemployed. Her mother works only part time, so the family is struggling financially. Her homelife is also unstable due to her parents' abusive relationship. They get into verbal altercations frequently and at times become physically violent with one another. On one occasion, she witnessed her father waving a gun in her mother's face, threatening to kill her. When Julia ran into the room, the father threatened to shoot her as well. Fortunately, he was able to calm down and leave the house without harming them, but Julia was terrified by the incident and still remains fearful of her father. She is also afraid of her mother's reactions to her, which range from cursing and screaming to crying and avoiding her children for days. While her brothers and sister tend to fight with their parents and to stay away from home as much as they can, Julia has learned to be silent at home, staying in her room and avoiding others. She never invites friends into her home and she does not get invited to very many social gatherings with peers. As a result of her isolation, she has poor social skills, particularly in the area of communicating her needs and wants to others.

At school, Julia prefers to stay in the background rather than being the center of attention. She lacks confidence in her appearance and in her personality, believing she will be the object of ridicule if anyone really gets to know her. Lately she is realizing that she is sexually attracted to other girls, but she is not sure what this means because she also has crushes on boys at her school as well. She feels guilt about her same-sex attractions and never acts on her feelings, and she realizes her parents would further reject her if she ever told them she was bisexual or a lesbian. After spending so much time witnessing her parents' conflicts, hiding in her room, and keeping all of her thoughts and feelings to herself, Julia often feels like she is going to internally explode.

One day she heard her sister discussing a friend who came to school with scars on her arms from NSSI. She said the girl was a follower of a certain Internet site about self-injury, and that the girl was gaining a lot of attention at school because of her scars and strange behaviors. Julia decided to Google "self-injury" and stumbled upon hundreds of sites and videos with demonstrations of how to self-injure, from cutting with razors and glass to burning herself. She was scared to try this out, but the next time her parents began a loud argument, Julia locked herself in her room, got a razor from the medicine cabinet, and cut the inside of her thighs (as the videos recommended so that no one could see her cuts). As the blood began to flow, Julia realized that she didn't really feel any pain, only relief that she could numb out her feelings, not hear her parents screaming, and just focus on the warm blood on her legs. She felt cleansed and relieved when it was over, and it wasn't until she began to clean the blood up from the floor that she realized what she had done. She felt guilty and ashamed, but she also felt refreshed, like she had just released some pent up pain. She began to cut herself on a regular basis, always feeling clean and fresh afterward. On one occasion she cut too deeply and had to drag herself into her parents' room to ask for help, and they both acted immediately to give her medical attention. Afterward they gave her increased attention and fought less when she was at home, so Julia hoped that her NSSI would help her parents to stop fighting with each other and to pay attention to her instead.

Discussion Questions

1. What are the factors that place Julia at risk for the development of NSSI? Based on the ecological model, what influence has she had from the larger culture, her peer group, and from her family that contribute to her NSSI?
2. What are intrapersonal factors that contribute to and maintain the problem? How is the problem reinforced (either positively or negatively) by inter- or intrapersonal factors?
3. If you were Julia's counselor, where would you start in your work with her?

TREATMENT FOR NSSI IN ADOLESCENT GIRLS

The first step in preparing to work with girls who engage in NSSI is for counselors to examine their own personal reactions to self-injury. This work can cause feelings of helplessness, disgust, and frustration, and the counselor needs to learn to manage his or her reactions and to closely monitor and set limits on his or her ability to work with this client problem (White, Trepal-Wollenzier, & Nolan, 2002). Counselors should refrain from attempts to force the client to eliminate NSSI behaviors before she has had an opportunity to develop more positive coping strategies that can adequately take the place of NSSI. Instead of pushing her to eliminate NSSI, counselors should focus on acceptance and helping her develop the desire to self-protect and to increase her quality of life. This is accomplished by reducing the frequency of self-injury episodes through increasing the use of positive behavior replacement skills, emotion-focused strategies, life skills development, and cognitive restructuring (Walsh, 2006). Counselors may find it helpful to engage in frequent consultation and supervision in order to remain objective and as neutral as possible (Zila & Kiselica, 2001).

Cognitive behavioral approaches have the most research support (Klonsky & Muehlenkamp, 2007) for NSSI, and forms of CBT include problem-solving therapy, manual-assisted cognitive therapy, DBT, and standard CBT. I will first describe the CBT approach in general, and then provide a more detailed discussion of DBT, a form of CBT treatment that provides the most promise for the treatment of adolescent NSSI.

In general, CBT approaches share common therapeutic strategies such as using functional assessment of the self-injury, teaching skills for replacing the self-injury, teaching life skills (e.g., problem solving, distress tolerance, assertive communication), and cognitive restructuring.

Assessment

Walsh (2006) recommends that the counselor take a low-key, inquisitive, but dispassionate stance during the assessment process, so as not to show the client that he or she is shocked or horrified by client disclosures, but also to refrain from reinforcing the behaviors by reacting in ways that are similar to significant others in the client's life (peer groups, parents). By asking questions and responding with interest but without alarm, clients will become more comfortable in disclosing their history with NSSI.

The initial evaluation can be conducted informally through clinical interview or formally through a structured interview or self-report instrument. Some of the commonly used structured instruments include: Suicide Attempt Self Injury Interview (SASII; Linehan, Comtois, Brown, Heard, & Wagner, 2006) and the Comprehensive Self Injurious Thoughts and Behaviors Interview (SITBI; Nock, Holmberg, Photos, & Michel, 2007). Recommended self-report instruments include the Functional Assessment of Self-Mutilation (FASM; Lloyd, Kelley, & Hope, 1997), the Inventory of Statements about Self Injury (ISAS; Glen & Klonsky, 2007), and the Deliberate Self-Harm Inventory (Gratz, 2001). When conducting an assessment on a more informal basis, the counselor should ask about such areas as:

- Onset of NSSI
- Methods used and instruments with which it is performed
- Frequency of NSSI behaviors
- Most recent instance of NSSI
- Medical severity
- Level of pain experienced

- Context in which it occurs (e.g., events, thoughts, and emotions that precede, accompany, and follow NSSI episodes)
- Factors that contribute to vulnerability (e.g., use of alcohol or drugs, sleep problems)
- Positive and negative intrapersonal and interpersonal reinforcement functions of the behavior (as reviewed previously)
- Related behaviors that also interfere with quality of life (e.g., substance abuse, eating disorders, impulsive sexual behaviors, staying in abusive relationships) (Hoffman & Kress, 2010; Nock, 2010; Walsh, 2006)

Replacement Skills

After assessment of the behavior, clients benefit from learning initial skills for replacing NSSI behaviors. Replacement skills are coping strategies that can be used instead of the impulsive use of NSSI to cope with emotional pain, numbness, or emptiness. Some suggestions for nine types of NSSI replacement skills are listed below.

NSSI REPLACEMENT SKILLS

1. Temporary, negative replacement skills:
   - Hold an ice cube until it melts or rub it across your skin
   - Chew on something with a strong taste (peppermint, grapefruit, chili peppers)
   - Take a very cold or very hot shower
   - Mark on skin with a red colored marker
   - Snap a rubber band on arm or leg
   - Apply a temporary tattoo, then scratch off with a fingernail
2. Mindful breathing:
   - Slow down breathing, take deep breaths
3. Visualization:
   - Guided imagery
   - Visualizing a calm, safe place
4. Physical movement and exercise:
   - Exercise vigorously
   - Punch a pillow or mattress
   - Scream into your pillow

(continued)

NSSI REPLACEMENT SKILLS (*continued*)

- Squeeze a stress ball or squish Play Doh
- Rip something up
- Make some noise
- Massage neck, hands, and feet
5. Writing:
   - Express feelings in a journal
   - Compose a poem or song about your feelings
   - Write your negative feelings and then rip the paper to shreds
6. Artistic expression:
   - Paint, draw, or scribble on a big piece of paper with red ink
7. Playing and listening to music:
   - Listen to music that expresses your emotional state
   - Play or listen to calming music
8. Communicating with others:
   - Call someone from your support system
   - Visit a supportive online resource
9. Diversion techniques
   - Watch TV or a movie
   - Take a bath or hot shower
   - Spend time with a pet dog or cat
   - Wrap yourself in a warm blanket
   - Physically leave the setting

Sources: Cornell Research Program on Self-Injurious Behavior (2012), Kilburn & Whitlock (2010), Walsh (2006)

It should be noted that the negative replacement behaviors category (no. 1 in the text box) represents examples of behaviors that can be used *temporarily* until the client develops a full repertoire of positive behavioral, emotional, and cognitive coping strategies. Suggesting these types of behaviors can be helpful to some clients early in their treatment because they seem similar to their typical NSSI behaviors and might serve the same symbolic representation and coping function as NSSI but without the actual tissue damage (Walsh, 2006). However, Walsh cautions that these behaviors should only be used as a temporary bridge to overcome initial urges for NSSI episodes, and that that they might be contraindicated for certain clients. For some clients, the stimulus cues of these replacement behaviors might be too similar to self-injury rituals and might serve as a trigger for an actual self-injury episode. Therefore, it is recommended that these skills be used only in the early transitional stage of treatment when clients have not yet developed other more functional skills (Walsh, 2006).

Clients should develop a set of coping skills from multiple categories listed in the text box. For example, clients need coping skills that are not simply based on distractions (no. 9 in the box). Distractions (e.g., television watching, reading a book) do not solve problems, but they distract the client long enough to overcome the urge to engage in NSSI. Therefore, the client is not able to learn that she can manage her emotions directly or take actions to make the situation better for herself. For additional behaviors and strategies, visit the Cornell Research Program on Self-Injurious Behavior (CRPSIB) at www.crpsib.com/userfiles/File/Coping-Alt%20Strat-REV-ENGLISH.pdf.

Cognitive Restructuring Skills

In addition to teaching replacement skills, life skills such as communication skills, assertiveness, and distress tolerance are also taught in the CBT approach (these skills are reviewed in the following sections on DBT). Cognitive restructuring is also a life skill emphasized throughout CBT approaches. The counselor begins by examining the types of beliefs the adolescent girl might hold, including such thoughts as: "NSSI gives me a sense of control I don't have anywhere else." "If I don't act on my urge to cut, I feel like I am going to explode and do something crazy!" "NSSI is acceptable and necessary. I have to do something to reduce my unpleasant feelings." "I hate my body and it is my enemy; it is disgusting and should be punished." "Nobody notices or believes how badly I feel until I start doing NSSI." "I am generally numb and empty, but NSSI reminds me that I am real and that I can feel something" (Newman, 2009; Walsh, 2006).

The counselor first works to understand the adolescent's beliefs and then reflects them to her in a way that validates her experience. Next the counselor can help the client recognize the connection between her thoughts and her NSSI episodes. Once this connection is made, the client can begin to modify her maladaptive beliefs by replacing them with more positive, less self-destructive thoughts (Newman, 2009; see Walsh, 2006 for a manualized approach to teaching cognitive restructuring to clients experiencing NSSI).

DIALECTICAL BEHAVIOR THERAPY

While I have reviewed the general treatment elements of CBT, DBT is a more specific yet comprehensive approach to treatment. DBT, currently the treatment with the most empirical support for NSSI, is a therapy approach first developed by Marsha Linehan for clients with Borderline Personality Disorder (BPD; Linehan, 1993a). DBT is considered the gold standard for reducing suicidal and self-destructive behaviors in clients with BPD, with demonstrated treatment effectiveness in at least seven randomized controlled trials that were conducted by four independent research teams (Linehan et al., 2006; Lynch & Cozza, 2009). Although developed for adults with BPD, Linehan's DBT model has also been adapted for use with suicidal and self-injuring adolescents, yielding highly promising results in reducing NSSI (Miller, Rathaus, & Linehan, 2007). The treatment model was not designed specifically for girls, but has been successful with adolescents of both genders. The treatment model described in the paragraphs to follow is based upon Miller et al.'s (2007) research-based adaptation of outpatient DBT for adolescent clients at high risk for self-injury. While a complete description of the model is beyond the scope of this chapter, the reader is referred to the treatment manuals of Miller et al. (2007) and Linehan (1993a).

The comprehensive, multimodal, 16-week treatment approach comprises sessions that serve to: (a) directly address skills for interpersonal effectiveness, self-regulation, and distress tolerance; (b) provide the structure necessary to motivate, reinforce, individualize, and generalize these new skills; and (c) identify and interrupt learned behavioral sequences that lead to NSSI. It incorporates the use of individual therapy, multifamily training groups, family therapy, telephone consultations for both adolescents and family members, and a consultation team to provide ongoing support for counselors (Miller et al., 2007).

Individual Therapy With Adolescents

The DBT approach for adolescents involves a relationship with a primary counselor who conducts weekly individual counseling sessions. The counselor-client relationship is paramount in assisting the client to increase motivation for change and to learn new strategies for coping with his or her stressful thoughts, feelings, and events. The counselor's role is to be active, supportive, and collaborative throughout the process. The counselor works to convey acceptance of clients by taking their responses seriously, by providing validation of their pain, and by displaying an understanding of their choices to cope with this distress through the use of NSSI as a highly effective but self-destructive strategy (Muehlenkamp, 2006). The counselor's role is also to instill hope, to encourage the client, and to focus on client strengths.

Client acceptance, however, must also be balanced with a commitment to change, so that the counselor continuously challenges clients to eliminate NSSI and other behaviors that greatly interfere with their quality of life. As stated earlier, many adolescents will be reluctant to give up a behavior that works so effectively in so many ways and may be in treatment only at the insistence of their parents, so the counselor may need to spend several sessions building the relationship and employing strategies to enhance the client's commitment to change.

JULIA'S DBT TREATMENT, PART ONE

Julia's counselor focused initially on validation of her thoughts, feelings, and choices to use NSSI as a method for coping. As Julia was not familiar with expressing herself or with having a caring adult to validate her feelings, this was very effective in establishing initial trust and rapport. Over time, Julia began to trust the counselor's assertion that there might be other strategies for coping with her feelings rather than always turning to NSSI, and she began to believe that she did deserve a better quality of life.

As part of establishing a therapeutic relationship, it also critical for counselors to discuss issues of confidentiality. When working with clients who engage in NSSI, the counselor should establish a balance between the ethical principles of protecting client autonomy versus nonmaleficence (the principle of *doing no harm*). The client has a right to choose NSSI as a preferred coping strategy, but the counselor also has the obligation to protect the client from harm (Hoffman & Kress, 2010). In working with adolescents, there is also an ethical issue of protecting client confidentiality versus the need to disclose information to parents (White Kress, Drouhard, & Costin, 2006). Adolescents will be reluctant to trust the counselor if they believe that the counselor will call their parents every time they discuss an episode of self-injury. Miller et al. (2007) recommend that counselors can assure clients that a parent will not be contacted each time they self-injure, but that a parent will be notified if the counselor deems that the behaviors are escalating in frequency or in level of severity. To preserve client respect, adolescents can also be assured that they will be involved as much as possible in the process of parental disclosure (Hoffman & Kress, 2010). This helps in building trust as well as in meeting ethical and legal obligations for protecting client dignity, respecting parental rights, and promoting client well-being. However, if the behaviors are detected within a school, state and local laws may dictate whether or not student confidentiality and parent contact apply (White Kress et al., 2006). The American School Counseling Association asserts that parents should be contacted when any student is clearly at risk for harm, and the Cornell Research Program on Self-Injurious Behavior for Adolescents and Young Adults further indicates that elementary or secondary school staff should inform parents about their child's NSSI even if the student is not an immediate threat to herself (Bubrick, Goodman, & Whitlock, 2010). The school counselor and relevant staff also have the responsibility to ensure that the parents will make an effort to seek outside counseling or help for their child (Bubrick et al., 2010).

Initial sessions should be comprised of a thorough assessment of problem behaviors and skill deficits (see the preceding assessment section). According to the DBT model, the counselor can integrate the results of this assessment within four DBT treatment target areas: (a) decreasing life-threatening behaviors (e.g., NSSI, suicidal thoughts); (b) decreasing therapy-interfering behaviors (e.g., dropout, noncompliance, canceling sessions, leaving early); (c) decreasing behaviors that interfere with the quality of life, and (d) increasing behavioral skills (addressed primarily through the multifamily skills groups, described in the next section). These broad areas and specific behaviors can then be written into an initial treatment plan with accompanying goals and objectives.

JULIA'S DBT TREATMENT, PART TWO

In the example of Julia, her list of behaviors in need of change could be prioritized as follows: (a) decreasing NSSI, (b) decreasing her tendency to cancel sessions at the last minute, (c) decreasing her tendency to isolate at home and at school, and (d) developing new coping skills, assertiveness skills, and social skills.

Treatment Onset

As treatment commences, the primary objective of the individual sessions is to assist the client in eliminating NSSI behaviors by teaching clients to first identify relevant antecedent events, thoughts, and feelings that precede NSSI and the consequences that follow it. As described by Miller et al. (2007) and Linehan (1993b), clients are asked to complete weekly diary cards to address these aspects. The diary cards assess the following: (a) the specific problem behavior(s); (b) the specific precipitating event (e.g., What were you doing, thinking, or feeling at that moment? Why did the NSSI happen on that day instead of some other time?); (c) vulnerability factors (e.g., alcohol or drugs, poor sleep or eating, stressful event); (d) the entire chain of events that led up to the NSSI; and (e) consequences of the behavior (What happened next? What effect did the NSSI have on you or your environment?).

Finally, the last part of the diary card asks the client to begin identifying solutions that will disrupt the chain of antecedent behaviors, reduce vulnerability factors, or extinguish reinforcers of the behavior. The client can examine the specific chain of behaviors that happened before the NSSI and can examine what she could have done differently at each step that might have avoided the problem.

JULIA'S DBT TREATMENT, PART THREE

Julia engaged in NSSI late one night after her parents began a loud argument at the dinner table about their lack of finances and blamed her for running up such a high tab with her counselor. She ran to her room and shut the door, but looked at NSSI sites on the Internet and waited until they had gone to sleep to engage in NSSI so that they would not try to stop her. After cutting herself with a razor, she felt more in control, less tense, and was able to go to sleep. In reviewing the diary card with her counselor, she recognized that she could have disrupted the chain of events by leaving the table as soon as her parents began to argue, or even eating alone so that she would not have to eat with her parents. She realized that hiding in her room and looking at NSSI sites only made things worse. In brainstorming possible solutions, she stated that she could have called her counselor, talked to one of her siblings if they had been home, or left the house to go for a walk. She also saw this as an impetus to make a few friends so that she would have a supportive person with whom to talk.

In sum, the diary card is an essential part of the individual therapy process, as it assists with self-monitoring throughout the week, helps to structure sessions through a review of problems, and assists in the generation of potential solutions.

Multifamily Skills Training Groups

While the individual therapy counseling sessions described previously help to address the chain of behaviors that precede and follow NSSI episodes in order to generate solutions for disrupting this process, adolescent girls also need specific skills in order to be able to implement these new solutions. If they are to learn to employ adaptive coping strategies, they need the ability to gain awareness of their thoughts, feelings, and actions, to tolerate the pain or stress that often occurs with life circumstances, to regulate their emotional states more effectively, and to become more effective in communicating their needs and wants in relationships. Therefore, the DBT approach recommends skills training groups to assist clients in mastering four essential skills: *mindfulness, distress tolerance, emotion regulation,* and *interpersonal effectiveness* (Linehan, 1993b). A fifth skill set, *walking the middle path,* was added by Miller et al. (2007) to specifically address the extreme, polarized thinking that is typical in adolescent/parent conflicts. These will be described briefly in the sections that follow.

Miller recommends that the skills training groups involve both adolescents and at least one member of her family, so that there are five to seven adolescents and five to seven parents in every group. While these are intended to be mixed gender groups, there is also a benefit for girls to have girls-only groups so that they can feel freer to share gender-related experiences. The same family member should attend each time so that a consistent parent can learn the skills, practice, help his/her child implement the skills at home, and learn new skills that can help strengthen his/her parenting practices and provide more effective responses to meet his or her child's needs. The groups meet weekly and are structured as follows: warm up practice consisting of mindfulness exercises, homework review, learning a new skill, and a wrap up exercise. In the first sessions of the groups, issues of confidentiality and risks of contagion should be addressed. Because discussions and displays of NSSI can be triggers for members, the leaders can inform members that the purpose of the group is a place to learn new skills and how to apply them in daily life. Members are not to discuss the specifics of NSSI and are urged to reduce the public display of scars, wounds, or bandages by keeping them covered during group sessions (Walsh, 2006). If members want to talk about NSSI incidents, they can be reminded that their individual sessions are the appropriate place for these types of discussions.

Skill Set One: Core Mindfulness Skills.   Mindfulness involves paying attention to one's emotions, thoughts, and physical experiences without necessarily trying to end them, numb them, or avoid them. It involves observing, describing, and experiencing emotions in the moment in a nonjudgmental way and learning to be in control of one's attention. As clients become more mindful of the present, they learn to understand the ebb and flow of their emotions (McCabe et al., 2004).

The DBT model teaches mindfulness by introducing three states of mind: (a) reasonable mind, a state in which one's behaviors are controlled primarily by rationality and logic; (b) emotion mind, a mind state in which one's behaviors are determined by emotions; and (c) wise mind, a mind state that synthesizes all ways of knowing, which produces knowing through intuition, or what can be described as an inner experience of truth or deep inner wisdom. These three mind states can be taught in session through a game of charades, with leaders first enacting one of the three states of mind and asking members to guess which one was being portrayed. Members can also take turns acting out scenarios, having other members select the appropriate mind state, and then asking them to describe how they arrived at their decision.

Members are then taught skills for observing their thoughts with awareness. For example, in the *wordless watching* exercise, members are asked to practice mindfully watching their thoughts and feelings come and go as if they are on a conveyor belt. Next, they learn skills for labeling their thoughts and reactions in a nonjudgmental manner. For example, members might be asked to use a wordless watching exercise by describing their experiences without placing judgment on their observations. They are also taught to approach tasks *one-mindfully*, learning to control their attention by just focusing on just one thing at a time. Instead of multitasking, they are asked to focus attention on only the task at hand. A mindfulness exercise that incorporates one-mindfulness is to ask members to mindfully unwrap a Hershey's Kiss, keeping their attention on the foil, the unwrapping process, and on the feel of the chocolate. This exercise can also be replicated with holding an ice cube, mindfully observing how it feels as the ice melts in one's hand. These exercises are repeated in each session and members are also asked to practice mindfulness throughout the week. These skills are deemed essential for gaining awareness of what one is experiencing in order to make mindful decisions that will disrupt the typical sequence of thoughts, feelings, and behaviors that lead to NSSI.

JULIA'S DBT TREATMENT, PART FOUR

Julia attended the group sessions with her mother, who reluctantly agreed to participate. Julia learned to become more aware of her thoughts and feelings, and practiced trying to observe them rather than cutting them off or numbing them. She realized how mindlessly she had been going throughout her day and how out of touch she had been with her emotions. She liked the one-mindfully exercises where she would focus intently on one activity at a time, rather than feeling scattered and unaware of what she was doing.

Skill Set Two: Emotion Regulation.   In this module, members learn how to identify, observe, and describe emotions, regulate intense or painful emotions, increase positive emotions, and reduce vulnerability to negative emotions. As they practice emotion regulation, clients recognize that they do have control over how they react to emotional experiences and that they can change their emotional responses.

Some specific skills for emotion regulation include processes for observing and describing emotions. This can be taught experientially by asking members to examine all of the aspects of what goes on for them when an emotion gets triggered. The group leaders can play music or movie clips designed to provoke emotional reactions, and members are asked to listen or watch nonjudgmentally, directing their attention to their inner experiences in response to the clip. They are then asked to describe the emotions that emerged in addition to thoughts, body changes, urges, observations that were associated with those emotions. In addition, they are asked to notice the secondary emotions that might have been associated with the primary emotion elicited. For example, Julia might label her emotional response to caring so much about what other girls think about her as "stupid," feel guilty about having the emotion in the first place, or try to block the emotion. Instead, members are taught to respond to negative or uncomfortable feelings with understanding and self-compassion. Responding to emotions and their associated effects in this way will decrease emotional intensity and lead to an increased sense of mastery (Safer et al., 2009).

Other skills include *reducing vulnerability* (i.e., decreasing the likelihood of negative emotions by caring for oneself physically, eating a balanced diet, getting enough sleep and exercise, and avoiding mood-altering drugs), *increasing positive emotions* (i.e., increasing daily pleasant events), *building mastery* (i.e., completing daily activities that contribute to a sense of competence and mastery), and *acting opposite to current emotions* (i.e., learning to change emotional reactions by acting in a manner opposite to the emotion one is currently experiencing, such as approaching a feared situation instead of avoiding it).

JULIA'S DBT TREATMENT, PART FIVE

In session, Julia learned that she could reduce her vulnerability to NSSI by planning for and eating well-balanced meals, avoiding too much caffeine, and exercising at least several times per week. She also felt better when she spent some time with her siblings or peers each day, so she became more committed to developing peer relationships at school. She also tried to include daily activities that she enjoyed, although this took some experimentation to learn what she does and does not like to do. She also decided to try harder in school, making a commitment to making better grades and even planning for college.

Skill Set Three: Interpersonal Effectiveness. The interpersonal effectiveness module emphasizes skills for maintaining one's personal values and beliefs while striving to improve overall relationships. For example, members learn the acronym DEAR MAN to help them remember the components of assertiveness: Describe (describe situation in factual manner), Express (express feelings using I statements), Assert (ask clearly for what you want or do not want), Reinforce (explain the benefits to the other person if he or she complies with your request), stay Mindful (keep your focus on what you want), Appear confident (make eye contact, use a confident tone), and Negotiate (ask for feedback, offer alternative solutions, and be mindful of when to agree to disagree). Miller et al. (2007) recommend that interpersonal skills can best be learned through group role plays. First, one of the facilitators can role play a hypothetical conflict he or she is having with someone outside of the group, and members can coach him or her in making effective responses. Next, either two adolescents or an adolescent/parent pair can role play in front of the group, with members providing coaching based on the interpersonal skills learned in the group.

JULIA'S DBT TREATMENT, PART SIX

Julia realized that she needed to assert herself more in all of her relationships, as she had never had this modeled for her. The next time she had a specific conflict with her mother, she tried the DEAR MAN strategy: D: Mom, My curfew is now 9 p.m. and I believe this is too early; E: I have a new friend and I like spending time with her, and I believe I am responsible enough to handle a later curfew; A: I would like a new curfew of 10 p.m. starting this Saturday; R: If this works, I think we will have a lot less fighting between us and we will be able to focus on more important things; M: I know that you are worried about my self-injury but I would like to keep this discussion about my new curfew, which will help me have better relationships with friends; A: (Looks mom in the eye, does not become defensive); N: What do you think about this idea? How can I help you make your decision?

Skill Set Four: Distress Tolerance. Distress tolerance is the ability to effectively tolerate emotional pain in situations that cannot be changed, at least in the present moment. By accepting a situation that cannot be changed and not struggling against it, a client is able to cope with it more effectively (Safer et al., 2009). Further, distress tolerance skills help a client to self-soothe and distract if necessary in order to prevent impulsive decisions or actions.

Distress tolerance skills are divided into two components: skills for accepting reality and skills for crisis survival. Accepting reality skills assist clients in accepting life in the moment, just as it is, even when it is painful or uncomfortable. These skills include *observing one's breath* through deep breathing and *half-smiling* (triggering positive emotions associated with a smile). Skills for crisis survival involve engaging in activities that help a client remain functional without resorting to behaviors that make things worse. These could involve doing activities to improve the moment in a small way, whether it is through prayer, taking a break, or using positive thoughts. These might also include ways to provide self-nurturance through self-soothing strategies. In DBT, these strategies are presented to members through using the five senses (with examples): vision (art, nature), hearing (soft, pleasant music), smell (scented candles), taste (herbal teas, chocolates), or touch (velvet pillows). In Miller's groups, the leaders set up these types of objects on a table and ask members to select one object that appeals to them. As the leaders lower the lighting and play soft music, group members engage in self-soothing by mindfully engaging with the selected object. Following this exercise, leaders ask members to describe how they felt before, during, and after the experience, including how they might incorporate self-soothing into their daily routines outside of the group.

JULIA'S DBT TREATMENT, PART SEVEN

Julia learned that she tended to avoid her painful feelings, especially because she felt there was nothing she could do to feel better other than use NSSI to numb them. She liked the concept of trying to improve the moment in a small way, because many times her stressors occurred at home and she could not change the situation. When she felt distress at school regarding her insecurity and sexual feelings, she also liked having a repertoire of self-soothing strategies on which to rely. At school she chose to take deep breaths and get a drink of water, leave the situation to go to the bathroom, or change her thoughts to more positive ones. While at home she learned to put on headphones and listen to music, take a walk through her neighborhood, cuddle with the family dog, or to light a scented candle. She also learned to write about her feelings in a journal and to openly share her feelings during her counseling sessions.

Skill Set Five: Walking the Middle Path. This skill-training module helps adolescents and family members to address unbalanced, polarized thinking and behaviors among teens and family members in order to achieve a more balanced lifestyle. Members are encouraged to move away from black/white, either/or thinking, to consider others' perspectives, to realize that there are multiple ways to view any situation, and to practice examining all sides of a situation. These concepts are then applied to three common parent–teen dilemmas: (a) being too loose versus being too strict; (b) making light of a particular problem behavior versus making too much of typical adolescent behaviors; and (c) pushing away versus holding on too tightly. Members are directed to identify the point where they currently are on a balance scale for each of these dilemmas and where their family member is, and to describe a middle path that might create a more successful outcome for both adolescent and parent.

The module also teaches members to achieve a balance between acceptance- and change-oriented skills. Acceptance skills are taught through encouraging members to use validating responses. These involve active-listening skills: the ability to communicate to another individual that you have considered the person's feelings seriously, that his or her feelings make sense and have been communicated clearly to you, and that you are trying to understand his or her perspective. Members practice active-listening skills by applying them to scenarios in group and then practicing them with their family members. In contrast, change-oriented skills are taught through basic behavioral principles (e.g., reinforcers, shaping, extinction, punishment) that operate to either increase or decrease particular behaviors. Members practice specific exercises using principles for decreasing behaviors and emphasize differences between extinction and punishment. They also practice exercises to better understand how positive reinforcement serves to increase behaviors.

JULIA'S DBT TREATMENT, PART EIGHT

Julia and her mother greatly benefitted from completing this component together, as they were operating at extremes rather than taking the middle path in most of their decisions. Her parents were either too loose (not caring about her well-being or whereabouts) or too strict (forbidding her to leave the house when she had made specific plans to go spend time with a friend). They made little out of her tendency to spend time alone and to avoid them, but made too much out of her new assertiveness in asking for a later curfew or to spend more time with friends. They also tended to push her away because they were so focused on their problems with one another, while at other times her mother relied too heavily on Julia to meet her needs. Group members helped the two learn about the middle path so that their reactions to one another were more balanced and more in line with a normal adolescent developmental trajectory. They also helped Julia and her mother listen more effectively to one another and to validate the other's disclosures within the relationship.

Additional DBT Components

In addition to individual and group modalities, the DBT approach also provides for the use of telephone consultation for both adolescents and family members. By providing the option of telephone contact outside of regularly scheduled sessions, the primary counselor can provide coaching for skill generalization, provide emergency crisis intervention, and repair any ruptures in the therapeutic alliance that may have occurred in the previous session. In addition, clients are encouraged to call the counselor not just because they are in crisis, but also to relate when things are going well during the week.

Another component of DBT for adolescents is the provision of family counseling on an as-needed basis. In meeting with the parental unit, the counselor can first help educate parents about self-injury, its causes, and its treatment (e.g., CRPSIB Information for Parents; Self Abuse Finally Ends (SAFE) alternatives website; Selekman, 2006) so they will be better prepared to engage in the treatment process. When meeting with the family, the counselor identifies any aspects of the family environment that serve to either reinforce NSSI behaviors or that attempt to punish the adolescent's use of new coping strategies when they are actually practiced at home. The parents in particular might be undermining the adolescent's ability to develop healthy coping behaviors through their lack of support or through over-controlling behaviors. Family therapy can also address any family behaviors that regularly interfere with the adolescent's participation in treatment, or reduce family interactions that interfere with family's overall quality of life. This is important because family conflict is often a source of distress that serves as a trigger for NSSI, and family counseling might serve to assist the family in interacting in a more functional way in order to reduce the conflict. When the family works together to directly confront dysfunctional family interactions, provides more acceptance and open communication, and supports the adolescent in developing new skills, the family can be an essential asset to the recovery process (CRPSIB Information for Parents, 2012).

A final component of DBT is ongoing support for the counselor in the form of weekly team consultation meetings. Because working with adolescent girls who self-injure is extremely stressful work, team meetings provide an important opportunity for counselors to have their needs met by discussing their difficulties and frustrations with the treatment process. Team support and feedback may help a counselor maintain a nonjudgmental and supportive stance, and to generate alternative perspectives or solutions when the counselor feels stuck.

PREVENTION AND NSSI

Because of the overlap between NSSI and other impulsive, self-destructive behaviors such as eating disorders and substance abuse, many of these disorders share risk and protective factors that can be targeted in prevention programs. The primary skills necessary for preventing NSSI are life skills and assisting adolescents in developing positive coping skills. The relevant life skills reviewed in the DBT description provided in this chapter (e.g., mindfulness skills, distress tolerance, emotion regulation, interpersonal effectiveness, and decreasing polarized thinking) will help adolescent girls have a repertoire of skills to use to manage life stressors as they emerge.

In addition, parents of girls and adolescents can help to provide a family environment in which girls feel validated and can cope openly with any stress and negative feelings. Some suggestions for family prevention from CRPSIB Resource for Parents (2012) are as follows:

- Provide a protective home environment. Parents should seek open family communication and provide opportunities for quality family time. They should attempt to keep the atmosphere at home inviting, upbeat, and one that actively promotes positive emotions.
- The family should model healthy ways of managing stress and should practice positive coping skills together.
- Parents should provide expectations that the adolescent will contribute to family chores and be a contributing member of the family.
- Parents should set limits and consistently enforce consequences. As with any technology, parents should monitor their children's Internet usage and set firm guidelines around what sites are permitted.
- Parents should attempt to avoid overscheduling the adolescent's activities and putting too much pressure on her to achieve/ perform.

CONCLUSIONS AND FUTURE DIRECTIONS

Research indicates that adolescent girls who use NSSI have difficulty in recognizing and regulating their emotions; tolerating distressful thoughts, feelings, or circumstances; and influencing their relationships in an effective way. It is therefore understandable that some adolescents turn to NSSI as an effective but self-destructive coping strategy for managing these intra- and interpersonal problems. The CBT general components (and the DBT treatment approach in particular) as described in this chapter address these emotional and relational skill deficits by first emphasizing the counselor-client relationship in which the function of the NSSI behavior is accepted and validated. Using a collaborative style, they can then carefully examine the chain of behaviors that lead to specific NSSI episodes, identifying triggers and generating potential new solutions for disrupting the behavioral sequence. The DBT approach in particular also provides a structured method for teaching core mindfulness, emotion regulation, distress tolerance, and interpersonal effectiveness skills in a multifamily group setting. Additional components such as family counseling, telephone contact, and counselor collaboration meetings also serve to enhance the effectiveness of DBT.

However, there are also clear limitations to the DBT treatment approach. It would not be feasible in many treatment settings, as the multifamily groups would be difficult for some counselors to offer on a consistent basis. Miller et al. (2007) suggest that if the group modality is not possible, then the counselor should schedule twice weekly sessions with the client, with one session devoted to behavior analysis and problem solving, and the other dedicated to skills training and acquisition. Phone consultation and team meetings are also deemed essential for the program to be successful but may not be feasible for all counselors. Nevertheless, when working with adolescent clients who engage in NSSI, it is recommended that counselors should engage in some type of weekly supervision in order to help them manage the demands of working with this challenging population (Miller et al., 2007).

Future applications of the DBT approach for adolescent girls who self-injure can take greater account of the client's sociocultural context and can examine differential treatment effects for gender, race/ethnicity, and other cultural variables. For example, as stated previously, gender is not specifically accounted for in the treatment model, yet the needs of girls and boys will differ in the early adolescent period as girls encounter a greater number of stressors and pressures (Hilt et al., 2008a). Further, while DBT is currently the treatment approach with the most research support, it is not effective in all cases and there may be other approaches that are more beneficial for certain clients. Future research can examine other treatment models and how they may be best matched to specific client characteristics.

In conclusion, an alarmingly large number of today's adolescent girls turn to NSSI as a coping strategy for managing emotions, relationships, and life circumstances. Counselors need to be prepared to assist their clients in understanding the functions of this behavior, to help them generate more effective solutions to resolve their tensions and stressors, and to learn new skills that will enhance their overall quality of life. The model presented in this chapter is intended to provide guidance to counselors as they work to meet these complex and challenging treatment goals.

RESOURCES

www.crpsib.com

The Cornell Research Program on Self-Injurious Behavior in Adolescents and Young Adults is a research project at the Cornell University Family Life Development Center. The website provides links and resources for understanding, detecting, treating, and preventing self-injurious behavior (SIB) in adolescents and young adults. The CRPSIB team has also developed factsheets and web-based presentations about several therapies commonly used to treat self-injury.

www.self-injury.com/index.html

The Self Abuse Finally Ends (S.A.F.E) Alternatives treatment approach is a nationally recognized approach, a professional network, and an educational research base, which is committed to helping people achieve an end to SIB. The website provides general information and resources for professionals and clients, information on how to find a therapist, and a store to purchase resources.

www.selfinjury.org/indexnet.html

American Self-Harm Information Clearinghouse (ASHIC). The ASHIC seeks to improve treatment to those who self-harm by providing accurate and up-to-date information to the public, medical professionals, and psychological professionals.

www.selfinjuryfoundation.org/

The Self-Injury Foundation aims to provide funding for education, advocacy, support, and research for self-injurers. It contains information about self-injury and resources for self-injurers, parents, friends, medical professionals, schools, clergy, and crisis staff. There are also directions for those individuals interested in volunteering or donating to the Self-Injury Foundation.

7

Violated and Betrayed: Sexual Trauma and Dating Violence in Adolescent Girls

Sexual violence is a major problem experienced by girls and women worldwide, with long-term serious health consequences and significant social and public health costs. Because of the intimate nature of sexual violence, it is considered one of the most distressing types of trauma an individual can experience (Frazier, Conlon, & Glaser, 2001). Sexual violence includes a broad spectrum of nonconsensual sexual activities that are perpetrated upon a victim by partners, friends, acquaintances, family members, or strangers. It can include any of the following: rape (unwanted sexual acts that result in oral, vaginal, or anal penetration); unwanted sexual contact or touching; performance of sexual acts forced through threats of violence, intimidation, or coercion; sexual abuse, including childhood sexual abuse (CSA) and incest; sexual abuse of individuals who are physically or mentally disabled and unable to give consent; or forced prostitution and trafficking of individuals for the purpose of sexual exploitation (Jewkes, Sen, & Garcia-Moreno, 2002; Violence Against Women, 2009).

Unfortunately, adolescent girls are at high risk for sexual violence and for rape in particular. Available statistics indicate that it is a reality for many girls in middle and high school; 11% of high school girls (grades 9–12) report a history of forced sexual intercourse and over 50% report experiencing sexually coercive experiences (Black et al., 2011). Worldwide, over 33% of adolescent girls report that their first sexual experience was forced (Krug, Dahlberg, Mercy, Zwi, & Lozano, 2002). Further, of young women who have been raped, 25% experienced a first rape before age 12, and 34% experienced a first rape between the ages of 12 and 17 (Black et al., 2011). It should be noted that while males are also the victims of sexual violence, girls are disproportionately likely to experience all forms of sexual violence. Approximately 1 in 33 men (vs. 1 in 6 women) has experienced an attempted or completed rape in their life time (Tjaden & Thoennes, 2006).

It is not surprising that trauma resulting from sexual violence is associated with a host of negative health-related physical symptoms such as chronic pain, headaches, stomach problems, and higher rates of STDs and unwanted pregnancies. Survivors of sexual violence are also more likely to smoke, engage in risky sexual activity and physical fights, and to experience future victimization and physical dating violence (Basile et al., 2006). They are also more likely to experience mental health problems, including Posttraumatic Stress Disorder (PTSD) and associated anxiety, depression, eating disorders, low self-esteem, and substance abuse (Campbell, Dworkin, & Cabral, 2009; Resnick, Acierno, Holmes, Dammeyer, & Kilpatrick, 2000). Adolescents who have been sexually victimized and use substances are also at greater risk for suicide (Behnken, Le, Temple, & Berenson, 2010).

Because most girls develop PTSD-like symptoms within 2 weeks of a sexual assault (Resnick, Acierno, Holmes, Kilpatrick, & Jager, 1999); I will review the PTSD diagnosis briefly here. While most girls experience *symptoms* following an assault, many do not have symptoms that would meet criteria for a diagnosis of PTSD, especially after several weeks postassault. Full syndrome PTSD, however, develops in 17% to 65% of sexual trauma survivors (Kilpatrick, Amstadter, Resnick, & Ruggiero, 2007).

The *Diagnostic and Statistical Manual, Fifth Edition* (APA, in press), groups PTSD symptoms into four clusters: (1) intrusion (e.g., reexperiencing of the trauma through nightmares, flashbacks); (2) avoidance (e.g., avoiding thoughts, feelings, physical sensations, people, activities, places, or physical reminders that arouse recollection of the event); (3) negative alterations in cognitions and mood (e.g., inability to remember certain aspects of the event, persistent self-blame, strong and persistent negative emotional reactions, feelings of detachment); and (4) alterations in arousal and activities associated with the event (e.g., irritability, reckless or self-destructive behavior, exaggerated startle response, problems with concentration and sleep). To meet *DSM-5* criteria for PTSD, this constellation of symptoms must occur for at least 1 month and cause clinically significant distress or impairment in social, occupational, or other important areas of functioning (APA, in press). The frequency, severity, and duration of a client's PTSD symptoms may be influenced by many factors, and the primary influences are addressed in the sections to follow.

CONCEPTUALIZING SEXUAL TRAUMA

Recent research indicates the importance of understanding a survivor's responses to trauma as a complex interaction between the individual and her environment. In line with the other chapters in this book, sexual trauma can also be understood by examining the experience through an ecological systems lens. This approach describes ways in which an individual's adjustment to trauma can be influenced by multiple systems—including the characteristics of the assault, the immediate environment, the broader community, and the larger cultural context in which sexual violence is understood (Campbell et al., 2009; Messman-Moore & Long, 2003; Neville, Oh, Spanierman, Heppner, & Clark, 2004; Ullman, 2007). For the purposes of this chapter, I draw upon the ecological model of Campbell and colleagues for conceptualizing the impact of sexual trauma on a survivor's posttrauma functioning (Campbell et al., 2009) and also from my previous work (Choate, 2012). This systems model is based upon Bronfenbrenner's (1995) ecological theory of human development and consists of six levels, all of which are described in the paragraphs that follow.

Individual Level

This level refers to the individual survivor's particular sociodemographical characteristics. Although any individual can be a victim of sexual trauma, individual risk factors include: being female, reaching puberty at an earlier age, starting to date at an earlier age, having a sexually active peer group, living in a nontraditional setting (i.e., other than with biological parents), and experiencing CSA (see chronosystem level) (Freeman & Temple, 2010; Tjaden & Thoennes, 2006). Research highlighting other variables indicates that African American girls are more likely to report a history of rape than are Caucasian or Latina girls (Black et al., 2011). In one study of primarily African American young women in an urban medical setting, 30% of the young women who were seeking treatment for other medical reasons reported having unwanted verbal sexual coercion or attempted/completed rape during the past year (Rickert, Wiemann, Vaughan, & White, 2004). Other research indicates that individuals who are lesbian/gay/bisexual/transgender (LGBT) experience sexual violence at rates roughly equivalent to the heterosexual population (Tjaden & Thoennes, 2006). Further, it should be noted that individuals with disabilities are raped and sexually assaulted at high rates, although these crimes are highly underreported, so accurate data regarding this population are difficult to obtain (Violence Against Women, 2009).

Assault Characteristics Level

This level refers to the use of alcohol or other drugs during the assault, and also provides an understanding of the relationship of the survivor to the perpetrator. This section will also include a discussion of adolescent dating violence, which is also a risk factor for sexual assault.

Use of Alcohol and Drugs

Sexual assault is highly associated with alcohol use, both by the perpetrator and the victim, particularly for older adolescents and college students. In one survey of 7th to 12th grade students, alcohol was involved in approximately 12% to 20% of cases of reported unwanted sexual activity (Young, Grey, Abbey, Boyd, & McCabe, 2008). In college women, rapes in which alcohol and other drugs are involved occur five times more frequently than do forcible rapes in which alcohol was not used (Lawyer, Resnick, Bakanic, Burkett, & Kilpatrick, 2010). Of adolescent girls who have been sexually assaulted, approximately 18% report that drugs or alcohol were used by the perpetrator to facilitate the assault (McCauley et al., 2009). Frequently, a person is raped while she is unable to give consent for sexual activity due to intoxication or incapacitation, yet she is hesitant to label the incident as rape, questions her role in the assault, and tends to engage in self-blame (Schwartz & Leggett, 1999). For these reasons, individuals are far less likely to report alcohol-related sexual assaults than they are to report forcible rapes. Further, research indicates that girls who experience drug or alcohol-facilitated sexual assault are significantly more likely than survivors with other abuse histories to report past-year alcohol abuse and drug use (McCauley et al., 2009).

Relationship to Perpetrator

The assault characteristics level also provides an examination of the survivor's previous relationship with the perpetrator. Sexual trauma is generally classified as spousal/marital, partner, date, acquaintance, stranger, and incest. There is a pervasive stereotype that sexual assault is most likely to be perpetrated by a stranger, while data indicate that sexual assault is most likely to be perpetrated by someone whom the survivor knows. Eighty to 90% of survivors of rape report that they knew the perpetrator, either through a dating relationship, friends, friends of friends, or through meeting the perpetrator within a social context (Centers for Disease Control and Prevention [CDC], 2009). While the experience of sexual coercion occurs in all types of acquaintance relationships, actual rape most often occurs within the context of a dating relationship (Young, Grey, & Boyd, 2009). Sexual violence committed by an intimate partner is particularly traumatic, in that while rape by a stranger may be experienced as a singular event, survivors of date rape often endure multiple sexual assaults along with the continuous threat of repeated incidents of trauma, including other types of partner violence such as physical and psychological abuse (Temple, Weston, Rodriguez, & Marshall, 2007). Further, adolescent survivors of acquaintance or dating partner rapes tend to engage in more self-blame than do those who experience stranger rapes, although the negative psychological effects on survivors of both types of crimes are similar (Koss & Kilpatrick, 2001).

Adolescent Dating Violence

As stated, sexual violence often occurs in the context of a dating relationship. It is not surprising, then, that sexual violence is considered part of the definition of adolescent dating violence, defined as the physical, sexual, or psychological/emotional violence within a relationship with a current or former dating partner. Dating violence is considered to include any abusive behavior aimed at controlling or hurting a dating partner; includes threats, acts of intimidation, stalking; and can occur both in person or electronically (Black et al., 2011). Therefore, adolescent dating violence is an important aspect of understanding an adolescent client's sexual trauma history and is discussed in the paragraphs that follow.

Most studies report that between 10% and 30% of adolescent girls have experienced physical, emotional, or verbal abuse from a dating partner (Davis, 2008; Teten, Ball, Valle, Noonan, & Rosenbluth, 2009). In an examination of physical dating violence alone, nearly 25% of 7th grade girls reported being a victim of physical dating violence in the past year (Swahn, Simon, Arias, & Bossarte, 2008), indicating that dating violence is prevalent even in early middle school. With both sexes combined, around 10% of all high school students report being hit, slapped, or physically hurt on purpose by a boyfriend or girlfriend in the past year (CDC, 2009). African American adolescents are at particularly high risk for dating violence, as they are 1.5 times more likely to have experienced physical dating violence when compared to their Caucasian peers (Howard, Wang, & Yan, 2008). When examining dating violence and sexual orientation, adolescents in same-sex relationships experience very similar rates of violence as adolescents in heterosexual relationships. Approximately 1 in 3 adolescents who are in same-sex romantic or sexual relationships report dating violence victimization in the past year (Halpern, Young, Waller, Martin, & Kupper, 2004; Swahn et al., 2008).

Unlike other forms of violence, most studies demonstrate that girls engage in aggressive behavior toward their dating partners at rates comparable to boys, so girls and boys are equally likely to be both perpetrators and victims of dating violence (CDC, 2009). In fact, the majority of adolescents who have experienced dating violence describe it as mutual aggression. This may not be surprising in our current culture in which violence has become increasingly normalized among both sexes and female aggression is encouraged and in many cases glamorized (Garbarino, 2006). As evidence of this trend, a recent survey by the Substance Abuse and Mental Health Services Administration (SAMHSA) indicated that 26.7% of adolescent girls participated in a serious fight at school or work, group-against-group fight, or an attack on another individual with the intent to inflict serious harm during the past year (SAMHSA, 2010). In addition to physically fighting one another, partners may use various forms of verbal abuse, including peer pressure (spreading rumors, telling lies about her to her friends); emotional abuse (name calling, humiliation); using social status; intimidation (destroying property, displaying weapons); minimizing or denying the abuse; making threats to harm her, leave her, or to commit suicide if she leaves; manipulating or making threats to get sex; controlling what she does, who she sees and talks to, and where she goes (National Center on Domestic and Sexual Violence, 2012). For example, 29% of adolescents report that they have been in a relationship with someone who wanted to keep them from seeing friends and family, had partners who acted jealously, and who demanded to know their whereabouts at all times (Tween and Teen Dating Violence and Abuse Study, 2008).

Dating abuse increasingly involves digital harassment, which refers to an adolescent using cell phones, social networks, and other communication devices to bully, threaten, and aggressively badger a dating or former dating partner. Adolescents frequently report such behavior as excessive texting, being pressured for their online or cell phone passwords, being pressured to send sexy photos, being forced to unfriend people whom the abuser doesn't like, and being impersonated online (MTV's A Thin Line Campaign, 2011).

While adolescents may view their aggressive behavior toward one another as mutual aggression, it is important for counselors to examine both the motivations for and consequences of the violence used in a dating relationship. Both sexes cite anger as a primary motivating factor for using violence, but boys are more likely to cite the need to use violence to exert control, while girls often report self-defense as a motivating factor. In addition, boys are more likely to react with laughter when their partner is physically aggressive, while girls rarely report this reaction. Most importantly, girls are significantly more likely to suffer long-term consequences from dating violence than are boys (Mulford & Giordano, 2008). For example, girls are more likely to be injured, are more likely to be sexually assaulted by their dating partner, and are more likely to experience mental health problems than are their male peers (CDC, 2009). Adolescent dating violence in girls is associated with PTSD, depression, suicidality, substance use problems, disordered eating behaviors, low relationship satisfaction, negative views of school, fears of pregnancy due to forced sex, low social support, and general emotional distress (Ackard & Neumark-Sztainer, 2001; Banyard & Cross, 2008; Wolitzky-Taylor et al., 2008).

It is also important to note how abusive experiences during early dating relationships can disrupt normal developmental processes for girls, including the development of a stable self-concept and body image (Ackard & Neumark-Sztainer, 2001). Adolescent girls' bodies are undergoing tremendous changes that require her to integrate her rapidly changing weight, shape, and appearance into her overall sense of self. If she is harmed by physical or sexual abuse during this time, it is harder for her to view her body in a positive way, which thereby impedes her attainment of a positive body image. In addition, due to her age, it is difficult for a girl to understand the difference between what is normal or expected behavior in a dating relationship and what is considered abuse. Unfortunately, adolescent dating violence can represent a chronic trend in a girl's relationships throughout her lifetime, as adolescents who are abused as children by their parents are more likely to become involved in teen dating violence (Laporte, Jiang, Pepler, & Chamberland, 2011), and adult women experiencing intimate partner violence report that they have been involved in violent dating relationships since their early adolescent years (Black et al., 2011). Therefore, teaching girls effective interpersonal relationship skills, including assertiveness, healthy boundaries, and communication strategies at an early age can help to prevent a pattern of abusive relationships and even sexual violence from occurring later in her life. These strategies are discussed in the prevention programs highlighted later in the chapter.

Chronosystem Level

This level refers to the cumulative effects of multiple developmental transitions in a survivor's life. In cases of sexual trauma, it refers to an adolescent girl's particular history of victimization. There is a considerable line of research indicating that CSA is a significant risk factor for revictimization as an adolescent or adult (Fortier et al., 2009; Koss & Kilpatrick, 2001; Tjaden & Thoennes, 2006; Walsh, Blaustein, Knight, Spinazzola, & van der Kolk, 2007). CSA survivors are two to three times more likely to be sexually assaulted in adolescence and adulthood than are individuals from the general population (Tjaden & Thoennes, 2006; Walsh et al., 2007), and there is some indication that there are even higher revictimization rates among LGBT individuals who experienced CSA (Heidt, Marx, & Gold, 2005).

Counselors need to assess for and understand a survivor's victimization history, as girls who have been victimized previously are more likely to have differing treatment needs than other survivors. Revictimization is associated with increased levels of PTSD symptoms compared to a single incident of trauma, and those who experience revictimization report greater levels of depression, PTSD, dissociation, anxiety, and substance abuse than do other survivors of sexual trauma (Fortier et al., 2009).

While there are multiple factors involved in revictimization, most of the recent research in this area has centered upon microsystem factors. Some studies have examined interpersonal factors such as engaging in high-risk activities that increase exposure to potential perpetrators (e.g., binge drinking, having two or more current sexual partners; Brener, McMahon, Warren, & Douglas, 1999; Grauerholz, 2000). Other studies have identified specific intrapersonal factors that may be related to revictimization, including psychological distress, relationship insecurity, low self-esteem, self-blame, low self-efficacy, use of avoidant coping styles, and deficits in risk appraisal and situational coping. All of these factors can reduce an individual's ability to assess, assertively cope with, and escape from potentially dangerous situations; these factors also can increase the likelihood that a perpetrator may act with aggression (Walsh et al., 2007).

Recent research in this area has examined the specific impact of coping strategies and chronic trauma symptoms on whether or not an individual becomes revictimized. Those individuals who have experienced CSA are likely to employ avoidant coping strategies (e.g., denial, avoidance, numbing, or detachment). The use of these types of avoidant coping strategies is related to increased PTSD symptoms that develop over time. The resulting PTSD symptoms, in turn, have been shown to interfere with information processing, accurate risk perception and assessment, failures to react appropriately to threats, and the ability to engage in self-protective responses (Fortier et al., 2009). These responses are all related to increased risk of future victimization (Fortier et al., 2009).

Exosystem Level

This level refers to a survivor's contact with medical, legal, law enforcement, or mental health systems. It is common for survivors to report that their contacts with formal systems were quite negative and caused them to experience guilt, mistrust, and reluctance to seek further help (Campbell & Raja, 2005). These interactions can result in what often is termed a *secondary victimization*, which is the experience of insensitivity, victim blaming, minimization, and negative reactions from medical, legal, law enforcement, and mental health professionals, and which often exacerbates a survivor's trauma symptoms (Campbell, 2006; Feldman, Ullman, & Dunkel-Schetter, 1998). Victim blame and negative social reactions are common for all survivors, but are particularly likely to occur in the cases of acquaintance, date, or partner rape (Resnick et al., 2000).

It is not surprising, then, that fully two thirds of adolescents never report sexual violence to social services or law enforcement. There are many reasons for this reluctance, including fear she won't be believed because she had voluntary social interactions with the perpetrator before the assault occurred, guilt or confusion about her prior relationship with the perpetrator, whether or not her actions contributed to the assault, worries that her parents will impose restrictions that keep her from going to future social events, or hesitancy because she has little memory of assault due to alcohol or date rape drugs (Kaufman, 2008). Further, her family may be hesitant to seek help from formal service providers due to their cultural attitudes and experiences. This might include membership in a racial or ethnic group that has experienced a history of not being believed by law enforcement officials, or those who have developed a mistrust of agencies based on both personal experiences and historical experiences of violations perpetrated by such agencies. Some also may be hesitant to seek services due to their immigration status and fears of deportation (Bryant-Davis, Chung, & Tillman, 2009).

A final reason a girl might avoid seeking help is in order to protect herself from psychological harm (Patterson, Greeson, & Campbell, 2009; Ullman, 2007). After a sexual trauma, survivors may try to suppress their memories and emotions, deny the impact of the trauma on their current functioning, and fear that if they experience the memories and feelings, they may become overwhelmed. They may delay seeking help from professionals until they can no longer suppress their emotions or when their symptoms become intolerable. As a result, many survivors may delay seeking mental health treatment for years, and even when they do, they often present for counseling with a different presenting problem (Patterson et al., 2009).

It is also important to note that when survivors and their families do attempt to seek assistance, there may be significant barriers for them in receiving needed services. Formal services tend to be less available and accessible for survivors who are disabled, non-English speaking, or who have low levels of education; such individuals often are unaware of available resources or have limited access to hospitals or rape crisis centers (Bryant-Davis et al., 2009). In addition, many social services are not designed to meet the needs of LGBT individuals (Gold, Dickstein, Marx, & Lexington, 2009).

Microsystem Level

This level refers to a girl's social support system. As stated previously, many survivors experience negative reactions from others, and they often are blamed for bringing the traumatic event upon themselves. Negative reactions from others, however, can be buffered by the availability of positive social support. Research indicates that social support can strongly affect a survivor's reactions to trauma and the ability to recover from sexual violence (Ullman, 2007). The availability of social support increases the likelihood of early disclosure, which is related to more positive recovery. Adolescent girls who disclose an act of sexual violence to significant others within the first month are at reduced risk for developing depression and for committing acts of delinquency compared to those survivors who waited longer than 1 month. Disclosure to mothers in particular is related to more positive mental health outcomes (Broman-Fulks et al., 2007; Camacho, Ehrensaft, & Cohen, 2012). Overall, survivors with strong support systems, and who disclose to supportive family and friends, have more positive physical and mental health following sexual trauma (Camacho et al., 2012; Kimerling & Calhoun, 1994; Ullman, 2007). In contrast, adolescent girls who do not disclose their experience to others have more symptoms of depression, PTSD, and other psychological problems than those survivors who do share their experience (Ahrens, Stansell, & Jennings, 2010).

Macrosystem Level

This level refers to broader community and societal factors such as cultural differences in responding to rape and the acceptance of rape myths that exist in a particular culture. It is important to understand a survivor's reactions to sexual violence within a sociocultural context, examining the meaning of sexual assault not only to the individual, but also in terms of how it is perceived within the individual's community.

When examining rape from a societal, gendered context, it is viewed not as a crime about sex but about power, which serves to devalue women, limit their freedom, and maintain their inequality (Brownmiller, 1975; Low & Organista, 2000). According to Bryant-Davis et al., (2009), the sexual assault of ethnic minority girls and women should be understood within the broader context of *societal trauma*, considering that an individual's previous experiences with racism, sexism, classism, heterosexism, cultural violence, or historical violence are cumulative and contribute to the way in which a survivor experiences sexual violence when it occurs. Culture also impacts the decisions a girl and her family might make about reporting an act of sexual violence. For example, Asian American families may place pressure on survivors to remain silent about their experiences so as not to bring the family shame or dishonor. African American women may subscribe to a perceived cultural mandate to protect African American male perpetrators so that males from their communities will not be incarcerated (Bryant-Davis et al., 2009).

For adolescent girls in particular, sexual violence is fostered in a culture in which girls are sexually objectified (i.e., viewed as objects that are only valued for their sexual appeal). It is also bred in a culture in which images of violence and sexuality are often linked (e.g., in movies, video games, music videos). As explored in Chapter 1 of this book, today's girls are growing up in a climate in which both objectification and sexualized images of violence are widespread and even glamorized in popular culture. These cultural messages are then internalized by boys and girls alike, and they are manifested throughout middle and high schools, the places, where adolescents spend most of their time. Girls regularly experience sexual harassment as part of their daily school experiences. For example, according to the most recent American Association of University Women (AAUW) and Kearl Report (2011), fully half of students experienced some form of sexual harassment during the 2010 to 2011 school year and 87% of these students said it had a negative effect on them. Girls are more likely to be sexually harassed than boys (56% vs. 40%) both in person and via electronic means. Thirteen percent of girls said they had been touched in an unwelcome, sexual way; 9% were physically intimidated in a sexual way; and 4% report that they were forced to do something sexual.

Further, girls are more likely than boys to say they have been negatively affected by sexual harassment and were most affected by unwanted sexual comments, gestures, and having sexual rumors spread electronically about them. Girls were more likely than boys to report that these behaviors caused them to have trouble sleeping, to not want to go to school, to feel sick or nauseated, to find it hard to concentrate and to study, and to change the way they went to or came home from school (AAUW et al., 2011). It is not difficult to imagine that these frequent experiences and negative outcomes have a cumulative effect on both perpetrators and victims of harassment. Based on widespread harassment by peers and potential romantic partners, students may become desensitized toward viewing girls only according to their sexual appeal and what they have to offer sexually. In turn, both boys and girls may experience increasing difficulty in determining what constitutes consensual and nonconsensual sexual activity (Young et al., 2008).

In addition to sexual harassment within schools, myths about rape may exist within particular communities or neighborhoods that influence both survivors' and others' reactions to acts of sexual violence. Women in particular are harmed when the following types of commonly accepted rape myths are endorsed: "She must have deserved it, because of the way she dressed and where she was when it happened"; "She must have wanted it, because she didn't say no or didn't put up a struggle"; "If a woman sexually teases a man, she deserves to be raped"; "When she says 'no' she really means 'yes' and is just playing hard to get"; "Women who accuse a man of rape are doing it to get back at him for not going out with her"; or, "It is not really rape if a woman has had many sexual partners" (Burt, 1991; Haworth-Hoeppner, 1998).

It is clear that accepting rape-related myths perpetuated by society can lead to greater levels of negative reactions from others, to minimization by the survivor, and to the likelihood of increased victim blaming. All of these can have an impact on an individual's ability to recover from sexual trauma (Campbell et al., 2009).

CASE EXAMPLE, PART ONE

Nia is a 13-year-old girl who lives with her mother and a 16-year-old brother. She has recently gone through puberty and has developed a curvaceous figure. Her mother is religious and takes her to church weekly, and she makes average grades at school. Last summer, her brother told her that he and his friends were going to have a party at the local pool after hours. He said that they like to sneak in while it is closed so they can hang out, drink, and swim. He told her that one of his friends (Robert) thought she was "hot" and wanted her to come hang out with them that night. Even though Nia did not usually disobey her mother, this time she decided to go because she was flattered that an older guy liked her and that her brother wanted to include her in his party. She left the house after her mother had gone to bed. She was proud to wear her new push-up bikini to the party, and enjoyed the stares she received when she got there. Soon after she arrived, Robert offered her a beer and asked her if she wanted to swim with him. He paid her a lot of attention, gave her several additional beers, then invited her into the locker room so that they could be alone. Although she didn't want to be alone with him, she also didn't want him to stop hanging out with her, so she agreed. They began to kiss, which she liked, but soon he forced her on the ground and raped her. She was too scared to scream, so she froze until it was over. She immediately ran out of the room and rushed home, sneaking back into her house at 1 a.m. She felt stupid and guilty because she went out late at night, she felt she had led Robert on with her bikini and kissing, and she had agreed to go into the locker room with him. She grew up believing that things like this only happen to "bad" girls, so she believed that she too must be bad and that the rape must have been entirely her fault. She did not tell anyone about it for over a month.

After the rape, she made excuses so that she would not have to go back to the pool, and she began dressing in baggy t-shirts and gym shorts. She did not return her friends' calls and avoided her peers. She also began to experience nightmares, recurrent stomachaches, and remained terrified around all males who came over to their house. She could not face her brother and tried to avoid him as well. As the end of the summer neared, she began to dread having to go back to school and wondered if she would ever function normally again.

(continued)

CASE EXAMPLE, PART ONE (*continued*)

Discussion Questions

1. When conceptualizing Nia's experiences according to the ecological systems model, which of the levels seem most relevant for her case (e.g., chronosystem, macrosystem, etc.)? How does it help to take a multisystemic view of her problem?
2. If you were a counselor, where would you want to start your work with Nia? What most needs to be changed?

TREATMENT FOR SEXUAL TRAUMA

As highlighted in the previous sections, it is important for counselors to be prepared with the knowledge and skill to provide contextually sensitive treatment for adolescent survivors of sexual violence. To this end, I describe treatment approaches that are most effective for counseling adolescent girls who have experienced sexual assault and rape.

When counselors work with an adolescent girl who has experienced sexual trauma, they first should work to develop a trusting therapeutic alliance with both the girl and her family, as survivors may have great reluctance to discuss their memories of the trauma and families may have had negative experiences with other service providers. Counselors should demonstrate empathy and positive regard for clients as they carefully assess client concerns through the multisystemic lens described in this chapter. This type of assessment is imperative in developing a treatment approach that is tailored to the adolescent client's specific needs.

The treatment components outlined in the following are drawn from expert consensus guidelines for the treatment of PTSD (Foa, Davidson, & Frances, 1999; Foa, Keane, & Friedman, 2000) and the treatment of child and adolescent PTSD (Cohen et al., 2010), and are adapted specifically for rape-related trauma. For a complete discussion of these components, see Trauma-Focused Cognitive Behavior Therapy (TF-CBT) (Cohen, Mannarino, & Deblinger, 2006; Choate, 2008; and Foa et al., 1999).

At the outset of treatment, it is important to provide psychoeducation to parents/caregivers and their daughter regarding commonly experienced reactions to sexual assault (e.g., guilt, anger, shame, powerlessness, helplessness, fear) and the symptoms of PTSD as described previously (Marotta, 2000). Many survivors express that they feel relief when they realize they are not "crazy" but are rather experiencing an expected reaction to a highly traumatic event (Rauch, Hembree, & Foa, 2001). The counselor should be prepared to provide information and resources about medical and legal decisions and assist her in accessing the services of the local rape crisis center, as appropriate. They should also explain the rationale for treatment services they plan to provide.

Trauma-Focused Cognitive Behavioral Therapy (TF-CBT)

The most effective treatment for children and adolescents experiencing PTSD symptoms is TF-CBT. TF-CBT is a brief and effective treatment approach for children with diverse backgrounds, is administered in as few as 12 sessions, and is based on the premise that treatment should be focused directly on resolving reactions to the traumatic event (Cohen et al., 2006). It has been effectively tested in several randomized controlled trials and is deemed efficacious for children ages 3 to 17 by the American Academy of Child and Adolescent Psychiatry (Cohen et al., 2010).

TF-CBT Components. TF-CBT treatment components can be described using the PRACTICE acronym:

P. In addition to pychoeducation to establish the therapeutic relationship with the family, *parenting skills* are provided to parents (e.g., use of effective parenting interventions such as praise, positive attention, appropriate consequences), so that the adolescent receives the needed amount of structure, support, and boundaries during this time.

R. *Relaxation skills* are taught to help reduce symptoms of anxiety and to prepare for the exposure-based techniques to follow. Meadows and Foa (1998) suggest teaching clients coping skills to reduce anxiety-related symptoms such as hypervigilance, hyperarousal, sleep disturbances/nightmares, and difficulty in concentration. These coping strategies include progressive muscle relaxation training and controlled breathing exercises. Clients can become empowered as they learn to employ these and other anxiety management strategies that promote recovery from sexual trauma.

A. *Affective modulation skills* assist in feelings identification, use of positive self-talk, thought stopping, positive imagery, and the ability to recognize and regulate negative affective states.

C. *Cognitive coping and processing* help the adolescent to recognize the relationships among her thoughts, feelings, and behaviors, and to help her to change inaccurate and unhelpful thoughts. As clients identify these thoughts and beliefs related to the trauma, they become aware of cognitive distortions related to sexual trauma, learn to evaluate distortions, to challenge them, and to eventually replace them with more rational or beneficial thoughts (Meadows & Foa, 1998). One specific form of CBT that is designed specifically for rape-related trauma is cognitive processing therapy (CPT; Resick & Schnicke, 1993). In CPT, survivors learn to identify and challenge "stuck points" in five specific areas: self-blame and guilt (blaming self for actions that contributed to or could have prevented the event), power and control (taking back power and control over her life), self-esteem (learning to feel lovable and worthwhile following the event), trust (learning to trust others following the betrayal of her trust in the perpetrator), and intimacy (taking risks to establish close relationships with others again). While the CPT approach was designed for adult survivors, the reader is referred to the manual to determine if material related to these five areas might be relevant for a particular adolescent client.

T. The *trauma narrative component* involves creating a narrative of the adolescent's traumatic experiences and placing the experience within the context of her entire life. To create a trauma narrative, exposure-based techniques are needed to assist a survivor in working through painful memories, situations, thoughts, and emotions associated with the traumatic event and which currently evoke anxiety and fear. As noted previously, many adolescents engage in avoidant coping strategies in order to avoid this intense anxiety and fear (Fortier et al., 2009), and it is understandable that they will be resistant to this strategy when it is presented to them in counseling. To encourage clients to undertake this difficult work, counselors should express empathy and acknowledge a survivor's fear, spend time educating her about the rationale for this treatment strategy, and convey positive expectations for recovery (Draucker, 1999). As suggested by Foa, Rothbaum, and Steketee (1993) and as adapted by Choate (2008, p. 177), counselors can explain the use of exposure therapy to clients and their families in the following way:

1. Memories, people, places, and activities now associated with the rape make you highly anxious, so you avoid them.
2. Each time you avoid them you do not finish the process of digesting the painful experience, and so it returns in the form of nightmares, flashbacks, and intrusive thoughts.
3. You can begin to digest the experience by gradually exposing yourself to the rape in your imagination and by holding the memory without pushing it away.

4. You will also practice facing those activities, places, and situations that currently evoke fear.
5. Eventually, you will be able to think about the rape and resume your normal activities without experiencing intense fear.

When the client is ready to begin the process, the counselor can use *imaginal exposure* to assist the client in repeatedly recounting memories associated with the sexual trauma until the memories no longer cause intense anxiety and fear (Foa et al., 1999). These techniques will vary depending upon the client' age and developmental level. In general, clients are asked to close their eyes, to imagine the traumatic event in vivid detail, and to describe it as if it were happening in the present. This is an extremely difficult phase of treatment for clients as they face the thoughts, feelings, and images associated with the event that they have been attempting to avoid out of fear. Counselors should acknowledge this difficulty and encourage clients in their willingness to process gradually in order to cope with their fears. The adolescent client should practice telling this narrative so that she will be able to repeat it to her parents/caregivers (if they are viewed as a source of support and if they are not the perpetrators).

I. *In vivo exposure* is a process through which clients are asked to focus on activities and situations associated with the event that they currently avoid because it evokes intense fear and disrupts daily functioning. The client lists all avoided situations and activities, ranking them from least to most distressing. It should be noted that the counselor should review this list to ensure that these situations or activities are actually safe and that it includes only those things that are interfering with the client's ability to engage in her daily routines. Starting with the activity or situation that is least distressing, the client remains in this particular environment for a minimum of 30 minutes. This time period is recommended because it is long enough for the client to experience fear, evaluate the actual level of danger present in the situation, and to allow the fear and anxiety to decrease (Foa et al., 1999). The counselor might accompany the client if feasible or a parent might also assist in this process. Relaxation techniques (as described previously) can be used during this time. Over the course of counseling, the client can progress through the hierarchy until she is able to resume daily routines and functioning.

C. The *conjoint child/parent session* component involves joint sessions in which the adolescent shares her trauma narrative with parents. At this time, other family issues can also be addressed. As stated previously, the adolescent girl prepares for these sessions by creating and practicing her trauma narrative in individual sessions with the counselor.

E. The *enhancing future safety and development* component addresses safety concerns related to the prevention of future trauma (based on the research that indicates a high level of revictimization in adolescent girls, as reviewed previously). This component also examines ways in which she can return to a normal developmental trajectory after this disruption in her growth.

The TF-CBT treatment manual is located in the book, *Treating Trauma and Traumatic Grief in Children and Adolescents* (Cohen et al., 2006). A no-cost, online training course is available at www.musc. edu/tfcbt, and an intensive skills based training is also offered (see the Resource section of www.musc.edu/tfcbt).

TF-CBT has also been adapted for use in schools (cognitive behavior intervention for trauma in schools; CBITS, 2012). The components are the same except CBITS does not include the parental component. Instead, it provides a component for teachers regarding the impact of trauma on a student's ability to learn and behave in the classroom following a trauma. The components are conducted in a group format, while the trauma narrative component is conducted individually.

In sum, the recommended treatments for sexual violence in adolescent girls are trauma focused; in other words, the counselor helps the client to address the trauma directly in counseling rather than avoiding it as the client will typically do to avoid the anxiety and psychological pain associated with the traumatic experience. By processing memories, evaluating distortions, and engaging in previously avoided activities, the client is able to begin the process of healing from the traumatic event.

CASE EXAMPLE, PART TWO

Before school started again, Nia decided that she had to tell her mother about what happened at the pool. Because she was still losing weight, feeling constant anxiety, and not sleeping, she felt her mother might be able to assist her in getting some help. She didn't describe the details, but just told her mother that she had been hurt by a boy at the pool. Her mother reacted initially with anger ("How could you betray my trust by sneaking out at night? What kind of daughter have I raised?"), but then felt compassion for her daughter and told her that she would support her in getting some help for coping with the rape. Her mother took her to a counselor who specialized in TF-CBT.

After conducting an initial ecological systems assessment (asking about family beliefs and values, history of assault, context of assault, etc.), the counselor learned that Nia's own beliefs about the rape were keeping her stuck (i.e., she blamed herself, not the perpetrator; denied her feelings about it; and accepted that she must be a "bad" person because this happened to her). Her beliefs had also prevented her from accessing needed support from her family and others during this time, and they also contributed to her continued PTSD symptoms (nightmares, anxiety). Following the TF-CBT PRACTICE model, the counselor targeted the following areas:

P. While providing psychoeducation to Nia and her mother regarding the typical reactions following a sexual assault and how Nia's symptoms were normal and expected following this type of trauma, the counselor also educated them about the treatment model she would be using. The counselor then provided Nia's mother with some positive parenting practices, including validation, affirmation, and support balanced with appropriate structure and limits. While Nia was not asking to go out with her friends right now, she and her mother talked about curfews, monitoring of her activities, and appropriate consequences for future social outings.

R. To help Nia with her anxiety, she learned some relaxation techniques such as progressive muscle relaxation, controlled breathing, meditation, and prayer. She learned to practice them several times per day as a regular routine so that they could be easily implemented during times of anxiety or stress.

A. Through her disclosures to her counselor, Nia began to recognize her thoughts and feelings about the rape and to put words to what happened to her. She realized that she had only been pushing her feelings away as an attempt to cope, but now needed to understand and face her feelings so that she could move past them. When her feelings became overwhelming, she learned how to use thought stopping and how to institute more positive self-talk.

C. An important part of cognitive processing for Nia was to identify her cognitive distortions related to the sexual trauma. She learned that she was "stuck" in her beliefs related to self-blame and guilt (that she could have prevented the rape), power and control (that she is out of control in her relationships with men and that they will always have power over her), self-esteem (she believes she is "bad" and undesirable now that this has happened to her), trust (she believes that she can't trust others because she has been betrayed), and intimacy (she doesn't want to get close to others because they will reject her if they find out what happened to her). Through therapy, Nia learned to evaluate and challenge each of these beliefs, and to slowly replace them with more rational and beneficial thoughts.

(continued)

CASE EXAMPLE, PART TWO (*continued*)

T. During the sessions, Nia reluctantly agreed to create a trauma narrative in collaboration with her counselor. After providing a rationale for why she should do this work, Nia trusted her counselor enough to begin imaginal exposure, repeatedly relaying her memories about the chain of events leading to the rape, the rape itself, and the aftermath of the rape. She described it in vivid detail, trying to imagine herself in the actual scene again (rather than retelling it as a story from the past). This was quite painful for Nia, and she cried multiple times during these sessions. However, at the end of this period she said that she felt a catharsis now that she had expressed her thoughts and feelings that had been bottled up for months.

I. As Nia was ready, the counselor suggested that she use in vivo exposure to help her resume her normal daily functioning. The primary place she had been avoiding was the pool, so Nia agreed to sit with her mother in the pool parking lot for 30 minutes until her anxiety was reduced. They also went to a skateboard park where her brother and a lot of boys his age were hanging out, and just sat in the parking lot while observing the boys. Nia felt a lot of fear initially, but the longer she sat there, the anxiety began to subside. She had already decided that it was unsafe for her to see Robert and she did not want to include that scenario in her in vivo exercises. She was adamant that she did not want to see him and that she did not want to report the rape. She counselor respected her decision, but told her that she could change her mind at any time.

C. During the conjoint session, Nia invited her mother into the session where she shared everything that had happened to her. Her mother sobbed throughout the story, but Nia felt better now that they had no secrets between them. Nia also thought it was important for her to begin speaking to her brother again, so he was invited into the session as well. She did not give him all of the details of what happened, but she explained to him why she had been avoiding him all summer. He asked for her forgiveness for inviting her to the pool that night, and admitted that he was partly to blame for the experience. Family communication was greatly improved after this session as all members felt that they could communicate more openly without hiding secret resentments toward one another.

E. Finally, the counselor helped Nia focus on the future: Now that she no longer believes that she is a bad person and that she got what she deserved, Nia feels empowered to make decisions to protect herself and to practice self-care. She wants to set boundaries with others but also to be able to trust significant others in the future. She also wants to move past this trauma with enhanced compassion for others, and she has plans to volunteer at the local rape crisis center when she is old enough to do so.

PREVENTION/RISK REDUCTION PROGRAMS

Because girls often experience sexual violence perpetrated by a dating partner or someone they know, the emphasis of prevention programs is currently to reduce the risk of sexual violence, while also providing adolescents with the skills to prevent dating violence. The programs Safe Dates, Choose Respect, and Expect Respect are highlighted here.

Safe Dates

Safe Dates (Foshee & Langwick, 2010; Foshee et al., 2005) is a research-based program with strong long-term outcomes and effectiveness with diverse populations of adolescents. It has been identified as a model program in the National Registry of Evidence–Based Programs and Practices. The overall goals of the program are to (a) raise student awareness of what constitutes healthy versus abusive dating relationships; (b) raise awareness of dating abuse, its causes, and its consequences; (c) provide students with skills and resources to help themselves or friends in abusive dating relationships; and (d) equip students with skills to develop healthy dating relationships, including positive communication, anger management, and conflict resolution. Research studies of program participants (compared to students who did not attend the program) indicate that both male and female participants report reductions in rates of perpetration (among teens already engaging in violence against their dating partners), less likelihood of being a victim of physical dating violence, lower reported levels of acceptance of dating violence and gender stereotypes, stronger communication and anger management skills, and greater awareness of community services for dating abuse (Foshee et al., 2005).

Choose Respect

Another commonly used program is the *Choose Respect* initiative offered by the Centers for Disease Control and Prevention (available: www. chooserespect.org). Available at no cost, it is a web-based resource containing information, resources, educational videos, TV and radio ads, print resources, and a facilitator's guide for prevention education. One of its newer programs is Dating Matters, a no-cost, 60-minute online training program designed to help educators, youth-serving organizations, and others working with teens to understand the risk factors and warning signs associated with adolescent dating violence. The training covers adolescent dating violence and its consequences, information on how to identify risk factors for dating violence, strategies for communicating with adolescents about the importance of healthy relationships, and provides resources to prevent dating violence. The Dating Matters training program is available at www.vetoviolence. org/datingmatters/index.html.

Expect Respect

A school-wide dating violence prevention approach that incorporates the Choose Respect initiative is the *Expect Respect* program (Ball, Kerig, & Rosenbluth, 2009). It incorporates five components: (a) administering a needs assessment of the school climate regarding dating relationships; (b) establishing a school policy for defining and reporting adolescent dating violence; (c) conducting an awareness campaign based on the Choose Respect initiative (see the preceding), which includes awareness training for parents and teacher a well a students; (d) developing a Safe Teens youth leadership training program in which students in the school are invited to take action and become actively involved in creating a prevention project regarding sexual harassment and dating violence; (e) establishing Expect Respect support groups for students who have experienced dating violence or sexual abuse. These are separate gender groups held for 24 weekly sessions throughout the school year. The goal of the group is to prevent at-risk adolescents from becoming future victims and/ or perpetrators of violence (Ball et al., 2009). By using a top-down, multisystemic approach, all stakeholders are more likely to become involved in prevention efforts.

CONCLUSION

In summary, the purpose of this chapter was to provide an overview of sexual violence in adolescent girls, as conceptualized through an ecological systems framework. It is important for counselors to consider a girl's life history within these multiple systems in order to fully understand her sexual trauma experience and to provide developmentally sensitive treatment. Adolescent dating violence was also included as part of a system that can contribute to the onset of intimate partner violence, which is often related to sexual assault and rape. Treatments for sexual trauma are intentionally trauma focused so that the adolescent client has an opportunity to face her memories, experiences, and fears directly, process them, and experience a subsequent reduction in her associated anxiety and other trauma-related symptoms. Because sexual violence is one of the most difficult types of trauma a person can undergo, prevention programs designed to reduce risks for both sexual and dating violence are essential to prevent the potential development of a pattern of victimization and abusive relationships.

RESOURCES

In addition to the resources provided in the chapter, the following resources will also be helpful for counselors:

National Child Traumatic Stress Network: www.NCTSN.org
The purpose of the network is to improve access to services for traumatized children, their families and communities throughout the United States. According to its stated vision, the network provides resources to raise public awareness of the scope and serious impact of child traumatic stress, to advance a broad range of effective services and interventions by creating trauma-informed developmentally and culturally appropriate programs, and to work with established systems of care to ensure that there is a comprehensive trauma-informed continuum of accessible care for traumatized children.

Seeking Safety: www.seekingsafety.org
Because so many adolescent survivors of sexual violence cope with their feelings through using alcohol and other drugs, the Seeking Safety program was developed for adolescents with PTSD and comorbid substance use. It is an evidence-based and widely used group model that focuses on establishing safety in all life areas. It includes sequential interventions for (a) affective modulation and stabilization, (b) substance abuse risk reduction, and (c) trauma specific cognitive processing and coping skills. There are 25 topics covered in the manual, with each topic independent of the others so that groups can remain open.

National Center for Injury Prevention and Control: www.cdc.gov/ViolencePrevention/sexualviolence/index.html
The National Center for Injury Prevention and Control (NCIPC) site provides facts and statistics regarding sexual violence, provides links

to relevant research, describes effective prevention and training programs for professionals, and lists links to resources for survivors.

National Sexual Violence Resource Center: www.nsvrc.org
The National Sexual Violence Resource Center provides a clearinghouse of information on sexual violence intervention and prevention strategies.

Rape, Abuse, and Incest National Network: www.rainn.org/
Rape, Abuse, and Incest National Network (RAINN) is currently the nation's largest antisexual assault organization. RAINN created and operates the National Sexual Assault Hotline and National Sexual Assault Online Hotline (800.656.HOPE and Rainn.org) in partnership with over 1,100 local rape crisis centers across the country. RAINN also carries out programs to prevent sexual assault, help victims, and ensure that rapists are brought to justice.

8

Hope for the Future: Strengthening Resilience in Adolescent Girls

One of the primary goals of this book was to provide an analysis of adolescent girls' lived experiences as viewed through an ecological systems lens. Starting with the macrosystem, the book began with an overview of current cultural trends that are impacting girls at increasingly younger ages. In childhood, a girl learns that to have value, she must look hot, sexy, and older than she is; act like a diva; be materialistic, competitive, and aggressive; plaster herself online with the right image; and be perfect in all areas. Clearly, this is a lot for a girl to absorb as she is trying to figure out who she is and what she wants to become.

Adding to this pressure from the larger culture, she is also entering a period in which she faces multiple physical and psychosocial developmental challenges. As reviewed in Chapter 2, a girl simultaneously experiences massive changes in her brain and body, with gains in enhanced cognitive, emotional, and relational complexity. At the same time, she also faces changes in friendships, pressures around attracting a romantic partner, academic stressors and harassment at school, and transitions in her family relationships. Often these combined factors become more than girls can manage at one time. In addition, cultural messages may impede her mastery of developmental tasks (e.g., encouraging her to dress and act hot and sexy before she is psychologically prepared for actual sexual activity, or causing conflict between her desire to maintain relationships with friends and the message that she should be competitive with other girls). Often without adequate problem solving and coping skills and parenting and/or peer support, girls' development becomes derailed, placing them at risk for negative outcomes, including the mental health problems reviewed in Chapters 3 to 7.

The specific mental health problems addressed in these chapters (depression, Chapter 3; eating and weight related problems, Chapter 4; substance use disorders, Chapter 5; self-injury, Chapter 6; and sexual assault/dating violence, Chapter 7) are common in adolescent girls. Because the expectations for girls have shifted in recent years, treatments should be sensitive to the current cultural context. It is my hope that this book provides a step toward both the dissemination of evidence-based practices for girls experiencing these problems, as well as for assisting practitioners in recognizing external and developmental influences on girls' mental health.

I have also emphasized the importance of prevention for each of these mental health concerns, and have provided general prevention components and specific program highlights as part of each chapter. In many cases, if girls can learn the coping, problem solving, and social skills they need to navigate the minefields of adolescence, they will be far better equipped to manage initial problems as they arise rather than having them evolve into symptoms or even future disorders. These components presented in each chapter were drawn from targeted prevention programs designed to prevent the onset of further problems in girls who are already at high risk for the particular problem or disorder.

Because our goal as mental health professionals is to build resilience in *all* girls so that they develop optimal mental health during the adolescent years, the purpose in this final chapter is to focus on the development of girls' life skills that will enable them to remain resilient against the pressures of contemporary adolescent life. Drawing from components in selected prevention programs described throughout the chapters in this book (Penn Resiliency Program, Girls in Transition, Body Image Resilience model, Body Project, Life Skills Training), as well as several current primary prevention programs and resources for girls, in the following section I provide 12 resilience-building skills, practices, and supports that girls need in order not only to survive but also to thrive during their adolescent years.

LIFE SKILLS FOR RESILIENCE IN ADOLESCENT GIRLS

Quality Parenting

Parents play a critical role in fostering girls' resilience and for providing a foundation for the development of all the skills described in the following. As reviewed in Chapter 2, a girl needs a warm, supportive relationship with parents or caregivers in which she is fully accepted based on who she is, not based upon her appearance, behaviors, accomplishments, or parental expectations. In addition to unconditional acceptance, girls also need parents who provide clear and consistent structure, boundaries, and limits. Monitoring their daughter's whereabouts, setting family rules, enforcing consequences, and remaining informed regarding their daughter's activities and peer group are all positive parenting practices that contribute to girls' success. While many girls do not have access to this type of parenting, counselors working with girls can provide parental education regarding these practices to their clients' families, and when this is not possible, counselors can work to ensure that girls are surrounded by as many positive adult mentors who can provide this structure to the greatest extent possible.

Problem-Solving and Decision-Making Skills, Resourcefulness

Levine (2012) identifies an essential skill for resilience: resourcefulness, which is the ability to solve daily life problems independently and to know how to seek help from others when we can't solve problems on our own. Many adolescents today do not have the internal organization necessary to solve their own dilemmas and instead turn to parents or others to handle their problems for them. In addition, girls are more likely to ruminate about problems, and when they discuss their problems with others they tend to co-ruminate rather than to use their combined resources to solve the problem. Therefore, while parents and trusted adults can assist girls in brainstorming possible solutions, girls need the skills to be resourceful by problem solving on their own in order to become confident and self-reliant (Levine, 2012).

As discussed throughout this book, if girls can learn to implement basic problem-solving strategies in situations where action is needed, they can eliminate many initial stressors or problems before they become worse. As reviewed in Chapter 3, the following is a five-step problem-solving model that is helpful for girls to learn:

1. Specify and operationalize the problem—What is the problem? What are the various contributors to the problem? What are the reasons that this is causing problems for you? Out of all possible problems you are facing, which is the one that needs immediate attention? Try to narrow down the problem.
2. Define goals—Ideally, what would you like to have happen in this situation?
3. Formulate possible solutions—identify and brainstorm a wide range of possible solutions. This aspect can call upon creativity as the adolescent learns to look at the problem from different perspectives, trying to generate innovative ways to solve a problem. For example, you can consider times in which you have faced similar problems and how you handled the situations at other times.
4. Evaluate possible solutions—After compiling a list of possibilities, weigh the possible pros and cons of each option. What are the advantages and disadvantages of each? What are the potential outcomes for each?
5. Choose a solution—After a careful analysis of the pros/cons list you created, choose a solution based on its compatibility with your ideal outcome for the situation, your ability to actually take the steps needed to act on the plan, and any barriers to achieving the plan.

These skills are also helpful for decision making (e.g., making a list of pros and cons for each option, weighing them carefully, and choosing an option), especially when a girl might tend to make decisions based upon what is easiest, what is most popular among her peers, or based solely on her emotions. When she has a structure to use and adult guidance to help her put these steps into practice, she can learn to problem solve more easily and will feel in greater control of her life.

Coping Skills for Emotion Regulation and Distress Tolerance

While problem-solving skills are essential for times when a girl needs to take action, she also needs skills for coping with situations that may be out of her control to change. People in her life will disappoint her, unexpected crises may occur, and her life may be changing too rapidly for her to comfortably manage. Girls need coping skills for identifying, expressing, and regulating their emotions by interrupting the chain of events leading to distressing emotions and for tolerating distress in situations that cannot be changed by implementing self-soothing responses.

Emotion Regulation Skills

Emotion regulation strategies are used to reduce emotional vulnerability and change intense and painful emotions. A girl can learn to recognize that she does have control over how she reacts to emotional experiences. She begins to learn the function her emotions serve and how she can better manage her reactions.

Some specific skills for emotion regulation (as reviewed in Chapter 6) include:

- Identifying the trigger of the emotion
- Reducing vulnerability to intense reactions by caring for herself physically, eating a nutritious, balanced diet, getting enough sleep and exercise
- Increasing positive emotions through increasing daily pleasant events
- Building mastery through completing daily activities that contribute to a sense of competence
- Acting opposite to current emotions by acting in a manner opposite to the emotion she is currently experiencing

Distress Tolerance Skills

Distress tolerance is the ability to effectively tolerate emotional pain in situations that cannot be changed, at least in the present moment. By accepting a situation that cannot be changed and not struggling against it, a client is able to cope with it more effectively. These coping skills can be presented to girls in terms of five categories, as presented in Chapter 3: (a) do something fun and relaxing; (b) do something that uses energy; (c) do something soothing and relaxing; (d) talk to someone; and (e) change the way you think about it. The self-soothing strategies can also be developed in terms of the five senses: vision (art, nature), hearing (soft, pleasant music), smell (scented candles), taste (herbal teas, chocolates), or touch (velvet pillows). Some additional coping strategies also include:

- Mental imagery
- Deep breathing
- Prayer, connecting to religious and spiritual resources
- Taking a break
- Using positive thoughts
- Progressive muscle relaxation
- Seeking social support

Social Skills: Communication, Assertiveness, Conflict Resolution

Girls are socialized to be indirect with their communication with others, particularly regarding confrontation over differences. Many girls are concerned about jeopardizing a relationship if they attempt to express their true thoughts and feelings, and many have never learned the skills for open, assertive communication or for effective conflict resolution. While these skills are relatively straightforward, in reality their implementation will be difficult for girls when they fear the results of a new communication style.

Therefore, girls will benefit from skills training in the areas of assertiveness (e.g., avoiding passivity and aggression); compromise (e.g., active listening, reflection, negotiation, conflict resolution); social interaction skills (e.g., starting conversations, joining groups, listening, using "I" statements); and family communication (e.g., reducing blame, clearly identifying problems without name calling, increasing trust) (Kennard et al., 2009).

Simmons (2009) presents a helpful, specific five-step model of conflict resolution that incorporates the value that girls place on their relationships:

CONFLICT RESOLUTION MODEL

1. Affirm the positive aspects of the relationship (say something positive about the relationship: "I really like working with you on this project").
2. Avoid using the word "but" to move between steps. Use "and" instead.
3. Use an "I" statement: Define the specific problem and how you feel about it. Try using a feeling word and a "who, what, where, when, and

why" of what's bothering you. "I am feeling frustrated because of the number of hours that I am putting into this project."
4. Say your contribution; explain what you did to make the problem bigger or worse: "I know that I didn't approach you about this earlier, so we have not been communicating well about the problem."
5. Ask how you can solve this together: Say what you need from the other person and also offer to do something yourself. "I would like for you to complete your part of the project by Tuesday so I can have time to combine it with my part. I will be glad to edit the whole paper to make sure it fits together well. How does that sound?"

To be assertive, a girl will need to learn that it is acceptable to express how she feels (even if it differs from others), to say no directly, to say what she thinks, and to ask for what she needs (Silverman, 2010). Because this way of communicating is so different from the way she might have been socialized, these skills might require modeling, role playing, and considerable practice before she feels comfortable and confident in her newfound assertiveness.

Cognitive Skills: Cognitive Restructuring, Self-Regulation

As a girl begins to develop abstract thinking skills, she is better able to identify any negative automatic thoughts and her cognitive distortions about self, others, and the future. It is helpful for her to uncover her core beliefs and the guidelines or rules for living she has developed based on these beliefs (e.g., "I am unlovable, therefore, I must work hard to look perfect in order for people to like me"). She can also identify her automatic thoughts (her internal running dialogue) that can become distorted and self-critical. In addition, she needs to be aware of any cognitive distortions she has developed, such as mindreading (jumping to conclusions, assuming she knows what others are thinking about her), fortune telling (believing she can foretell what is going to happen in the future), and all-or-nothing thinking.

Once she has identified any tendencies toward distorted thinking, she can learn to become more aware of these cognitive biases and to challenge them as they occur. As she does so, she can learn to recognize how her reactions to events are a result of her *interpretation* of the situation. It is her thoughts or interpretation of events (often based upon automatic thoughts or cognitive distortions) that cause her distress, not the events themselves.

Next, she can then learn to generate possible alternative interpretations, moving away from black/white, either/or thinking, to consider others' perspectives, to realize that there are multiple ways to view any situation, and to practice examining all sides of a situation (Miller et al., 2007). For example, when she has a negative thought, she can ask herself the following questions:

1. Is there any evidence that this belief is true? Is my belief realistic?
2. Is there another way to think about it?
3. Is this belief helping me or harming me?
4. If this were true, what would be the best and the worst thing that might happen?
5. Is my thinking extreme or self-critical?
6. Would a good friend say this to me?

As part of this process, she can continue to practice challenging negative self-talk, and to substitute these with more positive, affirming, balanced, and realistic thoughts.

In addition to cognitive restructuring skills, a girl will also need to develop a greater capacity for self-regulation. The ability to delay gratification and to control impulsivity, to be able to have internal restraint rather than always relying on external rules and monitors, can protect her from many problems (Levine, 2012). To help her learn the benefits of self-regulation, she will benefit from ongoing conversations about the multiple alternatives in any situation and the costs/benefits and consequences of each. As she rehearses the practice of pausing and thinking through her options, she can gradually learn to do this in actual life situations. She can also learn self-regulation as adults provide her with increasing levels of age-appropriate responsibility and require that she experience the consequences of her decisions.

Authenticity: Self-Awareness, Standing Up for Her Convictions

As has been emphasized throughout this book, cultural trends encourage girls to look and act in increasingly complex ways, leaving girls confused in terms of their identity development. A girl learns that she is expected to fulfill others' expectations but also to live up to her own, resulting in a double bind: If she disconnects from her authentic self in pursuit of connections with others, she experiences a loss of self-esteem; if she attempts to disconnect from others in pursuit of autonomy, she feels a loss when she does not feel supported by others (Anderson & Choate, 2008). To resolve this tension, often a girl will try to conform and act the part that she believes is expected of her (and that will bring the most approval) rather than first defining who she is and what she believes, and subsequently making life choices based on this core sense of self.

Instead the process may require a "different way of being in the world with others" (Brown, 1991, p. 83) that includes the development of a responsibility to both self and others. To be able to do this, first she needs to know herself. She needs opportunities to discover the answers to such questions as "Who am I?" "What do I believe?" "What do I like? Dislike?" "What are my standards for friendships? For romantic partners?" "What are my strengths? What are my areas for growth?" Instead of conforming to the beliefs and values of peers and family, what does she believe for herself? This can occur with adult guidance and conversations to help her recognize and affirm these values (Simmons, 2009). It can also occur through having adequate downtime for self-reflection; instead of remaining busy rushing from activity to activity (or of spending inordinate amounts of time with peers), she needs time alone to reflect on her core values and dream about what she wants for her future (Hartstein, 2012).

Once she has started to define what is most meaningful to her, she then needs the skills for standing up for her beliefs, and for living by her convictions, despite pressure from others who try to compromise these values (Silverman, 2010). She begins to believe in her power to make her own choices, despite what others might think. Some girls refrain from taking a stand because she believes that her role is to keep the peace in relationships. She fears that others might be hurt if she disagrees with them or tries to go her own way. In contrast, Simmons (2009) distinguishes between this type of "nice girl" and a "real girl"—a girl that stays connected to her strong inner core of thoughts, feelings, desires, and then is able to act on it. An authentic "real girl" does not ignore others' needs, but can manage the needs of others without sacrificing the integrity of her own. She can defend her interests in a relationship or advocate on her own behalf (Simmons, 2009, p. 11).

This balance between caring for self versus caring for others is important, because many girls lean to one extreme or the other—either they express a "me-first" attitude of selfishness and aggression (as described in Chapter 1) or they deny their own thoughts and feelings in order to please others at all costs. She needs to develop an authentic sense of self that is able to incorporate compassion and empathy for others. This is not easy when there are few role models in the media that represent this image of an empowered, assertive, authentic, yet caring woman. It is also difficult because girls and women who are assertive and share how they feel or what they have accomplished are often maligned with pejorative labels. According to Simmons (2009), "Despite every door that has opened, girls continue to grapple with confusing, conflicting messages about personal authority: be successful, but say nothing about it, or about yourself; be strong but don't make anyone angry; and be confident, but do it quietly" (p. 250). Girls need to learn that speaking the truth may not always be popular or easy, but it is vitally important to her growth and optimal development (Silverman, 2010).

PROGRAM HIGHLIGHT: FULL OF OURSELVES

Full of Ourselves. A wellness program to advance girl power, health, and leadership (Steiner-Adair & Sjostrom, 2006) is a primary prevention program intended to enhance girls' mental, physical, and social health and to decrease their vulnerability to the development of negative body image and eating-related problems. Research to evaluate the program indicates that it promotes positive changes in girls' body satisfaction, body image, and body esteem. It is also effective in increasing girls' knowledge about health, nutrition, weightism, and puberty. The three primary components of the curriculum are power, health, and leadership.

Power. Girls learn how to accept their bodies as sources of strength; they learn how to state their own opinions in an assertiveness manner, use positive self-talk, and understand the power that comes from creating healthy relationships with others.

Health. Girls gain tools to build and maintain the well-being of the body, mind, and spirit; they learn to have a healthy, nutritious diet (vs. dieting), and learn to replace "good" and "bad" food labels with the idea of "powerful foods"; they also learn to refrain from using food as a coping mechanism; they learn healthy stress-reduction techniques, such as journaling and yoga, to help them cope in any situation.

Leadership. Girls have opportunities to experience themselves as leaders and agents of change. The curriculum provides multiple opportunities to put girls' ideas into action with family, peers, and community. In the second phase of the program, girls have a chance to become leaders—mentors by leading activities for younger girls.

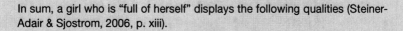

In sum, a girl who is "full of herself" displays the following qualities (Steiner-Adair & Sjostrom, 2006, p. xiii).

- I know who I am.
- I know that I matter.
- I know what matters to me.
- I pay attention to what I feel and what I need.
- I make choices and decisions that are good for me.
- I take good care of my body.
- I stand up for what I believe in.
- I let people know what I think, even when I'm angry or confused or in disagreement with everyone else.
- I am a valuable friend.
- I know I can make a positive difference in the world in my own unique way.

Self-Worth and Self-Efficacy

For a girl to thrive in today's culture, she needs a sense of self-worth that is unconditional—not based upon her appearance, her material possessions, or how well she lives up to external expectations. She needs to believe she is worthwhile and that she has a purpose. This requires that she develops an authentic core, a foundation, that helps her feel good about herself even in the face of challenges, negative feedback, or occasional setbacks (Hartstein, 2012). Self-worth comes from confidence in who she is as well as from her competence to handle life challenges. This sense of competence, also termed self-efficacy, is the belief that she is a capable, active agent in her own life story, and the belief that her actions and decisions play a role in how things will turn out for her. She knows that she is not a passive victim in life, but has the capability to make positive choices and to determine how her life is shaped (Anderson & Choate, 2008).

Wellness and Balance

A girl needs holistic wellness and balance in her life in order to thrive. Although societal messages encourage her to value primarily one area—her appearance—she can learn to value all aspects of herself and to develop a range of skills in multiple life areas. She can appreciate her strengths in the intellectual, fitness/health, social, career, and spiritual dimensions, placing greater emphasis on her character than on external appearance or accomplishments. She can remember that when she overemphasizes any one area of her life, or neglects certain other areas, her overall wellness is compromised; she will feel out of balance, much as when one spoke on a wheel is broken, the entire wheel does not roll effectively (Myers & Sweeney, 2005).

At the core of wellness is spirituality, a core aspect of overall mental health. Spirituality encompasses personal and private beliefs that enhance one's life, hope, and optimism, purpose in life, moral values, transcendence, and overall spiritual well-being (Myers & Sweeney, 2005). It also includes one's awareness of a being or force that transcends the material aspects of life and gives a deep sense of wholeness or connectedness to the universe (Myers & Sweeney, 2005). If a girl draws her sense of meaning from a spiritual force that goes beyond herself and provides her with a sense of coherence and purpose, she will find less need to focus on appearance or accomplishments when searching for happiness or life satisfaction. Viewing life through a spiritual perspective gives her a sense of meaning and purpose, helping her to see that she is part of something larger than herself and her own problems. This helps her cultivate a sense of gratitude for what she does have (instead of comparing herself with others and feeling that she does not measure up), and gives her compassion and empathy for others. When a girl is grateful for the positives in her life, believes in a greater purpose for her life, and experiences interconnectedness with others, she is better at rejecting current cultural trends toward materialism and entitlement. As a girl decreases emphasis on appearance and conformity, not basing her sense of worth as contingent on unattainable standards, she can begin to dedicate her time and energy to the pursuit of goals in all areas of wellness (Choate, 2008).

Positive Support Systems: Adults, Peers, Dating Partners

Girls need supportive relationships during this time of rapid change and instability in their lives. Positive support systems should include relationships with parents and other caregivers, who can provide a much-needed network of encouragement, warmth, and security. Parents can seek to ensure that a girl has access to adult mentors throughout her life (e.g., school, community, religious leaders) who can also provide guidance and wisdom as she develops the skills for resilience described in this chapter.

A girl's support system should also include positive friendships that can affirm her, support her, and accept her as she is. Friends who engage in prosocial (vs. deviant) behaviors are a strong influence on her decision-making processes and actual behaviors. As a girl's peer group expands into potential romantic partners, she also needs the skills for developing trusting relationships that involve open communication, where she can assert her own needs, and have these needs respected. She also needs to have an awareness of potential warning signs for unhealthy relationships so that she can remove herself from these situations before she becomes fully entrenched in them (see Chapter 7).

PROGRAM HIGHLIGHT: GO GRRRLS PROGRAM

The Go Grrrls Program (LeCroy & Daley, 2001) is a research-based primary prevention program designed to help girls develop a lifelong perspective about living as a female in society. Sessions comprise a wide range of topics, including:

1. Self-awareness, learning to describe oneself
2. Being a girl in today's society, stereotypes, and talking back to media messages
3. Establishing a positive body image, body acceptance
4. Establishing a positive mindset, identifying strengths
5. Making and keeping friends, understanding what makes a good friend
6. Establishing independence through problem solving and decision making
7. Establishing independence through assertiveness
8. Establishing a sexual identity and setting sexual limits
9. Establishing an awareness of warning signs and knowing how to reach out for help, knowing resources in community
10. Planning for the future: career aspirations, dreams for the future

Positive Physical Self-Concept: Body Acceptance, Physical Changes, Self-Care

Despite all of the messages she will receive regarding her body and appearance that encourage her to believe that she will never measure up to the current societal standard, a girl should be encouraged to accept her body, to continually see it in a positive light, and to appreciate her unique physical attributes. A girl can grow to understand that her perception of her body is not a reflection of her overall worth, but is the home for her authentic self. A broader, more fluid definition of beauty can encompass such qualities as self-respect, assertiveness, compassion, wisdom, confidence, individuality, and motivation (National Eating Disorders Association [NEDA], 2012). She should protect herself from worrying excessively about what others might think about her appearance, and should maintain a realistic image of herself that is not influenced by comparisons to unrealistic standards.

In addition to body acceptance, a girl needs basic education regarding the physical and psychological changes that are occurring in her body as she transitions through adolescence; she needs assistance in understanding her physical development, puberty, menstruation, sexual identity and feelings, and her cognitive and emotional changes. Girls also need to be aware of the normative nature of weight gain during this time and develop the ability to challenge the inconsistencies between the media-generated thin ideal and their maturing bodies (see website resources at the end of this chapter).

Further, girls need basic information to guide their decisions around self-care, including health, nutrition, exercise, and sleep. In particular, girls need to learn skills for healthy weight management, not dieting, which will include healthful eating and moderate exercise. In particular, they need to learn about the negative effects of dieting (slowed metabolism, increased likelihood of binge eating, eventual weight gain), and ways to learn how to take a nondieting approach to healthful eating. Finally, girls highly benefit from their participation in physical activity. Girls should be encouraged to participate in a variety of physical activities that they enjoy; however, their motivations should be for the purposes of health and improved fitness rather than for weight control or body shape changes (NEDA, 2012).

Media Literacy Skills

Media literacy involves the ability to identify, evaluate, and resist media messages so that one becomes an active consumer rather than a passive victim of media influences. Literacy involves a four-step process: (a) Identify harmful cultural images, (b) explore and deconstruct underlying messages, (c) resist the message being sent, and (d) actively work to change these messages. She will need assistance in recognizing the unrealistic, unattainable nature of media images, and then will need education regarding the process of how these images are created (e.g., through strategies such as digital editing). She can begin to question the values embedded in these images, through the following inquiries used for deconstructing an advertisement:

- Do real girls and women look like these models?
- What is the real purpose of the advertisement?
- Will buying this product help me look like this?
- If I did use/wear this product, would my life really become like the life portrayed in the ad?
- Does the model really use this product to help her look like this?
- What are the consequences of these messages for girls?

Girls need skills to actively resist and challenge these messages and to generate positive alternatives to messages conveyed. It is helpful for parents and adult mentors to co-view media and to help guide a girl through deconstructing advertisements and media themes. Adults can highly influence adolescents' choices regarding how they will allow media messages to influence their personal lifestyles, beliefs, and values (Lamb & Brown, 2006). Consult the Center for Media Literacy and Media Education Foundation to view downloadable activities, resources, handouts, and study guides.

Develop Goals, Pursue Them With Perseverance

As discussed in Chapter 2, many girls are overly involved in multiple activities, but may be participating only due to parental pressure for resume building. On the other hand, many other girls are under-involved, trying to remain unnoticed and preferring to be left alone. Both extremes can lead to girls' boredom and lack of fulfillment, which places them at risk for depression and other problems. Girls do best when they find an interest, talent, skill, or dream that excites them and inspires them to pursue their passion (Silverman, 2010). Pursuing a dream creates an enthusiasm and a healthy zest for living (Levine, 2012). In order to find her passion, she must try out new things, spend time pursuing various interests, and take healthy risks that might involve multiple successes and setbacks. As she finds her interest area, she can learn to develop a strong work ethic, spending time and effort in persisting toward her passion, and going after goals to create the future she truly wants for herself (Levine, 2012; Silverman, 2010).

PROGRAM HIGHLIGHT: GIRLS ON THE RUN

Girls on the Run (GOTR) is a research-based primary prevention program that has demonstrated positive effects on the physical, emotional, social, and intellectual development in 3rd through 8th grade girls (Girls on the Run International, 2012). Evaluations of the program indicate that girls complete the 12-week program with a stronger sense of identity, greater self-confidence, a healthier body image, and a better knowledge of what it means to be a member of a team and a community (Gabriel, DeBate, High, & Racine, 2011). The culminating event of the 12-week season is the opportunity for the girls to participate in a noncompetitive 5K running event, a goal that often seems out of reach to many of the participants at the beginning of the program. The 24-session program combines both physical activities with experiential learning about a variety of topics, highlighted below.

Highlights of the GOTR curriculum include:

1. Self-awareness and discovery
2. Positive team building and cooperation
3. Identifying self-talk, increasing positive self-talk
4. Emphasis on healthy eating, nutrition, moderate exercise
5. Emotion regulation skills
6. Taking time for self-reflection, self-care, gratitude
7. Positive body image, broadening definitions of beauty
8. Assertiveness skills, managing peer pressure
9. Skills for positive friendships and for managing relational aggression
10. Media literacy skills
11. Importance of community service and action
12. Goal setting, perseverance in attaining a positive goal (in this case, training for a 5K race and successfully completing it)

CONCLUSION: HOPE FOR THE FUTURE

This book was intended to provide a guide for mental health professionals and others interested in working with adolescent girls. It is my hope that presenting a portrait of girls' experiences from an ecological systems perspective will enlighten our understanding of the pressures and changes that girls are experiencing during this period in their lives. My intention was to present changes that are occurring not only on an individual level (physical, psychosocial developmental shifts) but also on micro (family, peer, school) and macro (cultural) levels. These changes are becoming increasingly intense for girls, particularly when they experience them simultaneously and do not find the support they need for navigating these new pathways. It is not surprising that girls are developing problems in coping with these challenges, and they (and their parents) are turning to counselors for assistance. I hope that this book can be a valuable resource for counselors as they consider multiple systems operating in girls' lives and how these in turn can influence the development of and treatment for various mental health concerns.

Just as important as the goal to provide a resource for treatment, I hoped to present prevention components that would help deter the onset of many of these problems in girls. Because of the current cultural climate that seems increasingly toxic for younger girls, it is especially important that counselors become involved in prevention efforts to work with girls *before* they reach the onset of puberty and the multiple challenges it poses. If counselors can find ways to partner with parents, schools, and youth organizations to enhance these life skills for resilience, girls would be better able to resist cultural pressures and to manage the changes that are occurring in their lives. Today's girls do have the strengths and qualities to thrive despite the complex and often contradictory cultural climate. As counselors, our work is to collaborate with girls and their support systems to empower them and to help develop their skills for holistic wellness and balance, healthy relationships, problem solving, assertive communication, and for coping with negative emotions. Finally, we wish to provide girls with flexible boundaries, responsibility, and guidance on their journey toward adulthood.

RESOURCES

TheGirlEffect.org
A site that promotes awareness about issues that affect girls and encourages them to get involved to change negative messages that limit girls' achievement.

Empoweragirl.org
An international nonprofit organization that helps girls interact with other girls internationally and become social change agents.

Girlsforachange.org
A site that encourage girls to use their own voice to become activists in their own communities.

Girlsontherun.org
As reviewed in this chapter, this program encourages girls to be physically healthy while teaching lessons about empowerment and self-esteem.

Braincake.org
A site that encourages girls to pursue activities, interests, and careers in the fields of math, science, and technology.

Girlstart.org
A site for parents, teachers, and all educators that want to help girls explore science, technology, engineering, and mathematics projects. The site also contains interesting projects and experiments for girls to conduct.

GirlsInc.org
Girls Inc. inspires all girls to be "strong, smart, and bold" through programs and experiences that help girls navigate gender, economic, and social barriers. According to their website, research-based curricula, delivered by trained, mentoring professionals in a positive all-girl environment, equip girls to achieve academically; lead healthy and physically active lives; manage money; navigate media messages; and discover an interest in science, technology, engineering, and math. The network of local Girls Inc. nonprofit organizations serves 125,000 girls ages 6 to 18 annually across the United States and Canada.

References

Abela, J. R. Z., & Hankin, B. L. (2008a). Cognitive vulnerability to depression in children and adolescents: A developmental psychopathology perspective. In J. R. Z. Abela & B. L. Hankin (Eds.), *Handbook of depression in children and adolescents* (pp. 35–78). New York, NY: The Guilford Press.

Abela, J. R. Z., & Hankin, B. L. (2008b). Depression in children and adolescents: Causes, treatment, and prevention. In J. R. Z. Abela & B. L. Hankin (Eds.), *Handbook of depression in children and adolescents* (pp. 3–5). New York, NY: The Guilford Press.

Abela, J. R. Z., & Hankin, B. L. (2008c). *Handbook of depression in children and adolescents.* New York, NY: The Guilford Press.

Ackard, D. M., & Neumark-Sztainer, D. (2002). Date violence and rape among adolescents: Associations with disordered eating behaviors and psychological health. *Child Abuse & Neglect, 26*, 455–473.

Ackard, D. M., Neumark-Sztainer, D., Story, M., & Perry, C. (2003). Overeating among adolescents: Prevalence and associations with weight-related characteristics and psychological health. *Pediatrics, 111*(1), 67–74. doi:10.1542/peds.111.1.67

Adrian, M., Zeman, J., Erdley, C., Lisa, L., & Sim, L. (2011). Emotional dysregulation and interpersonal difficulties as risk factors for nonsuicidal self-injury in adolescent girls. *Journal of Abnormal Child Psychology, 39*, 389–400.

Ahrens, C. E., Stansell, J., & Jennings, A. (2010). To tell or not to tell: The impact of disclosure on sexual assault Survivors' Recovery. *Violence & Victims, 25*(5), 631–648. doi:10.1891/0886-6708.25.5.631

Alegria, M., Woo, M., Cao, Z., Torres, M., Meng, X., & Striegel-Moore, R. (2007). Prevalence and correlates of eating disorders in Latinos in the United States. *International Journal of Eating Disorders, 40*, 15–21. doi:10.1002/eat.20406

American Academy of Child and Adolescent Psychiatry. (2005). Practice parameter for the assessment and treatment of children and adolescents with substance use disorders. *Journal of the American Academy of Child & Adolescent Psychiatry, 44*, 609–621.

American Academy of Child and Adolescent Psychiatry. (2007). Practice parameter for the assessment and treatment of children and adolescents with depressive disorders. *Journal of the American Academy of Child and Adolescent Psychiatry, 46*(11), 1503–1526. doi:10.1097/chi.0b013e318145aelc

American Association of University Women, Hill, C., & Kearl, H. (2011). *Crossing the line: Sexual harassment at school.* American Association of University Women, Washington, D.C.

American Psychiatric Association. (2000). *Diagnostic and statistical manual of mental disorders (DSM-IV-TR)* (4th ed., text revision). Washington, DC: American Psychiatric Association.

American Psychiatric Association. (2006). Practice guidelines for the treatment of patients with eating disorders [revision]. *American Journal of Psychiatry, 157,* 1–39.

American Psychiatric Association. (2012). *DSM-5 development.* Retrieved from www.dsm5.org.

American Psychiatric Association. (2012). *DSM-5 development.* Retrieved from http://www.dsm5.org/Pages/Default.aspx

American Psychological Association. (2007a). *Report of the American Psychological Association task force on the sexualization of girls.* Retrieved from www.apa.org.

American Psychological Association. (2007b). *Report of the APA task force on the sexualization of girls.* Washington, DC: Author.

Anderson, K., & Choate, L. (2008). Beyond the crossroads: A cognitive behavioral model to promote adolescent girls' self-esteem. In L. Choate (Ed.), *Girls' and women's wellness: Contemporary counseling issues and interventions* (pp. 89–116). Alexandria, VA: American Counseling Association Publications.

Arim, R., Tramonte, L., Shapka, J., Susan Dahinten, V. V., & Douglas Willms, J. J. (2011). The family antecedents and the subsequent outcomes of early puberty. *Journal of Youth & Adolescence, 40*(11), 1423–1435. doi:10.1007/s10964-011-9638-6

Arteaga, I., Chen, C., & Reynolds, A. (2010). Childhood predictors of adult substance abuse. *Children & Youth Services Review, 32*(8), 1108–1120.

Avenevoli, S., Knight, E., Kessler, R. C., & Merikangas, K. R. (2008). Epidemiology of depression in children and adolescents. In J. R. Z. Abela & B. L. Hankin (Eds.), *Handbook of depression in children and adolescents* (pp. 6–34). New York, NY: The Guilford Press.

Babor, T. F., Higgins-Biddle, J. C., Saunders, J. B., & Monteiro, M. G. (2001). Audit: Alcohol Use Disorders Identification Test. Geneva, Switzerland: World Health Organization. Retrieved from http://whqlibdoc.who.int/hq/2001/who_msd_msb_01.6a.pdf

Baker, F. (2003). Media Literacy Clearinghouse: Resources for K-12 Educators. Media Literacy Clearinghouse: Resources for K-12 Educators. Retrieved from http://www.frankwbaker.com/

Ball, B., Kerig, P., & Rosenbluth, B. (2009). "Like a family but better because you can actually trust each other": The expect respect dating violence prevention program for at-risk youth. *Health Promotion Practice, 10*(1), 45S–58S. doi:10.1177/1524839908322115

Bandura, A. (1991). Social cognitive theory of self-regulation. *Organizational Behavior and Human Decision Processes, 50,* 248–287.

Banyard, V., & Cross, C. (2008). Consequences of teen dating violence: Understanding intervening variables in ecological context. *Violence Against Women, 14*(9), 998–1013.

Barr Taylor, C., Bryson, S., Celio Doyle, A. A., Luce, K. H., Cunning, D., Abascal, L B., & Rockwell Wilfley, D. E. (2006). The adverse effects of negative comments about weight and shape from family and siblings on women at high risk for eating disorders. *Pediatrics, 118,* 731–738. doi:10.1177/02724316 030230002002

Basile, K., Black, M., Simon, T., Arias, I., Brener, N., & Saltzman, L. (2006). The association between self-reported lifetime history of forced sexual inter-course and recent health-risk behaviors: Findings from the 2003 National Youth Risk Behavior Survey. *Journal of Adolescent Health, 39*(5), 752.e1–e7.

Basow, S. A. (2006). Gender and role development. In J. Worell & C. D. Goodheard (Eds.), *Handbook on girls' and women's psychological health* (pp. 242–251). New York, NY: Oxford University Press.

Baumrind, D. (1991). The influence of parenting style on adolescent competence and substance use. *Journal of Early Adolescence, 11*(1), 56–95.

Becker, A., Franko, D., Speck, A., & Herzog, D. (2003). Ethnicity and differential access to care for eating disorder symptoms. *International Journal of Eating Disorders, 33*(2), 205–212. doi:10.1002/eat.10129

Behnken, M., Le, Y., Temple, J., & Berenson, A. (2010). Forced sexual intercourse, suicidality, and binge drinking among adolescent girls. *Addictive Behaviors, 35*(5), 507–509. doi:10.1016/j.addbeh.2009.12.008

Belsky, J., Houts, R. M., & Fearon, R. M. (2010). Infant attachment security and the timing of puberty: Testing and evolutionary hypothesis. *Psychological Science, 21*(9), 1195–1201. doi:10.1177/0956797610379867

Belsky, J., Steinberg, L. D., Houts, R. M., Friedman, S. L., DeHart, G., Cauffman, E., ... Susman, E. (2007). Family rearing antecedents of pubertal timing. *Child Development, 78*(4), 1302–1321.

Bem, S. L. (1993). *Lenses of gender: Transforming the debate on sexual inequality.* Yale University Press. New Haven, CT.

Berg, K. C., & Peterson, C. B. (2013). Assessment and diagnosis of eating disorders. In L. Choate (Ed.), *Eating disorders and obesity: A counselor's guide to prevention and treatment* (pp. 193–231). Alexandria, VA: American Counseling Association Press.

Bingham, C., & Crockett, L. (1996). Longitudinal adjustment patterns of boys and girls experiencing early, middle, and late sexual intercourse. *Developmental Psychology, 32,* 647–658.

Biro, F. M., Galvez, M. P., Greenspan, L. C., Succop, P. A., Vangeepuram, N., Pinney, S. M., ... Wolff, M. S. (2010). Pubertal assessment method and baseline characteristics in a mixed longitudinal study of girls. *Pediatrics, 126*(3), E583–E590.

Bissell-Havran, J. M., Loken, E., & McHale, S. M. (2012). Mothers' differential treatment of adolescent siblings: Predicting college attendance of sisters versus brothers. *Journal of Youth and Adolescence, 41*(10), 1267–1279. doi:10.1007/s10964-011-9727-6

Black, M., Basile, K., Breiding, M., Smith, S., Walters, M., Merrick, ... Stevens, M. R. (2011). *The National Intimate Partner and Sexual Violence Survey (NISVS)*. Atlanta, GA: National Center for Injury Prevention and Control, Centers for Disease Control and Prevention.

Blair, J. (2003). New breed of bullies torment their peers on the Internet. *Education Week, 22*, 6–8.

Blodgett Salafia, E. H., & Gondoli, D. M. (2011). A 4-year longitudinal investigation of the processes by which parents and peers Influence the development of early adolescent girls' bulimic symptoms. *Journal of Early Adolescence, 31*(3), 390–414.

Blueprints for Healthy Youth Development – Center for the Study and Prevention of Violence – Institute of Behavioral Science. (2012). *University of Colorado Boulder*. Retrieved from http://www.colorado.edu/cspv/blueprints/

Blumenthal, H., Leen-Feldner, E. W., Babson, K. A., Gahr, J. L., Trainor, C. D., & Frala, J. L. (2011). Elevated social anxiety among early maturing girls. *Developmental Psychology, 47*(4), 1133–1140. doi:10.1037/a0024008

Bolton, P., Bass, J., Betancourt, T., Spellman, L., Onyango, G., Clougherty, K. F., ... Verdeli, H. (2007). Interventions for depression symptoms among adolescent survivors of war and displacement in Northern Uganda. *Journal of the American Medical Association, 298*(5), 519–527.

Bond, E. (2012). Virtually anorexic—Where's the harm? A research study on the risks of pro-anorexia websites. Retrieved from www.ucs.ac.uk/virtuallyanorexic.

Botvin, G. J., & Griffin, K. W. (2002). Life skills training as a primary prevention approach for adolescent drug abuse and other problem behaviors. *International Journal of Emergency Mental Health, 4*(1), 41–48.

Brener, N. D., McMahon, P. M., Warren, C. W., & Douglas, K. A. (1999). Forced sexual intercourse and associated health-risk behaviors among female college students in the United States. *Journal of Consulting and Clinical Psychology, 67*, 252–259.

Brent, D. A., Polig, K. D., & Goldstein, T. R. (2011). *Treating depressed and suicidal adolescents: A clinician's guide*. New York, NY: The Guildford Press.

Briggs, C. A., & Pepperell, J. L. (2009). *Women, girls, and addiction: Celebrating the feminine in counseling treatment and recovery*. New York, NY: Routledge/Taylor & Francis Group.

Broman-Fulks, J. J., Ruggiero, K. J., Hanson, R. F., Smith, D. W., Resnick, H. S., Kilpatrick, D. G., & Saunders, B. E. (2007). Sexual assault disclosure in relation to adolescent mental health: Results from the National Survey of Adolescents. *Journal of Clinical Child and Adolescent Psychology, 36*(2), 260–266.

Bronfenbrenner, U. (1995). Developmental ecology through space and time: A future perspective. In P. Moen, G. H. Elder, Jr., & K. Luscher (Eds.),

Examining lives in context: Perspectives on the ecology of human development (pp. 619–647). Washington, DC: APA Books.

Bronfenbrenner, U. (1977). Toward an experimental ecology of human development. *American Psychologist, 32,* 513–531. doi:10.1037/0003-066X.32.7.513

Bronfenbrenner, U. (1979). *The ecology of human development: Experiments by nature and design.* Cambridge, MA: Harvard University Press.

Bronstein, P. (2006). The family environment: Where gender role socialization begins. In J. Worell & C. D. Goodheart (Eds.), *Handbook of girls' and women's psychological health* (pp. 262–271). Oxford, NY: Oxford University Press, Inc.

Brown, J., Halpern, C., & L'Engle, K. (2005). Mass media as a sexual super peer for early maturing girls. *Journal of Adolescent Health, 36*(5), 420–427. doi:10.1016/j.jadohealth.2004.06.003

Brown, L. M. (1991). Telling a girl's life: Self-authorization as a form of resistance. In C. Gilligan, A. Rogers, & D. Tolman (Eds.), *Women, girls, and psychotherapy: Reframing resistance* (pp. 71–86). Binghamton, NY: Haworth Press.

Brown, S., McGue, M., Maggs, J., Schulenberg, J., Hingson, R., Swartzwelder, S., & Murphy, S. (2008). A developmental perspective on alcohol and youths 16 to 20 years of age. *Pediatrics, 121,* 290–310.

Brownmiller, S. (1975). *Against our will: Men, women, and rape.* New York, NY: Bantam Books.

Bryant-Davis, T., Chung, H., & Tillman, S. (2009). From the margins to the center: Ethnic minority women and the mental health effects of sexual assault. *Trauma, Violence, & Abuse, 10*(4), 330–357. doi:10.1177/1524838009339755

Bubrick, K., Goodman, J., & Whitlock, J. (2010, June). *Developing and implementing a school protocol for non-suicidal self-injury.* Poster session presented at the 5th annual meeting of the International Society for the Study of Self-Injury (ISSS), Chicago, IL.

Bukstein, O. G., & Horner, M. S. (2010). Management of the adolescent with substance use disorders and comorbid psychopathology. *Child and Adolescent Psychiatric Clinics of North America, 19*(3), 609–623. doi:10.1016/j.chc.2010.03.011

Bulik, C. M., Berkman, N. D., Brownley, K. A., Sedway, J. A., & Lohr, K. N. (2007). Anorexia nervosa treatment: A systematic review of randomized controlled trials. *International Journal of Eating Disorders, 40*(4), 310–320. doi:10.1002/eat.20367

Burt, M. (1991). Rape myths and acquaintance rape. In A. Parrot & L. Bechhofer (Eds.), *Acquaintance rape: The hidden crime.* New York, NY: John Wiley & Sons.

Bussey, K., & Bandura, A. (1999). Social cognitive theory of gender development and differentiation. *Psychological Review, 106*(4), 676.

Byrne, S. M., Fursland, A., Allen, K. L., & Watson, H. (2011). The effectiveness of enhanced cognitive behavioural therapy for eating disorders: An open trial. *Behaviour Research and Therapy, 49*(4), 219–226. doi:10.1016/j.brat.2011.01.006

Cachelin, F. M., & Striegel-Moore, R. H. (2006). Help seeking and barriers to treatment in a community sample of Mexican American and European American women with eating disorders. *International Journal of Eating Disorders, 39*, 154–161. doi:10.1002/eat.20213

Camacho, K., Ehrensaft, M. K., & Cohen, P. (2012). Exposure to intimate partner violence, peer relations, and risk for internalizing behaviors: A prospective longitudinal study. *Journal of Interpersonal Violence, 27*(1), 125–141.

Campbell, M., & Schmidt, U. (2011). Cognitive-behavioral therapy for adolescent bulimia nervosa. In D. LeGrange & J. Lock (Eds.). *Eating disorders in children and adolescents: A clinical handbook* (pp. 305–318). New York, NY: Guilford Press.

Campbell, R., Dworkin, E., & Cabral, G. (2009). An ecological model of the impact of sexual assault on women's mental health. *Trauma, Violence, & Abuse, 10*(3), 225–246. doi:10.1177/1524838009334456

Campbell, R., & Raja, S. (2005). The sexual assault and secondary victimization of female veterans: Help-seeking experiences with military and civilian social systems. *Psychology of Women Quarterly, 29*, 97–106.

Carlo, G., McGinley, M., Hayes, R., Batenhorst, C., & Wilkinson, J. (2007). Parenting styles or practices? parenting, sympathy, and prosocial behaviors among adolescents. *Journal of Genetic Psychology, 168*(2), 147–176.

Castro-Fornieles, J., Díaz, R., Goti, J., Calvo, R., Gonzalez, L., Serrano, L., & Gual, A. (2010). Prevalence and factors related to substance use among adolescents with eating disorders. *European Addiction Research, 16*(2), 61–68. doi:10.1159/000268106

Center on Alcohol Marketing and Youth (2013). Women, girls, and alcohol. Retrieved: www.camy.org/factsheets/sheets/Women_Girls_and_Alcohol.html

Center on Media and Child Health (2011). Cell phone use. Retrieved www.cmch.tv/mentors/hotTopic.asp?id=70

Centers for Disease Control and Prevention. (2009a). *Physical dating violence among high school students.* Retrieved from http://www.cdc.gov/ViolencePrevention/intimatepartnerviolence/teen_dating_violence.html

Centers for Disease Control and Prevention. (2009b). *Selected health risk behaviors and health outcomes by sex, National Youth Risk Behavior Survey 2009.* Atlanta, GA: Centers for Disease Control.

Chao, Y. M., Pisetsky, B. A., Dierker, L. C., Dohm, F., Rosselli, F., May, A. M., & Striegel-Moore, R. H. (2008). Ethnic differences in weight control practices among U.S. adolescents from 1995-2005. *International Journal of Eating Disorders, 41*: 2, 124–133. doi:10.1002/eat.20479

Choate, L. H. (2008). *Girls' and women's wellness: Contemporary counseling issues and interventions.* Alexandria, VA: American Counseling Association.

Choate, L. H. (2010). Counseling college women experiencing eating disorder not otherwise specified: A cognitive behavior therapy model. *Journal of College Counseling, 13*, 73–86. doi:10.1002/j.2161-1882.2010.tb00049.x

Choate, L. H. (2011). Negotiating contradictory cultural pressures: A treatment model for binge eating in adolescent girls. *Women & Therapy, 34*(4), 377–392. doi:10.1080/02703149.2011.591668

Choate, L. H., & Curry, J. R. (2009). Addressing the sexualization of girls through comprehensive programs, advocacy and systemic change: Implications for professional school counselors. *Professional School Counseling, 12*(3), 213–221. doi:10.5330/PSC.n.2010-12.213

Chung, T., & Martin, C. S. (2011). Prevalence and clinical course of adolescent substance use and substance use disorders. In Y. Kaminer & K. C. Winters (Eds.), *Clinical manual of adolescent substance abuse treatment* (pp. 1–24). Arlington, VA: American Psychiatric Publishing.

Clarke, G. N., & DeBar L. L. (2010). Group cognitive-behavioral treatment for adolescent depression. In J. K. Weisz & A. E. Kazdin (Eds.), *Evidenced-based psychotherapies for children and adolescents* (pp. 110–125). New York, NY: The Guilford Press.

Cognitive behavior interventions for trauma in schools. (2012). Retrieved from http://cbitsprogram.org

Cohen, J. A., Bukstein, O., Walter, H., Benson, R., Chrisman, A., Farchione, T. R., ... Medicus, J. (2010). Practice parameter for the assessment and treatment of children and adolescents with posttraumatic stress disorder. *Journal of the American Academy of Child & Adolescent Psychiatry, 49*(4), 414–430.

Cohen, J. A., Mannarino, A. P., & Deblinger, E. (2006). *Treating trauma and traumatic grief in children and adolescents.* New York, NY: Guilford Press.

Commission on Adolescent Depression and Bipolar Disorder. (2005). Defining depression and bipolar disorder. In D. L. Evans, E. B. Foa, R. E. Gur, H. Hendin, C. P. O'Brien, M. E. P. Seligman, & B. T. Walsh (Eds.), *Treating and preventing adolescent mental health disorders: What we know and what we don't know* (pp. 3–27). New York, NY: Oxford University Press.

Commission on Adolescent Eating Disorders. (2005). Treatment of eating disorders. In D. L. Evans, E. B. Foa, R. E. Gur, H. Hendin, C. P. O'Brien, M. P. Seligman, & T. Walsh (Eds.), *Treating and preventing adolescent mental health disorders: What we know and what we don't know: A research agenda for improving the mental health of our youth* (pp. 283–301). New York, NY: Oxford University Press.

Commission on Adolescent Substance and Alcohol Abuse (CASAA). (2005). Treatment of substance use disorders. In D. L. Evans, E. B. Foa, R. E. Gur, H. Hendin, C. P. O'Brien, M. E. P. Seligman, & B. T. Walsh (Eds.), *Treating and preventing adolescent mental health disorders: What we know and what we don't know: A research agenda for improving the mental health of our youth* (pp. 391–410). New York, NY: Oxford University Press.

Constantino, M. J., Arnow, B. A., Blasey, C., & Agras, W. (2005). The association between patient characteristics and the therapeutic alliance in cognitive-behavioral and interpersonal therapy for bulimia nervosa. *Journal of Consulting and Clinical Psychology, 73*(2), 203–211. doi:10.1037/0022-006X.73.2.203

Cornell Research program on Self-Injurious Behavior (2012). Resources. Retrieved: www.crpsib.com/resources.asp

Crick, N. R., & Grotpeter, J. K. (1995). Relational aggression, gender, and social-psychological adjustment. *Child Development, 66*, 710–722. doi:10.2307/1131945

Crow, S. J., Peterson, C. B., Swanson, S. A., Raymond, N. C., Specker, S., Eckert, E. D., & Mitchell, J. E. (2009). Increased mortality in bulimia nervosa and other eating disorders. *American Journal of Psychiatry, 166,* 1342–1346. doi:10.1176/appi.ajp.2009.09020247

Crowther, J., Sanftner, J., Bonifazi, D., & Shepherd, K. (2001). The role of daily hassles in binge eating. *International Journal of Eating Disorders, 29*(4), 449–454. doi:10.1002/eat.1041

Csikszentmihalyi, M. (1990). *Flow: The psychology of optimal experience.* New York, NY: Harper.

Cummings, A. L. (2000). Teaching feminist counselor responses to novice female counselors. *Counselor Education and Supervision, 40*(1), 47–57. doi:10.1002/j.1556-6978.2000.tb01798.x

Curry, J. R., & Choate, L. H. (2010). The oversexualization of young adolescent girls: Implications for middle grades educators. *Middle School Journal, 42*(1), 6–15.

David-Feron, C., & Kaslow, N. J. (2008). Evidence-based psychosocial treatments for child and adolescent depression. *Journal of Clinical Child & Adolescent Psychology, 37*(1), 62–104. doi:10.1080/15374410701817865

Davies, P. G., Spencer, S. J., Quinn, D. M., & Gerhardstein, R. (2002). Consuming images: How television commercials that elicit stereotype threat can restrain women academically and professionally. *Personality and Psychology Bulletin, 28,* 1615–1628. doi:10.1177/014616702237644

Davila, J., Stroud, C. B., Starr, L. R., Miller, M. R., Yoneda, A., & Hershenber, R. (2009). Romantic and sexual activities, parent-adolescent stress, and depressive symptoms among early adolescent girls. *Journal of Adolescence, 32,* 909–924. doi:10.1016/j.adolescence.2008.10.004

Davis, A. (2008). Interpersonal and physical dating violence among teens. The National Council on Crime and Delinquency Focus. Retrieved from http://www.nccd-crc.org/nccd/pubs/2008_focus_teen_dating_violence.pdf

Davison, K., Werder, J., Trost, S., Baker, B., & Birch, L. (2007). Why are early maturing girls less active? Links between pubertal development, psychological well-being, and physical activity among girls at ages 11 and 13. *Social Science & Medicine, 64*(12), 2391–2404.

Deas, D. (2008). Evidence-based treatments for alcohol use disorders in adolescents. *Pediatrics, 121,* 348–354.

Deas, D., & Clark, A. (2009). Current state of treatment for alcohol and other drug use disorder in adolescents. *Alcohol Research & Health, 32*(1), 76–82.

Dellasega, C., & Nixon, C. (2003). *12 Strategies that will end female bullying: Girl wars.* New York, NY: Simon & Schuster.

Dennis, M., Godley, S. H., Diamond, G., Tims, F. M., Babor, T., Donaldson, J., & Funk, R. (2004). The Cannabis Youth Treatment (CYT) Study: Main findings from two randomized trials. *Journal of Substance Abuse Treatment, 27*(3), 197–213.

Dietz, L. J., Mufson, L., Irvine, H., & Brent, D. A. (2008). Family-based interpersonal psychotherapy for depressed preadolescents: An open-treatment trial. *Early Intervention in Psychiatry, 2*(3), 154–161. doi:10.1111/j.1751-7893.2008.00077.x

Doherty, W. J. (2002). *Take back your kids*. Notre Dame, IN: Sorin Books.

Douglas, S. (2010). *Enlightened sexism: The seductive message that feminism's work is done*. New York, NY: Times Books.

Draucker, C. B. (1999). The psychotherapeutic needs of women who have been sexually assaulted. *Perspectives in Psychiatric Care, 35*(1), 18–28.

Durbin C. E., & Shafir, D. M. (2008). Emotion regulation and risk for depression. In J. R. Z. Abela & B. L. Hankin (Eds.), *Handbook of depression in children and adolescents* (pp. 149–176). New York, NY: The Guilford Press.

Durham, G. (2008). *The Lolita effect: The media sexualization of young girls and what we can do about it*. New York, NY: Overlook Press.

Eaton, D. K., Kann, L., Kinchen, S., Shanklin, S., Ross, J., Hawkins, J., ... Wechsler, H. (2010). Youth risk behavior surveillance–United States, 2010. *MMWR Surveillance Summaries, 59*(SS05), 1–142.

Eisenberg, N., Guthrie, I. K., Murphy, B. C., Shepard, S. A., Cumberland, A., & Carlo, G. (1999). Consistency and development of prosocial dispositions: A longitudinal study. *Child Development, 70*(6), 1360–1372.

Elkind, D. (1967). Egocentrism in adolescence. *Child Development, 38*, 1025–1034.

Elkind, D. (1981). *The hurried child: Growing up too fast too soon*. Reading, MA: Addison-Wesley Publishing Company.

Erikson, E. H. (1968). *Identity: Youth and crisis*. New York, NY: W. W. Norton & Company.

Essau, C. A., & Chang, W. C. (2009). Epidemiology, comorbidity, and course of adolescent depression. In C. A. Essau (Ed.), *Treatments for adolescent depression: Theory and practice* (pp. 3–26). Oxford, NY: Oxford University Press.

Evans, D. L., Foa, E. B., Gur, R. E., Hendin, H., O'Brien, C. P., Seligman, M. E. P., & Walsh, B. T. (2005). *Treating and preventing adolescent mental health disorders: What we know and what we don't know*. New York, NY: Oxford University Press.

Fairburn, C. G. (1995). *Overcoming binge eating*. New York, NY: Guilford Press.

Fairburn, C. G. (1997). Interpersonal psychotherapy for Bulimia Nervosa. In D. M. Garner & P. E. Garfinkel, Handbook of treatment for eating disorders (pp. 278–294). New York: Guilford Press.

Fairburn, C. G. (2008). *Cognitive behavior therapy and eating disorders*. New York, NY: Guilford Press.

Fairburn, C. G., Cooper, Z., Doll, H. A., O'Connor, M. E., Bohn, K., Hawker, D. M., ... Palmer, R. L. (2009). Transdiagnostic cognitive-behavioral therapy for patients with eating disorders: A two-site trial with 60-week follow-up. *American Journal of Psychiatry, 166*(3), 311–319. doi:10.1176/appi.ajp.2008.08040608

Fairburn, C. G., Cooper, Z., & Shafran, R. (2003). Cognitive behaviour therapy for eating disorders: A "transdiagnostic" theory and treatment. *Behaviour Research and Therapy, 41*(5), 509–528. doi:10.1016/S0005-7967(02)00088-8

Fairburn, C. G., Marcus, M. D., & Wilson, G. T. (1993). Cognitive-behavioral therapy for binge eating and bulimia nervosa: A comprehensive treatment manual. In C. G. Fairburn & G. T. Wilsons (Eds.), *Binge eating: Nature, assessment, and treatment* (pp. 361–404). New York, NY: Guilford Press.

Feldman, P. J., Ullman, J. B., & Dunkel-Schetter, C. (1998). Women's reactions to rape victims: Motivational processes associated with blame and social support. *Journal of Applied Social Psychology, 28*, 469–503.

Fisher, L., Miles, I., Austin, S., Camargo, C., & Colditz, G. (2007). Predictors of initiation of alcohol use among US adolescents: Findings from a prospective cohort study. *Archives of Pediatrics & Adolescent Medicine, 161*(10), 959–966.

Foa, E. B., Davidson, J. R. T., & Frances, A. (1999). Expert consensus guideline series: Treatment of posttraumatic stress disorder. *The Journal of Clinical Psychiatry, 60* (Suppl.16), 1–31.

Foa, E., Keane, T., & Friedman, M. (2000). *Effective treatments for PTSD: Practice guidelines from the International Society for Traumatic Stress Studies.* New York, NY: Guilford Press.

Foa, E. B., Rothbaum, B. O., & Steketee, G. S. (1993). Treatment of rape victims. *Journal of Interpersonal Violence, 8*, 256–276.

Fortier, M. A., Peugh, J., DiLillo, D., DeNardi, K. A., Gaffey, K. J., & Messman-Moore, T. L. (2009). Severity of child sexual abuse and revictimization: The mediating role of coping and trauma symptoms. *Psychology of Women Quarterly, 33*, 308–320.

Forum on Child and Family Statistics. (2011). America's children in brief: Key national indicators of well-being. Retrieved from www.childstats.gov/americaschildren.

Fosco, G. M., Stormshak, E. A., Dishion, T. J., & Winter, C. E. (2012). Family relationships and parental monitoring during middle school as predictors of early adolescent problem behavior. *Journal of Clinical Child and Adolescent Psychology, 41*(2), 202–213. doi:10.1080/15374416.2012.651989

Foshee, V. A., Bauman, K. E., Ennett, S. T., Suchindran, C., Benefield, T., & Linder, G. (2005). Assessing the effects of the dating violence prevention program 'Safe Dates' using random coefficient regression modeling. *Prevention Science, 6*, 245–258. doi:10.1007/s11121-005-0007-0

Foshee, V. A., & Langwick, S. (2010). *Safe dates curriculum.* Retrieved from www.hazelden.org

Frazier, P., Conlon, A., & Glaser, T. (2001). Positive and negative life changes following sexual assault. *Journal of Consulting and Clinical Psychology, 69*(6), 1048–1055. doi:10.1037//0022-006X.69.6.1048

Frederickson, B. L., Roberts, T. A., Noll, S. M., Quinn, D. M., & Twenge, J. M. (1998). That swimsuit becomes you: Sex differences in self-objectification, restrained eating, and math performance. *Journal of Personality and Social Psychology, 75*, 269–284. doi:10.1037/0022-3514.75.1.269

Freeman, D. R., & Temple, J. (2010). Social factors associated with history of sexual assault among ethnically diverse adolescents. *Journal of Family Violence, 25*(3), 349–356. doi:10.1007/s10896-009-9296-6

Fursland, A., & Watson, H. J. (2013). Enhanced cognitive behavioral therapy approach to counseling clients with eating disorders. In L. Choate (Ed.), *Eating disorders and obesity: A counselor's guide to prevention and treatment* (pp. 504–537). Alexandria, VA: American Counseling Association Press.

Gabriel, J., DeBate, R. D., High, R. R., & Racine, E. F. (2011). Girls on the run: A quasi-experimental evaluation of a developmentally focused youth sport program. *Journal of Physical Activity and Health, 8*, 285–294.

Garbarino, J. (2006). *See Jane hit: Why girls are growing more violent and what we can do about it.* New York, NY: Penguin Press.

Garber, J., Clarke, G. N., Weersing, V. R., Beardslee, W. R., Brent, D. A., Gladstone, T. R. G., ... Iyengar, S. (2009). Prevention of depression in at-risk adolescents. *Journal of the American Medical Association, 301*(21), 2215–2224.

Garner, D. (2004). *Eating disorder inventory-3.* Torrance, CA: Western Psychological Services.

Garner, D. M., Vitousek, K. M., & Pike, K. M. (1997). Cognitive-behavioral therapy for anorexia nervosa. In D. M. Garner & P. E. Garfinkel (Eds.), *Handbook of treatment for eating disorders* (2nd ed., pp. 94–144). New York, NY: Guilford Press.

Gault-Sherman, M. (2012). It's a two-way street: The bidirectional relationship between parenting and delinquency. *Journal of Youth & Adolescence, 41*(2), 121–145. doi:10.1007/s10964-011-9656-4

George, J. B. E., & Franko, D. L. (2010). Cultural issues in eating pathology and body image among children and adolescents. *Journal of Pediatric Psychology, 35*(3), 231–242. doi:10.1093/jpepsy/jsp064

Gerbner, G. (1998). Cultivation analysis: An overview. *Mass Communication and Society*, Volume 1 (3/4), 175–194.

Gilbert, L. A., & Sher, M. (1999). *Gender and sex in counseling and psychotherapy.* Needham Heights, MA: Allyn & Bacon.

Gillham, J. E., Brunwasser, S. M., & Freres, D. R. (2008). Preventing depression in early adolescence: The Penn resiliency program. In J. R. Z. Abela & B. L. Hankin (Eds.), *Handbook of depression in children and adolescents* (pp. 309–332). New York, NY: The Guilford Press.

Gillham, J. E., & Chaplin, T. M. (2011). Preventing girls' depression during the transition to adolescence. In T. J. Strauman, P. R. Costanzo, & J. Garber (Eds.), *Depression in adolescent girls: Science and prevention* (pp. 275–317). New York, NY: The Guilford Press.

Gilligan, C. (1982). *In a different voice.* Harvard University Press. Cambridge, MA.

Gilligan, C. (1991). Women's psychological development: Implications for psychotherapy. In C. Gilligan, A. Rogers, & D. Tolman (Eds.), *Women, girls, and psychotherapy: Reframing resistance* (pp. 5–32). Binghamtom, NY: Haworth Press.

Girl Scout Research Institute. (2009). Beauty redefined: Girls and body image [Fact sheet]. Retrieved from http://www.girlscouts.org/research/pdf/beauty_redefined_factsheet.pdf

Girl Scout Research Institute. (2010). Who's that girl? Image and social media [Fact sheet]. Retrieved from http://www.girlscouts.org/research/pdf/gsri_social_media_fact_sheet.pdf

Girl Scout Research Institute. (2011a). Real to me: Girls and reality tv [Fact sheet]. Retrieved from http://www.girlscouts.org/research/pdf/real_to_me_factsheet.pdf

Girl Scout Research Institute. (2011b). Tips for parents: Real to me: Girls and reality tv. Retrieved from http://www.girlscouts.org/research/pdf/real_to_me_tip_sheet_for_parents.pdf

Girls on the Run International. *The girls on the run program.* Retrieved from December 11, 2012, http://www.girlsontherun.org/theprogram.html

Glenn, C. R., & Klonsky, E. D. (2007). *The functions of non-suicidal self-injury: Measurement and structure.* Presented at the annual meeting of the Association of Psychological Science, Washington, DC.

Gold, S. D., Dickstein, B. D., Marx, B. P., & Lexington, J. M. (2009). Psychological outcomes among lesbian sexual assault survivors: An examination of the roles of internalized homophobia and experiential avoidance. *Psychology of Women Quarterly, 33,* 54–66.

Goldston, D. B., Sergeant, S. S., & Arnold, E. M. (2006). Suicidal and nonsuicidal self-harm behaviors. In D. A. Wolfe & E. J. Mash (Eds.), *Behavioral and emotional disorders in adolescents: Nature, assessment, and treatment.* New York, NY: Guilford Press. GOldston.

Grabe, S., & Hyde, J. S. (2006). Ethnicity and body dissatisfaction among women in the United States: A meta-analysis. *Psychological Bulletin, 132,* 622–640. doi:10.1037/0033-2909.132.4.622

Grabe, S., & Hyde, J. (2009). Body objectification, MTV, and psychological outcomes among female adolescents. *Journal of Applied Social Psychology, 39*(12), 2840–2858. doi:10.1111/j.15591816.2009.00552.x

Grabe, S., Ward, L. M., & Hyde, J. S. (2008). The role of the media in body image concerns among women: A meta-analysis of experimental and correlational studies. *Psychological Bulletin, 134,* 460–476. doi:10.1037/0033-2909.134.3.460

Graber, J. A., Nichols, T. R., & Brooks-Gunn, J. (2010). Putting pubertal timing in developmental context: Implications for prevention. *Developmental Psychobiology, 52*(3), 254–262.

Gratz, K. L. (2001). Measurement of deliberate self-harm: Preliminary data on the deliberate self-harm inventory. *Journal of Psychopathology and Behavioral Assessment, 23,* 253–263.

Grauerholz, L. (2000). An ecological approach to understanding sexual revictimization: Linking personal, interpersonal, and sociocultural factors and processes. *Child Maltreatment, 5,* 5–17.

Green, C. A. (2006). Gender and use of substance abuse treatment services. *Alcohol Research & Health, 29*(1), 55–62.

Greenfield, S., Back, S., Lawson, K., & Brady, K. (2010). Substance abuse in women. *Psychiatric Clinics of North America, 33*(2), 339–355. doi:10.1016/j.psc.2010.01.004

Griffin, K. W., Botvin, G. J., Nichols, T. R., & Doyle, M. M. (2003). Effectiveness of a universal drug abuse prevention approach for youth at high risk for substance use initiation. *Preventive Medicine, 36,* 1–7.

Griffin, K., Samuolis, J., & Williams, C. (2011). Efficacy of a self-administered home-based parent intervention on parenting behaviors for preventing adolescent substance use. *Journal of Child & Family Studies, 20*(3), 319–325. doi:10.1007/s10826-010-9395-2

Grilo, C. M., Crosby, R. D., Masheb, R. M., White, M. A., Peterson, C. B., Wonderlich, S. A., ... Mitchell, J. E. (2009). Overvaluation of shape and weight in binge eating disorder, bulimia nervosa, and sub-threshold bulimia nervosa. *Behaviour Research and Therapy, 47,* 692–696. doi:10.1016/j.brat.2009.05.001

Groesz, L. M., Levine, M. P., & Murnen, S. K. (2002). The effect of experimental presentation of thin media images on body satisfaction: A meta-analytic review. *International Journal of Eating Disorders, 31,* 1–16. doi:10.1002/eat.10005

Grube, B., & Lens, V. (2003). Student-to-student harassment. *Children and Schools, 25,* 173–185. doi:10.1093/cs/25.3.173

Guerry, J. D., & Prinstein, M. J. (2010). Longitudinal prediction of adolescent nonsuicidal self-injury: Examination of a cognitive vulnerability-stress model. *Journal of Clinical Child & Adolescent Psychology, 39*(1), 77–89. doi:10.1080/15374410903401195

Gunlicks-Stoessel, M., Mufson, L., Jekal, A., & Turner, B. (2010). The impact of perceived interpersonal functioning on treatment for adolescent depression: IPT-A versus treatment as usual in school-based health clinics. *Journal of Consulting and Clinical Psychology, 78*(2), 260–267. doi:10.1037/a0018935

Hall, J. A., Smith, D. C., & Williams, J. K. (2008) Strengths Oriented Family Therapy (SOFT): A manual guided treatment of substance involved teens and their families. In C. W. Lecroy (Ed.), *Handbook of evidence-based treatment manuals for children and adolescents* (2nd ed., pp. 491–545). New York, NY: Oxford University Press.

Hall, J. A., & Valente. T. W. (2007). Adolescent smoking networks: The effects of influence and selection on future smoking. *Addictive Behaviors, 32,* 3054–3059.

Hall, P. C., West, J. H., & Hill, S. (2012). Sexualization in lyrics of popular music from 1959–2009: Implications for sexuality educators. *Sexuality & Culture, 16,* 103–117. doi:10.1007/s12119-011-9103-4

Halpern, C., Young, M., Waller, M., Martin, S., & Kupper, L. (2004). Prevalence of partner violence in same-sex romantic and sexual relationships in a national sample of adolescents. *Journal of Adolescent Health, 35*(2), 124–131.

Halpern, D. F. (2006). Girls and academic success: Changing patterns of academic achievement. In J. Worell & C. Goodheart (Eds.), *Handbook of girls' and women's psychological health* (pp. 272–282). New York, NY: Oxford University Press.

Hankin, B. L., & Abramson, L. (2001). Development of gender differences in depression; the elaborative cognitive vulnerability-transition stress theory. *Psychological Bulletin, 127,* 773–796.

Hankin, B. L. Wetter, E., & Cheely, C. (2008). Sex differences in child and adolescent depression: A developmental psychopathological approach. In J. R. Z. Abela & B. L. Hankin (Eds.), *Handbook of depression in children and adolescents* (pp. 377–415). New York, NY: The Guilford Press.

Hanley, S., Ringwalt, C., Ennett, S., Vincus, A., Bowling, J., Haws, S., & Rohrbach, L. (2010). The prevalence of evidence-based substance use prevention curricula in the nation's elementary schools. *Journal of Drug Education, 40*(1), 51–60. doi:10.2190/DE.40.1.d

Harris, A. (2004). *All about the girl: Culture, power, and identity.* New York, NY: Routledge.

Harrop, E. N., & Marlatt, G. (2010). The comorbidity of substance use disorders and eating disorders in women: Prevalence, etiology, and treatment. *Addictive Behaviors, 35*(5), 392–398.

Harter, S., & Buddin, B. (1987). Children's understanding of the simultaneity of two emotions: A five-stage developmental acquisition sequences. *Developmental Psychology, 23,* 388–399.

Hartstein, J. L. (2012). *Princess Recovery. A How-to guide to raising strong, empowered girls.* Avon, MA: Adams Media.

Haworth-Hoeppner, S. (1998). What's gender got to do with it: Perceptions of sexual coercion in a university community. *Sex Roles: A Journal of Research, 38,* 757–780.

Haworth-Hoeppner, S. (2000). The critical shapes of body image: The role of culture and family in the production of eating disorders. *Journal of Marriage and Family, 62,* 212–227. doi:10.1111/j.1741-3737.2000.00212.x

Healey, A. C., Trepal, H. C., & Emelianchik-Key, K. (2010).Nonsuicidal self-injury: Examining the relationship between diagnosis and gender. *Journal of Mental Health Counseling, 32*(4), 324–341.

Heidt, J. M., Marx, B. P., & Gold, S. D. (2005). Sexual revictimization among sexual minorities: A preliminary study. *Journal of Traumatic Stress, 18*(5), 535–540. doi:10.1002/jts.20061

Heilbron, N., & Prinstein, M. J. (2008). Peer influence and adolescent nonsuicidal self-injury: A theoretical review of mechanisms and moderators. *Applied and Preventive Psychology, 12,* 169–177. doi:10.1016/j.appsy.2008.05.004

Henggler, S. W., Schoenwald, S. K., Borduin, C. M., Rowland, M. D., & Cunningham, P. B. (2009). *Multisystematic therapy for antisocial behavior in children and adolescents.* New York, NY: Guilford Press.

Hernandez, L. Barnett, N., Sindelar-Manning, H., Chun, T., & Spirito, A. (2011). Alcohol Problems. In S. Naar-King & M. Suarez (Eds.), *Motivational interviewing with adolescent and young* adults (pp. 85–91). New York, NY: Guilford Press.

Hill, C., Kearl, H., & American Association of University Women. (2011). *Crossing the line: Sexual harassment at school.* American Association of University Women Publications. Retrieved from http://www.aauw.org/learn/research/upload/CrossingTheLine.pdf

Hilt, L. M., Cha, C. B., & Nolen-Hoeksema, S. (2008a). Nonsuicidal self-injury in young adolescent girls: Moderators of the distress–function relationship. *Journal of Consulting and Clinical Psychology. 76*(1), 63–71. doi:10.1037/0022-006X.76.1.63

Hilt, L. M., Nock, M. K., Lloyd-Richardson, E. E., & Prinstein, M. J. (2008b). Longitudinal study of nonsuicidal self-injury among young adolescents: Rates, correlates, and preliminary test of an interpersonal model. *Journal of Early Adolescence, 28*(3), 455–469. doi:10.1177/0272431608316604

Hinduja, S., & Patchin, J. W. (2010). Bullying, cyberbullying, and suicide. *Archives of Suicide Research, 14*(3), 206–221. doi:10.1080/1311118.2010

Hinshaw, S. P. (2009). *The triple bind: Saving our teenage girls from today's pressures*. New York, NY: Ballantine Books.

Hoffman, R. M., & Kress, V. E. (2010). Adolescent nonsuicidal self-injury: Minimizing client and counselor risk and enhancing client care. *Journal of Mental Health Counseling, 32*(4), 342–347.

Horigan, V. E., Suarez, S., Morales, L., Robbins, M. S., Zarata, M., Mayorga, C. C., Mitrani, V. B. et al., (2005). Brief strategic family therapy for adolescent behavior problems. In J. L. Lebow, (Ed.), Handbook of clinical family therapy (pp. 73–102). New York: Wiley.

Howard, D., Wang, M., & Yan, F. (2008). Psychosocial factors associated with reports of physical dating violence victimization among U.S. adolescent males. *Adolescence, 43*(171), 449–460.

Hudson, J. I., Hiripi, E., Pope, H. G., & Kessler, R. C. (2007). The prevalence and correlates of eating disorders in the national comorbidity survey replication. *Biological Psychiatry, 61*, 348–358. doi:10.1016/j.biopsych.2006.03.040

Huebner, L. A., Weitzman, L. M., Mountain, L. M., Nelson, K. L., Oakley, D. R., & Smith, M. L. (2006). Development and use of an eating disorder assessment and treatment protocol. *Journal of College Counseling, 9*(1), 72–78. doi:10.1002/j.2161-1882.2006.tb00094.x

Huh, D., Tristan, J., Wade, E., & Stice, E. (2006). Does problem behavior elicit poor parenting?: A prospective study of adolescent girls. *Journal of Adolescent Research, 21*(2), 185–204. doi:10.1177/0743558405285462

Hurst, K., Read, S., & Wallis, A. (2012). Anorexia nervosa in adolescence and maudsley family based treatment. *Journal of Counseling & Development, 90*, 339–345. doi:10.1002/j.1556-6676.2012.00042.x

Institute of Medicine and National Research Council, Committee of Science of Adolescence. (2011). *The science of adolescent risk-taking* [Workshop report]. Washington DC: National Academics Press.

International Society for the Study of Self-injury. (2007). *Definitional issues surrounding our understanding of self-injury*. Conference proceedings from the actual meeting. Montreal, Quebec, Canada.

Jacobson, C. M., & Mufson, L. (2010). Treating adolescent depression using interpersonal psychotherapy. In J. K. Weisz & A. E. Kazdin (Eds.), *Evidenced-based psychotherapies for children and adolescents* (pp. 140–158). New York, NY: The Guilford Press.

Jaffee, S., & Hyde, J. (2000). Gender differences in moral orientation: A meta-analysis. *Psychological Bulletin, 126*(5), 703.

Jewkes, R., Sen, P., & Garcia-Moreno, C. (2002). Sexual violence. In E. G. Krug, L. L. Dahlberg, J. A. Mercy, A. B. Zwi, & R. Lozano (Eds.), *World report on violence and health* (pp. 147–182). Retrieved from http://whqlibdoc.who.int/publications/2002/9241545615_chap6_eng.pdf

Johnston, L. D., O'Malley, P. M., Bachman, J. G., & Schulenberg, J. E. (2012). *Monitoring the Future national results on adolescent drug use: Overview of key findings, 2011*. Ann Arbor, MI: Institute for Social Research, The University of Michigan.

Jones, S. M., & Dindia, K. (2004). A meta-analytic perspective on sex equity in the classroom. *Review of Educational Research, 74*(4), 443–471.

Jordan, J. V. (2003). Relational-cultural therapy. In K. Kopala & M. A. Keitel (Eds.), *Handbook of counseling women* (pp.22–30). Thousand Oaks, CA: Sage.

Jordan, J. V. (2010). *Relational-cultural therapy.* Washington, DC: American Psychological Association.

Kaltiala-Heino, R., Kosunen, E., & Rimpela, M. (2003). Pubertal timing, sexual behavior, and self-reported depression in middle adolescence. *Journal of Adolescence, 26,* 531–545.

Kaminer, Y., & Slesnick, N. (2006). Evidence-based cognitive-behavioral and family therapies for adolescent alcohol and other substance use disorders. In M. Galanter (Ed.), *Alcohol problems in adolescents and young adults: Epidemiology, neurobiology, prevention, and treatment* (pp. 383–405). New York, NY: Springer Science + Business Media.

Kassel, J., & Jackson, S. (2001). Twelve-step-based intervention. In E. Wagner & H. Waldron (Eds.), *Innovations in adolescent substance abuse interventions* (pp. 333–352). Oxford, UK: Elsevier Science Ltd.

Katzman, D. K. (2005). Medical complications in adolescents with anorexia nervosa: A review of the literature. *International Journal of Eating Disorders, 37,* 52–59. doi:10.1002/eat.20118

Kaufman, M. (2008). Care of the adolescent sexual assault victim. *Pediatrics, 122*(2), 462–470. doi:10.1542/peds.2008-1581

Kennard, B. D., Clarke, G. N., Weersing, V. R., Asarnow, J. R., Shamseddeen, W., Porta, G., ... Brent D. A. (2009). Effective components of TORDIA cognitive-behavioral therapy for adolescent depression: Preliminary findings. *Journal of Consulting and Clinical Psychology, 77*(6), 1033–1041. doi:10.1037/a0017411

Kerr, P. L., & Muehlenkamp, J. J. (2010).Features of psychopathology in self-injuring female college students. *Journal of Mental Health Counseling, 32*(4), 290–308.

Kilburn, E., & Whitlock, J. (2010). Distraction techniques and alternative coping Strategies. *Cornell Research Program on Self-Injurious Behavior in adolescents and young adults, 1–3.* Retrieved from http://www.crpsib.com/userfiles/File/Alternative%20Strategies.pdf/

Kilpatrick, D. G., Amstadter, A. B., Resnick, H. S., & Ruggiero, K. J. (2007). Rape-related PTSD: Issues and interventions. *Psychiatric Times, 24*(7), 50.

Kimerling, R., & Calhoun, K. S. (1994). Somatic symptoms, social support, and treatment seeking among sexual assault victims. *Journal of Consulting and Clinical Psychology, 62,* 333–340.

Klerman, G. L., Weissman, M. M., Rounsaville, B. J., & Chevron, E. S. (1984). *Interpersonal psychotherapy of depression.* New York, NY: Basic Books.

Klonsky, E. D., & Muehlenkamp, J. J. (2007). Self-injury: A research review for the practitioner. *Journal of Clinical Psychology, (63)*11, 1045–1056. doi:10.1002/jclp.20412

Knight, J., Sherritt, L., Shrier, L., Harris, S., & Chang, G. (2002). Validity of the CRAFFT Substance Abuse Screening Test among adolescent clinic patients. *Archives of Pediatrics & Adolescent Medicine, 156*(6), 607–614.

Kochel, K. P., Ladd, G. W., & Rudolph, K. D. (2012). Longitudinal associations among youth depressive symptoms, peer victimization, and low peer acceptance: An interpersonal process perspective. Child Development, 83(2), 637–650.

Kohlberg, L. (1972). Moral stages and moralization: The cognitive developmental approach. In T. Lickona (Ed.) *Moral development and behavior: Theory, research, and social issues*. New York, NY: Holt, Rinehart, and Winston.

Koss, M. P., & Kilpatrick, D. G. (2001). Rape and sexual assault. In E. Gerrity, T. Keane, & F. Tuma (Eds.), *Mental health consequences of torture* (pp. 177–193). New York, NY: Plenum Publishers.

Kosterman, R., Hawkins, J. D., Haggerty, K. P., Spoth, R., & Redmond, C. (2001). Preparing for the drug free years: Session-specific effects of a universal parent-training intervention with rural families. *Journal of Drug Education, 31*(1), 47–68.

Krug, E. G., Dahlberg, L. L., Mercy, J. A., Zwi, A. B., & Lozano, R. (Eds.). (2002). *World report on violence and health*. Geneva: World Health Organization.

LaGreca, A. M., Mackey, E. R., & Miller, K. B. (2006). The interplay of physical and psychological development. In J. Worell & C. D. Goodheart (Eds.), *Handbook of girls' and women's psychological health* (pp. 252–261). Oxford, NY: Oxford University Press, Inc.

Lamb, S. & Brown, L. M. (2006). *Packaging girlhood: Rescuing our daughters from marketers' schemes*. New York, NY: St. Martin's Griffin Press.

Laporte, L., Jiang, D., Pepler, D. J., & Chamberland, C. (2011). The relationship between adolescents' experience of family violence and dating violence. *Youth & Society, 43*(1), 3–27.

Laser, J. A. & Nicotera, N. (2011). *Working with adolescents: A guide for practitioners*. New York, NY: Guilford Press.

Latzman, R. D., Gratz, K. L., Young, J., Heiden, L. J., Damon, J. D., & Hight, T. L. (2010). Self-injurious thoughts and behaviors among youth in an underserved area of the southern united states: Exploring the moderating roles of gender, racial/ethnic background, and school-level. *Journal of Youth Adolescence, (39)*, 270–280. doi:10.1007/s10964-009-9462-4.

Lawyer, S., Resnick, H., Bakanic, V., Burkett, T., & Kilpatrick, D. (2010). Forcible, drug-facilitated, and incapacitated rape and sexual assault among undergraduate women. *Journal of American College Health, 58*(5), 453–460.

LeCroy, C. W., & Daley, J. (2001). *The go grrrls workbook*. New York, NY: W.W. Norton Publishers.

Le Grange, D., Crosby, R. D., Rathouz, P. H., & Leventhal, B. L. (2007). Randomized controlled comparison of family-based treatment and supportive psychotherapy for adolescent bulimia nervosa. *Archives of General Psychiatry, 64*, 1049–1056. doi:10.1001/archpsyc.64.9.1049

Le Grange, D., & Lock, J. (2007). *Treating bulimia in adolescents: A family-based approach*. New York, NY: Guilford Press.

Levin, D. E., & Kilbourne, J. (2008). *So sexy so soon: The new sexualized childhood and what parents can do to protect their kids*. New York, NY: Ballantine.

Levine, M. P. (2012). *Teach your children well: Parenting for authentic success*. New York, NY: Harper Collins Publishers.

Levine, M. P., & Piran, N. (2004). Role of body image in the prevention of eating disorders. *Body Image, 1,* 57–70. doi:10.1016/S1740-1445(03)00006-8

Levine, M. P., & Smolak, L. (2002). Body image development in adolescence. In T. F. Cash & T. Pruzinsky (Eds.), *Body image: A handbook of theory, research, and clinical practice* (pp. 74–82). New York, NY: Guilford Press.

Lewis, S. P., Heath, N. L., St Denis, J. M., & Noble, R. (2011). The scope of nonsuicidal self-injury on youtube. *Pediatrics, 127*(3), e552–e557. doi:10.1542/peds.2010-2317.

Liddle, H. A. (2002). Multidimensional family therapy for adolescent cannabis users, cannabis youth treatment series. *Center for Substance Abuse Treatment, Substance Abuse and Mental Health Services Administration, 5.*

Liddle, H. A. (2010). Treating adolescent substance abuse using multidimensional family therapy. In J. R. Weisz, A. E. Kazdin, J. R. Weisz, & A. E. Kazdin (Eds.), *Evidence-based psychotherapies for children and adolescents* (2nd ed., pp. 416–432). New York, NY: Guilford Press.

Liddle, H. A., Dakof, G., Turner, R., Henderson, C., & Greenbaum, P. (2008). Treating adolescent drug abuse: A randomized trial comparing multidimensional family therapy and cognitive behavior therapy. *Addiction, 103*(10), 1660–1670.

Liddle, H. A., Dakof, G. A., Parker, K., Diamond, G. S., Barrett, K., & Tejeda, M. (2001). Multidimensional family therapy for adolescent drug abuse: Results of a randomized clinical trial. *American Journal of Drug & Alcohol Abuse, 27*(4), 651.

Liddle, H. A., Rodriguez, R. A., Dakof, G. A., Kanzki, E., & Marvel, F. A. (2005). Multidimensional family therapy: A science-based treatment for adolescent drug abuse. In J. L. Lebow (Ed.), *Handbook of clinical family therapy* (pp. 128–163). Hoboken, NJ: John Wiley & Sons.

Liddle, H. A., Rowe, C. L., Dakof, G. A., Henderson, C. E., & Greenbaum, P. E. (2009). Multidimensional family therapy for young adolescent substance abuse: Twelve-month outcomes of a randomized controlled trial. *Journal of Consulting and Clinical Psychology, 77*(1), 12–25. doi:10.1037/a0014160

Lindberg, S. M., Grabe, S., & Hyde, J. S. (2007). Gender, pubertal development, and peer sexual harassment predict objectified body consciousness in early adolescence. *Journal on Research on Adolescence, 17,* 723–742. doi:10.1111/j.1532-7795.2007.00544.x

Linehan, M. M. (1993a). *Cognitive behavioral treatment of borderline personality disorder.* New York, NY: Guilford Press.

Linehan, M. M. (1993b). *Skills training manual for treating borderline personality disorder.* New York, NY: Guilford Press.

Linehan, M. M., Comtois, K. A., Brown, M. Z., Heard, H. L., & Wagner, A. (2006). Suicide attempt self-injury interview (SASII): Development, reliability, and validity of a scale to assess suicide attempts and intentional self-injury. *Psychological Assessment, 18,* 303–312.

Lloyd, E. E., Kelley, M. L., & Hope, T. (1997). *Self-mutilation in a community sample of adolescents: Descriptive characteristics and provisional prevalence rates.* Poster presented at the annual meeting of the Society for Behavioral Medicine, New Orleans, LA.

Lock, J., & LeGrange, D. (2006). Eating disorders. In D. A. Wolfe & E. J. Mash (Eds.), *Behavioral and emotional disorders in adolescence* (pp. 485–504). New York, NY: Guilford Press.

Lock, J., LeGrange, D., Agras, W. S., & Dare, C. (2001). *Treatment manual for anorexia nervosa: A family-based approach* New York, NY: Guilford Press.

Lock, J., LeGrange, D., Agras, S. W., Moye, A., Bryson, S. W., & Booil, J. (2010). Randomized clinical trial comparing family-based treatment with adolescent-focused individual therapy for adolescents with anorexia nervosa. *Archives of General Psychiatry, 67*(10), 1025–1032. doi:10.1001/archgenpsychiatry.2010.128

Loeb, K. L., Lock, J., Le Grange, D., & Greif, R. (2012). Transdiagnostic theory and application of family-based treatment for youth and eating disorders. *Cognitive and Behavioral Practice, 19*(1), 17–30. doi:10.1016/j.cbpra/2010.04.005

Low, G., & Organista, K. C. (2000). Latinas and sexual assault: Towards culturally sensitive assessment and intervention. *Journal of Multicultural Social Work, 8*, 131–157.

Lynch, T. R., & Cozza, C. (2009). Behavior therapy for nonsuicidal self-injury. In M. K. Nock (Ed.), *Understanding nonsuicidal self-injury: Origins, assessment, and treatment* (pp. 222–250). Washington, DC: American Psychological Association.

March, J., Silva, S., & Vitiello, B. (2006). The treatment for adolescents with depression study (TADS): Methods and message at 12 weeks. *Journal of the American Academy of Child and Adolescent Psychiatry, 45*(12), 1393–1403.

March, J. S., & Vitiello, B. (2009). Clinical messages from the treatment for adolescents with depression study (TADS). *American Journal of Psychiatry, 166*(10), 1118–1123.

Marotta, S. A. (2000). Best practices for counselors who treat post-traumatic stress disorder. *Journal of Counseling and Development, 78*, 492–495.

Martin, C. E. (2007). *Perfect girls, starving daughters: The frightening new normalcy of hating your body.* New York, NY: Free Press.

Martino, S. C., Collins, R. L., Elliot, M. N., Strachman, A., Kanouse, D. E., & Barry, S. H. (2006). Exposure to degrading versus nondegrading music lyrics and sexual behavior among youth. *Pediatrics, 118*, E430–E441. doi:10.1542/peds.2006-0131

Mason, M., & Posner, M. (2009). Brief substance abuse treatment with urban adolescents: A translational research study. *Journal of Child & Adolescent Substance Abuse, 18*(2), 193–206.

Mason, W. A., Kosterman, R., Hawlins, J. D., Haggerty, K. P., & Spoth, R. L. (2003). Reducing adolescents' growth in substance use and delinquency: Randomized trial effects of a preventive parent-training intervention. *Prevention Science, 4*(3), 203–212.

Matlin, M. W. (2004). *The psychology of women* (5th ed.). Belmont, CA: Wadsowrth/Thomson Learning, Inc.

McCabe, E. B., LaVia, M. C., & Marcus, M. D. (2004). Dialectical behavior therapy for eating disorders. In J. K. Thompson (Ed.), *Handbook of eating disorders and obesity* (pp. 232–244). Hoboken, NJ: John Wiley & Sons, Inc.

McCauley, J. L., Conoscenti, L. M., Ruggiero, K. J., Resnick, H. S., Saunders, B. E., & Kilpatrick, D. G. (2009). Prevalence and correlates of drug/alcohol-facilitated and incapacitated sexual assault in a nationally representative sample of adolescent girls. *Journal of Clinical Child and Adolescent Psychology, 38*(2), 295–300.

McCormick, P. (2011). Cut. New York: Push Publications.

McDonough, P. (2009, October 26). TV viewing among kids at an eight-year high. Retrieved from http://blog.nielsen.com/nielsenwire/media_entertainment/tv-viewing-among-kids-at-an-eight-year-high

McKinley, N. M. (1999). Women and objectified body consciousness: Mothers' and daughters' body experience in cultural, developmental, and familial context. *Developmental Psychology, 35*, 760–769. doi:10.1037/0012-1649.35.3.760

McKinley, N. M. (2002). Feminist perspectives and objectified body consciousness. In T. F. Cash & T. Pruzinsky (Eds.), *Body image: Handbook of theory, research, and clinical practice* (pp. 55–64). New York, NY: Guilford Press.

McWhirter, P. (2008). Enhancing adolescent substance abuse treatment engagement. *Journal of Psychoactive Drugs, 40*(2), 173–182.

Meadows, E. A., & Foa, E. B. (1998). Intrusion, arousal, and avoidance: Sexual trauma survivors. In V. Follette, I. Ruzek, & F. Abueg (Eds.), *Cognitive-behavioral therapies for trauma* (pp. 100–123). New York, NY: Guilford Press.

Merten, M. J., & Henry, C. S. (2011). Family structure, mother-daughter relationship quality, race and ethnicity, and adolescent girls' health risks. *Journal of Divorce & Remarriage, 52*(3), 164–186. doi:10.1080/10502556.2011.556966

Messman-Moore, T. L., & Long, P. J. (2003). The role of childhood sexual abuse sequelae in the sexual revictimization of women: An empirical review and theoretical reformulation. *Clinical Psychology Review, 23*, 537–571. doi:10.1016/S0272-7358(02)00203-9

Miller, A. L., Rathaus, J. H., & Linehan, M. M. (2007). *Dialectical behavior therapy with suicidal adolescents.* New York, NY: Guilford Press.

Miller, F. G., & Lazowski, L. E. (2001). *The adolescent SASSI-A2 Manual: Identifying substance user disorders.* Springville, IN: The SASSI Institute.

Miller, L., Gur, M., Shanok, A., & Weissman, M. (2008). Interpersonal psychotherapy with pregnant adolescents: Two pilot studies. *The Journal of Child Psychology and Psychiatry, 49*(7), 733–742. doi:10.1111/j.1469-7610.2008.01890.x

Miller, S., Loeber, R., & Hipwell, A. (2009). Peer deviance, parenting and disruptive behavior among young girls. *Journal of Abnormal Child Psychology, 37*(2), 139–152.

Miller, W. R., & Rollnick, S. (2002). *Motivational interviewing: Preparing people for change* (2nd ed.). New York, NY: Guilford Press.

Moran, P., Coffey, C., Romaniuk, H., Olsson, C., Borschmann, R., Carlin, J., & Patton, G. (2011). The natural history of self-harm from adolescence to young adulthood: A population-based cohort study. *The Lancet, 379*(9812), 236–243.

MTV's A Thin Line. (2011). MTV-AP 2011 Digital abuse research study. Retrieved from http://www.athinline.org/pdfs/MTV-AP_2011_Research_Study-Exec_Summary.pdf

Muehlenkamp, J. J. (2006). Empirically supported treatments and general therapy guidelines for non-suicidal self-injury. *Journal of Mental Health Counseling, (28)*2, 166–185.

Muehlenkamp, J. J., Engel, S. G., Wadeson, A., Crosby, R. D., Wonderlich, S. A., Simonich, H., & Mitchell, J. E. (2009). Emotional state preceding and following acts of non-suicidal self-injury in bulimia nervosa patients. *Behaviour Research and Therapy, (47),* 83–87. doi:10.1016/j.brat.2008.10.011

Muehlenkamp, J. J., Williams, K. L., Gutierrez, P. M., & Claes, L. (2009).Rates of non-suicidal self-injury in high school students across five years. *Archives of Suicide Research, 13,* 317–329. doi:10.1080/13811110903266368

Mufson, L. (2010). Interpersonal psychotherapy for depressed adolescents (IPT-A): Extending the reach from academic to community settings. *Child and Adolescent Mental Health,15*(2),66–72.doi:10.1111/j.1475-3588.2009.00556.x

Mufson, L., & Dorta, K. P. (2000). Interpersonal psychotherapy for depressed adolescents: Theory, practice and research. *Adolescent Psychiatry, 35,* 139–167.

Mufson, L., Dorta, K. P., Moreau, D., & Weissman, M. M. (2004). *Interpersonal psychotherapy for depressed adolescents.* New York, NY: The Guilford Press.

Mufson, L. H., Dorta, K. P., Olfson, M., Weissman, M. M., & Hoagwood, K. (2004). Effectiveness research: Transporting interpersonal psychotherapy for depressed adolescents (IPT-A) from the lab to the school-based health clinic. *Clinical Child and Family Psychology Review, 7*(4), 251–261.

Mufson, L., Dorta, K. P., Wickramarante, P., Nomura, Y., Olfson, M., & Weissman, M. M. (2004). A randomized effectiveness trial of interpersonal psychotherapy for depressed adolescents. *Archives of General Psychiatry, 61,* 577–584.

Mufson, L., Gallagher, T., Dorta, K. P., & Young, J. F. (2004). A group adaptation of interpersonal psychotherapy for depressed adolescents. *American Journal of Psychotherapy, 58*(2), 220–237.

Mulford, C., & Giordano, P. (2008). Teen dating violence: A closer look at adolescent romantic relationships. *NIJ Journal, 261,* 34–40.

Myers, J., & Sweeney, T. J. (Eds.).(2005). *Counseling for wellness: Theory, research, and practice.* Alexandria, VA: American Counseling Association Publications.

Naar-King, S., & Suarez, M. (2010). Motivational interviewing with adolescents and young adults. New York: Guilford Press.

National Center for Education Statistics. (2012). Fast facts: Back to school statistics. Retrieved from http://nces.ed.gov/fastfacts/display.asp?id=372

National Center on Addiction and Substance Abuse. (2011). *Adolescent substance use: America's #1 problem.* Columbia University. New York, NY.

National Center on Domestic and Sexual Violence. (2012). Wheels adapted from the Power and Control Wheel. Retrieved from http://www.ncdsv.org/publications_wheel.html

National Federation of State High School Associations. (2012, August 23). High school sports participation achieves all-time high [Press release]. Retrieved from http://www.nfhs.org/content.aspx?id=7495

National Institute on Drug Abuse (2010). NIDA for Teens: Drug Facts. Retrieved: http://teens.drugabuse.gov/drug-facts

National Registry of Evidence Based Programs and Practices (2008). Life Skills Training Intervention Summary. Retrieved: nrepp.samhsa.gov/viewintervention.aspx?id=109.

National Science Foundation, Division of Science Resources Statistics. (2011). *Women, minorities, and persons with disabilities in science and engineering: 2011* (Special Report NSF 11–309). Arlington, VA. Retrieved from http://www.nsf.gov/statistics/wmpd

National Survey of Family Growth. (2011). *Key statistics from the National Survey of Family Growth.* Retrieved from http://www.cdc.gov/nchs/nsfg/abc_list_u.htm#unwantedsex

National Survey on Drug Use and Health. (2012). Depression triples between the ages of 12 and 15 among adolescent girls. Retrieved from http://www.samhsa.gov/data

Neville, H. A., Oh, E., Spanierman, L. B., Heppner, M. J., & Clark, M. (2004). General and culturally specific factors influencing black and white rape survivors' self-esteem. *Psychology of Women Quarterly, 28,* 83–94.

Newman, C. F. (2009). Cognitive therapy for nonsuicidal self-injury. In M. K. Nock (Ed.), *Understanding nonsuicidal self-injury: Origins, assessment, and treatment* (pp. 201–220). Washington, DC: American Psychological Association.

Nielsen Company. 2010. US teen mobile report: Calling yesterday, texting today, using apps tomorrow. Retrieved April 16, 2011, from http://blog.nielsen.com/nielsenwire/online_mobile/u-s-teen-mobile-report-calling-yesterday-texting-today-using-apps-tomorrow

Nishina, A., Ammon, N. Y., Bellmore, A. D., & Graham, S. (2006). Body dissatisfaction and physical development among ethnic minority students. *Journal of Youth and Adolescence, 25,* 179–191.

Nock, M. K. (2010). Self-injury. *Annual Review of Clinical Psychology. 6,* 339–363. doi:10.1146/annurev.clinpsy.121208.131258

Nock, M. K., & Cha, C. B. (2009). Psychological models of nonsuicidal self-injury. In M. K. Nock (Ed.), *Understanding nonsuicidal self-injury: Origins, assessment, and treatment* (pp. 65–78). Washington, DC: American Psychological Association.

Nock, M. K., & Favazza, A. R. (2009).Nonsuicidal self-injury: Definition and classification. In M. K. Nock (Ed.), *Understanding nonsuicidal self-injury: Origins, assessment, and treatment* (pp. 9–18). Washington, DC: American Psychological Association.

Nock, M. K., Holmberg, E. B., Photos, V. I., & Michel, B. D. (2007). The Self-injurious thoughts and behaviors interview: Development, reliability, and validity in an adolescent sample measure. *Psychological Assessment, 19,* 309–317.

Nock, M. K., & Mendes, W. B. (2008). Physiological arousal, distress tolerance, and social problem-solving deficits among adolescent self-injurers. *Journal of Consulting and Clinical Psychology, (76)*1, 28–38. doi:10.1037/0022-006X.76.1.28

Nock, M. K., Prinstein, M. J., & Sterba, S. K. (2009). Revealing the form and function of self-injurious thoughts and behaviors: A real-time ecological assessment study among adolescents and young adults. *Journal of Abnormal Psychology, (118)*4, 816–827. doi:10.1037/a0016948

Nock, M. K., Teper, R., & Hollander, M. (2007). Psychological treatment of self-injury among adolescents. *Journal of Clinical Psychology, 63*(11), 1081–1089. doi:10.1002/jclp.20415

O'Donnell, L., Stueve, A., Duran, R., Myint-u, A., Agronick, G., Doval, A., & Wilson-simmons, R. (2008). *Parenting practices, parents' underestimation of daughters' risks, and alcohol and sexual behaviors of urban girls.* St Paul, Minnesota, US: Minnesota Department of Health (MDH).

O'Hara, R., Gibbons, F., Gerrard, M., Li, A., & Sargent, J. D. (2012). Greater exposure to sexual content in popular movie predicts earlier sexual debut. *Psychological Science, 20*, 1–10.

O'Keeffe, G. S., Clarke-Pearson, K., & Council on Communications and Media. (2011). Clinical report-the impact of social media on children, adolescents, and families. *Pediatrics: Official Journal of the American Academy of Pediatrics, 127*, 800–804. doi:10.1542/peds.2011-0054

Oppliger, P. A. (2008). *Girls gone skank: The sexualization of girls in American culture.* Jefferson, NC: McFarlan & Co.

Orenstein, P. (2011) *Cinderella ate my daughter: Dispatches from the front lines of the new girlie-girl culture.* New York, NY: Harper

Orenstein, P. (2012, June 11). Too young for status updates: Social media for tweens? No. It's better to keep things face to face. *Los Angeles Times.* Retrieved from http://articles.latimes.com/2012/jun/11/opinion/la-oe-orenstein-facebook-tween-20120611

Ormerod, A., Collinsworth, L., & Perry, L. (2008). Critical climate: Relations among sexual harassment, climate, and outcomes for high school girls and boys. *Psychology of Women Quarterly, 32*(2), 113–125.

Parkes, A., Strange, V., Wight, D., Bonell, C. Copas, A., Henderson, M., … Hart, G. (2011). Comparison of teenagers' early same-sex and heterosexual behavior: UK data from the SHARE and RIPPLE studies. *Journal of Adolescent Health, 48*, 27–35.

Patterson, D., Greeson, M., & Campbell, R. (2009). Understanding rape survivors' decisions not to seek help from formal social systems. *Health & Social Work, 34*(2), 127–136.

Paxton, S. J., Schutz, H. K., Wertheim, E. H., & Muir, S. L. (1999). Friendship clique and peer influences on body image and concerns, dietary restraint, extreme weight loss behaviors, and binge eating in adolescent girls. *Journal of Abnormal Psychology, 108*, 255–266. doi:10.1037/0021-843X.108.2.255

Pea, R., Nass, C., Meheula, L., Rance, M., Kumar, A., Bamford, H., … Zhou, M. (2012). Media use, face-to-face communication, media multitasking, and social well-being among 8- to 12-year-old girls. *Developmental Psychology, 48*(2), 327–336. doi:10.1037/a0027030

Perepletchikova, F., Krystal, J. H., & Kaufman, J. (2008). Practitioner review: Adolescent alcohol use disorders—Assessment and treatment issues. *Journal of Child Psychology and Psychiatry, 49*(11), 1131–1154.

Perry, D. G., & Bussey, K. (1979). The social learning theory of sex differences: Imitation is alive and well. *Journal of Personality & Social Psychology, 37*(10), 1699–1712.

Pew Research Center. (2011). Trends in teen communication and social media use: What's really going on here? [PDF document]. Retrieved from http://www.pewinternet.org/Presentations/2011/Feb/~/media/Files/

Presentations/2011/Feb/Pew%20Internet_Girl%20Scout%20Webinar%20 PDF.pdf

Piaget, J. (1972). Intellectual evolution from adolescence to adulthood. *Human Development, 15*, 1–12.

Pike, K. M., Loeb, K. L., & Vitousek, K. (1996). Cognitive-behavioral therapy for anorexia nervosa and bulimia nervosa. In J. K. Thompson (Ed.), *Body image, eating disorders, and obesity: An integrative guide for assessment and treatment* (pp. 253–302). Washington, DC: American Psychological Association.

Pipher, M. (1994). *Reviving ophelia: Saving the selves of adolescent girls*. New York, NY: The Berkley Publishing Group.

Piran, N., Jasper, K., & Pinhas, L. (2004) Feminist therapy and eating disorders. In J. K. Thompson (Ed.), *Handbook of eating disorders and obesity*. Hoboken, NJ: Wiley.

Piran, N., & Ross, E. (2006). From girlhood to womanhood: Multiple transitions in context. In J. Worell & C. D. Goodheart (Eds.), *Handbook of girls' and women's psychological health* (pp.301–311). Oxford, NY: Oxford University Press, Inc.

Polivy, J., & Herman, C. P. (2002). Causes of eating disorders. *Annual Review of Psychology, 53*, 187–213. doi:10.1146/annurev.psych.53.100901.135103

Prinstein, M. J., Heilbron, N., Guerry, J. D., Franklin, J. C., Rancourt, D., Simon, V., & Spirito, A. (2010). Peer influence and nonsuicidal self injury: Longitudinal results in community and clinically-referred adolescent samples. *Journal of Abnormal Child Psychology, (38)*, 669–682. doi:10.1007/s10802-010-9423-0

Prothrow-Stithand, D., & Spivak, H. (2005, November 20). *Beyond mean girls: Why young females are fighting more*. The Boston Globe. Boston, MA.

Psychological Assessment Resources. (2012). *Welcome to PAR — Home.* Retrieved from http://www4.parinc.com/

Rauch, S. A. M., Hembree, E. A., & Foa, E. B. (2001). Acute psychosocial preventive interventions for post-traumatic stress disorder. *Advances in Mind-Body Medicine, 17*, 160–196.

Reinecke, M. A., & Ginsburg, G. S. (2008). Cognitive-behavioral treatment of depression during childhood and adolescence. In J. R. Z. Abela & B. L. Hankin (Eds.), *Handbook of depression in children and adolescents* (pp. 179–206). New York, NY: The Guilford Press.

Remley, T. P., & Herlihy, B. (2010). *Ethical, legal, and professional issues in counseling* (3rd ed.). New York, NY: Merrill/Pearson.

Remmel, E., & Flavell, J. H. (2004). Recent progress in cognitive developmental research: Implications for clinical practice. In H. Steiner (Ed.). Handbook of mental health interventions in children and adolescents: An integrated developmental approach (pp. 73–97). New York: Jossey-Bass.

Resick, P. A., & Schnicke, M. K. (1993). *Cognitive processing therapy for rape victims: A treatment manual.* Newbury Park, CA: Sage Publications.

Resnick, H., Acierno, R., Holmes, M., Dammeyer, M., & Kilpatrick, D. (2000). Emergency evaluation and intervention with female victims of rape and other violence. *Journal of Clinical Psychology, 56*, 1317–1333.

Resnick, H., Acierno, R., Holmes, M., Kilpatrick, D., & Jager, N. (1999). Prevention of post-rape psychopathology: Preliminary findings of a controlled acute rape treatment study. *Journal of Anxiety Disorders, 13,* 359–370.

Reynolds, B. M., & Repetti, R. L. (2006). Adolescent girls' health in the context of peer and community relationships. In J. Worell & C. D. Goodheart (Eds.), *Handbook of girls' and women's psychological health* (pp. 292–300). Oxford, NY: Oxford University Press, Inc.

Rich, S. S., & Thomas, C. R. (2008). Body Mass Index, disordered eating behavior, and acquisition of health information: Examining ethnicity and weight-related issues in a college population. *Journal of American College Health, 56,* 623–628. doi:10.3200/JACH.56.6.623-628

Rickert, V. I., Wiemann, C. M., Vaughan, R. D., & White, J. W. (2004). Rates and risk factors for sexual violence among an ethnically diverse sample of adolescents. *Archives of Pediatrics & Adolescent Medicine, 158*(12), 1132–1139.

Robin, A., & Le Grange, D. (2010). Family therapy for adolescents with anorexia nervosa. In J. Weisz & A. Kazdin (Eds.), *Evidence-based psychotherapies for children and adolescents* (2nd ed., pp. 345–358). New York, NY: The Guilford Press.

Rodham, K., & Hawton, K. (2009). Epidemiology and phenomenology of nonsuicidal self-injury. In M. K. Nock (Ed.), *Understanding nonsuicidal self-injury: Origins, assessment, and treatment* (pp. 37–62). Washington, DC: American Psychological Association.

Rodin, J., Silberstein, L. R., & Streigel-Moore, R. H. (1984). Women and weight: A normative discontent. In T. B. Sonderegger (Ed.), *Psychology and gender: Nebraska symposium on motivation* (pp. 267–307). Lincoln, NE: University of Nebraska Press.

Rose, A. J., & Rudolph, K. D. (2006). A review of sex differences in peer relationship processes: Potential trade-offs for the emotional and behavioral development of girls and boys. *Psychological Bulletin, 132*(1), 98–131. doi:10.1037/0033-2909.132.1.98

Rudolph, K. D., Flynn, M., & Abaied, J. L. (2008). A developmental perspective on interpersonal theories. In J. R. Z. Abela & B. L. Hankin (Eds.), *Handbook of depression in children and adolescents* (pp. 79–102). New York, NY: The Guilford Press.

Rudolph, K. D., Hammen, C., & Daley, S. E. (2006). Mood disorders. In D. A. Wolfe & E. J. Mash (Eds.), *Behavioral and emotional disorders in adolescents: Nature, assessment, and treatment* (pp. 300–342). New York, NY: Guilford Press.

S.A.F.E. Alternatives | Locations. (2013). *S.A.F.E. Alternatives: Self Abuse Finally Ends.* Retrieved from http://www.selfinjury.com/

Safer, D. L., Lock, J., & Couturier, J. L. (2007). Dialectical behavior therapy modified for adolescent binge eating disorder: A case report. *Cognitive and Behavioral Practice, 14,* 157–167. doi:10.1016/j.cbpra.2006.06.001

Safer, D. L., Telch, C. F., & Chen, E. Y. (2009). *Dialectical behavior therapy for binge eating and bulimia.* New York, NY: Guilford Press.

Salk, R., & Engeln-Maddox, R. (2011). "If you're fat then I'm humongous!": Frequency, content and impact of fat talk among college women. *Psychology of Women Quarterly, 35*, 18–28. doi:10.1177/0361684310384107

Sampl, S., & Kadden, R. M. (2001). Cannabis Youth Treatment Series Vol. 1. DHHS Publication No. (SMA) 01-3486. Rockville, MD: Center for Substance Abuse Treatment.

SASSI Institute. Retrieved from http://www.sassi.com

Sax, L. (2010). *Girls on the edge: The four factors driving the new crisis for girls.* New York, NY: Basic Books.

Schinke, S., Di Noia, J., Schwinn, T., & Cole, K. (2006). Drug abuse risk and protective factors among black urban adolescent girls: A group-randomized trial of computer-delivered mother-daughter intervention. *Psychology of Addictive Behaviors, 20*(4), 496–500. doi:10.1037/0893-164X.20.4.496

Schinke, S., Fang, L., & Cole, K. (2008). Substance use among early adolescent girls: Risk and protective factors. *Journal of Adolescent Health, 43*(2), 191–194.

Schneider, B., & Stevenson, D. (1999). *The ambitious generation: American teenagers motivated but directionless.* New Haven, CT: Yale University Press.

Schor, J. B. (2005). *Born to buy: The commercialized child and the new consumer culture.* New York, NY: Scribner Books.

Schwartz, M. D., & Leggett, M. S. (1999). Bad dates or emotional trauma? The aftermath of campus sexual assault. *Violence Against Women, 5*, 251–271.

Schwinn, T., Schinke, S., & Trent, D. (2010). Substance use among late adolescent urban youths: Mental health and gender influences. *Addictive Behaviors, 35*(1), 30–34. doi:10.1016/j.addbeh.2009.08.005

Schwitzer, A. M., Rodriguez, L. E., Thomas, C., & Salimi, L. (2001). The eating disorders NOS diagnostic profile among college women. *Journal of American College Health, 49*, 157–166. doi:10.1080/07448480109596298

Selekman, M. D. (2006). *Working with self-harming adolescents; a collaborative, strengths-based therapy approach.* New York, NY: W.W. Norton Books.

Sexton, T. L., & Alexander, J. F. (2005). Functional family therapy for externalizing disorders in adolescents. In J. L. Lebow (Ed.), *Handbook of clinical family therapy* (pp. 164–191). Hoboken, NJ: John Wiley & Sons.

Shapiro, J. R., Woolson, S. L., Hamer, R. M., Kalarchian, M. A., Marcus, M. D., & Bulik, C. M. (2007). Evaluating binge eating disorder in children: development of the children's binge eating disorder scale (C-BEDS). *International Journal of Eating Disorders, 40*(1), 82–89. doi:10.1002/eat.20318

Shaw, H., & Stice, E. (2013). Eating disorders prevention with adolescents and young adults. In L. Choate (Ed.), *Eating disorders and obesity: A counselor's guide to prevention and treatment* (pp. 396–428). Alexandria, VA: American Counseling Association Press.

Shisslak, C. M., Mays, M. Z., Crago, M., Jirsak, J. K., Taitano, K., & Cagno, C. (2006). Eating and weight control behaviors among middle school girls in relationship to body weight and ethnicity. *Journal of Adolescent Health, 38*, 631–633. doi:10.1016/j.jadohealth.2005.03.006

Sierra-Baigrie, S., Lemos-Giraldez, S., & Fonseca-Pedrero, E. (2009). Binge eating in adolescents: Its relation to behavioural problems and family-meal patterns. *Eating Behaviors, 10*(1), 22–28. doi:10.1016/j.eatbeh.2008.10.011

Silverman, R. (2010).*Good girls don't get fat: How weight obsession is messing up our girls and how we can help them thrive despite it.* New York, NY: Harlequin Publications.

Simmons, R. (2002). *Odd girl out.* Orlando, FL: Harcourt.

Simmons, R. (2009). *The curse of the good girl: Raising authentic girls with courage and confidence.* New York, NY: Penguin Press.

Simpson, A. R. (2001). *Raising teens: A synthesis of research and a foundation for action.* Boston, MA: Center for Health Communication, Harvard School of Public Health.

Smith, D., & Hall, J. (2010). Implementing evidence-based multiple-family groups with adolescent substance abusers. *Social Work With Groups, 33* (2–3), 122–138. doi:10.1080/01609510903366236

Smolak, L., & Chun-Kennedy, C. (2013). Sociocultural influences on the development of eating disorders and obesity. In L. Choate (Ed.), *Eating disorders and obesity: A counselor's guide to prevention and treatment* (pp.44–75). Alexandria, VA: American Counseling Association Press.

Smolak, L., & Murnen, S. K. (2004). A feminist approach to eating disorders. In J. J. Thompson, (Ed.), *Handbook of eating disorders and obesity* (pp. 590–605). New York, NY: John Wiley and Sons.

Snapp, S., Choate, L., & Ryu, E. (2012). A body image resilience model for first year college women. *Sex Roles, 67,* 1–11. doi:10.1007/s11199-012-0163-1

Sontag, L. M., Graber, J. A., & Clemans, K. H. (2011). The role of peer stress and pubertal timing on symptoms of psychopathology during early adolescence. *Journal of Youth and Adolescence, 40*(10), 1371–1382.

Spoth, R. L., Randall, G., Trudeau, L., Shin, C., & Redmond, C. (2008). Substance use outcomes 5 1/2 years past baseline for partnership-based, family-school preventive interventions. *Drug and Alcohol Dependence, 96*(1–2), 57–68. doi:10.1016/j.drugalcdep.2008.01.023

Stanton, M., & Shadish, W. R. (1997). Outcome, attrition, and family–couples treatment for drug abuse: A meta-analysis and review of the controlled, comparative studies. *Psychological Bulletin, 122*(2), 170–191. doi:10.1037/0033-2909.122.2.170

Stark, K. D., Hargrave, J., Hersh, B., Greenberg, M., Herren, J., & Fisher, M. (2008). Treatment of childhood depression: The action treatment program. In J. R. Z. Abela & B. L. Hankin (Eds.), *Handbook of depression in children and adolescents* (pp. 224–249). New York, NY: The Guilford Press.

Stark, K. D., Hargrave, J., Sander, J., Custer, G., Schnoebelen, S., Simpson, J., & Molnar, J. (2006). Treatment of childhood depression: The ACTION treatment program. In P. C. Philip (Ed.), *Child and adolescent therapy: Cognitive-behavioral procedures* (pp. 169–216). New York, NY: The Guilford Press.

Stark, K. D., Sander, J., Hauser, M., Simpson, J., Schnoebelen, S., Glenn, R., & Molnar, J. (2006). Depressive disorders during childhood and adolescence.

In E. J. Mash & R. A. Barkley (Eds.), *Treatment of childhood disorders* (pp. 336–410). New York, NY: The Guilford Press.

Stark, K. D., Streusand, W., Krumholz, L. S., & Patel, P. (2010). Cognitive-behavioral therapy for depression: The ACTION treatment program for girls. In J. K. Weisz & A. E. Kazdin (Eds.), *Evidenced-based psychotherapies for children and adolescents* (pp. 93–109). New York, NY: The Guilford Press.

Starr, C. R., & Ferguson, G. M. (2012). Sexy dolls, sexy grade schoolers? Media and maternal influences on young girls' self-sexualization. *Sex Roles, 67*(7/8), 463–476. doi:10.1007/s11199-012-0183-x

Starr, L. R., & Davila, J. (2009). Clarifying co-rumination: Associations with internalizing symptoms and romantic involvement among adolescent girls. *Journal of Adolescence, 32*, 19–37. doi:10.1016/j.adolescence.2007.12.005

Steinberg, L., Darling, N. N., Dornbusch, S. M., & Lamborn, S. D. (1992). Impact of parenting practices on adolescent achievement: Authoritative parenting, school involvement, and encouragement to succeed. *Child Development, 63*(5), 1266–1281.

Steinberg, L., & Silk, J. S. (2002). Parenting adolescents. In M. H. Bornstein (Ed.), *Handbook of parenting: Vol. 1: Children and parenting* (2nd ed., pp. 103–133). Mahwah, NJ: Lawrence Erlbaum Associates Publishers.

Steiner-Adair, C., & Sjostrom, L. (2006). *Full of ourselves: A wellness program to advance girl power, health, and leadership*. New York, NY: Teachers College Press.

Stevens, S., Andrade, R., & Ruiz, B. (2009). Women and substance abuse: Gender, age, and cultural considerations. *Journal of Ethnicity in Substance Abuse, 8*(3), 341–358.

Stewart, S., Gavric, D., & Collins, P. (2009). Women, girls, and alcohol. In K. Brady, S. Back, & S. Greenfield (Eds.), *Women and addiction* (pp. 341–359). New York, NY: Guilford Press.

Stice, E., & Bearman, S. K. (2001). Body-image and eating disturbances prospectively predict increases in depressive symptoms in adolescent girls: A growth curve analysis. *Developmental Psychology, 37*(5), 597–607. doi:10.1037/0012-1649.37.5.597

Stice, E., Bohon, C., Marti, C. N., & Fischer, K. (2008). Subtyping women with bulimia nervosa along dietary and negative affect dimensions: Further evidence of reliability and validity. *Journal of Consulting and Clinical Psychology, 76*, 1022–1033. doi:10.1037/a0013887

Stice, E., Davis, K., Miller, N. P., & Marti, C. N. (2008). Fasting increases risk for onset of binge eating and bulimic pathology: A 5-year prospective study. *Journal of Abnormal Psychology, 117*, 941–946. doi:10.1037/a0013644

Stice, E., Killen, J. D., Hayward, C., & Taylor, C. B. (1998). Support for the continuity hypothesis of bulimic pathology. *Journal of Consulting and Clinical Psychology, 66*, 787–790. doi:10.1037/0022-006X.66.5.784

Stice, E., Marti, C. N., Shaw, H., & Jaconis, M. (2009). An 8-year longitudinal study of the natural history of threshold, subthreshold, and partial eating disorders from a community sample of adolescents. *Journal of Abnormal Psychology, 118*, 587–597. doi:10.1037/a0016481

Stice, E., Mazotti, L., Weibel, D., & Agras, W. S. (2000). Dissonance prevention program decreases thin ideal internalization, body dissatisfaction, dieting, negative affect, and bulimic symptoms: A preliminary experiment. *International Journal of Eating Disorders, 27,* 206–217. doi:10.1002/(SICI)1098-108X(200003)27:2<206::AID-EAT9>3.0.CO;2-D

Stice, E., & Presnell, K. (2007). *The body project: Promoting body acceptance and preventing eating disorders facilitator guide.* New York, NY: Oxford University Press.

Stice, E., Presnell, K., & Spangler, D. (2002). Risk factors for binge eating onset in adolescent girls: A 2-year prospective investigation. *Health Psychology 2,* 131–138. doi:10.1037/0278-6133.21.2.131

Stice, E., Rohde, P., Shaw, H., & Gau, J. (2011). An effectiveness trial of a selected dissonance-based eating disorder prevention program for female high school students: Long-term effects. *Journal of Consulting and Clinical Psychology, 79,* 500–508. doi:10.1037/a0024351

Stice, E. & Shaw, H. (2003) Prospective relationship of body image, eating, and affective disturbances to smoking onset in adolescent girls: How Virginia slims. *Journal of Consulting and Clinical Psychology, 71,* 129–135. doi:10.1037/0022-006X.71.1.129

Stopbullying gov. (2012). What is cyberbullying? Retrieved from http://www.stopbullying.gov/cyberbullying/what-is-it/index.html

Straus, M. B. (2006). *Adolescent girls in crisis.* New York, NY: W. W. Norton & Company.

Striegel-Moore, R. H., Dohm, F., Pike, K. M., Wilfley, D. E., & Fairburn, C. G. (2002). Abuse, bullying, and discrimination as risk factors for binge eating disorder. *American Journal of Psychiatry, 159*(11), 1902–1907. doi:10.1176/appi.ajp.159.11.1902

Striegel-Moore, R. H., Wilfley, D. E., Pike, K. M., Dohm, F., & Fairburn, C. G. (2000). Recurrent binge eating in Black American women. *Archives of Family Medicine, 9,* 83–87. doi:10.1001/archfami.9.1.83

Strong, M. (1998). *A bright red scream: Self-mutilation and the language of pain.* New York, NY: Viking Press.

Substance Abuse and Mental Health Services Administration. (2010). *Violent behaviors among adolescent females.* Retrieved from http://oas.samhsa.gov/2k9/171/171FemaleViolence.cfm

Substance Abuse and Mental Health Services Administration. (2012, July 19). Depression triples between the ages of 12 and 15 among adolescent girls. Retrieved from http://www.samhsa.gov/data/spotlight/Spot077Girls Depression2012.pdf

Suldo, S. M., McMahan, M. M., Chappel, A. M., & Loker, T. (2012). Relationships between perceived school climate and adolescent mental health across genders. *School Mental Health, 4*(2), 69–80. doi:10.1007/s12310-012-9073-1

Sussman, S., Skara, S., & Ames, S. L. (2008). Substance abuse among adolescents. *Substance use & misuse, 43*(12/13), 1802–1828.

Swahn, M. H., Simon, T. R., Arias, I., & Bossarte, R. M. (2008). Measuring sex differences in violence victimization and perpetration within date and same-sex peer relationships. *Journal of Interpersonal Violence, 23*(8), 1120–1138. doi:10.1177/0886260508314086

Swanson, S. A., Crow, S. J., LeGrange, D., Swendsen, J., & Merikangas, K. R. (2011). Prevalence and correlates of eating disorders in adolescents: Results from the national comorbidity survey replication adolescent supplement. *Archives of General Psychiatry, 68*(7), 714–723. doi:10.1001/archgenpsychiatry.2011.22

Swarr, A. E., & Richards, M. H. (1996). Longitudinal effects of adolescent girls' pubertal development, perceptions of pubertal timing, and parental relations on eating problems. *Developmental Psychology, 32*(4), 636–646. doi:10.1037/0012-1649.32.4.636

TADS Team. (2009). The treatment for adolescents with depression study (TADS): Outcomes over 1 year of naturalistic follow-up. *American Journal of Psychiatry, 166*(10), 1141–1149.

Taffel, R. (2009). *Childhood unbound.* New York, NY: Free Press.

Talleyrand, R. (2013). Clients of color and eating disorders: cultural considerations. In L. Choate (Ed.), *Eating disorders and obesity: A counselor's guide to prevention and treatment* (pp. 116–155). Alexandria, VA: American Counseling Association Press.

Tanner-Smith, E. (2010). Negotiating the early developing body: Pubertal timing, body weight, and adolescent girls' substance use. *Journal of Youth & Adolescence, 39*(12), 1402–1416. doi:10.1007/s10964-009-9489-6

Tanofsky-Kraff, M., Wilfley, D. E., Young, J. F., Mufson, L., Yanovski, S. Z., Glasofer, D. R., & Salaita, C. G. (2007). Preventing excessive weight gain in adolescents: Interpersonal psychotherapy for binge eating. *Obesity, 15*(6), 1345–1355. doi:10.1038/oby.2007.162

Telch, C. F., Agras, W., & Linehan, M. M. (2000). Group dialectical behavior therapy for binge-eating disorder: A preliminary, uncontrolled trial. *Behavior Therapy, 31,* 569–582. doi:10.1016/S0005-7894(00)80031-3

Temple, J. R., Paul, J., van den Berg, P., Le, V., McElhany, A., & Temple, B. (2012). Teen sexting and its association with sexual behaviors. *Archives of Pediatrics & Adolescent Medicine, 166*(9), 828–833. doi:10.1001/archpediatrics.2012.835

Temple, J. R., Weston, R., Rodriguez, B. F., & Marshall, L. L. (2007). Differing effects of partner and nonpartner sexual assault on women's mental health. *Violence Against Women, 13*(3), 285–297. doi:10.1177/1077801206297437

Teten, A., Ball, B., Valle, L., Noonan, R., & Rosenbluth, B. (2009). Considerations for the definition, measurement, consequences, and prevention of dating violence victimization among adolescent girls. *Journal of Women's Health (15409996), 18*(7), 923–927. doi:10.1089/jwh.2009.1515

Tjaden, P., & Thoennes, N. (2006). Extent, nature, and consequences of rape victimization: Findings from the National Violence Against Women Survey. Retrieved from www.ojp.usdoj.gov/nij

The Center for Eating Disorders at Sheppard Pratt. (2012). *Public survey conducted by The Center for Eating Disorders at Sheppard Pratt finds Facebook use impacts the way many people feel about their bodies.* Baltimore, MD: Author.

The Ophelia Project. (2007). Retrieved from http://www.opheliaproject.org/main/index.htm

Thompson, J. K., Heinberg, L., Altabe, M., & Tantleff-Dunn, S. (1999). *Exacting beauty: Theory, assessment, and treatment of body image disturbance.* Washington DC: American Psychological Association.

Toddlers and Tiaras. (2012). Retrieved from http://tlc.howstuffworks.com/tv/toddlers-tiaras

Tolman, D. L., Impett, E. A., Tracy, A. J., & Michael, A. (2006). Looking good, sounding good: Femininity ideology and adolescent girls' mental health. *Psychology of Women Quarterly, 30,* 85–95. doi:10.1111/j.1471-6402.2006.00265.x

Travis, C. B. (2006). Risks to healthy development: The somber planes of life. In J. Worell & C. D. Goodheart (Eds.), *Handbook of girls' and women's psychological health* (pp. 15–24). Oxford, NY: Oxford University Press, Inc.

Treasure, J., Claudino, A., & Zucker, N. (2010). Eating disorders. *Lancet, 375,* 583–593. doi:10.1016/S0140-6736(09)61748-7

Trepal, H., Boie, I., Kress, V., & Hammer, T. (2013). A relational cultural approach to working with clients with eating disorders. In L. Choate (Ed.), *Eating disorders and obesity: A counselor's guide to prevention and treatment* (pp. 396–428). Alexandria, VA: American Counseling Association Press.

Tuchman, E. (2010). Women and addiction: The importance of gender issues in substance abuse research. *Journal of Addictive Diseases, 29*(2), 127–138. doi:10.1080/10550881003684582

Turkle, S. (2011) *Alone together: Why we expect more from technology and less from each other.* New York, NY: Basic Books.

TV.com. (2013) *TV.com — Free Full Episodes & Clips, Show Info and TV Listings Guide.* Retrieved from http://www.tv.com

Tween and Teen Dating Violence and Abuse Study, Teenage Research Unlimited for Liz Claiborne Inc. and the National Teen Dating Abuse Helpline. (2008). Retrieved from http://www.loveisnotabuse.com/pdf/Tween%20Dating%20Abuse%20Full%20Report.pdf

Ullman, S. E. (2007). Relationship to perpetrator, disclosure, social reactions, and PTSD symptoms in child sexual abuse survivors. *Journal of Child Sexual Abuse, 16*(1), 19–35. doi:10.1300/J070v16n01_02

Underwood, M. K. (2003). *Social aggression among girls.* New York, NY: Guilford Press.

Unger, J. B., Ritt-Olson, A., Teran, L., Huang, T., Hoffman, B. R., & Palmer, P. (2002). Cultural values and substance use in a multiethnic sample of California adolescents. *Addiction Research & Theory, 10*(3), 257–279. doi:10.1080/16066350290025672

Upadhyaya, H., & Gray, K. (2009). Adolescent substance se and the role of gender. In K. Brady, S. Back, & S. Greenfield (Eds.), *Women and addiction* (pp. 421–421). New York, NY: Guilford Press.

U.S. Department of Commerce. (2011). United States Census Bureau *Data Access Tools.* Retrieved from http://www.census.gov/main/www/access.html

U.S. Department of Education. (2012). *Office of Safe and Drug-Free Schools.* Retrieved from http://www2.ed.gov/about/offices/list/osdfs

U.S. Department of Labor, & Bureau of Labor Statistics. (2011). *Women in the labor force: A databook* (2010 ed.). Retrieved from http://www.bls.gov/cps/wlf-databook-2011.pdf

Violence Against Women Online Resources. (2009, August). *Research in brief: The facts about sexual violence.* Retrieved from http://www.vaw.umn.edu/documents/inbriefs/domesticviolence/domesticviolence-color.pdf

Vitousek, K., Watson, S., & Wilson, G. T. (1998). Enhancing motivation for change in treatment-resistant eating disorders. *Clinical Psychology Review, 18*, 391–420. doi:10.1016/S0272-7358(98)00012-9

Wade, T., Bergin, J., Tiggemann, M., Bulik, C., & Fairburn, C. G. (2006). Prevalence and long term course of eating disorders in an adult Australian cohort. *Australian and New Zealand Journal of Psychiatry, 40*(2), 121–128. doi:10.1080/j.1440-1614.2006.01758.x

Waldron, H., & Turner, C. W. (2008). Evidence-based psychosocial treatments for adolescent substance abuse. *Journal of Clinical Child and Adolescent Psychology, 37*(1), 238–261.

Wallace, J. M., Brown, T. N., Bachman, J. G., & LaVeist, T. A. (2003). Religion, race, and abstinence from drug use among African American adolescents. *Monitoring the Future Occasional Paper, 58*, 1–25.

Waller, G., Cordery, H., Corstorphine, E., Hinrichsen, H., Lawson, R., Mountford, V., & Russell, K. (2007). *Cognitive behavioral therapy for eating disorders: A comprehensive treatment guide.* Cambridge, UK: Cambridge University Press.

Walsh, B. T., & Garner, D. M. (1997). Diagnostic issues. In D. M. Garner & P. E. Garkinkel (Eds.), *Handbook of treatment for eating disorders* (pp.25–34). New York, NY: The Guilford Press.

Walsh, B. W. (2006). *Treating self-injury: A practical guide.* New York, NY: Guilford Press.

Walsh, K., Blaustein, M., Knight, W. G., Spinazzola, J., & van der Kolk, B. A. (2007). Resiliency factors in the relation between childhood sexual abuse and adulthood sexual assault in college-age women. *Journal of Child Sexual Abuse, 16*(1), 1–17. doi:10.1300/J070v16n01_01

Walvoord, E. (2010). The timing of puberty: Is it changing? Does it matter?. *Journal of Adolescent Health, 47*(5), 433–439. doi:10.1016/j.jadohealth.2010.05.018

Want, S. C. (2009). Meta-analytic moderators of experimental exposure to media portrayals of women on female appearance satisfaction: Social comparisons as automatic processes. *Body Image, 6*, 257–269. doi:10.1016/j.bodyim.2009.07.008

Ward, L. M., & Friedman, K. (2006). Using TV as a guide: Associations between television viewing and adolescents' sexual attitudes and behavior. *Journal of Research on Adolescence, 16*, 133–156. doi:10.1111/j.1532-7795.2006.00125.x

Weil, E. (2012). *Puberty before age 10: A new 'normal'?.* New York, NY, US: New York Times Company.

Weissman, M. M., Markowitz, J. C., & Klerman, G. L. (2000). *Comprehensive guide to interpersonal psychotherapy.* New York, NY: Basic Books.

Weisz, J. R., & Hawley, K. M. (2002). Developmental factors in the treatment on adolescents. *Journal of Consulting and Clinical Psychology, 70*(1), 21–43. doi:10.1037/0022-006X.70.1.21

Werth, J. L., Wright, K. S., Archambault, R. J., & Bardash, R. J. (2003). When does the 'duty to protect' apply with a client who has anorexia nervosa? *The Counseling Psychologist, 31*(4), 427–450.

Wertheim, E. H., Paxton, S. J., & Blaney, S. (2009). Body image in girls. In L. Smolak & J. K. Thompson (Eds.), *Body image, eating disorders, and obesity in youth: Assessment, prevention, and treatment*, (2nd ed., pp. 47–76). Washington DC: American Psychological Association.

White, M., & Epston, D. (1990). *Narrative means to therapeutic ends*. New York, NY: W.W. Norton.

White, V., Trepal-Wollenzier, H., & Nolan, J. (2002). College students and self-injury: Intervention strategies for counselors. *Journal of College Counseling, 5*, 105–113.

White Kress, V. E., Drouhard, N., & Costin, A. (2006). Students who self-injure school counselor ethical and legal considerations. *Professional School Counseling, 10*(2), 203–209.

Whitlock, J. L. (2009). The cutting edge: Non-suicidal self-injury in adolescence. *ACT for Youth Center Excellence Research Facts and Finding*, 1–7.

Whitlock, J. L., Eckenrode, J., & Silverman, D. (2006). Self-injurious behaviors in a college population. *Pediatrics, 117*, 1939–1948.

Whitlock, J. L., Lader, W., & Conterio, K. (2007). The internet and self-injury: What psychotherapists should know. *Journal of Clinical Psychology, 63*, 1135–1143.

Whitlock, J. L., Muehlenkamp, J., Purington, A., Eckenrode, J., Barreira, J., Baral-Abrahms, G., … Knox, K. (2009). *Primary and Secondary Non-Suicidal Self-Injury Characteristics in a College Population: General Trends and Gender Differences*. Manuscript submitted for publication.

Whitlock, J. L., Purington, A., & Gershkovich, M. (2009).Media, the internet, and nonsuicidal self-injury. In M. K. Nock (Ed.), *Understanding nonsuicidal self-injury: Origins, assessment, and treatment* (pp. 139–156). Washington, DC: American Psychological Association.

Wilfley, D. E., Kass, A. E., & Kolko, R. P. (2011). Counseling and behavior change in pediatric obesity. *Pediatric Clinics of North America, 58*, 1403–1424. doi:10.1016/j.pcl.2011.09.014

Wilfley, D. E., MacKenzie, K. R., Welch, R. R., Ayers, V. E., & Weissman, M. M. (2000). *Interpersonal psychotherapy for group*. New York, NY: Basic Books.

Williams, R. J., Chang, S. Y., & Addiction Centre Adolescent Research Group. (2000). A comprehensive and comparative review of adolescent substance abuse treatment outcome. *Clinical Psychology: Science and Practice, 7*(2), 138–166. doi:10.1093/clipsy/7.2.138

Wilson, G. T., Fairburn, C. G., & Agras, W. S. (1997). Cognitive-behavioral therapy for bulimia nervosa. In D. M. Garner & P. E. Garfinkel (Eds.), *Handbook of treatment for eating disorders, second edition* (pp. 67–93). New York, NY: The Guilford Press.

Wilson, G. T., Grilo, C. M., & Vitousek, K. M. (2007). Psychological treatment of eating disorders. *American Psychologist, 62,* 199–216. doi:10.1037/0003-066X.62.3.199

Wilson, G. T., & Pike, K. M. (2001). Eating Disorders. In D. H. Barlow (Ed.), *Clinical handbook of psychological disorders: A step-by-step treatment manual* (pp. 332–375). New York, NY: The Guilford Press.

Wisdom, J. P., Cavaleri, M., Gogel, L., & Nacht, M. (2011). Barriers and facilitators to adolescent drug treatment: Youth, family, and staff reports. *Addiction Research & Theory, 19*(2), 179–188. doi:10.3109/16066359.2010.530711

Wisniewski, L., & Kelly, E. (2003). The application of dialectical behavior therapy to the treatment of eating disorders. *Cognitive and Behavioral Practice, 10*(2), 131–138. doi:10.1016/S1077-7229(03)80021-4

Wolitzky-Taylor, K. B., Ruggiero, K. J., Danielson, C., Resnick, H. S., Hanson, R. F., Smith, D. W., ... Kilpatrick, D. G. (2008). Prevalence and correlates of dating violence in a national sample of adolescents. *Journal of the American Academy of Child & Adolescent Psychiatry, 47*(7), 755.

Worell, J. (2006). Pathways to healthy development: Sources of strength and empowerment. In J. Worell & C. D. Goodheart (Eds.), *Handbook of girls' and women's psychological health* (pp.3–14). New York, NY: Oxford University Press.

Worell, J., & Remer, P. (2002). *Feminist perspectives in therapy* (pp. 173–202). Hoboken, NJ: Wiley.

Yates, T. M. (2009). Developmental pathways from child maltreatment to nonsuicidal self-injury. In M. K. Nock (Ed.), *Understanding nonsuicidal self-injury: Origins, assessment, and treatment* (pp. 117–138). Washington, DC: American Psychological Association.

Yates, T. M., Tracy, A. J., & Luthar, S. S. (2008). Nonsuicidal self-injury among "privileged" youths: Longitudinal and cross-sectional approaches to developmental process. *Journal of Consulting and Clinical Psychology, 76*(1), 52–62. doi:10.1037/0022-006X.76.1.52

Young, A., Grey, M., Abbey, A., Boyd, C. J., & McCabe, S. (2008). Alcohol-related sexual assault victimization among adolescents: Prevalence, characteristics, and correlates. *Journal of Studies on Alcohol and Drugs, 69*(1), 39–48.

Young, A., Grey, M., & Boyd, C. J. (2009). Adolescents' experiences of sexual Assault by peers: Prevalence and nature of victimization occurring within and outside of school. *Journal of Youth & Adolescence, 38*(8), 1072–1083. doi:10.1007/s10964-008-9363-y

Young, J. F., Mufson, L., & Davies, M. (2006). Efficacy of interpersonal psychotherapy–adolescent skills training: An indicated preventive intervention for depression. *Journal of Child Psychology and Psychiatry, 47*(12), 1254–1262. doi:10.1111/j.1469-7610.2006.01667.x

Young, J. F., Mufson, L., & Gallop, R. (2010). Preventing depression: A randomized trial of interpersonal psychotherapy-adolescent skills training. *Depression and Anxiety, 27,* 426–433. doi:10.1002/da.20664

Youth Risk Behavior Survey. (2011). US Department of Health and Human Services, Centers for Disease Control. Retrieved from http://www.cdc.gov/HealthyYouth/yrbs/index.htm (Original work published 2009).

Zila, L., & Kiselica, M. S. (2001). Understanding and counseling self-mutilation in female adolescent and young adults. *Journal of Counseling and Development, 79*(1), 46–52.

Zilberman, M. (2009). Substance abuse across the lifespan in women. In K. Brady, S. Back, & S. Greenfield (Eds.), *Women and addiction* (pp. 3–13). New York, NY: Guilford Press.

Index

African American families
  characteristics of, 33
  sexual violence and culture, 231
African American girls
  binge eating, 127
  sexual trauma, 223–224
African American mothers,
      substance abuse prevention
      program for, 186
age of onset and SUD, 155–156
aggression
  adolescent dating violence and, 226
  female competition and, 13
Alcoholics Anonymous (AA) groups
      and adolescent substance use
      treatment, 166
alcohol use, 149, 150
  screening instruments for, 161–162
  and sexual violence, 224
Alcohol Use Disorders Identification
      Test (AUDIT), 161
American Academy of Child and
      Adolescent Psychiatry Best
      Practice Guidelines for Child
      and Adolescent Depression
      (2007), 94
American Association of University
      Women (AAUW) report, 23
amplified reflection, 180
anorexia nervosa (AN), 102
  diagnostic criteria
    DSM-5, 109
    DSM-IV-TR, 108, 109
  FBT for, 137–140
antidepressant medication, 67, 93–95
anxiety
  disorders, 154
  presentation, 15
appearance of girls, 9, 14
  "hot and sexy," 5–7
Asian American women, sexual
      violence and culture, 231
assault characteristics level, sexual
      trauma, 224
  adolescent dating violence, 225–228
  alcohol and drug use, 224
  relationship to perpetrator, 225

assertiveness skills, 250–251
attitudes and behaviors, 35–36
attributional style, negative, 75–76
AUDIT. See Alcohol Use Disorders
      Identification Test
authenticity/authentic self, 252–254
authoritative parenting style, 58

balance in girls
  caring for self versus others, 253
  wellness and, 255–256
Bandura's Social Learning Theory, 19
Beck's schema construct, 75
BED. See binge eating disorder
behavioral activation, 78
behaviors
  attitudes and, 35–36
  delinquent, 35–36, 58
  goal-oriented, 45
  maladaptive, 194, 197
  negative adolescent, 59
  risk-taking, 44, 45
  sex role, 50
  weight loss, 102
belief systems, 45–47
Belsky, Steinberg, and Draper (BSD)
      theory, 42
binge eating
  subtype of AN, 109
  treatment model for, 128
    CBT, 130–131
    DBT, 131–133
    feminist therapy approaches,
      129–130
    IPT, 134–137
  treatments for, 125–128
binge eating disorder (BED), 102,
      110–111
Black female students, substance
      use, 156
Black women, binge eating, 127
BN. See bulimia nervosa
body acceptance, 257–258
body dissatisfaction, 4, 104–105
  and disordered eating, 101, 146
  peer influences, 105–106

family prevention
  for parents, suggestions, 218
  substance use, 184
family structure, 29
  adolescent girls, current trends in,
    30–33
  current trends in, 30–33
family support, positive body
    image, 142
father–daughter relationships, 33
FBT. *See* family-based treatment
female role, traditional, 51
feminist therapy and eating
    disorders, 129–130
FFT. *See* family focused therapy
fluoxetine, 67, 93
forbidden foods, 122
friendships, 49
  development and maintenance
    of, 33
  lack of quality group, 34
Full of Ourselves program, 254–255
functional family therapy, 150

gender-balanced identity, 53
gender difference
  in comorbidity, 155
  and depression, 68
  in family influence, 73
  and NSSI, 192–193
  in substance abuse, 167
gender gaps, 37
gender identity, 49
gender schemas, 50
gender stereotypes, 22
genetic factors, eating disorders, 102
genetics, 41
Gilligan and crossroads, 51
"girl power," 11, 19
girls and depression, 65–98
girls and physical violence, 226
girls' identity, 157
girls in transition (GT) program, 96–97
girls' media consumption, 4–5
Girls on the Run (GOTR), 260
girl's perception, girl's appearance, 105

girls' sociocultural context
  ethnicity and culture, 72
  family influences, 72–75
  gender differences, 68
  girls and life stressors, 68–69
  interpersonal vulnerability, 69–71
goal-oriented behavior, 45
goals development, girls, 259
Go Grrrls Program, 257
grief, 86–88
group modalities and substance
    abuse treatment, 166
GT program. *See* girls in transition
    program
Guiding Good Choices, prevention
    program, 185

half-smiling skills, DBT, 133, 214
Halloween costumes, 6
harm reduction, 166
Harvard Project on Raising Teens, 54
  parenting adolescents. *See*
    parenting tasks
healthful eating, 258
high-risk sexual behaviors, substance
    usage, 158
Hispanic girls
  binge eating, 127
  substance use, 156
holistic wellness and balance, 143
home environment, protective, 218
homework, 77
hormonal changes, eating
    disorders, 103
"hot and sexy" appearance, 5–9
human development, ecological
    study of, 2

ideal body weight (IBW), 109
identity development, adolescent, 30,
    49, 51
imaginal exposure, 237
imaginary audience, 43
indicated prevention programs,
    binge eating, 143